Well Informed

D1542490

Medical and Health Contributors and Reviewers

We acknowledge the following professionals for their contributions to this publication:

William B. Baun, M.S., F.A.W.H.P.

Susan Blair, M.B.A., F.A.W.H.P.

John M. Carpenter, M.D.

Alice Y. Chang, M.D.

David L. Chesler, M.D.

Philip Chicon, M.D.

William C. Clair, M.B.A., F.A.W.H.P.

Allen Douma, M.D.

Camille F. Deckert, M.Ed.

Fleming Edwards, R.P.

Robin Fuller Foust

John N. Hall, M.D.

Carolyn Helmly, M.D.

Don S. Hillier

John Hong, M.D.

Alan L. Kimmel, M.D.

Ronald M. Lather, M.D.

Donald MacKay

R. Michael Morse, M.D.

Lynn Ostrowski, M.Ed.

George J. Pfeiffer, M.S.E., F.A.W.H.P.

Michael E. Pfeiffer, D.D.S.

Marti Remmell, R.N.

Elin Silveous

Andrew Scibelli, M.S.E.

Philip Smeltzer, M.A.

Judith Webster, R.N., M.S.

Michael Wood, M.S., M.P.H.

A publication of

The WorkCare Group, Inc.

Charlottesville, Virginia

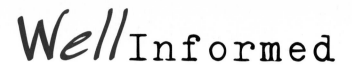

WellInformed

Distributed in the United States by
The WorkCare Group, Inc.®
P.O. Box 2053, Charlottesville, Virginia 22902

ISBN Number: 1-893567-09-5

Printed in the United States of America

Publisher:	George J. Pfeiffer
Editor:	Jeanne Rashap
Production and Design:	Catalina McChesney
Internal Illustrations:	Scott Emond
Cover Design:	Barbee Graphics, Inc.

Limits of Liability

Well Informed: Your Guide to Health and Vitality is intended to increase awareness of health and medical care issues. None of the information in this text is intended to be a substitute for appropriate physician diagnosis and medical care. The WorkCare Group, Inc. has thoroughly researched the materials contained herein, which are deemed accurate as of the publication date. Additional research and findings, subsequent to the publication date, may affect the representations made.

Contents

Contents

Look for the blue page edges on the top of the closed book.

Contents

"An ounce of prevention is worth a pound of cure."

Although medical advances have improved our chances for living longer, the health decisions we make every day influence our future health more. In fact, quality health care is more than good medical care, it means taking personal responsibility for managing your health by practicing positive lifestyle behaviors and working with your doctor to make informed health decisions.

As you take an active role in your health decisions, the *Well Informed* self-care guide will help you and your family improve your health and well-being.

Taking Charge of Your Health, One Step at a Time

Research has shown that even modest changes in your lifestyle habits, such as increasing your physical activity and eating more fruit and vegetables, can reduce your risk for heart disease and certain cancers. And, it's never too late to start improving your health:

- **Step #1:** Decide to make a change, no matter how small. With each success, you'll feel more confident about taking control of your health.

- **Step #2:** Develop a partnership with your doctor to make the medical decisions that affect you. This may include deciding when medical interventions are necessary.

Regardless of your health status, it's important to be informed and take an active role in your health care decisions. This includes:

- Understanding and practicing self-care skills that help prevent and/or manage lifestyle-related disorders.

- Selecting a doctor based on your needs.

- Knowing when common problems can be treated at home or when medical care is necessary.

- Talking confidently with your doctor, including discussing available treatment options and the benefits, risks, and costs of each option.

- Talking with your doctor to evaluate the need for hospitalization.

- Knowing your rights as a patient.

How *Well Informed* Can Help

Well Informed provides an introduction to the principles of prevention, medical self-care, and health care consumerism. *Well Informed* will help you:

- Prevent and/or manage major health problems using positive lifestyle skills.

- Treat common medical complaints with medical self-care (HomeCare™).

- Make medical care decisions with skill and confidence.

- Improve the quality of health care you receive.

When you have a health problem, consult this book first as part of your overall health management plan.

> This book is not intended to replace professional medical treatment when it's needed or to replace treatment already recommended by your doctor. If you have any questions or concerns, always consult your doctor first.

Remember, when it comes to your health, you can never be too Well Informed.

Lifestyle and Health

In this section:

- Lifestyle skills for reducing your risk of illness and disease

- Adding regular physical activity to your life

- Eating for good health

- Making stress work for you

- Skills for losing weight

- Medical screening tests for you and your family

- Good dental care

- Immunizations for you and your family

- Preventing or managing high blood pressure and high cholesterol

- Substance abuse and getting help for an alcohol or drug problem

- Family planning

- AIDS and other sexually transmitted diseases

- Keeping your child healthy and safe

Lifestyle Skills for Your Health

This chart shows the positive lifestyle skills that have the greatest influence on your health and longevity. Making wise choices every day increases your vitality and reduces your risk for disease and disability.

Skill	Ideas that Work	Benefits	Resources
Staying Active	• Try physical activity a minimum of 30 minutes/day, 5 days/week. Strive for a regular exercise routine. • Involve large muscles, (e.g., walking, cycling, swimming, and yard work). • Strengthen shoulders, arms, back, abdomen, and leg muscles with resistance exercises, twice a week. • Maintain joint flexibility with daily stretching.	• Protects against heart disease, cancer, diabetes, osteoporosis, and depression. • Helps control your weight. • Increases your energy level. • Maintains muscle strength and endurance needed for everyday activities. • Protects major muscle groups and joints. Enhances performance.	• Local YMCA/YWCA • Recreation centers • Health clubs • Company fitness centers • Pages 6-15
Eating Wisely	• Aim for 5 to 9 servings of fruit and vegetables each day. • Eat proteins such as leaner cuts of red meat, poultry, eggs, and plant-based proteins such as nuts and legumes. • Choose whole-grain products. • Eat fatty fish twice a week. • Choose low-fat dairy products. • Limit saturated fat, trans fat, sweets, and refined carbohydrates.	• Provides a balance of nutrients, vitamins, minerals, and fiber for overall health. • Provides energy for mental and physical activities. • Protects against heart disease, hypertension, cancer, diabetes, and obesity.	• American Cancer Society • American Dietetic Association • See the 5-A-Day Plan on page 16 • American Heart Association
Staying at a Healthy Weight	• Keep your weight within 10 percent of the ideal for your height and weight. See the BMI chart on page 23. • Avoid fad diets. • Balance calorie intake with activity level.	• Reduces risk of heart disease, hypertension, diabetes, and cancer. • Reduces stress on joints.	• American Dietetic Association • Pages 22–23
Drinking Alcohol in Moderation, or Not at All	• Allow a maximum of one drink for women and two drinks for men per day. • Pregnant women should not drink alcohol. • Don't drink and drive. • Don't operate equipment or machinery while under the influence of alcohol. • Be aware that a family history of alcoholism increases your risk for alcoholism.	• Lowers risk of liver disease and certain cancers. • Reduces risk of on-the-job accidents and motor vehicle accidents. • Moderate alcohol use is linked to a lower risk for heart disease.	• Your company's employee assistance program (EAP) • Alcoholics Anonymous • Pages 39–42

Lifestyle Skills for Your Health

Skill	Ideas that Work	Benefits	Resources
Using Drugs Wisely	• Don't use Illegal drugs. • Use prescription and over-the-counter medications only as recommended. • Don't use someone else's prescription medications.	• Helps prevent the spread of disease. • Prevents drug dependence. • Decreases adverse drug reactions.	• Narcotics Anonymous • Your pharmacist • Pages 35-38
Practicing Safe Sex	• Maintain monogamous relationships. • Use latex condoms.	• Helps prevent sexually transmitted diseases.	• Your personal physician • Local health department • Page 50
Using Your Seat Belt	• Always use your seat belt. • Small adults should sit as far from an air bag as possible. • All passengers should buckle up before you start your vehicle. • Secure children under age 12 in the back seat, in child safety seat, or buckled up appropriately.	• Reduces death and injury.	• National Safety Council • Local police
Getting Scheduled Immunizations and Medical Screenings	• Follow recommended schedules based on age, gender, family history, and health status.	• Identifies health risks. • Prevents and/or manages disease.	• Your personal physician • Immunizations, page 44 • Screenings, page 43
Limiting Exposure to the Sun	• Avoid sun during peak hours. • Apply sunscreen: SPF 15 or higher. • Wear a hat and other protective clothing. • Protect your children—a single significant burn before age 5 increases the lifetime risk of skin cancer. • Wear UV protective sunglasses.	• Prevents skin cancer. • Prevents premature aging. • Reduces your risk of developing cataracts.	• American Cancer Society • American Academy of Ophthalmology
Living Tobacco-Free	• Don't start using tobacco. • Establish a quit date no more than 30 to 45 days away. • Before you quit, practice positive behaviors such as exercising, eating wisely, watching your weight, and managing stress. • Seek support from family, friends, or a group smoking cessation program. • Once you quit, avoid situations that trigger your old habit.	• Reduces the risk of lung cancer, emphysema, oral cancers, heart disease, hypertension, osteoporosis, and stroke. • Prevents premature aging of the skin.	• American Cancer Society • American Lung Association

Walking: Possibly the Best Exercise

Whether you want to lose weight, manage stress, or reduce your health risks, walking is perhaps the best way to add regular exercise to your life. Walking is inexpensive, requires little equipment, can be done almost anywhere, rarely causes injury, and is good for young and old alike.

Ideas that Work

Discuss your exercise plans with your doctor before starting if you have a medical condition such as high blood pressure, heart disease, or joint problems, or if you are over 40 years old and have been inactive.

■ **Wear the proper shoes.** There are several walking shoes on the market designed to help the heel-to-toe motion of walking and provide good support for the heel. Shop for shoes in the afternoon when your feet may be larger from the day's activities.

■ **Use proper form.** Walk tall, but keep your upper body relaxed. Foot contact with the ground should be heel to toe. Pump your arms forward and back. *Note: Using hand weights may stress your joints.*

■ **Map your course.** To ensure your personal safety, find an interesting walking route that is out of the way of traffic, is safe and well-lit at night, and has an even surface. Shopping malls are excellent places to walk, especially in bad weather.

■ **Road rules.** If you walk at night, wear reflective clothing and use a flashlight. Carry your ID, a cell phone, or change for a pay phone. If you must walk in the street, always walk facing traffic.

■ **Start on the right foot.** Begin your program slowly. Gradually increase the duration (time) of your walk before increasing the speed (intensity).

■ **Walk with a family member, friend, or co-worker.** Ideally, try to walk with someone at your fitness level.

■ **Schedule your walk and make it a habit.** This is your time for doing something enjoyable for yourself.

■ **Add variety.** Although having a regular walking route is a good idea, try to vary your walking course once you've reached a level of comfort and regularity. Map out additional safe walking routes that vary in distance, terrain, and scenery.

■ **Gain health benefits.** To begin achieving health benefits, walk at least 5 days a week, for a total of 30 minutes per day. If you can walk for only 10 minutes before needing a rest—that's OK. Three 10-minute walks spread out over the day are just as beneficial. Gradually add a few minutes to the length of your walk until you're able to walk for 30 minutes without stopping. A rule of thumb is that if you can carry on a normal conversation without being out of breath, then you are not exercising too vigorously.

■ **If weight loss is your goal,** you'll need to walk for 30 minutes, 5 days per week, and reduce calories as well. Walking for 20 to 40 minutes also helps reduce anxiety and tension.

■ **Drink water before walking.** It's wise to carry a bottle of water along with you.

Walking: Possibly the Best Exercise

■ **Use sunscreen.** Also, wear a brimmed hat and sunglasses on sunny days.

■ **Have fun!** Vary your walking routes, change the distance, play with the tempo, walk through city parks or botanical gardens, have a company noon-hour walk program, or participate in a community walkathon for charity.

■ **Rewards all around.** Set up an incentive program for your progress, or establish an office or family walking fund. For every mile walked, contribute to the walk fund. Then treat yourself or the group to movie tickets or donate the money to charity.

Walking Through the Day

■ **Ride and walk.** If you commute by mass transit, get off before your usual stop and walk the additional distance to work.

■ **Park and walk.** Park your car farther from your place of work or at the back of the parking lot.

■ **Break walk.** Get out of the office and walk during your scheduled breaks.

■ **Lunch and walk.** If you pack a brown bag for lunch, walk to a nearby park that's 5 to 7 minutes from the office. Enjoy your lunch and walk back.

■ **Form a walking group.** Form a lunch-hour walking group. Have members take turns choosing the route of the day.

■ **Walk after dinner.** Take a stroll for 20 to 30 minutes by yourself or with a member of your family.

■ **Count 'em!** A pedometer is a small, battery-powered device that attaches to your waistband and measures the number of steps you take. Most people walk between 900 and 3,000 steps per day, which is significantly fewer than the 10,000 often recommended. Increasing your total to 10,000 steps throughout the day will give you approximately the same health benefits as 30 minutes of moderate physical activity, such as slow jogging or cycling. The best part about using a pedometer with your walking program is that you get "credit" for all walking—through the hallways at work, down the aisles at the store, or up and down the stairs at home.

Resource

President's Council on Physical Fitness and Sports, www.fitness.gov
American College of Sports Medicine, www.acsm.org

For Your Information

Fit Activity Into Your Day

The Surgeon General's Report on Physical Activity and Health recommends that people of all ages engage in 30 minutes of physical activity of moderate intensity on most, if not all, days of the week. See page 8.

Rating Popular Fitness Activities

Regular physical activity is an important part of a healthy lifestyle. The *Surgeon General's Report on Physical Activity and Health* recommends that adults take part in moderate physical activities for a total of 30 minutes per day, most days of the week, in order to experience health benefits.

Daily physical activity may include manual labor, household chores, structured fitness programs, and recreational or sports activities. For most of us, a combination of these activities will provide health benefits and improve our overall fitness level. Formal, scheduled exercise provides more consistent benefits and results.

In choosing activities that suit you, consider mixing your activities—you'll avoid the seasonal peaks and valleys of any one pursuit, reduce boredom, and achieve a higher level of fitness.

The chart below ranks fitness benefits for some popular activities. Activities are ranked 1 through 10, with 10 having the greatest benefit. In the "Risk of Injury" column, 1 represents the least risk and 10 represents the highest risk.

Note: Benefits can vary greatly among individuals. Personal skill levels and the intensity, duration, and frequency of the activity influence its effects. Therefore, use the chart only as a guideline.

Remember: It's a good idea to talk with your doctor before starting any physical activity program, especially if you've been inactive or have a health problem.

Rating Popular Fitness Activities

Activity	Aerobic Fitness**	Muscle Toning	Flexibility	Weight Control	Risk of Injury***
Aerobics (low impact)	6	7	7	6.5	5
Cycling*	6	6	3	6	5-9
Cross-country skiing*	9	8	7	9	5-7
Golf (walking)	5	5	6	4	5
In-line skating	5	6	6	5	8
Jogging	8.5	6	3	8	7
Rowing*	7	8	6	7	5
Singles tennis	6	6	7	6	6-7
Stair-climbing exercise	7	6	6	7	4
Swimming (lap)	8	7	7-9	8	3
Walking (4 mph)	5	5	4	5	3
Weight training	4	8-10	6	5	7
Yoga	2	6	8-10	2	2

*   Includes both stationary equipment and outdoor activity. Outdoor activity increases the chances of injury.

**   Approximates exercising at a moderate intensity for 30 minutes.

*** Reduce injury with proper conditioning, warm-up and cool-down, using proper technique, using appropriate equipment, and following proper safety procedures.

Improving Your Flexibility

lexibility is the ability of a joint to move smoothly and easily. Outside of acute injury or chronic conditions such as arthritis, the biggest reason for lack of flexibility is lack of use. How far and how easily a joint will move (range of motion) depends on a number of factors, such as its structure and the condition of supporting ligaments, tendons, and muscles. If a joint area is not moved through its full range of motion on a regular basis, mobility will decrease and the risk of injury will increase.

Flexibility is especially important if you take part in sports and recreational activities that place repeated stress on muscles and joints. Even if you're not an athlete, joint flexibility is an important part of physical health, especially as you age. By doing the exercises on the following pages, you can improve and maintain your range of motion, reduce stiffness in your joints, reduce post-exercise soreness, reduce the risk of injury, and improve your overall mobility and performance.

General Guidelines for Stretching

- If you have a health condition that limits your activity, consult your doctor before doing these exercises. Take this book with you and show your doctor what you intend to do.
- Start with a large-muscle warm-up such as brisk walking for 5 to 10 minutes before stretching.
- Don't bounce or jerk when you stretch. Gently stretch to a point of tension.
- Hold the stretch for 15–30 seconds. Concentrate on relaxing the muscles while you're stretching.
- Breathe normally. Don't hold your breath.

For Your Information

Exercise to Your Heart's Content

How hard should you exercise? One gauge of exercise intensity is your heart rate. To maximize your workout, your heart rate should be elevated and maintained within your exercise heart rate zone for a total workout time of 30 minutes. Here's how to calculate your zone:

■ Subtract your age from 220.

■ Multiply this number by .6 to find the low end of your zone.

■ Multiply the first number by .8 to find the high end of your zone.

If you're a beginning exerciser, work out at the low end of your zone and increase intensity as your fitness level improves. Check your pulse right after you finish your workout to see if you're exercising at the appropriate intensity. Place your ring and middle fingers gently on your pulse point, just below your jaw or on your wrist below your thumb. Count the number of beats—the first is zero—for 10 seconds. Then multiply by 6. Adjust the intensity of your next exercise interval or workout if necessary.

Stretching for Health

Neck Stretch:
Chin to Chest

- Sitting or standing, lower your chin to your chest with control.
- Hold for 15 seconds, then lift your head up.
- Repeat 3 to 5 times.

Head Rotation

- Sitting or standing, turn your head in a controlled movement, first to the right (hold) and then to your left (hold).
- Repeat 3 to 5 times.

Note: Do not tilt your head back. This puts dangerous stress on the cervical joint.

Seated Back Stretch

- From a seated position, bend at the waist with control, sliding your hands to your feet.
- Lower your head between your arms.
- Relax your shoulders and neck until you feel the stretch.
- Do not bounce to extend your reach.
- Hold for 15 seconds. Breathe normally.
- Repeat 3 times.

Back Extension

- Stand with your feet shoulder-width apart and your knees relaxed.
- Place your hands on the small of your back.
- Extend your shoulders backward with control until you feel tension.
- Hold for 15 seconds and then relax.
- Repeat 3 times.

"With control" means keeping tension on the muscle as you move through the stretch and as you return to the starting position.

Stretching for Health

Shoulder/Arm Stretch

- Sit or stand with your back straight but relaxed.
- Place your hands above your head—arms behind your ears—with your fingers interlaced and your palms facing the ceiling.
- Press your hands toward the ceiling, with control, until you feel the stretch.
- Hold the stretch for 15 seconds.
- Repeat 3 times.

Side Stretch

- Sitting or standing with hands together, reach overhead.
- Keeping your back straight, bend from the waist, with control, to one side.
- Breathe normally.
- Hold the stretch for 15 seconds.
- Repeat 3 times on each side.

Triceps and Shoulder Stretch

- Place your right palm on your back, just below your neck, with your elbow pointing toward the ceiling.
- Place your left hand on your right elbow and push gently until you feel tension.
- Hold for 15 seconds.
- Repeat 3 times with each arm.

"The Rack"

- Lie on the floor on your back with your arms extended above your head.
- Stretch by extending your arms and legs.
- Hold for 15 seconds. Breathe normally.
- Repeat 3 times.

Stretching for Health

Back Press (pelvic tilt)

- Lie on your back on the floor with your knees bent and feet flat on the floor.
- Tighten your abdominal muscles and press the small of your back to the floor.
- Hold for 15 seconds. Breathe normally.
- Repeat 3 times.

Hip/Gluteal Stretch

- Lie on your back on the floor with both knees bent.
- Keep your shoulders and head on the floor.
- With your hands behind and slightly above one knee, pull gently toward your chest until you feel tension.
- Hold for 15 seconds.
- Repeat 3 times with each leg.

Hamstring/Lower Leg Stretch

- Lie on your back on the floor with both knees bent.
- Raise one leg, with control, until it is perpendicular to the floor. Stretch to a point of tension and hold for 15 seconds.
- Next, flex your foot to stretch your calf, then point your toes to stretch the front of your lower leg.
- Repeat 3 times with each leg.

Building Strong Muscles

Research shows that strength training is beneficial for most adults. In fact, for older adults or those with such problems as arthritis, osteoporosis, heart disease, and hypertension, the benefits of strength training include increasing muscle mass, protecting the major joints from injury, improving balance, reducing falls, and improving the ability to do work.

The exercises on the following pages help condition the major muscle groups of the body. These exercises can be done in your home—equipment is limited to dumbbells and ankle weights. Even soup cans or detergent bottles (with handles) filled with water or sand to a desired weight will provide adequate resistance for upper body toning. Finally, consider joining a local fitness facility that has resistance equipment and trained supervision that can help you develop a safe and effective weight-training program.

For Your Information

General Guidelines for Strength Training

- Talk with your doctor before starting this or any exercise program.

- Begin by warming up the muscles you will be exercising.

- Use weights that are not too heavy for you to handle with control. If possible, join a health club that has fitness trainers who can help you lift weights safely.

- Concentrate on moving through the full range of motion with control—keeping steady tension on the muscle as it works—for 10 to 15 repetitions (one set).
  Note: Jerking the weights or rocking your body to lift the weights will increase your risk of injury. Use lighter weights.

- Exhale as your muscles work (exertion) and inhale as you return to the starting position (recovery).

- Start with one set per exercise for at least 2 weeks. When one set feels effortless—and you have no soreness or injury—add another set. You'll know you're working the muscle hard enough if the last two repetitions in the set feel difficult to complete; your muscle should not hurt or burn, but should feel challenged. Rest 2 to 3 minutes between sets.

- After your strength-training session, perform flexibility stretches (longer stretches of the muscles you worked).

- If you injure a muscle or have significant muscle soreness, rest this muscle group until discomfort is gone.

- Do weight training 2 to 3 days per week with a day of rest in between.

Building Strong Muscles

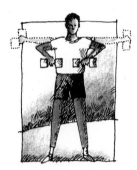

Triceps Fly

Strengthens the backs of the upper arms

- Stand with your back straight and your knees relaxed.
- Hold a weight in each hand with elbows bent at shoulder level. Keep your shoulders down and relaxed (not hunched).
- Extend both arms away from your body in a controlled motion until they are parallel to the floor and your elbows are straight but not locked.
- Repeat 10 to 12 times for 2 to 3 sets.

Biceps Curl

Strengthens the biceps, located at the front of the upper arms

- Sit on a bench or sturdy chair with a weight in each hand and arms straight down at your sides.
- Bend your elbow and lift the weight to your shoulder with control. Then lower it to the starting position, again with control.
- Alternate arms.
- Do 10 to 12 repetitions.
- Repeat for 2 or 3 sets.

Upright Row

Strengthens the shoulders

- Stand with your back straight, abdominal muscles tight, and knees relaxed.
- Hold a weight in each hand at the front of your thighs.
- Lift both weights, with control, to armpit level. Keep your elbows higher than your hands. Now shrug your shoulders to work trapezius muscles as well.
- Next, lower the weights, with control, to the starting position.
- Repeat 10 to 12 times for 2 to 3 sets.

Shoulder Press

Strengthens the upper back and shoulders

- Sit with a weight in each hand at shoulder level.
- Push one weight upward to full extension, then lower it and push the other one upward. Remember to keep a controlled tension on the muscles.
- Alternate 10 to 12 repetitions with each arm for 2 to 3 sets.

"With control" means keeping tension on the muscle as you move through the lift and as you return to the starting position.

Standing Leg Curl

Strengthens the hamstrings, located at the backs of the thighs

- Stand upright with weights fastened around each ankle. Hold on to a table or the top of a chair for support.
- Lift one heel in a controlled motion toward your buttocks. Then lower it to the starting position, keeping tension on the muscle.
- Do 10 to 12 repetitions with each leg.
- Repeat for 2 or 3 sets.

Leg Extension

Strengthens the quadriceps, located at the fronts of the thighs

- Sit on a bench with a weight fastened around each ankle.
- Extend both legs with control until they are parallel to the floor.
- Lower your legs back to the starting position, keeping tension on the muscles.
- Do 10 to 12 repetitions.
- Repeat for 2 or 3 sets.

Abdominal Crunch

Strengthens the abdominal muscles

- Lie on your back on the floor, with your knees bent and your feet flat on the floor.
- Place your arms across your chest.
- While exhaling, lift your head and shoulders together—without bending your neck—while pressing your lower back against the floor.
- Return to the starting position, with control, while inhaling.
- Do 15 to 20 repetitions.

Nutrition and You

Nutrition is one of the most important tools for health and longevity. Following a few simple nutritional guidelines can help you and your family lower your risks for disease, maintain your ideal body weight, and have more energy.

Food for Thought

■ **Balance the food you eat with regular physical activity to maintain your ideal body weight.** Good nutrition and regular physical activity make a powerful combination for managing body weight. Obesity is a significant risk factor for such conditions as hypertension, diabetes, and heart disease.

■ **Choose a diet low in saturated fat, trans fat, and cholesterol.** Saturated fats are found in marbled red meats, organ meats, whole milk, margarine, many cheeses (e.g., cheddar and brie), and coconut and palm oils. Trans fats are found in processed foods such as cakes, cookies, crackers, and other snacks. Instead:

–Choose lean meats, poultry, and fish.

–Increase your consumption of fish and skinless poultry to two to three servings per week.

–Try low-fat cooking methods such as broiling, baking, and steaming.

–When oils are needed, use those with monounsaturated fat, such as olive oil.

–Avoid processed snacks and baked goods high in trans fat.

■ **Choose plenty of whole-grain products, vegetables, and fruits.** Eat more whole-grain products (e.g. whole-grain bread, brown rice), fruits, vegetables, and legumes (e.g., kidney and lima beans).

For Your Information

The 5-A-Day Plan recommends that Americans eat a variety of fruits and vegetables every day and aim for five to nine servings of fruits and vegetables every day:

1. Eat at least one vitamin A-rich selection every day (e.g., apricots, cantaloupe, carrots, spinach, squash).
2. Eat at least one vitamin C-rich selection every day (e.g., orange, grapefruit, tomato juice, broccoli).
3. Eat at least one high-fiber selection every day (e.g., figs, prunes, dried peas, beans).
4. Eat cabbage family (cruciferous) vegetables several times per week (e.g., broccoli, cauliflower).

For variety, try for as many colors as you can each day. For example, yellow banana, green spinach, red tomato, blue berries, white onion, and orange mango. Plan a rainbow on your plate and feel good about your nutritious choices.

Source: U.S. Department of Agriculture

■ **Limit refined grains and sugar.** Snacks and baked goods made with white flour and sugar generally are high in calories and saturated and trans fats. These foods are high-glycemic carbohydrates that cause rapid increases in blood sugar that in turn, trigger cravings for more carbohydrates. This cycle may prompt you to eat more than you would otherwise.

■ **Limit foods with sodium (salt) and chemicals.** Limit salt-cured, smoked, and nitrite-cured foods (e.g., bacon, hot dogs), and sodium-laden processed foods and snacks.

■ **Moderate your alcohol consumption.** Men should drink no more than two drinks per day; no more than one drink per day for women; pregnant women should not drink alcohol. Moderate alcohol use has been linked to a lower risk of heart disease, but do not start drinking alcohol to lower your health risks. Heavy use of alcohol increases the risk of cancer, liver disease, osteoporosis, and alcoholism.

For Your Information

Calcium-Rich Foods

Adequate dietary calcium helps prevent osteoporosis and, perhaps, hypertension. Adult men and women need a minimum of 1,000 milligrams (mg) of calcium per day. Pregnant or lactating women require 1,300 mg, and postmenopausal women who are not taking estrogen, 1,500 mg per day.

Food	Serving Size	Calcium (mg)
Plain, low-fat yogurt	8 ounces	415
Canned sardines, with bones	3 ounces	371
Part skim-milk ricotta cheese	1/2 cup	334
Skim milk	1 cup	302–316
Two percent low-fat milk	1 cup	297–313
Swiss cheese	1 ounce	272
Dried figs	10 figs	269
Tofu	1/2 cup	258
Spinach	1 cup boiled	244
Raw oysters	4–6 medium	226
Nonfat dry milk	1/4 cup	209
Cheddar, muenster, or part skim-milk mozzarella	1 ounce	203–207
Cooked, chopped collards	1/2 cup	178
Cooked broccoli	3/4 cup	108

Source: National Women's Health Information Center

Nutrition and You

A balanced diet plays a major role in the prevention of many chronic illnesses such as cancer, heart disease, and diabetes. And, with a healthful diet, you'll have more energy, stamina, and be more alert all day long. A healthful diet should always include food that is nutritionally dense, low in saturated fats, and high in fiber. Many of the vitamins, minerals, and fiber frequently are removed during the processing of manufactured foods. When possible, use fresh or fresh-frozen ingredients.

- **Breakfast** is your most important meal of the day:
  - Instead of high-fat eggs, bacon, and doughnuts, try whole-grain cereal, low-fat yogurt or cottage cheese, or a whole-grain bagel with a low-fat spread. Always try to include a piece of fruit.
  - If it's hard to find time for a sit-down breakfast at home, grab a piece of fruit and a whole-grain bagel for the commute. Try getting to work a little earlier and eating a "brown-bag" breakfast.
  - If you don't like regular breakfast foods, try lunch or dinner food instead.

- **Lunch:** No matter where you eat lunch—your desk, the cafeteria, a restaurant—you can make it nutritious and enjoyable. A lunch that's lower in refined carbohydrates (e.g., white bread, cookies) will help you avoid mid-afternoon sluggishness. Here are a few suggestions:
  - Pack a balanced brown-bag lunch: a vegetable such as celery or carrots; a sandwich on whole-grain bread with turkey, chicken, or tuna; a piece of fruit; fig bars or graham crackers.
  - If you eat in the cafeteria, try the salad bar. Be aware that salads made with heavy dressings usually are high in fat.

For Your Information

Your daily food choices should include the following:

• Whole-grain foods	For fiber, vitamins, minerals
• Vegetables and fruit	For vitamins, antioxidants, fiber
• Nuts, legumes	For protein, fiber, beneficial fats
• Plant-based oils	For mono- and unsaturated fat
• Lean meat, fish, poultry, eggs	For protein
• Low-fat dairy	For calcium, vitamin D

Limit or use sparingly	Drawbacks
• Sweets, refined carbohydrates (e.g., white bread, white rice, white pasta, white potatoes)	May be high in calories and fat; low in fiber and vitamins
• Processed foods and snacks (e.g., cookies, pastry, pretzels)	May contain harmful trans fats that increase bad cholesterol (LDL) and lower good cholesterol (HDL)

Nutrition and You

–In restaurants, try to select main dishes that are broiled or steamed instead of fried. Also, try to include a vegetable dish or order a main-dish salad. Most fast-food restaurants now post nutritional information—some of it may surprise you.

■ **Snacks:** Snacking can help you meet your daily dietary requirements and give you a satisfying pick-me-up. Try these ideas:
–raisins or other dried fruit
–pretzels, popcorn
–fresh fruit or vegetables, canned fruit packed in water or unsweetened fruit juice
If you make regular trips to the vending machine, find out what's in the food you select. Is it high in calories, saturated fat, trans fat, and sodium?

■ **Dinner:** Try to plan before you go to the grocery store. Stock up on fresh or frozen fruit and vegetables, whole-grain bread, nuts, and lean meat to have on hand for quick meal preparation. Also, consider these suggestions:
–To cut down on saturated fat, broil meats instead of frying. Trim all visible fat from meat before cooking.
–Round out your daily recommended servings of fruits and vegetables (aim for five to nine).
–Help reduce your intake of high-fat foods by preparing two to three plant-based meals per week with no meat, poultry, or fish.
–Be aware that there is hidden fat in cheeses, sauces, gravies, and dressings.

■ **Beverages:** Try to moderate your consumption of caffeine, alcohol, and sugary drinks. Water, sparkling water, and decaffeinated tea make good substitutes.

■ **Take frequent water breaks:** We can survive for months without food, but only a few days without water. Essential body fluids such as saliva, tears, digestive juices, and the fluid in your joints are made up primarily of water. Water in the form of sweat regulates body temperature. Water serves many other purposes:
–aids digestion and circulation
–prevents urinary tract infections and constipation
–protects against colds, coughs, flu, and sore throats

■ **How much water should you drink?** Most of us need six to eight cups of fluid each day. This can include fluids consumed in foods such as soup and vegetables. Certain conditions require that you drink more: hot environments, physical activity and exercise, dieting, high altitudes (including airplane trips), pregnancy, illness and fever, vomiting, and diarrhea.

■ **Supplements:** Taking a multivitamin may be a good idea for making sure you are getting the nutrients you need. Pregnant and nursing women, the elderly, athletes, teenagers with irregular eating habits, people with deficiency diseases or absorption disorders, vegetarians, dieters, smokers, and those taking certain prescription medications may benefit from taking vitamin supplements.

Resource

American Dietetic Association
Nutrition Hotline 800.366.1655
www.eatright.org

Reading Food Nutrition Labels

How many crackers are in one serving? How many calories per serving? How much salt is in those pretzels? How do you know if the food you're eating really is good for you? It's easy when you know what to look for. The U.S. Food and Drug Administration requires that all packaged foods carry nutrition labels that assess the "Percent Daily Value" (%DV) of the food.

Nutrition Facts

Serving Size: 1 cup (228g)
Servings Per Container: 2

Amount Per Serving

Calories 260   Calories from Fat 120

	% Daily Value *
Total Fat 13g	20%
Saturated Fat 5g	25%
Cholesterol 30mg	10%
Sodium 660mg	28%
Total Carbohydrate 31g	10%
Dietary Fiber 0g	0%
Sugars 5g	

Protein 5g

• Vitamin A 4%   • Vitamin C 2%
• Calcium 15%   • Iron 4%

*Percent Daily Values are based on a 2,000 calorie diet. Your daily values may be higher or lower depending on your calorie needs:

Calories:		2,000	2,500
Total Fat	Less than	65g	80g
Saturated Fat	Less than	20g	25g
Cholesterol	Less than	300mg	300mg
Sodium	Less than	2,400mg	2,400mg
Total Carbohydrate		300g	375g
Dietary Fiber		25g	30g

Tells you the serving size upon which the amounts below are based, and the number of servings in the container.

Tells you the total calories per serving and the total calories from fat per serving. The ratio of these two is a good indication of whether or not the food is high fat.

Limit these.

Eat enough of these nutrients that are essential to your overall health. Choose whole grains and aim for at least five servings a day of fruit and vegetables.

This information is the same on all food labels. (It is sometimes omitted if the label is too small.) Your ideal DV may vary depending on your individual needs (e.g., age, gender, weight, general health, and cultural preferences).

How much is a serving?

Nutritional information on food labels refers to the serving size listed, which may not be the same as the amount you serve yourself. A recommended serving is probably less than you think!

■ 1 cup (8 oz) = Size of a baseball   ■ 1/2 cup (4 oz) = Size of a computer mouse
■ 1/4 cup (2 oz) = Fits in the palm of your hand

Understanding Food Labels

*I*n the past, it was difficult to keep track of all we needed to know about nutrition. Food labels didn't always help: Is "lite" really light? What's considered "high fiber"? To bring standards to food labeling, the Food and Drug Administration now requires that all products conform to set criteria before they can use such terms as "sodium-free" or "fat-free" on packaging. Below are some common label descriptions and their requirements.

TERM	DEFINITION
"Light"	One-third fewer calories, or fat and/or sodium reduced by 50%
"Fresh"	Raw; never frozen, processed, or preserved
"Free"	Per serving: Calorie free: less than 5 calories Sugar free: less than 0.5 g of sugar Sodium free: less than 5 mg of sodium Fat free: less than 0.5 g of fat Cholesterol free: less than 2 mg of cholesterol Saturated fat free: less than 0.5 g of saturated fat Trans fat free: less than 0.5 g of trans fat
"High"	Provides more than 20% of the recommended daily consumption of the nutrient, as in "high fiber"
"Lean"	Cooked meat or poultry with less than 10.5 g of fat, of which less than 3.5 g is saturated fat, and with less than 94.5 mg of cholesterol per 100 g
"Extra Lean"	Cooked meat or poultry with less than 4.9 g of fat, of which less than 1.8 g is saturated fat, and with less than 94.5 mg of cholesterol per 100 g
"Less"	At least 25% less sodium, calories, fat, saturated fat, or cholesterol than in the regular product
"Low"	Per 100 g or 3.5 ounces: Low sodium: less than 140 mg of sodium Low calorie: less than 40 calories Low fat: 3 g or less of fat Low saturated fat: 1 g or less of saturated fat and not more than 15% of calories from saturated fat Low cholesterol: 20 mg or less of cholesterol
"More"	At least 10% more of the nutrient than in the regular product
"Source of"	Provides 10% to 20% of the recommended daily consumption of the nutrient

Source: U.S. Food and Drug Administration

Maintaining a Healthy Weight

If you're overweight, losing weight—and keeping it off—can improve your health by reducing your risk of stroke, heart disease, arthritis, and diabetes. There's no effective quick-fix diet plan that works for the long term. These approaches will help you manage your weight for the long term:

- **Lose weight gradually**

- **Stay with it for the long haul**

- **Keep a vision of your success**

Forget About "Dieting"

Losing weight rapidly with fad diets usually leads to a gradual return of body fat within 6 months. Sometimes, weight loss and gain becomes a repeating cycle called "yo-yo dieting." Research suggests that this practice increases the risk of coronary heart disease, especially among men. To keep weight off permanently, it's best to lose no more than 2 pounds per week.

In most cases, successful weight management comes from making small changes in your everyday eating and activity patterns.

Make a Long-Term Commitment

A safe and effective way to reach your weight loss goal is to approach weight loss as a gradual process of changing your behavior for the long run—not as a quick-fix program. Try to think of weight management as a permanent change in your lifestyle that won't end once you've reached your goal.

Imagine Success

Someone once said: "When it comes down to willpower vs. imagination, imagination always wins." Do you blame your weight problem on a lack of willpower? Perhaps what's really needed is some positive thinking. No matter what you're trying to change, it's important to focus on the benefits of that change (e.g., more energy, less pain, improved health) and not on what you're giving up. Treat any progress toward your goal as a mini-victory. And don't get discouraged if your progress levels off for a time—it happens. Stick with your plan and focus on the positive.

Ideas that Work

For most people, weight gain can be traced to two things: too much food intake and/or lack of physical activity.

- **Balance your diet.** The most successful weight-loss plans are based on a sensible, balanced diet that includes a variety of vegetables, fruit, and whole-grain products. See pages 16-21.

- **Reduce total caloric intake.** It doesn't matter where your calories come from, if you eat too many of them and don't exercise, your weight will increase. You'll lose weight by reducing total calories and increasing your physical activity.

- **Keep an eye on fat content.** Because fats contain a lot of calories, trimming fat from your diet is a sensible way to reduce total calories.

Maintaining a Healthy Weight

- **Limit refined grains and sugars.** Snacks and baked goods (e.g. cake, crackers, cookies, and white bread) raise your blood sugar rapidly, which then drops, causing you to feel hungry again.

- **Choose high-fiber foods** (e.g., fruits, vegetables, whole grains, beans) that delay the return of hunger.

- **Beware of "low-fat" and "sugarless" items**—they may still be high in calories. Read the labels.

- **Watch your serving sizes.** Even "healthy" choices such as fruit can add unwanted calories if you serve yourself large portions. See page 20.

- **Drink plenty of water.** Six to eight 8-ounce glasses a day is ideal. Ironically, if you drink sufficient water, your body won't try to retain so much of it.

- **Keep a diary.** Write down your eating habits: when and what you eat, who's with you, and your mood, to help you identify your eating triggers.

- **Hide your scale.** Inches lost serves as a better measure than pounds lost. Checking the scale every day can be misleading and discouraging.

- **Increase your daily physical activity.** Exercise burns calories and fat during your activity and keeps your body burning calories for hours after you stop. Exercise also increases your muscle mass, which burns calories even while your body is at rest. Moderate, sustained activity such as walking 40 minutes, 5 days a week, can produce significant weight loss within 12 weeks. See pages 6 through 15.

Note: Consult your doctor before starting a weight loss and exercise program.

Resources

The Duke University Medical Center Book of Diet and Fitness, by Michael Hamilton, et al. New York: Fawcett Columbine, 1993.

Eat, Drink, and Be Healthy, by Walter C. Willett, M.D. New York: Simon and Schuster, 2001.

Your Body Mass Index (BMI)

BMI shows how body weight relates to height. A high BMI usually means extra body fat—although some people who have a lot of muscle may have a high BMI without having higher health risks.

To find your BMI, draw a line from left to right from your "height." Next, draw a line up from your "weight" to the top of the chart. The point where the two lines cross will show you your BMI category.

It's important not to have too much fat around your waist. Your health risks—for diabetes, high blood pressure, osteoarthritis, gallbladder disease, certain cancers, sleep apnea, respiratory problems, stroke, and coronary artery disease—are much higher if:

- your waist measures more than 40 inches around if you're a man or 35 inches if you're a woman
- your body mass index (BMI) is high.

Source: National Heart, Lung and Blood Institute

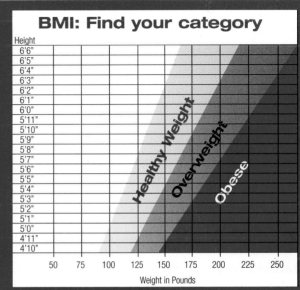

BMI: Find your category

Watching Your Blood Pressure

Blood pressure is the amount of force blood exerts against artery walls as it flows through them.

If your blood pressure is too high, your heart has to work too hard. Left untreated, high blood pressure increases your risk for heart disease, stroke, kidney disease, and blindness. See pages 271–272.

Essential hypertension, where the cause cannot be determined, accounts for 90 percent of hypertension cases. The remaining 10 percent are caused by such conditions as kidney disease and tumors.

Risk factors for high blood pressure include those you can control—being overweight, high alcohol consumption, a sedentary lifestyle, and stress—and those you cannot control—previous family history, age (risk increases with age), gender (affects more males than females), and race (affects African-Americans more than other ethnic groups).

Blood pressure is easily measured with a pressure cuff, gauge, and stethoscope, or computerized instrument. You should have your blood pressure measured at least once a year by a health professional.

Guidelines for High Blood Pressure

Your doctor may decide to evaluate you for high blood pressure based on these guidelines.

Category	Systolic		Diastolic
Normal	<120	and	<80
Prehypertension	120-139	or	80-89
Stage 1 Hypertension	140-159	or	90-99
Stage 2 Hypertension	≥160	or	≥100

Source: National Heart, Lung, and Blood Institute

Ideas that Work

- **Prevent and maintain.** Dietary Approaches to Stop Hypertension, or the DASH Diet, is useful if you already have high blood pressure, or if you want to prevent it. Key features include:
  - Eating a diet rich in fruits, vegetables, and whole grains, which are naturally low in sodium.
  - Limiting daily sodium intake to no more than about 1 teaspoon. Limit cured food (bacon, ham), food packed in brine (pickles, olives), and salty condiments (ketchup, mustard).
  - Including foods that contain potassium (e.g., bananas, lentils, cantaloupe) each day.

- **A healthy lifestyle.** Other strategies to keep your blood pressure under control include maintaining your ideal weight and increasing aerobic activity. Aim for 30 minutes on most days. Don't smoke, practice stress management techniques, and if you drink alcohol, do so only in moderation.

- **Follow your doctor's recommendations.** In general, if you have been diagnosed with high blood pressure, your doctor will recommend lifestyle changes and prescribe medication.

- **Stick to it.** Don't change your treatment schedule without checking with your doctor first. Tell your doctor about any side effects from medications such as headaches, fatigue, cough, and extra or skipped heartbeats.

Resources

Your doctor.

The American Red Cross. Check your phone directory for your local chapter.

DASH Diet, page 272.

Checking Your Cholesterol

*C*holesterol is important for maintaining healthy cell function. While your liver manufactures most of the cholesterol in your blood, you get the rest from eating certain foods, especially those from animals—meat, poultry, shellfish, and whole-milk dairy products.

High *LDL*, the "bad cholesterol," and *low HDL*, the "good cholesterol," promote atherosclerosis (hardening of the arteries), the major cause of clogged arteries. If the blood flow becomes blocked in the narrowed arteries leading to the heart, a heart attack may occur. A stroke can result if the blood flow to the brain is blocked. If you have other risk factors for heart disease (e.g., inactivity, smoking, obesity, family history), unhealthy cholesterol levels pose an even greater threat.

What Are Your Risk Factors?

❏ Are you male over age 45? Female over age 55?

❏ Do you have a family history of premature coronary heart disease? (Heart attack or sudden death of a parent or sibling before age 55 for men, 65 for women.)

❏ Do you smoke cigarettes?

❏ Do you have high blood pressure?

❏ Do you have diabetes?

❏ Do you have a history of vascular disease (blocked arteries) in other parts of your body such as the head or legs?

❏ Are you more than 20 percent overweight?

❏ Are you physically inactive?

The more boxes you check, the greater your risk for coronary heart disease.

How Cholesterol Is Measured

Cholesterol is measured with a blood test. A sample taken from a simple finger-stick or drawn from a vein is analyzed for total cholesterol and for LDLs and HDLs. The test may also measure triglycerides, another blood component associated with elevated cholesterol and higher risk of heart disease and stroke. Your total cholesterol count, including LDL, HDL, and triglycerides, helps your doctor evaluate your level of risk. While these numbers can be significant in themselves, it is also important to consider them along with other risk factors you may have.

The chart below summarizes generally accepted values. Cholesterol is measured in milligrams per deciliter (mg/dL).

What Your Cholesterol Numbers Mean

Total Cholesterol Level	Category
Less than 200 mg/dL	Desirable
200-239 mg/dL	Borderline high
Above 240 mg/dL	High

LDL Cholesterol Level	Category
Less than 100 mg/dL	Optimal
100-129 mg/dL	Near/above optimal
130-159 mg/dL	Borderline high
160-189 mg/dL	High
Above 190 mg/dL	Very high

HDL Cholesterol Level	Category
Above 60 mg/dL	High–desirable
Less than 40 mg/dL	Low

Checking Your Cholesterol

The National Cholesterol Education Program emphasizes lowering LDL and raising HDL cholesterol levels. Today, experts recommend aiming for very low levels of LDL, especially for people with cardiovascular disease or diabetes. Therapeutic Lifestyle Changes (TLC) and, when necessary, cholesterol-lowering drug therapy may be recommended to bring your cholesterol levels into an acceptable range.

Therapeutic Lifestyle Changes

- **The TLC diet** (Therapeutic Lifestyle Changes diet) may be your first approach to lowering total and LDL cholesterol. This diet emphasizes low saturated fat, low cholesterol, and high fiber. It includes a balance of fruit, vegetables, whole grains, protein, and low-fat dairy products.
  – Limit such foods as butter, hard cheeses, meat fat, and coconut, palm, hydrogenated vegetable oils, and trans fats found in processed snack foods and baked goods.
  – Replace saturated fats with monounsaturated fats found in olive and canola oils.
  – Read food labels carefully. See page 20.

- **Increase your intake of soluble fiber** found in oat bran, apples, legumes, and other vegetables. In addition, increase your consumption of such foods as nuts, vegetable oils, corn, and whole-grain rice. A good guideline is to try to eat a minimum of five servings of fruits and vegetables daily. See page 16.

- **Increase your daily physical activity.** Regular physical activity, such as aerobic exercise or activities such as yard work and household chores, increases your level of the "good" HDL cholesterol. How often you exercise appears to be more important than how hard you work out.

- **Maintain your ideal weight.** People of normal weight generally have higher HDL concentrations and lower levels of LDL.

- **Learn to manage stress.** Unmanaged chronic stress may be associated with an increase in LDL cholesterol levels.

Ideas that Work

- **Follow your doctor's advice.** Depending on your risk factors, your doctor may advise you to combine a cholesterol-lowering medication with Therapeutic Lifestyle Changes (TLC). Research has shown that all of the cholesterol-lowering drugs called "statins" are effective and safe. As with any therapy, it is important to follow the recommended schedule and dosage requirements in order to see results.

- **Watch your numbers.** Experts recommend that men have their cholesterol measured every 5 years from age 35, and from age 45 for women. On the other hand, if you have a family history of heart attack before age 50 or have other risk factors such as diabetes, high blood pressure, obesity, smoking, and a sedentary lifestyle, your doctor may recommend more frequent screening and at an earlier age.

Resources

Your primary care physician

You local chapter of the American Heart Association

National Heart, Lung, and Blood Institute, www.nhlbi.gov

TLC Diet, http://nhlbisupport.com

Going Tobacco-Free

Quitting tobacco use is the single best thing you can do for your health. Cigarette smoking is a major cause of lung disease, heart disease, and cancer. Secondhand smoke is dangerous to those around you and has even been linked to sudden infant death syndrome. Smokeless tobacco (e.g., dip, snuff, chew), cigars, and pipes are not an acceptable alternatives to smoking cigarettes because they also cause mouth and throat cancers.

Because nicotine is addictive, it's hard to give up, even for people with strong willpower. Quitting cold turkey works for some people. Others may need group support or self-help guidelines. Still others may require nicotine replacement therapy or other medications along with behavior modification to kick the habit.

Ideas that Work

Here are the five phases in a typical stop-smoking program:

- **Phase 1: Preconditioning.** Try to begin getting in shape before you quit.
  - Exercise most days of the week.
  - Develop good nutritional habits; watch your weight.
  - Practice relaxation techniques daily.
  - Focus on a list of benefits of being tobacco-free.

- **Phase 2: Establishing Your Quit Date.** Set your quit date, allowing no more than 30 to 45 days to cut down.

- **Phase 3: Preparing to Quit.** During the 30- to 45-day cutting down period:

  - Keep a record of how much you smoke each day.
  - Develop alternatives to smoking such as drinking a glass of water, playing with a pencil, or chewing gum.
  - Nicotine gum, a transdermal nicotine patch, or other medication may be appropriate for you. Consider talking with your doctor.

- **Phase 4: Stopping on Your Quit Date.** Once your quit date arrives, stop. Discard any remaining cigarettes. You are now a nonsmoker. This is a day to celebrate! Reward yourself with a new outfit or tickets to a sports event or concert.

- **Phase 5: Living as a Nonsmoker.** Take credit for a job well done. These approaches can help if you begin to slip:
  - Focus on a benefit of being a nonsmoker every day.
  - Avoid places where people will be smoking.
  - Chew sugarless gum.
  - Reduce stress and tension with regular exercise and relaxation techniques.
  - If you find yourself giving in to your craving to smoke—stop right away. Just one *will* hurt.
  - Remember, most people make five to seven attempts before they quit for good. Each attempt moves you closer to success, so don't be discouraged if you start again; keep trying!

Resources

American Cancer Society. Contact your local chapter for information and stop smoking programs.

American Lung Association. Contact your local chapter about their "Freedom from Smoking Program."

Making Stress Work for You

Stress, in itself, is not unhealthy. In fact, it is one of the many responses your body uses to help you survive. Stress is your body's response to what it believes is a threat. It begins as a physical reaction that prepares you to protect yourself from that threat.

Things that cause this kind of physical reaction are called stressors. Stressors that involve physical harm create this reaction in all of us. However, a perceived threat to your self-esteem, such as when someone criticizes you, may trigger the same feelings as if you were being attacked physically.

Stressors vary from person to person. Something that you consider threatening might not bother your co-worker at all. For example, while you might not like to work under deadline pressure, your friend may not mind that challenge. However, that person might hate it when his supervisor looks over his or her shoulder—something that doesn't bother you at all.

Fighting Imaginary Tigers

Whenever you meet a stressor (threat), your body instantly gets ready for physical danger. It automatically takes steps to help you deal with that danger, either by fighting off the attack or running away. This reaction, called the "fight-or-flight response" (also called the stress response), is part of your physical makeup, and you share it with all animal species. Anything your brain and nervous system perceives as a threat will put you on this same red-alert status.

Within a couple of seconds of encountering a perceived threat, you have extra strength, alertness, energy, and endurance to protect yourself from an attack.

However, do you need this reaction to face most day-to-day stressors? Probably not.

More About Stress

- **Many times the stress response has us overreacting to stressors** when a calmer, problem-solving approach would be more effective—and cause far less tension and distress.

- **Stress can be helpful.** The extra resources provided by the stress response can be useful in many situations. For example, the stress response can give you the inspiration that helps you perform at your best when making an important presentation or when meeting a tough production goal.

- **Too much uncontrolled stress** can limit your concentration, make you more prone to accidents, and affect your physical and mental well-being.

- **Chronic stress may become distress.** Normally, your body relaxes and returns to normal after a threat has passed. However, if stress doesn't go away, your body doesn't slow down and you're in a constant state of alert—or distress. If this constant tension persists and your symptoms get too bad to ignore, then your stress has become chronic.

What Is Chronic Stress?

When stress is frequent or ongoing, the effects can build up quickly and take a serious toll on your physical health and other aspects of your life.

■ **Physical health.** Risks include cardiovascular conditions such as high blood pressure, elevated cholesterol, and the sudden closing (spasm) of the blood vessels that supply the heart with oxygen. Repeated stress reactions can damage other organs including kidneys, stomach, skin and lungs, or lead to ulcers, chronic gastritis, skin rashes, and asthma.

■ **Mental and emotional health.** The self-protective reactions of alertness, fear, and aggression may become long-term conditions of anxiety, anger, and other mental disorders, such as depression. Some people try to relieve these feelings with food, alcohol, cigarettes, tranquilizers, painkillers, or other drugs. These kinds of behaviors are harmful in their own right and they also keep you from addressing the real cause of the problem.

■ **Relationships.** Your relationships with loved ones and your ability to enjoy leisure time may be impaired, leading to arguments with family, friends, co-workers, and supervisors. Your powers of concentration may be affected and you may be prone to excessive absenteeism or job burn-out.

■ **The way you feel about yourself.** Chronic stress can lead to poor self-esteem, fatigue, and depression.

Getting a Handle on Stress

You don't have to be a victim of uncontrolled stress. In fact, you have the power to reduce the effects of stress in your life.

The following pages provide an overview of stress management techniques. These can help you develop an understanding of your own stressors and how you react to them, and give you some strategies for reducing their impact.

How Do You Deal with Stress?

Answer the following questions about how you respond to stress. Then after you've read this section, review your answers. What changes could you make to handle the stressors in your life more effectively?

■ **How much stress do you have in your life?**

❑ Constant

❑ Too much

❑ Occasional

❑ I wish I had some

■ **What are your most common sources of stress? (check all that apply)**

❑ Other people

❑ Family problems (children, parents, spouse)

❑ Health problems

❑ Money problems

❑ Separation or divorce

❑ Job security

❑ Change

❑ Not enough authority to do my job

❑ Conflicts between work and family needs

❑ Lack of confidence in my own abilities and self-worth

❑ Boredom

❑ Overwork

❑ Loneliness

❑ Name your own: _____

Making Stress Work for You

■ **Which one of the stressors you listed is the most stressful for you?**

My main stressor is:

_____

■ **What is the source of your main stressor?** To what degree do you feel you contribute to it?

_____

_____

_____

■ **Who's in control?** How much control do you have over the situation?

❏ A lot of control

❏ Some control

❏ A little control

❏ None at all

■ **How do you react?** What emotions do you feel when you're faced with the stressor (e.g., anger, hurt, frustration, anxiety)? Do you hold them inside or do you express them? If you express your feelings, are you usually glad or sorry that you did?

_____

_____

_____

■ **How do you feel physically?** Do you feel tense or fatigued? Do you have headaches, insomnia, stomach problems, or trouble eating?

_____

_____

_____

■ **How do you act?** What do you do when you're faced with the stressor (e.g., ignore it, run away from the problem, deal with it directly)? How do you try to reduce the "threat" or pressure (e.g., use alcohol or drugs, exercise, overeat, try relaxation techniques)?

_____

_____

_____

_____

■ **Do you think your reactions and actions help or hurt you/the situation?** Do you consider your emotions and actions to be positive or negative? Would you do anything different the next time you experience the same stressor?

_____

_____

_____

_____

■ **Do you need help?** Do you think you need help or support to cope with this problem? Who do you think can help you?

_____

_____

_____

_____

What Does This Mean?

This exercise will help you begin to identify the stressors in your life, their sources, and how you tend to respond to them. You may have discovered that your reaction to stressful situations actually creates more stress. Go back and list some other stressors in your life and see how you would face each situation.

Making Stress Work for You

Coping with Stress

Two people who work side by side, or who live together, experience different kinds and amounts of stress. Why? Because the stress they experience is actually the result of a constantly changing relationship between two kinds of stressors:

1. **Job Stressors** that are a natural part of working

2. **Personal Stressors** that come from your family situation or social life

It's very difficult to leave your problems behind you at home or at the office. It's easy for your personal and job-related stress to spill into each other and have a negative effect on both areas of your life. Even if you can't control every stressful situation, you can have a big impact on how your stressors affect you. How? By identifying your job stressors and personal stressors, and understanding how they influence your behavior on and off the job.

Job Stressors

You may face things on the job that call up your stress response: deadlines, work conditions, an irritating boss or co-worker, a tragic or frightening event. Some jobs cause more stress than others, but every job produces at least some stress.

Some of that stress is helpful, of course. Deadlines help make sure you get the work done. A tough but fair supervisor can inspire you to achieve much more than you expected. In fact, having too little stress on the job has been shown to be just as harmful as being overloaded. Here are some ways to recognize if job stress is getting the best of you:

- Your job makes too many—or too few—demands on you.

- Your job is boring or routine, but you need to stay focused; for example, assembly-line work, data entry, and office reception.

- You have no input into, or control over, how your time or your work is managed.

- Your job duties are not well-defined.

- Management gives you no reason to feel valued or supported.

- You don't have the resources or the authority that are necessary to do your job.

- You get conflicting orders or mixed messages from supervisors.

- You have no guidance on how to do the job.

- You can suffer serious consequences for failure.

For Your Information

Experts have discovered that the most stressful jobs have one striking thing in common: They make you feel as though you have no control over the work that you're trying to do. On the other hand, the feeling that you are in charge of your work is the greatest source of job satisfaction.

Making Stress Work for You

Personal Stressors

Personal stressors are problems and feelings that you have about your life outside of work. Some, such as a need to earn more money, can motivate you to increase your job skills. Others, like a health problem or worries about your family, can make you less effective at work.

Every person brings different stressors to the workplace, but many stressors fall into specific groups:

- **Competence.** Lacking skills to do the job. Fear of learning new things.

- **Health.** Not enough energy to get through the shift. Effects of alcohol or drug use. Physical problems, such as back pain or chronic illness.

- **Interpersonal relations.** Shyness. Quick temper or lack of trust. Impatience. Inability to work on a team. Inability to listen actively.

- **Work/family.** Too much to do at home. Eldercare or childcare problems. An abusive or unsupportive partner. Upcoming move or divorce.

- **Finances.** Worrying about money. Debt. Living from paycheck to paycheck. Upcoming retirement.

- **Self-image.** Lack of confidence, or feeling overly important. Identifying too much with your job. Seeing yourself as a victim.

- **Attitude.** Being bored with your job. Having interest only in your paycheck. Doing things halfway because it's easier and takes less time. Believing that quality is someone else's job.

- **Fears.** Fearing change or learning new skills. Avoiding something necessary to the job, such as flying or public speaking. Fearing failure.

- **Poor coping behaviors.** Dealing with problems by using drugs or alcohol. Avoiding stress by vegging out in front of the TV, or taking it out on friends or family members.

Once you have identified your stressors, you have begun to take steps to understand the way you react to stressful situations (your "stress style").

The key to stress control is being able to manage day-to-day stressors before they reduce your personal effectiveness. The following self-care skills can help you avoid overload and reduce tension in your everyday life. When the cause of your stress is more serious, quick fixes are not enough. See "Resources" on pages 34 and 291.

Ideas that Work

- **Modify your perception.** Do you make a habit of "making a mountain out of a molehill?" When you're faced with a stressful situation, ask yourself: "What's the worst thing that can happen?"

- **Stop that thought!** When you have a stressful or negative thought, try this technique:
  - Stop the thought in midstream. Say to yourself: "Stop!"
  - Take a deep breath and exhale slowly.
  - Now, take another look at the situation objectively.
  - Ask yourself: "Am I overreacting (perception)?"
  - Then ask yourself: "What's a more positive, constructive way to approach this problem?"

Making Stress Work for You

- **Learn to accept and use change** to your advantage. Build flexibility into your work and personal life and view change as a part of life. Adapting to change can be a healthy experience that helps you grow, though there will be bumps in the road. Also, anticipate change and prepare for it before the change takes place (e.g., before an older relative comes to live with you, research community eldercare services).

- **Become a good communicator.** Poor communication is one of the main causes of stressful situations. Learn to be an active listener—try to understand what the other person is saying without interrupting. (Try to "walk in his or her shoes.") When responding, address the behavior or the problem; avoid attacking the individual.

- **Take charge of the home front.** Take steps to get problems at home under control. Seek counseling for marriage or financial difficulties; work on finding a reliable solution for childcare or eldercare needs.

- **Keep your job skills up to date.** You'll feel more confident about doing your job.

- **Appreciate that you and your abilities are unique.** Have the courage to take chances and risk failure. Before you leave work, name at least one thing that you feel good about in that day's work—paving a section of road, helping a customer handle a difficult problem, closing a sale, etc.

- **Pace yourself.** Pace your workflow—on and off the job—by staying organized, setting realistic timelines, and having needed resources available before you begin any project. Try to set aside 20 percent of your time for unplanned events or problems.

- **Be careful with caffeine.** Coffee, tea, and cola drinks are stimulants that increase your heart rate and can make you more irritable. Learn your individual tolerance for this powerful stimulant.

- **Use your imagination to relax.** In a quiet place, try this visualization exercise for 10 to 15 minutes:
  - Close your eyes and breathe normally.
  - Visualize yourself as a bag full of sand—full of tension.
  - Your feet are the bottom corners of the bag.
  - The corners suddenly burst open, and the sand begins to run out.
  - Feel the sand—and all the tension—run out of your feet.
  - Empty the bag of all the sand—all the tension.
  - Resume your normal activity.

- **Control your breathing to relax.** Most meditation exercises use breathing techniques to help relax the body and the mind. Try this simple technique:
  - Find a private spot where you can be quiet for 10 to 15 minutes.
  - Sit up straight, with your hands in your lap.
  - Close your eyes.
  - Inhale deeply, hold your breath for 5 seconds and exhale slowly.
  - Sit quietly, concentrating on your breathing.
  - As you exhale, say the word "calm."
  - With each exhalation, feel your mind becoming more still.
  - Don't fight other thoughts or distractions; let them come—let them go.
  - Just concentrate on your breathing.
  - After 10 to 15 minutes, open your eyes. Remain seated, and stay relaxed, for 2 to 3 minutes.

Making Stress Work for You

- **Tense, then relax.** Progressive relaxation has been a popular relaxation technique for years. The idea is to tense, then relax, specific muscle groups in a regular order. Try this technique when you begin to feel tense:
  - If possible, find a private, quiet room.
  - Lie on the floor. (If that's not possible, sit comfortably in an armchair.)
  - Loosen any tight clothing: belt, necktie, collar.
  - Remove your shoes.
  - Close your eyes and breathe normally.
  - For each muscle group, tense the muscles for 6 seconds, then relax. Repeat three times before going to the next group of muscles.
  - The sequence: feet, calves, thighs, buttocks, shoulders (bring shoulders to ears if sitting, up off the floor if lying down), hands, forehead, jaw (make a face, stick out your tongue).
  - Reverse the sequence.

- **Walk it off.** A simple 20- to 30-minute walk has been shown to reduce muscle tension as much as some tranquilizers.

- **Stretch it out.** Simple stretching exercises are an effective way to reduce built-up tension in the neck, shoulders, and back. See pages 10-12.

- **Have a good laugh.** Some experts call a good laugh "inner jogging." Keep a book of jokes or humorous short stories close by. If you begin to feel angry or tense, take a humor break.

- **Tune up!** Playing classical or other selections can help you relax and concentrate. There are also a number of relaxation tapes that combine nature sounds or soothing music with self-suggestion instructions that either ask you to visualize a specific scene or teach you to relax specific muscle groups.

- **Keep a journal.** A popular and effective way to manage stress is to keep a daily journal. Journal writing allows you to note your feelings on a given day: problems, insights, solutions, and outcomes. Many journal keepers find that they can blow off steam through writing. Your journal also can be a record of personal growth.

- **Pray or meditate.** Many experts have shown that prayer and meditation are very effective calming techniques for managing stress.

- **Play games.** Simple mental diversions such as puzzles and video and computer games can take the edge off seriousness, ease tension, and even release a creative urge or two.

Resources

Your employee assistance program

Your health care provider or local mental health agency

The Seven Habits of Highly Effective People, by Stephen R. Covey. New York: Simon and Schuster, 2001.

Stress Management for Wellness, by Walt Schafer. New York: Harcourt Brace Jovanovich, 1998.

Do you feel depressed?

Have you felt sad or blue lately? If you answered "yes," you may be depressed. The good news is that most symptoms of depression can be treated successfully with proper diagnosis and treatment (e.g., medication, talk therapy). Talk to your doctor. See page 207 to learn more.

Drug Abuse

urn on the television or read the newspaper, and the impact of drugs on our society will be very evident. But contrary to what you may hear or see, drug abuse is not limited to the crack houses of the inner city or the glamorous jet set. In fact, you may be working or living with a person who has a drug problem. Victims of drug abuse include:

- **Users.** Drug abuse leads to physical and/or psychological addiction. If people share needles for intravenous drug use, they put themselves and their sexual partners at risk of HIV or hepatitis infection.

- **Families.** Families of drug users may suffer neglect, financial ruin, and physical and mental abuse. Pregnant women who use drugs such as heroin, cocaine, and alcohol place their unborn children at greater risk for birth defects and infectious disease.

- **Co-workers.** Employees who work with a drug abuser may become victims of the abuser's unreliable job performance and unsafe work practices.

- **Employers.** Employees who abuse drugs cost companies money because of increased health and disability claims, defective products, and a damaged reputation in the marketplace.

- **Society.** Consumers may suffer from defective products or services: People who use public transportation are at risk from operators who may use drugs on the job. Drug abuse costs taxpayers billions of dollars for treatment and law enforcement.

How Do Drugs Work?

Drugs that alter the chemistry of the brain and nervous system are called psychoactive agents. They can act as stimulants, depressants, or hallucinogens. However, psychoactive substances are not limited to illegal "street drugs" such as cocaine, heroin, and marijuana. They also include prescription and over-the-counter medications, and the most widely used drugs: alcohol, nicotine, and caffeine. Each drug has a unique effect on the mind and body of the user and can lead to a physical and/or psychological dependence.

STIMULANTS: "Uppers" raise the metabolism, blood pressure, and heart rate. People use stimulants to stay alert, to get a rapid surge of energy, and to lose weight. "Household" stimulants include coffee, tea, cola drinks, and tobacco. Caffeine and nicotine both stimulate the central nervous system. Stimulants that are "controlled substances" (drugs that are strictly controlled or banned by federal laws) include cocaine and its highly addictive derivative, crack; amphetamines; and methamphetamine (speed).

DEPRESSANTS: "Downers" slow the central nervous system. They alter the user's perception of the outside world, causing slowed thinking, confusion, and other impairments. Users may become withdrawn and seem "spaced out." Alcohol is the most widely used depressant, although many think it's a stimulant because it tends to decrease people's inhibitions. See page 39.

Depressants include sedatives, sleep aids, and painkillers. Controlled substances classified as depressants include barbiturates; narcotic agents such as heroin, morphine, opium, OxyContin®, and codeine;

Drug Abuse

and other synthetic drugs. PCP, or "Angel Dust," is an especially dangerous depressant that often produces violent and unpredictable behavior. GHB ("liquid ecstasy") produces loss of consciousness and unknowing users may become victims of sexual assaults.

HALLUCINOGENS: These chemical agents alter a person's sense of reality. "Tripping" is the common term used to describe the effect hallucinogens have in enhancing and intensifying perception. LSD, mescaline (peyote), and psilocybin (magic mushrooms) produce hallucinogenic effects.

INHALANTS: Common household items—glue, butane, gasoline, felt-tip marker fluid, propane, room deodorizers—produce chemical vapors that cause mind-altering effects when inhaled. Young people are the most common abusers, probably because these substances are readily available and inexpensive. Using these substances can lead to heart failure or suffocation.

CANNABINOIDS: Cannabis products are taken from the leaves of the hemp plant and usually are sold as marijuana (grass, pot, or weed), hashish (hash), hashish oil, or the chemical derivative THC (tetrahydrocannabinol). Usually smoked, cannabis produces relaxation and a mild sense of euphoria. In specific cases, cannabis has been prescribed for cancer patients to counteract the effects of chemotherapy. Long-term use of cannabis has been linked to lung disease and a weakened immune system. Cannabis also affects memory, judgment, coordination, other sensory motor skills, and can impair a person's ability to drive and operate machinery.

STEROIDS: Anabolic steroids sometimes are abused by athletes or others who wish to enhance their physical strength and performance. While producing no intoxicating effects, these compounds cause a range of mental and physical health consequences from aggression and hostility to high blood pressure and certain cancers.

Do You Need Help?

It's common for abusers to feel they don't need help until the problem has compromised their lives seriously. If you think you have, or someone you care about has, a drug problem, it's important to get help right away.

The First Steps to Recovery

The first steps to overcoming drug dependence are the most difficult—first, admitting that there is a problem, and then, understanding that you need help in order to change. Rehabilitation treatment programs are tailored to individual needs, but with professional intervention, addicts can learn to control their condition and go on to lead normal, productive lives.

The following resources can provide professional support for drug treatment and recovery:

- If available, your company employee assistance program (EAP)

- Local or national drug hotlines

- "Anonymous" groups; e.g., Narcotics Anonymous (listed in the white pages)

Drug Abuse

- Local community drug rehabilitation centers (listed in the yellow pages)

- Your personal physician

- A member of the clergy

Recognizing Substance Abuse in Others

It's common for many people to attribute a person's erratic behavior to anything but drug abuse, especially if the individual is a co-worker or family member. When a person has a drug problem, he or she usually is sending out signals for help. Some signs are hard to detect, while others are more obvious. The following are indications that a person may have a drug problem:

- Increased absences or tardiness at work

- Poor health habits

- Physical symptoms such as red, glassy eyes and sleepiness (marijuana); a chronic runny nose and bad breath (cocaine); scars or needle marks and constricted pupils that don't respond to light (heroin)

- Presence of drug paraphernalia such as roach clips, pipes, rolling papers, syringes, razor blades, and straws

- Behavioral symptoms such as confusion, hyperactivity, excitability, mood swings, and explosive bouts of anger

- Taking extended breaks or being absent from the workstation

- Complaints about money; requests to borrow money from co-workers, friends, or family

- Strained or abusive relationships with co-workers, friends, or family

How to Help Drug Abusers

It's very difficult to confront someone about drug abuse. Family members and friends often become enablers by ignoring, denying, or even covering up the problem, making it possible for the drug user to continue his or her behavior. If you suspect that someone you know and care about has a drug problem, but you don't know what to do about it, try the following approaches:

- **Learn about the problem.** Contact resources such as your company employee assistance program, local drug rehabilitation center, or drug hotline. The professional will advise you how to communicate your concerns to the drug user and will offer possible options for referral.

- **Try an intervention.** With a trained drug counselor's help, family, friends, and, sometimes, co-workers can confront the drug user about his or her behavior. The goal is to help the person realize that he or she has a problem and to insist that he or she agree to go into rehabilitation immediately.

- **Expect denial.** It's common for a drug user to deny the problem when confronted. In fact, the threat of job loss and resulting loss of income may be the only thing that pushes a person to seek help.

- **Your efforts may fail at first.** Continue to voice your disapproval of the individual's behavior, but share your interest in supporting a decision to quit. Avoid becoming or remaining an enabler.

37

Drug Abuse

Working Through the Treatment Process

Recovery from drug dependence is a lifelong challenge. Although treatment depends on each person's individual needs and situation, the rehabilitation process may involve professional assessment and determination of a treatment plan, inpatient treatment, outpatient treatment, transitional care, and long-term follow-up.

There are three goals to drug abuse treatment:

1. **Stop or reduce drug use**

2. **Improve the person's ability to function in daily life**

3. **Reduce the medical and social complications of drug use**

Effective drug treatment programs may include:

■ **Outpatient drug-free treatment.** Patients visit clinics regularly and benefit from individual or group counseling. This treatment is appropriate for a wide variety of addictions and for those people with otherwise stable lives and only brief episodes of drug dependence.

■ **Short-term residential programs.** Referred to as chemical dependency units, these programs may involve intensive 3- to 6-week inpatient treatment, followed by extended outpatient support.

■ **Therapeutic communities (TCs).** Structured residential programs lasting as long as 1 year, TCs typically treat long-term drug abusers, those with criminal history, and others needing intensive rehabilitation to a drug-free, crime-free lifestyle.

Note: Because of the high costs of residential drug rehabilitation programs, make sure that the person's health insurance plan approves treatment before he or she is committed for a non-emergency. Check other options, such as outpatient care.

■ **Medication maintenance.** Individuals with opiate addictions may benefit from programs offering a synthetic drug, typically methadone, that blocks the effects of the heroin and reduces physical cravings. With appropriate counseling and support, individuals may be able to leave drug or criminal behavior behind and move toward a more productive life.

■ **Transitions.** The recovering person usually progresses from professionally led group therapy sessions to community-based self-help groups such as Narcotics Anonymous. Participants often follow a 12-Step Program that relies heavily on group support and commitment to lifelong recovery.

Resources

Your company employee assistance program, if available

American Council for Drug Education
800.488.3784
www.acde.org

Narcotics Anonymous. Check your phone directory's white pages.

Cocaine Hotline: 800.COCAINE

National Institute on Drug Abuse
800.662.HELP
www.drugabuse.gov

Alcohol Use

Since the beginning of civilization, alcohol has been used worldwide for cultural rituals and as part of other celebrations.

Classified as a depressant, alcohol is immediately absorbed through the stomach and affects every cell in the body. The brain, kidneys, liver, and lungs are especially affected by alcohol consumption.

How your body reacts to alcohol depends on a number of factors:

- **Dosage:** The higher the alcohol concentration, the faster your blood alcohol level will increase.

- **Drinking rate:** The more drinks you take within an hour, the faster the blood alcohol level will rise. Normally, the liver can metabolize one drink per hour with limited physical and mental effects on the user.

- **Alcohol and food:** Alcohol will be absorbed more slowly if you have food in your stomach.

- **Alcohol tolerance:** Since people with alcoholism burn alcohol at a faster rate than do non-alcoholics, they need more alcohol to get the same effects.

- **Body weight:** Usually the greater the body weight, the more alcohol a person needs to become intoxicated. However, even amounts of alcohol that are perceived as modest (e.g., three beers within an hour for an 180-pound person), can significantly impair judgment and motor skills for tasks such as driving a car. In fact, an 180-pound person who drinks three beers in 1 hour would have a blood alcohol level of .05, which in many states is grounds for arrest for "driving while intoxicated" (DWI) or "driving under the influence" (DUI).

Three Kinds of Drinkers

- **Social drinkers:** Millions of Americans are social drinkers. They use alcohol responsibly and not habitually—they can take it or leave it.

- **Problem drinkers:** Problem drinkers' use of alcohol interferes with their interpersonal relationships, health, and well-being. They may engage in periods

For Your Information

What's your attitude about alcohol?

The CAGE Questionnaire will help you assess whether you may have a problem with alcohol.
- Have you ever felt you should **C**ut down on your drinking?
- Have people **A**nnoyed you by criticizing your drinking?
- Have you ever felt bad or **G**uilty about your drinking?
- Have you ever had an **E**ye opener—a drink in the morning to steady your nerves or to get rid of a hangover?

What does this quiz mean?

If you answer yes to any of these questions, it's a good idea to discuss your alcohol use with your doctor, your EAP, if available, or try the resources listed on pages 42 and 288. *American Journal of Psychiatry*

of heavy drinking or binge drinking. They also may put themselves and others in danger due to their risky behaviors such as driving while under the influence of alcohol.

- **Alcoholics:** Alcoholism is an illness—not a simple lack of willpower. It is probably caused by a combination of genetics and a person's social and emotional environment. Alcoholics develop a psychological and physical dependence on alcohol, show an inability to limit their drinking, and have a high tolerance for alcohol—needing greater amounts of alcohol to feel the effects.

  Heavy drinking can cause:

  –Serious health consequences. Certain cancers, liver damage, immune system problems, brain damage, and harm to an unborn child may result from alcohol abuse.

  –A higher rate of on-the-job injuries, automobile accidents, homicides, and suicides.

  –Extraordinarily high costs to family, career, and personal relationships.

The First Step to Recovery

The first and most critical step in treating alcohol dependency is getting the problem drinker to admit there is a problem and that alchohol dependency is a behavioral problem as well as a medical condition. For long-term recovery to succeed, a problem drinker must admit that he or she has a problem with alcohol and, with guidance from a professional counselor, learn how to replace old drinking habits with more positive coping skills.

Start with These Resources

- Company employee assistance program, if available
- Local or national alcohol hotlines
- Local community alcohol rehabilitation centers (listed in the yellow pages)
- Anonymous groups; e.g., Alcoholics Anonymous (listed in the white pages)
- Your doctor
- Member of the clergy

Helping a Person with a Drinking Problem

It's very difficult to confront someone about his or her drinking, especially if there is a risk of mental and physical abuse. When friends, co-workers, and "drinking buddies" are reluctant to confront the person, they become enablers by ignoring or denying the problem and allowing it to continue. The more drinking behavior a person is exposed to, the more difficult it is for him or her to recognize normal behavior. This may be one of the reasons children of alcoholics may marry alcoholics; in the dating process they don't notice that the partner's drinking is abnormal.

Ideas that Work: Getting Involved

It's not easy to help an individual who has a serious drinking problem. In the short term you may be perceived as the enemy, especially if you persist. Here are some suggestions:

■ **Learn about the problem.** Contact such resources as your company employee assistance program, alcohol rehabilitation center, and Alcoholics Anonymous (AA).

■ **Confront the person when he or she is sober.**

■ **Focus on behavior only.** Focus on how the person's drinking affects his or her behavior, work, and interaction with family and friends. Be objective and stick to the facts: "When you were drunk last night, you threw a shoe at me. Do you remember that?"

■ **Expect denial.** It's common for problem drinkers to deny their problem until some event forces them to face it.

■ **Ease up.** If your first efforts fail to convince the person to seek help, ease up on your feedback. There will be other opportunities.

■ **Offer support.** Reinforce your interest in supporting the problem drinker when he or she decides to quit.

■ **Address abuse.** Never tolerate mental or physical abuse, either as a recipient or observer. Get help before someone gets hurt.

For Your Information

Depression hinders recovery

Men and women who are diagnosed with major depression with alcohol dependence are more likely to take that first drink and relapse than those who do not have depression with alcohol dependence. Alert your doctor if you, or someone you care about, shows signs of depression. See pages 264–265.

Archives of General Psychiatry

■ **Consider intervention.** A trained alcohol counselor joins family, friends, and, sometimes, co-workers to confront the person about his or her drinking behavior. The goal is to help the person realize that he or she has a problem and to agree immediately to rehabilitation.

Working Toward Sobriety

Staying sober is a day-to-day, lifelong commitment. Depending on the individual situation, treatment can range from a network such as Alcoholics Anonymous (AA) to outpatient or inpatient care using an intensive medical and behavioral approach.

■ **Alcoholics Anonymous.** Many alcoholics have been successful in staying sober through AA. This self-help approach guides a person through 12 carefully designed steps to becoming and remaining sober. There is continual emphasis on the need for recovering alcoholics to support and help one another. Studies show that the longer people attend AA, the longer they stay sober.

■ **Outpatient programs.** These community-based programs combine one-on-one counseling sessions and group sessions. Usually patients are referred to a local AA group for ongoing support and assistance.

■ **Inpatient programs.** An in-house treatment program through a local hospital or residential treatment center usually is recommended if the person with an alcohol problem has immediate medical needs (e.g., overdose, withdrawal) or psychological needs (e.g., suicidal thoughts) that place him or her in danger.

Alcohol Use

Note: Residential alcohol rehabilitation programs are expensive, so make sure that the person's treatment is approved by his or her medical benefit program before he or she is admitted for a non-emergency. Discuss other treatment options such as outpatient care.

■ **Family assistance.** There are many support organizations and services that assist family members in coping with a problem drinker. The first resource, if available, should be your company or union employee assistance program. Other organizations such as Al-Anon or Alateen help family members deal with the stresses of living with an alcoholic. MADD (Mothers Against Drunk Driving) sponsors programs against drunk driving (e.g., designated driver programs) and local support groups for families who have lost family members because of a drunk driver.

Resources

Your company or union employee assistance program, if available

Alcoholics Anonymous (AA)
212.870.3400
www.aa.org

Al-Anon/Alateen Family Group Headquarters
757.563.1600
www.al-anon.alateen.org

Mothers Against Drunk Driving (MADD)
511 E. John Carpenter Freeway, Suite 700
Irving, TX 75062
800.438.6233

Check your phone book's white pages for AA and Al-Anon groups near you.

For Your Information

Alcohol and Health

Evidence supports the value of moderate alcohol use in heart disease prevention because it's believed that alcohol increases HDL (good cholesterol). Moderate use is defined as no more than two servings per day for men and one serving per day for women. Pregnant women should never drink alcohol. A serving is defined as 12 ounces of beer, 1-1/2 ounces of alcohol, or 5 ounces of wine. Going beyond these levels eliminates the cardiovascular benefits and increases the risk of liver disease, cancer, and alcoholism. Finally, these recommendations do not encourage non-drinkers to start, and no one should drink alcohol and drive.

Preventive Health Screenings

COMMON HEALTH SCREENING TESTS: RECOMMENDED SCHEDULES

Test	Age 20–29	Age 30–39	Age 40–49	Age 50 and older
Blood Pressure*	• Every 1 to 2 years after age 18, unless part of a doctor visit for another purpose.			
Cholesterol*			• Once every 5 years from age ~~35~~ 25 for men, 45 for women*. See page 25.	
Dental Exam**	• Dental cleaning and exam recommended every 6 to 12 months.			
Pap Test and Pelvic Exam*	• First Pap test 3 years after sexual activity begins or by age 21, then annually up to age 30. Depending on risk factors, women age 30 and older may not need annual screening, although annual pelvic exams are recommended for all women. Consult with your doctor.			
Mammography***			• Every 1 to 2 years from age 40	• Every year. After age 75, talk to your doctor.
Clinical Breast Exam*	• Every 3 years		• Every year	
Breast Self-Exam	• Depending on risk factors, may be performed every month to establish familiarity with breast tissue.			
Fecal Occult Blood Sigmoidoscopy OR Colonoscopy OR Double Contrast Barium Enema				• Every year • Every 5 years • Every 10 years* • Every 5 to 10 years
Prostate Exam****				• Your doctor may recommend an annual digital rectal exam (DRE). Talk to your doctor about the risks and benefits of screening, including DRE and prostate-specific antigen (PSA).**** See pages 279-280.
Blood Glucose*				* Every 3 years if you are at high risk, at the discretion of your doctor.

* Patients with additional risk factors may be screened at an earlier age.

** Dental X-rays are generally recommended at 12- to 36-month intervals, depending on your clinical signs and symptoms (e.g., pain or trauma) and your individual risk factors (e.g., high number of previous cavities or poor oral hygiene). Talk to your dentist to determine your individual risk factors.

*** Physicians may determine that women younger than 40 with significant risk factors (e.g., sister or mother with breast cancer) may benefit from earlier intervention, including mammogram, ultrasound, and MRI.

**** African-American men and men with a family history of prostate cancer may want to consider screening at an earlier age.

Sources: Guide to Clinical Preventive Services: Report of the U.S. Preventive Services Task Force, American Cancer Society, American Diabetes Association, American Dental Association

Immunizations

RECOMMENDED IMMUNIZATION SCHEDULE FOR COMMON INFECTIOUS DISEASES

Protection from:	Abbreviation	Age
Diphtheria, tetanus, and pertussis	DTaP	2, 4, and 6 months; 15–18 months; 4–6 years
Polio	IPV (inactivated poliovirus)	2 months; 4 months; 6–18 months; 4–6 years
H. influenzae type b*	Hib	2, 4, and 6 months*; 12–18 months (booster)
Pneumococcal conjugate	PCV	2, 4, and 6 months; 12–15 months
Measles, mumps, rubella**	MMR	12–18 months; 4–6 years
Tetanus and diphtheria	Td	11–12 or 14–16 years; Every 10 years thereafter
Hepatitis B	Hep B	Birth; 1–4 months; and 6–18 months; Older individuals at high risk
Varicella zoster virus (chicken pox)	Var	12–18 months; Age 13 or older without a history of disease or vaccine: two doses 4–6 weeks apart
Influenza (yearly strain)	Influenza	Yearly for adults 50 or older; anyone over 6 months of age who wishes immunity or suffers from such chronic conditions as diabetes, heart disease, or lung disease, or has impaired immunity
Pneumonia	Pneumovac	Yearly from 6 months or older; anyone who wishes immunity; or those who suffer from certain chronic conditions or have impaired immunity

* Depending on which vaccine is used, an additional Hib may or may not be needed at 6 months. Also, Hib may be combined with DTP and given as Tetraimmune vaccine.

** Women and teenagers of childbearing age should be tested for antibodies against rubella (German measles). Immunization should be done if no antibodies are found. Talk to your health care provider.

Note: It's a good idea to check with your health plan for recommended immunization schedules.

Source: Centers for Disease Control and Prevention, Advisory Committee on Immunization Practices, 2003-2004

Breast Cancer

It is an important self-care practice to examine your breasts. Tumors found in the earliest stage of breast cancer are curable more than 90 percent of the time. Women should become familiar with their breasts and pay attention to the way their breasts look and feel.

If you are at average risk for breast cancer, you may choose to perform this self-exam occasionally. Depending on your individual risk for breast cancer, your doctor may recommend that you examine your breasts every month. Report any unusual new lumps, irregular thickening, surface irregularities or dimpling, or nipple discharge to your doctor immediately. See pages 256–257.

Testicular Cancer

Although relatively rare, testicular cancer is the most common cancer in men between the ages of 20 and 35. It also is one of the most curable cancers, especially if it is detected and treated early. Depending on your individual risk factors, your doctor may recommend you do a testicular self-exam every month after a warm bath or shower, feeling for any lumps, swelling, hardness, or other abnormalities you have not noticed before. It's normal for one testicle to be larger or slightly higher in the scrotum than the other. In addition, the cord-like structure on the back of the testicle also is normal. Report any lumps or abnormalities to your doctor immediately.

Skin Cancer

The incidence of skin cancer is on the rise. According to the American Cancer Society, half of all new cancers in this country are skin cancers.

Skin cancer is usually caused by bad sunburns and over-exposure to the sun's ultraviolet radiation over many years. In fact, getting just one severe sunburn in childhood increases your risk of developing skin cancer as an adult.

It's recommended that you examine your skin regularly, looking for any changes or abnormalities. Use a mirror, or have a partner or caregiver assist you in examining hard-to-see areas.

If you have any moles or dark spots that have any of these characteristics (remember **"ABCD"**), consult your doctor at once:

A–Asymmetry: one half of spot does not match the other

B–Border: edges are irregular or blurred

C–Color: variable in different shades or colors

D–Diameter: larger than a pencil eraser, which was not noticed before

For more information on cancer, see pages 258–259.

"Be true to your teeth or your teeth will be false to you," is an often-quoted dental proverb. Making a commitment to spending just 10 minutes a day to care for your teeth properly can mean the difference between keeping your teeth for the rest of your life, or keeping your teeth in a glass next to your bed at night.

Getting Checkups

You'll need to see your dentist any time your teeth need to be filled or repaired; otherwise a visit every 6 months for a thorough cleaning and checkup is all you'll need. During a dental exam, your dentist will check for dental decay and signs of gum disease and oral cancer, and examine your teeth for bite and alignment problems.

Your dentist will tell you what all of your options are—from describing state-of-the-art care and repair, to explaining the consequences if you choose to do nothing. If he or she recommends more dental work than you can afford, take care of the most pressing concerns first and get to the others as soon as you can afford it. Any recommended treatment should be accompanied by an itemized summary of the charges for any work your dentist recommends.

Brushing Up

Brushing your teeth is the first line of defense against the plaque that hardens into tartar (which only your dentist can remove) and leads to tooth decay, gum disease, and tooth loss. The entire brushing process should take 2 to 4 minutes. Here's how:

- **Brush at least twice a day,** and definitely brush before going to bed.

- **Toothbrush.** A brush with a small head fits better into your mouth's tight spaces than a bigger one. Bristles should be soft and rounded. Buy a new toothbrush every 2 months, or following an illness, because bristles harbor bacteria and tend to wear down with use.

- **Toothpaste.** Always use fluoride toothpaste.

- **Use the right touch.** Hold your toothbrush as you would a pencil, with the tips of your thumb and two or three fingers. Tilt the brush at a 45-degree angle toward your gums, then use a small, circular motion to clean the entire surface of each tooth, cheek-side and tongue-side. A light touch works best and will not damage your gums.

- **Brush your tongue too.** It only takes a few seconds to clean your tongue, which harbors bacteria just as gums and teeth do.

Flossing Away Plaque

Whatever plaque your toothbrush misses, your floss will find. Here are some tips for flossing correctly:

- **Work the curves.** The most important place for your floss to reach is the area where your gums curve around each tooth, where plaque harbors bacteria and hardens into tartar. With floss wrapped around each middle finger, gently work the floss between

Dental Health

your teeth to the gum line, then sweep the floss under the gumline around the curve of each tooth. Never use a sawing, back-and-forth motion, which can damage gums.

- **Floss is floss.** Thin floss may work better if your teeth are very close together. Dental tape may be comfortable for people whose teeth are not so tight-fitting. Waxed or unwaxed, flavored or plain—buy one you like and use it every day.

- **Water works.** Swish a mouthful of water around your teeth after you brush and floss. If you can't brush or floss after eating, a quick water rinse will at least remove food particles and wash away mouth acids. Water-jet appliances (e.g., WaterPik®) also remove food particles, but they don't replace flossing or brushing.

- **Mouthwash is optional.** Some studies have shown that rinsing with antiseptic mouthwash daily can reduce plaque buildup significantly. You can use a mouthwash that contains fluoride if your tap water doesn't contain fluoride.

Getting a Better Bite

Teeth that don't fit together properly can be hard to clean and may place harmful pressure on the structures that support the teeth, leading to dental problems later in life. If your dentist recommends braces or some other appliance to straighten your teeth, it can mean the difference between keeping or losing some or all of your teeth.

More Tooth Savers

- **Chew sugarless gum,** especially if you can't brush right away. Chewing gum neutralizes mouth acids and removes food particles from teeth. Don't chew gum all the time, though: You can damage the joint that attaches your lower jaw to your skull.

- **Don't use tobacco.** Besides giving you stained teeth and bad breath, tobacco—especially smokeless tobacco—can cause severe damage to gums and has been implicated in a number of mouth and throat cancers.

- **Limit sweets.** Candy and sweetened drinks increase acid in your mouth and contribute to tooth decay.

- **Never use your teeth as a tool.** Don't open bottles or try to tear things with your teeth. If you do break a tooth or have one knocked out, see your dentist immediately.

- **Get an early start.** Talk to your dentist about how to care for your children's teeth before and after their first teeth come in. He or she also can tell you how to teach your children to brush and floss properly, once your kids are old enough to handle the responsibility.

Resources

Your dentist

American Dental Association
312.440.2500
www.ada.org

National Institute of Dental and Craniofacial Research
301.496.4261
www.nidr.nih.gov

Birth Control

hoosing a method of birth control is one of the most important decisions that responsible, sexually active adults make. Both partners should be involved in the decision and should assess their sexual attitudes and practices when choosing one method over another. Before you rely on any birth control method, discuss the various options with your doctor. Remember to always practice safe sex.

Hormones

- **Oral contraceptives:** Birth control pills contain manufactured forms of female hormones that, when taken daily, stop a woman's ovaries from releasing an egg and/or change the cervical mucus to prevent sperm from entering.

- **Injections:** Hormone injections (shots) every 3 months (Depo-Provera®) are effective in preventing the ovaries from releasing eggs.

- **Emergency contraception:** The "morning after" pill is a backup contraception option if taken within 3 days of having unprotected intercourse. High doses of hormones are given to bring about changes in the lining of the uterus to prevent pregnancy.

- **Transdermal system:** "The patch," worn on the skin and changed periodically, delivers hormones directly through the skin.

- **Contraceptive ring:** This small ring (NuvaRing®) is inserted into the vagina near the cervix and releases hormones that prevent the egg from being released. It is discarded after 3 weeks and then replaced after menstruation.

Intrauterine Device (IUD)

The IUD is a small plastic device placed inside the uterus by a health care provider. The presence of the IUD creates changes in the uterus to make it inhospitable to a fertilized egg. IUDs may contain copper (Copper-T®) or hormones (Progestasert® or Mirena®) to further prevent pregnancy.

Barrier Methods

- **Spermicides:** Spermicides are chemical barriers that kill sperm on contact. They are most effective when used in combination with a physical-barrier method. Spermicides are available in foam, jelly, cream, foaming tablets, vaginal suppositories, and sponges.

- **Male condoms:** A sheath placed over the erect penis blocks passage of the sperm. Latex condoms are effective barriers against pregnancy and sexually transmitted diseases.

- **Female condoms:** A polyurethane sheath with a flexible ring on each end is inserted into the vagina. One ring covers the cervix while the other partially covers the outside of the vagina. The female condom may offer some protection against sexually transmitted diseases.

- **Diaphragm:** The diaphragm is a soft latex cup on a flexible ring. Before intercourse, it is filled with spermicide and inserted into the vagina to cover the cervix. It is available only through a health care provider, who can ensure a proper fit.

Birth Control

■ **Cervical cap:** The cervical cap covers the cervix like a diaphragm, but is smaller and somewhat more difficult to insert or remove. It must be fitted by a health care provider.

Natural Family Planning

Natural family planning methods (sometimes called rhythm methods) involve avoiding intercourse when a woman is likely to become pregnant.

■ **Periodic abstinence or fertility awareness:** A combination of taking a daily body temperature, keeping a calendar of the menstrual cycle, and watching for changes in vaginal mucus give a general indication of a woman's fertile periods each month. However, illness, stress, and other biochemical factors can throw off calculations by days or weeks.

■ **Lactational amenorrhea method (LAM):** This method is effective only if a woman breastfeeds her baby every 2 to 3 hours around the clock from birth, with no breaks. If menstruation resumes, the baby reaches 6 months of age, or the woman nurses less often or for shorter periods of time, this method may not be effective.

Sterilization

Sterilization is a permanent birth control option best suited to couples who know that they will not want to have another child in the future.

■ **Male sterilization (vasectomy):** The tube that leads from the testicles to the urethra is cut and sealed so that sperm cannot leave the body. The ejaculation and the quantity of semen produced are not altered by this procedure. A vasectomy can be reversed with another surgery, however fertility is not guaranteed.

■ **Female sterilization:** The fallopian tubes are cut or sealed surgically, or with tiny expandable coils (Essure®), to prevent eggs from reaching the uterus.

For Your Information

How Effective Are Contraceptive Methods?

The effectiveness of any birth control method depends on how appropriate the method is for you and how carefully it is used. The numbers below represent the number of pregnancies expected, per 100 women per year, using each method.

Method		Method	
Contraceptive ring	1	Male condom (without spermicide)	11
Transdermal system	1	Diaphragm (with spermicide)	17
Injections	less than 1	Cervical cap (with spermicide)	17
Sterilization	less than 1	Periodic abstinence	20
LAM (breastfeeding)	less than 1	No birth control method	more than 85
Intrauterine device (IUD)	less than 1	Spermicide only	20 to 50
Birth control pills	1 to 2	Female condom (without spermicide)	21
Emergency contraception	almost 80% risk reduction		

Source: Food and Drug Administration, 2002

Sexually Transmitted Diseases

Disease	Type of Infection	Symptoms
Chlamydia	Bacterial	Men usually have no symptoms. Sometimes, painful, burning urination; discharge from the penis. Most women have no symptoms until chlamydia progresses to pelvic inflammatory disease. Sometimes, painful urination, stomach pain, vaginal discharge
Genital warts	Viral	Small, hard, fleshy bumps on the genital or anal area. Warts inside the vagina are softer and reddish
Pubic lice	Parasitic	Severe itching that worsens at night; lice visible in pubic hair and on skin; eggs, called "nits," attached to pubic hair; hives
HIV	Viral	Swollen glands; unexplained weight loss and loss of appetite; weakness and fatigue; night sweats; unexplained, prolonged fever; chronic diarrhea; dry cough not associated with a cold or flu; tissue changes of the mouth, tongue, or vagina; shingles (a red, blistery rash); unusual illnesses; development of rare diseases (e.g., tuberculosis, certain cancers, pneumonia)
Gonorrhea	Bacterial	Men: painful, burning, and frequent urination; thick, milky discharge from the penis. Women: painful and frequent urination; thick vaginal discharge; but many women have no symptoms
Syphilis	Bacterial	Painless, open sores on the genitals, mouth, or anus; swollen lymph nodes, especially in the groin. Secondary symptoms include rash (especially on the palms or soles of the feet), fever, headache, and joint pain
Genital herpes	Viral	Intense itching in the genital or anal area, followed by the development of small, red bumps that blister, ulcerate, and then scab over. May be accompanied by fever, headaches, or flu-like symptoms. Women may have swollen labia and pain with urination.
Hepatitis B	Viral	Chronic flu-like symptoms, yellow skin and eyes, discolored urine
Trichomoniasis	Parasitic	Heavy (sometimes frothy) green or yellow vaginal discharge with a very strong, foul odor

Sexually Transmitted Diseases

Diagnosis	Treatment	Special Concerns
Microscopic examination and culture of vaginal or penile discharge; antibody test	Treated with antibiotics	Left untreated, chlamydia can cause infertility and pelvic inflammatory disease, urethritis, conjunctivitis, and arthritis-like swelling of the joints in men
Physical examination	May be removed surgically or with medication	Recurrence following treatment is common. Genital warts are linked with a higher incidence of some types of reproductive cancers in men and women
Physical examination	Medication to kill lice	None
Blood test	No cure. Antiretroviral drugs can slow the progression of disease	Left untreated, progresses to AIDS
Microscopic examination	Treated with antibiotics. However, new strains are becoming resistant to many common drugs	Left untreated, gonorrhea can cause infertility or arthritis-like joint pain, or it can develop into pelvic inflammatory disease
Physical examination; microscopic examination of fluid from sores; blood test	Treated with antibiotics. However, new strains are becoming resistant to many common drugs	Left untreated, syphilis can cause heart disease, blindness, brain damage, shortened life expectancy, or (in unborn children whose mothers have the disease) birth defects and fetal death
Physical examination and culture of fluid from blisters	No known cure, but medication (especially acyclovir) can shorten the duration or lessen the severity of symptoms	If the mother is infected, the baby may get the disease during childbirth, resulting in blindness, retardation, or even death
Physical examination and blood test	Restricted physical activity and dietary modifications; hospitalization	Left untreated, hepatitis B can lead to severe liver damage and even death. Hepatitis B can be prevented through immunization
Physical examination and microscopic examination	Metronidazole tablets. Sexual partners may need to undergo treatment with metronidazole to prevent re-infection	None

AIDS and HIV Facts

AIDS, or acquired immune deficiency syndrome, and HIV, human immunodeficiency virus, frighten everyone. However, unless you're involved in risky behaviors (see page 53) or are exposed to the virus accidentally, your chances of becoming infected are very low.

Today, the annual death rate for AIDS is less than half that of the earlier days of the epidemic in the 1980s. Two significant developments contribute to a more optimistic outlook regarding HIV/AIDS. First, because of strict screening and testing, all donated blood in the United States is considered safe. Second, medications can treat HIV and delay the onset of full-blown AIDS.

> Understanding what this disease is, how it is spread, and who is at risk can reduce your risk of getting it.

Drugs available to treat HIV cannot cure it; they can cause serious side effects; and they are very expensive. On the other hand, these new treatments help manage the condition, extend lives, and promise a more independent life. Because fewer people with HIV go on to develop AIDS, the number of people living with HIV is increasing.

Unfortunately, about 25 percent of HIV-infected people don't know they have it (it can take up to 10 years for symptoms to show), and about one-third of those with HIV are not receiving the treatment they need. Consequently, more cases of undiagnosed and untreated HIV mean the infection continues to be a serious threat.

HIV infection gradually damages the body's natural defenses against disease and can infect brain cells. Left untreated, HIV infection progresses to AIDS. With AIDS, life-threatening illnesses develop that do not affect people with normal immune systems.

Most people with HIV infection go through a series of stages:

■ **Acute primary infection.** This stage usually lasts 4 to 12 weeks. The person may experience mono-like symptoms such as sore throat, fever, fatigue, and swollen lymph glands. During this period, the body is producing antibodies, indicating that it is trying to fight the infection. Antibodies usually are present within 3 to 6 months of infection. A blood test (Elisa) is used to detect HIV antibodies. A positive test indicates the likelihood of HIV. A second, more sensitive test called the Western blot will confirm the first positive test. Infected persons can infect others. See "How is the AIDS virus spread?"

■ **Latent phase.** This period may last 10 to 12 years, during which the infected person has no symptoms. However, the person can transmit HIV. See "How is the AIDS virus spread?"

■ **Active phase.**
  –**ARC:** Some people develop a condition that is called "AIDS-related complex" (ARC). Symptoms include fever, feeling tired, loss of appetite, weight loss, diarrhea, night sweats, and swollen lymph nodes in the neck, armpits, or groin. They can have ARC-related symptoms for weeks or years, die from complications, or develop full-blown AIDS.
  –**AIDS:** The severe end stage of the disease has a variety of complications that further compromise the body's immune system. Two of the illnesses most often seen in AIDS patients are pneumocystis carinii pneumonia, a parasitic infection of the lungs, and Kaposi's sarcoma, a rare type of cancer.

AIDS and HIV Facts

How Is the HIV Virus Spread?

- The virus is spread through direct transmission during unsafe (unprotected) sexual contact, through sharing needles, from contaminated blood products, and by an HIV-positive mother to her baby during birth and breastfeeding.

- The virus is NOT spread through shaking hands, hugging, or other forms of casual contact. The virus dies very quickly when it comes into contact with air or light. Open-mouthed kissing is considered very low-risk unless blood passes between partners. However, the Centers for Disease Control and Prevention recommends against open-mouthed kissing with an infected partner.

- You can't get HIV from donating blood. The needles used are sterile and are never reused.

- HIV has never been shown to be transmitted through insect bites.

- Once outside the body, the HIV virus dies quickly, so you can't get it from drinking glasses, drinking fountains, or toilet seats.

Who Is at a Higher Risk?

- The fastest-growing group contracting HIV infection is heterosexual women. Traditionally, those with the highest risk for carrying HIV have been homosexuals and bisexuals, intravenous drug users, male and female prostitutes, and those who have sex or share needles with people in these high-risk groups.

- Anyone who has unprotected (unsafe) sex and who has not been in a mutually monogamous relationship for at least the last 10 years (HIV can exist for up to 10 years without symptoms).

- Anyone who received blood transfusions before early 1985. Since then, all blood used for transfusions in the United States has been screened for HIV. If you wish to reduce your anxiety regarding a possible blood transfusion, you can donate your own blood in advance of your scheduled procedure.

- Infants born to HIV-infected mothers have a 15 to 30 percent chance of developing HIV, but that risk can be as low as 8 percent if the mother takes antiviral medication.

- People in certain professions, such as police, firefighters, funeral home workers, emergency medical workers, dental personnel, prison staff, and medical workers, who are routinely exposed to blood and body fluids that may be contaminated, have a higher risk for contracting the virus.

How Can I Reduce My Risk of Getting HIV?

- Do not have unsafe (unprotected) sex. If you do, make sure your partner is not infected. Otherwise, use a latex condom.

- Consider abstinence or a monogamous relationship with an uninfected partner.

- If your job involves exposure to blood and body fluids, use precautions such as gloves, masks, gowns, and face shields.

- Do not share hypodermic needles for any reason.

Resources

STD National Hotline
800.227.8922

21 Tips for Your Child's Good Health

*C*hildren learn the basics of personal health at home, and the lifestyle habits they practice while they are young will influence them as they grow into adulthood. The following 21 tips will help you guide your child to a healthier and longer life.

1. **Make sure your child gets regular medical checkups,** including "well child" and preventive care. Don't wait until your child is sick to visit the doctor. Preventive visits as your child is growing and developing are important to record milestones such as height, weight, and developmental level, as well as to review immunization schedules, test hearing and vision, and talk about health concerns you, your child, or family may have.

2. **Have your child immunized.** You should be sure your child receives all his or her scheduled immunizations. (See page 44 for the recommended schedule.) This helps protect your child from infectious diseases that could affect his or her health and well-being. In addition to your doctor's office, county and city health departments and community clinics offer immunizations. Keep a record of your child's immunizations; you will need it when he or she enters school.

3. **Learn infant and child CPR.** Check with your local hospital or chapter of the American Red Cross for information on available classes. See pages 93.

4. **Have your child get regular dental checkups.** Teach your child how to brush and floss his or her teeth. Be sure your child brushes regularly, not only to take good care of the baby teeth but to establish good dental care habits as he or she grows older.

5. **Keep your child away from secondhand smoke.** If you or anyone in your family smokes, quit. If you can't, smoke only outdoors or away from your child. Don't smoke in the enclosed space of your car when traveling with your child. Be sure your child's caregiver doesn't smoke around him or her.

6. **Protect young children from home injuries,** the leading cause of death in young children. Do a safety audit of your home. Check to be sure that smoke detectors are working and that household chemicals and cleaners are stored where a child can't get to them. Store all medications away from your child. Install stairway gates, cabinet and drawer locks, electric outlet covers, and window guards. Be sure swimming pools are fenced in. Have your child wear a safety helmet when riding a bicycle. Store guns away from children and lock them up in a safe place. See pages 56–57.

7. **Take time out if you become frustrated by the stresses of parenting.** Never shake a baby or child as this can cause brain injury and death.

8. **Transport small children in approved child safety seats.** Buckle up your child at all times!

9. **Encourage your child to be physically active.** Offer opportunities to participate in sports. Cut down on the time you and your children watch TV. Exchange an hour of exercise for 1 hour in front of the TV. Make exercise a family affair. Walking, biking, swimming, running, or any other activity that increases heart rate is a good choice.

10. **Be aware of your child's exposure to direct sunlight.** Have him or her wear a hat, play in

the shade or indoors during the peak hours of sunlight, and wear sunscreen to minimize his or her risk of developing skin cancer in the future.

11. **Start your child's day with breakfast.** After a night without food, it gets him or her going for the rest of the day.

12. **Serve wholesome foods** including whole-grain breads and cereals, fresh fruits and vegetables, dairy products, and lean meats, poultry, and fish. Steer your child away from high-fat, high-sugar foods. Teach him or her how to select snacks wisely.

13. **Make sure your child gets enough rest and sleep.** Tired children are irritable, have more behavior problems, and have more difficulty concentrating in school.

14. **Allow your child to have some quiet time each day,** time when he or she can read or do creative activities.

15. **Help your child maintain a body weight that is right for him or her** by teaching him or her to get plenty of exercise and eat wisely.

16. **Make mealtime fun and pleasant.** Often it may be the only time your family is together during the entire day. Engage your child's enthusiasm by discussing positive activities of the day and interesting topics on his or her level. Try to hold off on arguing or discussing the pressures of daily life during mealtime.

17. **Demonstrate appropriate self-care** for treating minor medical conditions at home. Teach your child that medicine is not always the solution to a health problem. By your example, your child will learn good self-care skills and attitudes.

18. **When you do need to seek medical care, prepare your child ahead of time.** Tell your child what to expect and that it's all right for him or her to ask the doctor questions. This prepares your child to be a more active partner in his or her own medical care as an adult.

19. **Be a good role model.** Exercise sensibly, maintain an appropriate body weight, eat wholesome foods, use alcohol responsibly, and don't smoke. Your child will follow your example.

20. **Take time to talk with your child each day.** Arrange for a special time that you spend together, uninterrupted. Encourage him or her to let you know how things are going, and what problems he or she is having. Let your child know it's OK to speak up and talk about his or her feelings. Make sure you really take time and listen to your child. Reinforce and praise positive behavior and achievements. Offer advice and guidance, but be careful not to be critical.

21. **Last, but not least,** always show your child that you love him or her. The trust and care you give now will help your child develop healthy, loving relationships later in life.

Keeping Your Child Safe

Accidental injuries happen, but improving your accident-prevention skills can help keep your children safe. Children often are oblivious to dangers around them and count on you to keep them safe. The following table lists some common danger areas and preventive measures you can take to ensure your child's safety.

AGE	DANGER/RISK	SAFETY MEASURES
Birth to 1 year	Suffocation in crib	Keep pillows, plastic, and extra blankets out of the crib. Always put your baby to sleep on his or her back.
	Strangulation by objects around the neck	Keep cords and string away from infant. Do not hang pacifier by ribbon or cord.
	Choking from food, milk, or foreign objects	Don't leave your baby alone when eating. Don't give babies popcorn or peanuts. Check toys for small parts that can come loose. Keep small objects out of reach; everything goes in an infant's mouth. If it's small enough to fit inside a toilet paper roll, it's small enough to choke on.
	Falls	Keep sides of crib up when baby is unattended. Always keep a hand on the baby. Don't leave a baby alone on a bed or changing table, in a bath, high chair, swing, etc., where baby can fall, slip, or roll off. Place guard rails at the top of stairs; guards on windows. Do not leave a baby alone in a walker.
	Automobile accidents	Always use approved car safety seat.
	Burns	Test bath water before using; turn hot water heater temperature down to 120 F or less. Use back burners on kitchen stove; turn pot handles in. Don't smoke or drink hot beverages around infant. Protect your baby from excess sun exposure. Keep floor heaters out of reach.
	Cuts and bruises	Pad crib bars. Keep baby's fingernails short. Use plastic cups and bottles. Check toys for sharp edges. Keep fans, humidifiers, etc. out of reach.
	Electrical shock	Coil electric cords to keep out of reach. Cover electrical outlets.
	Poisoning	Lock or put childproof latches on cupboards. Keep poisonous substances and plants out of reach. Post Poison Control number next to phone.
1 to 3 years	Falls, cuts, banging into objects	Keep furniture with sharp edges (glass-topped tables) out of traffic flow. Place knives and sharp objects out of reach. Keep windows and balconies screened. Always supervise children.

Keeping Your Child Safe

AGE	DANGER/RISK	SAFETY MEASURES
1 to 3 years	Motor vehicle accident	Place child in car safety seat in the back seat of the car. Teach child not to ride tricycles in streets or around cars.
	Burns	Keep matches out of reach. Teach danger words ("no," "don't," "hot") and make sure child obeys. Teach child about the danger of fires, including charcoal fires. Test water before child's bath. Put pots on the back burners of the stove.
	Poisoning	Test for lead paint. Keep medicines, cleaning supplies, pesticides, and antifreeze locked up. Teach your child not to put objects in his or her mouth, and to take medicine only when a parent or caregiver gives it.
	Drowning	Do not leave a child alone in tub or pool. Keep water in the tub to minimum level. Fence in pools and install a self-closing gate with a self-locking latch. Do not let child play near deep ditches or wells. Put locks on toilets.
	Electrical shock	Keep outlets covered.
4+ years	Choking, putting foreign objects in ears and mouth, suffocation	Don't let your child run with objects (candy, gum) in the mouth. Teach your child not to put objects in ears, nose, or mouth. Remove doors from old freezers, refrigerators, etc., which can trap and suffocate a child.
	Injury from traffic	Teach children to play on the grass or sidewalk rather than in a driveway, street, or railroad tracks. Show child how to obey traffic signals and cross streets safely.
	Playground injury	Teach children not to walk in front of swings. Do not let your child push others off playground equipment. Encourage your child to put away his or her toys.
	Poisoning	Check Halloween candy for signs of tampering. Teach children not to eat any objects or plants. Remind your child not to take pills without parental permission.
	Drowning	Teach children over age 4 to swim.
	Fire and burns	Teach your child the danger of playing with matches or fire.
	Harm from other people	Teach your child to avoid strangers and to never go anywhere without asking a parent. Supervise your child at all times.
	Harm from animals	Teach your child to act and move quietly around animals. Don't let your child approach strange animals.
	Firearm accident	Teach your child not to play with guns or other weapons. Always keep firearms locked and out of reach.

In this section:

- Understanding common health care terms
- Selecting a primary care physician
- Talking with your doctor and asking important questions
- Locating health information and resources to make informed decisions

Simplifying Medspeak

Medical terms don't have to be a mystery. How a word begins or ends will give you a clue about its meaning. This list will help you piece together some of medicine's more puzzling vocabulary.

Ends with	Refers to	Example
-aholic	addiction	alcoholic
-algia	pain	neuralgia
-cele	tumor	hydrocele
-ectomy	removal of	hysterectomy
-emia	blood condition	leukemia
-itis	inflammation	sinusitis
-lysis	breaking down	dialysis
-natal	birth	prenatal
-oma	tumor	melanoma
-opia	sight	myopia
-opsy	medical examination	biopsy
-oscopy	viewing	colonoscopy
-osis	abnormal condition	cirrhosis
-pathy	abnormality	psychopathy
-plasia	growth	dysplasia
-plasty	rebuilding	rhinoplasty
-pnea	breathing	apnea
-rrhea	flow	diarrhea
-tomy	cutting	vasectomy
-uria	urine substances	pyuria

Starts with	Refers to	Example
adeno-	gland	adenoid
angio-	blood vessels	angina
arterio-	artery	arteriosclerosis
arthro-	joints	arthritis
broncho-	windpipe	bronchitis
carcino-	cancer	carcinoma
cardio-	heart	cardiovascular
cephalo-	head	hydrocephaly

Starts with	Refers to	Example
cranio-	skull	craniotomy
cysto-	bladder	cystitis
denti-	tooth	dentures
derma-	skin	dermatitis
dys-	impaired	dyslexia
entero-	intestines	enteritis
en- or endo-	inside, within	endoscopy
epi-	attached to	epidermis
gastro-	stomach	gastritis
geronto-	old age	geriatric
hemo-	blood	hemorrhage
hepato-	liver	hepatitis
hyper-	excessive	hypertension
hypo-	inadequate	hypoglycemia
intra-	within	intravenous
lipo-	fat	liposuction
masto-	breast	mastectomy
melano-	dark, black	melanoma
myelo-	bone marrow or spine	myelitis
myo-	muscle	myocardium
narco-	numbness, sleep	narcotic
nephro-	kidney	nephritis
neuro-	nerves	neuralgia
ortho-	straight, normal	orthopedic
osteo-	bone	osteoarthritis
ov-	eggs	ovaries
peri-	around	pericardium
poly-	many	polycystic
psycho-	mind	psychosis
pulmo- or pneumo-	lungs	pulmonary pneumonia
radio-	ray	radiology
rhino-	nose	rhinoplasty
scler-	hardening	arteriosclerosis
sero-	blood	serology
uro-, urino-	urine	urinalysis
vas-	vessel	vasectomy

Understanding Health Care Terms

As you and others, such as employers, insurance companies, and the government, try to manage increasing health care costs, new words and phrases are becoming part of the health care vocabulary. Here are some of the most common terms.

Types of Plans

- **Managed care:** A medical care delivery system that manages health care and costs through a variety of services. Most managed care programs use a network of primary care physicians, specialists, and hospitals.

- **Health Maintenance Organization (HMO):** A pre-paid medical system in which members receive medical services for one monthly fee, regardless of the severity of problems or number of visits. HMOs usually are one of two models:
  - Staff model: Specified clinics with employed staff located within the community that treat subscribers only and/or employees of the HMO.
  - Independent practice association (IPA), or network model: Physicians are contracted to provide services in their own offices or clinics. They may treat non-HMO patients.

- **Preferred Provider Organization (PPO):** A network of physicians and hospitals that agree to give discounts to companies when employees use their services.

- **Point-of-Service (POS):** A system in which a participant receives HMO benefits when care is managed by the primary care physician. However, services by non-network providers are subject to a deductible and coinsurance.

- **Indemnity Health Plan or "Fee-for-Service" plan:** The employer or insurance company pays a percentage (often 80 percent) of the reasonable cost of each medical service received by the eligible patient. Indemnity plans usually require the employee to pay a certain deductible before the employer or insurance company begins to contribute.

- **Consumer-Driven Health Plans (CDHP):** The employer contributes a fixed amount to an employee's personal health account. The employee decides how much to contribute to the account and usually may choose among various plans, selecting the features that best suit his or her needs. The employee makes all decisions about which doctors and services to use and pays for them out of this account. These plans also offer resources to help employees compare services and prices for doctors, drugs, medical devices, and hospitals. CDHPs may take a variety of different forms depending on amounts contributed, out-of-pocket expenses, and level of deductibles. Depending on the features offered, CDHPs may be called Medical Spending Accounts, Health Care Reimbursement Plans, or Health Reimbursement Arrangements, among others.

Fees and Expenses

- **Allowable charges:** The percentage of the charge an insurance carrier or company will pay for a specific medical or dental procedure. The individual is responsible for charges above this amount.

- **Coinsurance:** The amount patients have to pay for reasonable medical expenses after a deductible has been paid. Often insurance plans require the patient to pay 20 percent, while the insurance company pays 80 percent.

- **Copayment:** A flat fee paid by the patient to a provider or pharmacy for each visit or prescription.

- **Deductible:** A minimum payment made by an individual and/or family before the company or insurance carrier begins to pay for medical expenses.

- **Capitation:** A set dollar limit that a health plan pays to a group of physicians, regardless of how much you use their medical services.

- **Maximum dollar limit:** The maximum amount the employer or insurance company will pay within a specified period of time. That amount may be for a lifetime, for a year, or be specific to an illness, such as for psychiatric care or cancer treatment.

- **Out-of-pocket maximum:** The maximum amount a patient is required to pay through coinsurance before the employer or insurance company pays 100 percent of the reasonable medical expenses. This arrangement is common in fee-for-service plans.

Providers

- **Primary care physician (PCP):** A physician who is responsible for monitoring and treating your general health needs, including providing periodic health screenings and immunizations. See pages 43–44.

- **Nurse practitioner:** A registered nurse (RN) with advanced training who provides routine checkups and helps manage certain minor, acute, and chronic health problems under a physician's supervision.

- **Physician's assistant:** A health care professional with medical training who provides routine health checkups and manages certain acute and chronic health problems under a physician's supervision.

- **Specialist:** A physician trained and/or certified to treat a specific body system such as the heart (cardiologist) or women's reproductive system (gynecologist).

Other Terms to Know

- **Precertification or pre-admission review:** Patients with certain medical conditions are required to have pre-authorization for treatment from their insurers before payment for the services is approved.

- **Case management:** A service that assigns a health professional (usually a nurse) to assist and monitor the care plans of individuals who require extensive medical treatment. The case manager works to ensure that individuals receive the most appropriate and reasonable care.

- **Second opinion programs:** A process that requires patients to see a second physician for specific medical procedures that are elective; when there are other accepted treatment options; when the diagnosis is still in question; or when hospitalization or surgery is recommended.

Understanding Managed Care

Many of us are covered by managed care plans, yet understanding how they work can be confusing. The term "managed care" describes a method of financing, organizing, and delivering health care services. See page 61. Whether your plan is a PPO, POS, HMO, or consumer-driven health plan, your primary care physician (PCP) is the foundation of your care.

By emphasizing the role of the PCP, health plans focus on promoting health, not just treating disease. Similar to the traditional family doctor, your PCP gets to know you over time and helps you maintain your overall health and well-being. He or she provides health care services and consultation, and coordinates all your health care needs.

More than 80 percent of all medical conditions or concerns can be treated by a PCP. Because your PCP knows you, your health history, and your preferences, he or she is qualified to recommend a treatment plan tailored to meet your specific needs. However, if your condition requires the services of a specialist, your PCP will make an appropriate referral and consult with the specialist as necessary.

As you develop a relationship with your PCP, you will take a more active role in your health-related decisions and accept more responsibility for your treatment and lifestyle practices. The benefits? Improved confidence and satisfaction with your care.

Remember: Your *care* is being managed, not you. You and your doctor should work in partnership, no matter how the health care delivery system is organized. The information on pages 64–68 can help you develop a strong working relationship.

For Your Information

Is an HMO Right for You?

- Is the HMO a Staff Model or an IPA (Independent Practice Association)? (See page 61.)

- How do the premiums and copayments compare to those of other health plans in your area?

- What preventive screenings and programs are covered?

- How extensive is the HMO's network of primary care physicians (PCPs) and specialists? For an IPA, are there a number of PCPs close to your home? Is your current doctor a member?

- How easy is it for you to get an appointment? How long does it take?

- How difficult is it for you to change your primary care physician?

- How many of the HMO's PCPs and specialists are "board certified"? (Board certification is one indication of the quality of the physician network.)

- With what hospital is the HMO affiliated? What is the reputation of the hospital?

- What is the HMO's reputation among your friends and associates who may be members?

- What types of value-added services does the HMO offer?

Finding the Right Doctor

edicine has changed a lot over the last 40 years. The house call has been replaced by urgent care centers, 24-hour clinics, and doctor's office visits. Most Americans don't have a traditional family doctor who treats them from cradle to grave. Instead, more than 50 percent of Americans meet their doctors for the first time during a time of medical need or emergency. However, meeting in a crisis is not the best way to build a relationship, especially when you are trusting someone with your care and well-being. Therefore, an important first step toward being a wise medical consumer is finding a doctor you can trust.

Choosing a Health Care Provider

■ **Find a primary care physician (PCP).** Your primary care physician is responsible for your general health needs, such as periodic health screenings and immunizations, and treatment for common problems that don't require a specialist. Approximately 80 to 85 percent of all medical problems can be treated by a PCP. Because your PCP knows you, he or she can help you avoid unnecessary tests and procedures that might be expensive and possibly place you at greater risk. When a medical problem is more serious, your PCP may refer you to a specialist, but he or she should still be involved in your total care plan.

■ **Select your primary care physician according to your needs.** Depending on your health plan, choose a doctor who can meet most of your medical needs and those of your family. A primary care physician may be a family practitioner, general practitioner, internist, pediatrician, or obstetrician-gynecologist. Your family may need more than one PCP. For example, in a young family of three, the wife may have an obstetrician-gynecologist, the husband an internist, and the child a pediatrician. In general, your choice of physicians should be based on the qualities listed below.

For Your Information

Many health plans require members to choose a PCP from their list of providers. In this case, the PCP acts as your primary medical contact. Regardless, we recommend that everyone choose a PCP to act as his or her health advocate. Look for a PCP who:

❏ Is a person you respect who makes you feel confident about the care you'll receive.

❏ Has good communication skills: He or she is an active listener and takes time to talk with you and explain things.

❏ Promotes prevention and provides information to help you.

❏ Prescribes tests, procedures, and medication only when needed.

❏ Is willing to accept payment for "allowable charges."

❏ Has a reasonable waiting time for appointments.

❏ Can be contacted by phone and/or e-mail.

❏ Has office hours after your regular work hours.

Finding the Right Doctor

■ **Use your network.** Ask friends, family members, and co-workers to suggest doctors. Find out why they like a specific doctor or why they dislike others. Don't rule out someone automatically because of a negative comment.

■ **Ask the pros.** Contact your local hospital, medical society, or teaching hospital. Whenever possible, talk with nurses. They often have excellent views of a doctor's professional reputation, skills, and attitude toward patients. If you need a specialist, ask your PCP for at least two recommendations. Your local Better Business Bureau may know if there are malpractice claims filed against a certain physician. Also, professional medical organizations (e.g., American College of Family Physicians, American Academy of Orthopaedic Surgeons) can provide lists of board-certified physicians in your area.

■ **Call a physician line.** A number of "physician referral services" are available. When you call an advertised phone number, a consultant will help match you to a doctor based on your health needs, location, and personality preferences. Although these services can provide you with a list of doctors or even schedule an appointment for you, they usually are paid for by the doctors who support the service.

■ **Refer to your insurance plan.** If you belong to a Health Maintenance Organization (HMO), you may select or be assigned a PCP, or be referred to a doctor, depending on your medical needs. If you do not like your assigned physician's performance, request another doctor. If your company health plan is part of a Preferred Provider Organization (PPO), you may want to select a PCP from a "preferred list" of doctors. You will receive discounts if your doctor is part of the PPO.

■ **Ask about certification.** A board-certified physician has passed a national standardized test of competency in his or her field of medicine. Some studies suggest that board-certified doctors may provide more appropriate care.

■ **Check out the office staff.** How are you treated on the phone and in the office? A friendly, responsive office staff usually reflects a doctor with a similar manner.

■ **Evaluate the office environment.** Ask the front desk staff how appointments are scheduled: for example, four patients per hour or ten? Ask about the usual waiting time. Look at how many people are waiting in the reception area; this can give you a pretty good idea of office scheduling procedures.

The Quality Office Visit

A visit to the doctor's office can give rise to a range of feelings from relief and comfort to fear and confusion. It's easy to get frustrated by the long waits, the impersonal way patients are led to and from examining rooms, the lack of adequate time for talking with the doctor, and, of course, the high costs. The medical establishment is not insensitive to these issues. In fact, surveys indicate that doctors want to spend more time with their patients. By using the following strategies, you can improve the quality of your office visit.

Ideas that Work

■ **Evaluate the need.** Estimates show that at least 25 percent of all visits to the doctor are not necessary. Either there is little the doctor can do, as in the case of uncomplicated colds, or other health professionals can provide appropriate care, as in the case of routine screenings for blood pressure or cholesterol. So your first question should be: "Do I need to see my doctor, or do I have other options such as self-care?"

■ **Be prepared.** If you are going to your doctor with a new problem, try to provide as much information as you can to help narrow the diagnosis. Try to share your thoughts, feelings, and observations about your problem or other medical concerns (past or present). Always bring an up-to-date list that includes any prescribed and over-the-counter medications, herbal remedies, and dietary supplements you are using.

■ **Answer questions honestly and to the best of your ability.** Your doctor may ask detailed questions

Before your office visit, write down the answers to the following questions:

❏ **What is your problem?** Be specific by listing your symptoms, for example: I have had stomach cramps and diarrhea.

❏ **When did your problem begin?** Try to give the exact time. If you cannot pinpoint the exact date that a symptom appeared, try to remember the general period that you began to notice the problem.

❏ **What do you think may have caused the problem?** Did you eat some unusual food? Do any family members or co-workers have similar symptoms?

❏ **Learn your family history.** Is there a history of such diseases as heart disease, high blood pressure, diabetes, and breast cancer among your immediate family: parents, grandparents, brothers, or sisters?

❏ **What have you done to try to relieve the problem?** Have you used any medications? What kind? What happened?

❏ **Did you have this problem before?** When? What happened?

❏ **What makes the problem worse?** List the activities, medications, foods, or other situations that make your problem more serious.

❏ **Are you allergic to any medications?** If yes, what are they?

by body system (e.g., symptoms related to your skin, head, eyes, ears, throat, etc.) to see if there are any patterns to your problem. You also will be asked about your family life, emotional health, potential job-related exposures, and general health behaviors

The Quality Office Visit

such as alcohol consumption, drug use, tobacco use, exercise habits, and sexual activity. Although these questions are personal, it is important to be direct and honest with your answers.

■ **Be cooperative.** When your doctor has finished the interview, you usually receive a focused physical examination. You have the right to question or refuse any recommendations or procedures. State your concerns calmly and listen to your doctor's explanations.

■ **Ask about diagnostic tests.** Diagnostic tests can help the doctor determine either the cause of an illness or how serious it is. If tests are recommended, ask the doctor to explain about the risks, costs, and benefits (e.g., "If I have this test, will it change your diagnosis or my treatment?").

■ **Use the INFORMED Medical Decision-Making Process™.** If your problem is complex and requires extensive testing and treatment, a more formal

approach for deciding on your care plan may help you sort it out. The INFORMED process (see pages 78-82) can help you and your doctor consider your treatment options.

■ **Follow through with treatment.** To avoid complications and related additional procedures and treatments, it is important to understand and stick with the treatment plan you have chosen. Your medical problems are more likely to recur if you take shortcuts with your treatments or do not follow through with medications. See pages 98–104.

■ **Sometimes, less is more.** Finally, don't ignore suggestions that may seem simple. Recommendations such as drinking plenty of fluids, getting bed rest, eating a balanced diet, stopping smoking, exercising, or losing weight are just as sound as higher-tech medical advice. In fact, these can be the best medicine you'll ever give yourself!

For Your Information

Understanding Your Care Plan

It's important to follow through with your care plan as recommended by your doctor. Because most of us tend to forget details over time, it will be helpful to write down what your doctor tells you:

• Write down the diagnosis.

• Write down your treatment plan: medications (see "Medication Use Record," page 287), nutritional needs, activity restrictions, special exercises, and other specifics.

• Ask your doctor if any alternative or complementary therapies are appropriate. See page 71.

• Get a list of any possible medication side effects.

• List the warning signs (e.g., infection, high fever) that would require further medical evaluation.

• Finally, make sure your doctor clarifies any points you don't understand.

Communicating with Your Doctor

There may be a number of reasons you find it difficult to talk with your doctor. You may feel uncomfortable challenging someone who's had years of formal medical education. Perhaps you feel stupid asking a simple question. In certain instances, you may feel embarrassed about the health problem itself. However, instead of giving up control, most experts believe that the best way to get quality care is to be *more involved* in your care plan.

> The more information you have, the more active you will become in making decisions about your health. Remember, the first skill of a wise medical consumer is knowing the right questions to ask. But medicine is complex, so don't expect to get all your questions answered completely all the time.

Improving Communication Skills

Try the following tips for improving communication with your provider. And, when more complex medical procedures (e.g., surgery, hospitalization, diagnostic tests) are recommended, try using the INFORMED Medical Decision-Making Process™ and Worksheet (see pages 78-82).

■ **Write down your questions** and concerns before you visit your doctor.

■ **Don't be afraid to ask questions.** Ask your doctor to explain in simple, non-technical terms.

■ **When tests are recommended, ask about their value and need.** For example: "If I have this test, will it change your diagnosis or my treatment?"

■ **When a treatment is recommended, inquire about other options that may be available.** For each option, have your doctor explain the risks, benefits, and total expense.

■ **When medication is prescribed, ask about signs of adverse reactions.** Be sure you understand the recommended dosage and schedule.

■ **Consider e-mail.** If your doctor is available on-line, e-mail is an easy way to ask questions. You'll get written answers quickly and you can keep them. Also, it is easier for those who live far from medical facilities or are homebound to discuss nonemergent issues. And, your doctor can refer you to other health Web sites.

For Your Information

The Second Opinion

In cases of elective surgery, or when you aren't sure about your treatment plan, it makes sense to get a second opinion. Check with your insurance company or your primary care physician to find a specialist.

You may be required to contact your insurance carrier before you proceed with certain procedures. This precertification process helps ensure that your surgery or treatment is the best one for your needs. If a second opinion is required, your insurance carrier usually will pay the bill.

Choosing Mental Health Services

epression, anxiety, drug and alcohol abuse, grief, marital problems, feelings of helplessness and hopelessness, loss of control: Everyone handles life's less-than-perfect moments differently. Most of the time, you can get through tough times with coping skills you've learned along the way. You talk it out with friends or family; you take up a new hobby or start exercising to relieve stress; you take a vacation to give yourself a fresh perspective on the things that trouble you most.

However, there may be times when you could benefit from an objective point of view from someone who can act as a sounding board and offer solid, professional advice. To locate the best source for support, it helps to know what mental health services are available to you, and to be familiar with the type of professional or organization that can best serve your needs.

Who's Who?

The following is a quick rundown of how the National Mental Health Association defines the roles of mental health professionals:

■ **Psychiatrists** are medical doctors who specialize in mental disorders. They are licensed to practice medicine and can evaluate and diagnose all types of mental disorders. They carry out biomedical treatments and psychotherapy and work with people who have psychological problems associated with medical disorders. Of the mental health professionals, only psychiatrists can prescribe drugs and medical therapies. They have completed three years of specialty training after graduating from medical school. A board-certified psychiatrist has practiced for at least

2 years and passed the examinations of the American Board of Psychiatry and Neurology.

■ **Psychologists** practice psychotherapy and work with individuals, groups, or families to resolve problems. Licensed psychologists have earned an advanced degree from a program with specialized training and experience requirements; in addition, they have successfully completed an examination for a professional license from the state in which they practice.

■ **Psychiatric nurses** are registered nurses who have advanced academic degrees and professional certification. They specialize in the prevention, treatment, and rehabilitation of mental health-related problems. These nurses conduct individual, family, and group therapy, and also work in mental health consultation, education, and administration.

■ **Clinical social workers** are trained to provide individual therapy, group therapy, diagnosis, referral, and consultation. Psychiatric social workers have advanced degrees in social work and have completed special programs designed to train them in basic psychiatric techniques.

■ **Psychotherapists** are mental health professionals who offer a variety of counseling and therapy services. If you doubt the credentials of a therapist, check with one of the professional associations listed in the resource section of this book (pages 288 to 293) to see if he or she has had adequate training.

■ **Mental health counselors** provide counseling services involving psychotherapy, human development, learning theory, and group dynamics for individuals, couples, and families. Clinical mental health counselors have earned at least a master's degree and are required to have several years of clinical supervision before they are certified by the National Academy of Certified Clinical Mental Health Counselors.

- **Case managers and outreach workers** help severely or chronically mentally ill individuals access the services they need in order to live in the community. Most chronically mentally ill people need medical care, social services, and assistance from a variety of agencies, including those dealing with housing, Social Security, vocational rehabilitation, and mental health. Case managers will monitor a person's needs and ensure that appropriate agencies get involved. In many instances, they act as advocates for the client. Case managers can be nurses, social workers, or other mental health workers, and can be associated with mental health centers, rehabilitation programs, outpatient clinics, private and group practices, general hospitals, psychiatric hospitals, and prisons.

- **Marital and family therapists** are licensed to provide counseling to individuals, couples, or families. They specialize in relationships and other dynamics of marriage and family life.

Choosing the Right Service

How much you are helped by the mental health services you choose depends on the "fit" between your personality and that of the person you turn to for help.

- **Start with professionals you know.** Your family physician or the counselor with your employee assistance program are excellent starting points.

- **Check the credentials.** Don't be afraid to ask about a therapist's education, certification, years of experience, professional philosophy, and areas of expertise. Ask for references if you feel you need to verify a person's credentials or approach to counseling.

- **Ensure confidentiality.** If you hesitate to seek help because you are concerned that someone will find out, discuss your concerns up front. Every mental health professional is bound by a code of strict confidentiality according to professional association guidelines and federal and state laws. Information that some insurance companies require from the therapist as a condition for payment can be released *only* if the patient gives written permission. The employee assistance program at your workplace cannot tell your employer that you are asking for advice or referral.

- **Don't be afraid to switch.** If you are dissatisfied or feel you're not being helped by a particular mental health professional, seek help from someone else.

Resources

Check the Yellow Pages under "mental health," "health," or "social services."

For information on self-help organizations, contact the National Self-Help Clearinghouse at www.selfhelpweb.org

National Mental Health Association at www.nmha.org

Complementary and Alternative Medicine

mericans get more tests, see more doctors, use more drugs, and spend more time in hospitals than any other people in the world. However, some may argue that while our system of medicine and technology is effective in curing illnesses and injuries that improve with drugs or surgery, it falls short in disease prevention and in managing conditions that are related to lifestyle problems such as stress. Others believe that modern medicine does not address the connection between the mind, body, and spirit, and the role all three play in promoting overall health and well-being.

Complementary and Alternative Medicine (CAM) describes approaches to health care that usually are not included in conventional medicine in the United States. Sometimes, a care provider will use a combination of conventional medicine along with CAM therapies. Known as integrative medicine, this approach acknowledges that both methods can work in harmony to enhance a patient's health and well-being.

Today, almost 70 percent of Americans use at least one form of alternative or complementary therapy. They are choosing CAM approaches not because they are dissatisfied with conventional medicine, but because they find that many CAM approaches agree with their personal values and beliefs about health and life.

Some CAM therapies and practitioners may be covered by your medical plan, but many are not. If cost is an issue, be sure that you know what, if any, services your health plan will pay for before using this type of care. If you choose to use a CAM therapy or provider, it is important that you understand the care you can expect and the likely results of the treatment.

CAM Therapies

The National Center for Complementary and Alternative Medicine (NCCAM) at the National Institutes of Health is devoted to studying the safety and effectiveness of CAM. From the wide variety of medical and health care systems, practices, and products, researchers have developed five basic categories:

1. **Alternative medical systems** are built on complete systems of theory and practice (e.g., homeopathic medicine, naturopathic medicine, and traditional Chinese medicine).

   –Naturopathy uses natural remedies such as sun, water, heat, and air as the treatment for disease. Examples of naturopathic treatments include changes in diet (such as more fruits, no salt or caffeine), exercises, or steam baths.

   –Homeopathy is a holistically based system of treatment in which various animal, vegetable, or mineral substances are administered in minute quantities to alleviate specific symptoms and complaints.

2. **Mind-body interventions** include techniques that use the mind's ability to affect the body's functions and symptoms (e.g., meditation, prayer, creative therapies such as art, music, or dance).

   –Creative visualization, or imaging, uses positive thoughts and images to attain a certain result, such as being free of a disease or reducing pain.

3. **Biologically based therapies** use substances found in nature, such as herbs, food, vitamins, and other scientifically unproven therapies.

–Herbal medicine uses herbs to treat disease. Herbalists believe that herbs work differently, heal more quickly, and cause fewer side effects than purified manufactured drugs. Some plant extracts can have beneficial effects, but misuse or overuse of herbal preparations could lead to serious reactions. Some manufacturers do not monitor the purity or concentration of the extracts and the government does not regulate their safety and effectiveness. Always tell your doctor about herbals you are using; be sure to use the recommended amounts; be careful about using herbal and prescription remedies together (ask your doctor); be on the lookout for allergic reactions; avoid using herbal remedies when pregnant; and be sure to seek medical care if your symptoms continue or get worse.

4. **Manipulative and body-based methods** are based on the manipulation or movement of one or more body parts (e.g., chiropractic or osteopathic manipulation, or massage).

–Therapeutic massage employs various manual techniques, such as Swedish and deep-tissue massage, to return soft body tissues to an optimal state. It is frequently used for sports injuries, stress, or chronic pain.

–Chiropractors have a Doctor of Chiropractic (D.C.) degree. This method of treatment is based on the belief that misalignment of vertebrae can affect the health of other parts of the body. Chiropractors can use X-rays for making a diagnosis and manipulate the bones as treatment. Chiropractors cannot use prescription drugs or surgery to treat their patients. Chiropractors are licensed by their states with laws that define their scope of practice.

–Osteopaths are Doctors of Osteopathy (D.O.) rather than Doctors of Medicine (M.D.). Their training emphasizes disorders of the musculoskeletal system. They complete four-year programs in the basic medical, surgical, psychological, and pharmacological treatments. Their training emphasizes a holistic approach to healing that uses the hands, or manipulation, in diagnosis and treatment.

5. **Energy therapies** intend to affect the energy fields that may surround or penetrate the body (e.g., acupuncture, therapeutic touch).

–Acupuncture is based on the belief that energy circulating through the body controls health, and disruption in this cycle causes pain and disease. Long, thin needles are inserted at specific points in the body to rebalance the energy.

Are CAM Therapies Right for You?

Compare what the conventional medical system has to offer and what the CAM therapies claim. Check credentials and be wary of any treatment or practitioner claiming to be the "only" effective treatment or approach.

Resources

Your doctor

National Center for Complementary and Alternative Medicine
888.644.6226
www.nccam.nih.gov

Health and Healing, by Andrew Weil, M.D. Houghton Mifflin: Boston, 1998.

Avoiding Medical Quackery

No one likes being sick, and sometimes it seems that only a miracle could make us well again. Unfortunately, every year millions of individuals search for medical miracles that will never happen. It is estimated that Americans spend more than 10 billion dollars a year on unproven goods and services that not only cost a lot of money, but also take their toll in needless pain, worsening conditions, and, most of all, dashed hopes.

■ **Beware of good intentions.** Sometimes, medical advice, products, devices, or remedies are promoted by those who sincerely believe in what they are doing. For example, they may be sure that a certain vitamin will cure a specific ailment, or they may believe that a proven medical treatment is dangerous and should be avoided in favor of a natural cure. However, these promoters may be sharing misinformation based on personal experience and trying to convince you of the validity of concepts that are not scientifically sound.

■ **Preying on fears.** Individuals with conditions such as cancer or AIDS may be willing to embrace unproven and possibly worthless treatments in the hope that they may be cured. If that cure for baldness, smoking, or even cancer sounds too good to be true, it probably is. You may be just as likely harmed as helped by such products.

■ **Recognize the pitch.** Medical quackery can use a variety of methods to get you to buy something you "can't afford to be without." Sometimes individuals sell consumers cures, supplements, or even equipment, such as hearing aids, to improve health or stop disease. These people may not be qualified to advise you about your health. Also, they may make false or deceptive claims about their products—products peddled at greatly inflated prices and having no proven effect.

■ **Question group presentations.** The health lecture is another method used by promoters to sell you a product. They may rent a hall or hotel conference room and advertise a free lecture about a health topic or disease. There may just happen to be a line of health foods or special equipment that they are willing to sell to make or keep you free of disease.

■ **Beware of mail-order or on-line medicine.** The U.S. Chief Postal Inspector reports that mail-order fraud and quackery seem to be on the rise. On the Internet, search engines call up thousands of sites promoting products from nutritional cures to breast developers and weight reduction devices. Products sold through the mail or on the Internet frequently appear to be overpriced and of unproven effectiveness. The U.S. Food and Drug Administration warns that exaggerated and deceptive claims are common in mail-order and on-line health materials.

■ **Health information materials.** Read health books and printed material that you receive or purchase with a critical eye. Don't accept the printed word as absolute truth or be convinced that information is sound simply because you saw the author on a talk show or infomercial. Although there are laws prohibiting the publication of untrue statements about people, products, or events, clever wording can get around the law. Remember: Just because something is in print doesn't make it true.

Avoiding Medical Quackery

Protect Yourself from Quacks

■ **Be suspicious of miracle advertisements.** Avoid products advertised as secret remedies. Reliable organizations such as the American Cancer Society, the Arthritis Foundation, the National Center for Complementary and Alternative Medicine, and others listed in the resource section of this book keep track of unproven and ineffective treatments.

■ **Get it in writing.** Ask for written explanations and materials describing what the treatment does. What are the side effects? What documented evidence exists that proves the treatment works? Testimonials from users do not count. Are there published articles in reliable medical journals that support the effectiveness and safety of this method of treatment?

■ **Beware of requirements to pay up front.** Don't be too eager to part with your money, and keep in mind that insurance often won't pay for unproven therapies or remedies.

■ **Be cautious about new, cutting-edge tests or medical procedures.** Beware of new diagnostic tests that sound unorthodox to you. Blood tests for food allergies and hair analysis are examples of unproven diagnostic tests that sometimes are used

for recommending questionable treatments. Also, beware of advanced medical techniques that the promoter claims are being suppressed by the medical establishment.

■ **Talk to your medical doctor.** If in doubt about *any* treatment, consult with your doctor. Don't discontinue any elements of your current treatment plan in favor of a new cure without your physician's knowledge and approval. While many doctors *do* encourage and support complementary and alternative treatments such as relaxation, visualization, and chiropractic for certain conditions such as back problems, they can be your reality check against potentially dangerous and outrageous claims made by medical quacks. Also, don't hesitate to share with your doctor written material that you hold suspect or about which you need clarification.

Resources

Your doctor

U.S. Food and Drug Administration
800.INFO.FDA
www.fda.gov

National Council Against Health Fraud
617.332.3063
www.ncahf.org

Finding Medical Resources

To choose and use health and medical services wisely, you'll need to find accurate information concerning your health problem. Then, with a solid base of understanding, you'll be in a better position to work with your doctor and make decisions about available treatment options and their relative risks, benefits, and costs.

Ideas that Work

■ **Start with your primary care physician (PCP).** With your PCP, address the questions that are listed on the INFORMED Worksheets on pages 78–82. If your doctor doesn't have time, ask if a staff member can help you. Ask for pamphlets, videos, or other educational material describing your condition that is written for the layperson.

■ **Get a second opinion.** If you're uncomfortable with your doctor's recommendations, consult with another doctor. In the case of elective surgery, your insurance plan may require it.

■ **Telephone-based nurse service.** Your company or health plan may offer a telephone-based service through which professionals will help you prepare the questions you need to ask your doctor about your health problem.

■ **Telemedicine services.** Local hospitals and HMOs may provide educational services you can access by phone. Through an automated system, you can select audiotapes that will explain a health condition.

■ **College or a medical school library.** Try accessing the library of a nearby medical school or college.

■ **The Internet.** Web sites provided by government agencies, universities, not-for-profit groups, communication companies, pharmaceutical companies, managed care groups, and individuals offer access to a variety of health-related information. They may offer interactive health quizzes, health information and resources, and electronic bulletin boards. Because content on the Web is unregulated, it's best to be cautious when considering on-line health information, which may be misleading or false.

■ **Support groups.** Many support groups, such as for AIDS, mental health, or breast cancer, have their own resources. Check with your local hospital, health department, not-for-profit agencies, and on-line services for support groups near you or on-line.

■ **Government agencies.** Organizations such as the National Institutes of Health (NIH) and your state health department have publications and hotlines (e.g., cancer, AIDS) that provide educational assistance. You also can contact NIH regarding any clinical trials of experimental treatments and admission criteria for these government-financed studies.

■ **Not-for-profit groups.** Organizations such as the American Academy of Family Physicians, the American Cancer Society, the March of Dimes, the American Heart Association, the National Multiple Sclerosis Society, the Asthma Foundation, the American Diabetes Association, and the American Red Cross have their own educational materials and programs you can request.

Resources

Refer to pages 288-293 for organizations and other resources.

Medical Decision Making

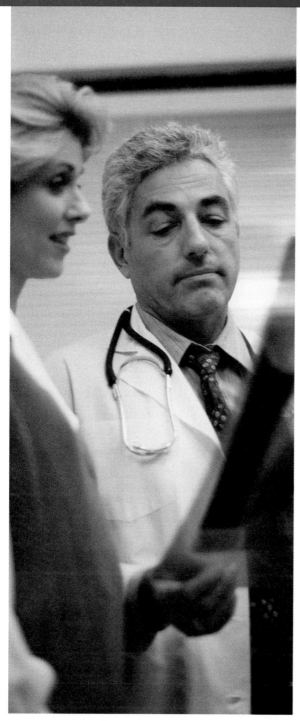

In this section:

- Using the INFORMED Medical Decision-Making Process™
- Being an active partner with your doctor in making treatment decisions
- Avoiding hospitalization
- Reducing your medical costs
- Your rights as a patient
- Important documents

Making Informed Medical Decisions

When you're facing a major health decision, the INFORMED Medical Decision-Making Process™ will help you and your doctor explore treatment options (i.e., further testing, medication, surgery) along with their benefits and risks.

The advantages of using INFORMED include:

■ **Better communication.** INFORMED will help guide your discussions with your doctor about the most important issues you face when you have a health problem.

■ **Increased participation.** INFORMED will help you become more active in making decisions about your medical treatment.

■ **Greater confidence, trust, and quality.** By learning more about your health problem and treatment options, you'll have more confidence and trust in your treatment plan. Also, your active participation in the decision-making process will make commitment to your treatment easier, and you'll feel more satisfied with your care.

The INFORMED Decision-Making Process™

INFORMED is your tool for becoming a more active participant in decisions about your medical care. It's easy to remember the **INFORMED** process—simply use the decision-making sequence below:

***I*nput:** Based on my symptoms and tests, what is my problem? What are my doctor's recommendations: further medical tests, medications, surgery, hospitalization?

***N*eed:** Why do I need this test or treatment? What happens if I do nothing? What outcome do I expect from my treatment?

***F*act-Finding:** Aside from my doctor, do I need additional resources and more information to make an informed decision? Do I need a second opinion? (See page 68.) Fact-finding includes learning more about your problem and exploring your treatment options.

***O*ptions:** Do other options exist for my problem? What are they? Can they be ranked from least intensive (e.g., "do nothing") to most intensive (e.g., surgery)? What are the risks for each option (e.g., infection, permanent disability, death)? What are the benefits of each option (e.g., complete recovery, lower cost, avoiding surgery, avoiding hospitalization)? How do the benefits of each option meet my needs (e.g., complete cure vs. minor disability or discomfort)?

***R*ecommended Treatment:** Based on my treatment options, what is my doctor recommending?

***M*anagement:** Based on my recommended treatment, what are my responsibilities for managing my health problem? For example, will I need to be on medication(s) for an extended period of time? Will I have to eliminate or reduce certain activities, including my work? Will I need rehabilitation? What can I do to help prevent my problem from happening again?

***E*xpense:** What is the total cost of my recommended treatment? Total cost includes medical costs, time off from work, lost wages, emotional distress, loss of independence, disfigurement due to scarring, etc.

***D*ecision:** Do I understand why a certain treatment is being recommended and what my responsibilities will be? Am I committed to my treatment plan?

INFORMED Questions

I nput: The first step toward learning about your health condition is understanding what your problem is and what your doctor is recommending, such as more tests, medications, hospitalization, and/or surgery.

Important Questions

- Based on the symptoms I provided, has my doctor diagnosed my condition or has he or she recommended further evaluation?
- If the diagnosis is not known, what could possibly be causing my symptoms?
- What tests is my doctor recommending?
- Is a treatment being recommended without discussing other options?

N eed: It's important that you understand the need for a procedure or test being recommended, and identify your own needs. Your doctor may suggest a need for further evaluation to make a diagnosis, or for specific treatment recommendations.

Important Questions

- Why do I need treatment?
- Why do I need a particular test(s)? How will it help my treatment or affect the outcome?
- What do I want (expect) from my treatment (e.g., a total cure, reduction in pain, etc.)?
- Are my expectations realistic?
- What do I need to do next to develop a treatment plan?

F act-Finding: Knowledge is power. Besides the information you receive from your primary care physician or health professional, it is important to learn as much as you can about your health problem and your current treatment options, and share what you learn with your doctor.

Important Questions

- Am I satisfied with how my doctor has explained my health problem? Do I understand what is being recommended? Do I need further explanation?
- Do I need a second opinion to confirm my diagnosis or recommended treatment?
- Besides my doctor, where else can I find out more about my problem (e.g., the Internet)? See page 75.

INFORMED Questions

Options: Your fact-finding will have helped you learn more about your problem and current approaches for treating it. Your next step is to discuss with your doctor what treatment options are available, based on your symptoms and need.

Important Questions

- What options are there for treating my problem? Together you and your doctor can compare the risks and benefits of each option side by side, using the INFORMED worksheet on page 82.
- What if I do nothing ("watchful waiting")?
- Can my doctor and I rank each treatment option based on how aggressive it is? "Watchful waiting" is the least aggressive approach, whereas surgery may be the most aggressive approach.

Recommended Treatment: Once you and your doctor have researched and discussed your treatment options using the INFORMED worksheet, it's time to develop a treatment plan.

Important Questions

- What treatment option are you recommending?
- Why are you recommending this course of action?
- What are the components of my treatment plan (e.g., medication, surgery, lifestyle changes)?

Management: Treatment goals depend on the severity of your health problem. Ideally, your goals for managing your problem are to reduce, then eliminate your symptoms, and ultimately avoid having symptoms return (relapse). In some cases, symptom management (e.g., reducing pain) may be the main goal. Whatever your treatment goals are, it is important to understand your responsibilities for managing your condition. Talk with your doctor to be sure you understand what is expected of you. In addition, don't hesitate to ask for help and support from your family or others who care about you.

Important Questions

- Will any short-term and/or long-term management be required (e.g., medication, therapy)?
- Will it help to eliminate or reduce certain activities, including those associated with my job?
- What lifestyle changes (exercising, quitting smoking, losing weight) do I need to make to help manage my problem?
- If medication(s) is prescribed, what is the dosage and schedule? See pages 98–104.
- What adverse reactions to medications might I experience? See page 99.
- What are my responsibilities for managing my health problem?

INFORMED Questions

Expenses: In addition to the monetary expenses of treating your problem, consider the emotional costs of loss of independence, and how your treatment may affect your relationships, career, overall health, and quality of life.

Important Questions

- What are the "ballpark" expenses (those from your doctor, any specialists, hospitalization, surgery, medications, etc.) for my recommended treatment?
- What are the potential ongoing costs of managing my problem (medications, rehabilitation)?
- What is covered under my health plan? What will I pay out of my pocket?
- Will I need to miss work or restrict activity because of my treatment? For how long?

Decision: Once you and your doctor have agreed on a treatment plan, make a commitment to follow through. Keep in mind that it may take time for medications to work and you may even have to change your plan to find what works best for you. If your treatment plan doesn't seem to be working, talk with your doctor before making changes. Asking these questions will help you commit to a plan, stick with it, and work with your doctor if changes are appropriate.

Based on the Questions Above:

- Have I discussed my treatment options with my doctor?
- Do I understand what options are appropriate for my situation?
- Do I understand why a specific treatment plan is being recommended?

Other Important Questions:

- Do I understand that my plan may change based on how I respond to treatment?
- If I have an additional health problem, do I understand how treating each problem can help me manage the other (e.g., diabetes and depression)?
- Do I have further questions about my recommended treatment?
- If I do, have I discussed these concerns with my doctor?
- Do I need more time to review other options?
- Have my doctor and I discussed and agreed on next steps?
- Am I committed to following my recommended treatment plan?

INFORMED Option Worksheet

	OPTION ONE	OPTION TWO	OPTION THREE
Treatment	Do nothing (watchful waiting*)		
Benefits			
Risks			
Management			
Expense			
Treatment your doctor is recommending	☐	☐	☐

* Watchful waiting involves no medical or surgical treatment, especially for someone with chronic illness. You continue to watch your symptoms to see if they improve, get worse, or stay the same over a specified period of time. Based on your observations, your doctor may advise further treatment.

Hospitalization

Hospitalization is the most expensive part of health care. Therefore, it is to everyone's advantage to try to reduce unnecessary hospital visits and find alternatives (e.g., home care, ambulatory surgical centers) that will still provide quality care, but at a lower cost.

Of course, there are many reasons hospitalization is necessary (e.g., emergency trauma, complicated surgical or treatment procedures). But, even in the best hospitals there are risks such as infection and complications during surgery. Therefore, avoiding hospitalization whenever possible is a logical goal. See the INFORMED process starting on page 78.

Discussing
Hospitalization and Surgery

Discuss these questions with your doctor when hospitalization is recommended.

■ **Outpatient vs. hospitalization?** If surgery or hospitalization is recommended, find out if there are any other methods of treating your condition, such as medication and outpatient surgery services.

■ **Explore all options whenever possible.** If there are alternatives, ask your doctor about their benefits, risks, and costs.

■ **Consider the total cost.** Besides the monetary costs of a specific treatment, talk with your doctor about the potential physical and emotional costs of a specific treatment plan (e.g., disabilities, scarring).

■ **Prepare for your surgery and treatment.** When surgery or other intensive treatments are recommended, learn about what to expect during the recovery or treatment phase. Ask:
–How much pain should I expect from the procedure?
–How long does it normally take to recover completely from this kind of surgery?
–What are the risks of disability from this surgery (e.g., nerve damage, limited mobility)?
–After surgery, what will my treatment be?
–What signs will indicate that my treatment is working?
–What complications are possible with this treatment?
–What signs would indicate that there is a problem?
–For what problems should I call the doctor?
–How long will I be out of work?
–Are there certain activities that I shouldn't participate in for a while after surgery? If yes, how long should I wait?

■ **If a surgical specialist is recommended, feel free to ask the following questions:**
–Are you board certified?
–How many surgeries similar to mine have you done? What is your success rate?
–Who will assist you?
–What is his or her experience?
–Will you or your assistant do the surgery?

Avoiding Medical Mistakes

Y ou can help prevent medical errors and assure your safety by staying closely involved in health care decisions that affect you.

Ideas that Work

Stand up for yourself. It's your right to question any and all health care you receive. See page 78. Do not go along with any treatment or procedure you have not authorized.

Medications. Inform your doctor of all prescribed and over-the-counter medications, and herbal or other supplements you are taking. Tell your doctor about any allergies or previous reactions you have had to medications. Make sure you understand the instructions for taking your medications. When you are given medications in the hospital, ask what the medication is, what it's for, and which doctor ordered it for you.

Diagnosis. Ask to see the results of diagnostic tests and have your doctor explain what they mean. If you have doubts about your diagnosis or the qualifications of the doctor, ask for a second opinion.

Hospitalization. If possible, select a hospital that has had a great deal of experience with your surgery, treatment, or procedure. Always feel free to speak up if you question any treatment, procedure, or medication given by anyone involved in your care. To lower your risk of infection, ask health care workers to wash their hands if they are going to touch you. Have a family member or other responsible person with you as much as possible to speak up for you if you can't communicate effectively. Get written instructions for follow-up care before you leave the hospital.

Surgery. Make sure you are scheduled for the correct surgery. Each caregiver and the surgeon should ask you to confirm what procedure you are supposed to have. You can help by marking the site of your surgery with a marking pen (e.g., left knee, right wrist).

For Your Information

Saving on Hospital Bills

- Make sure your doctor will accept the allowable charge. See page 61.
- Find out if you are required to get pre-approval from your insurance carrier before your treatment starts. See page 61.
- Find out if a certain procedure and any tests can be done on an outpatient basis. If hospitalization is required, avoid weekend admissions.
- On your bill, make sure your admission and discharge dates are correct.
- Keep a detailed record or log of the tests, drugs, supplies, and other services you receive on a day-to-day basis, or have a family member do it for you.
- Report discrepancies between your log and the itemized list of services performed.
- Check your insurance company's calculation of your deductible and out-of-pocket minimum.
- If you feel you have been overcharged and are getting nowhere with the hospital billing department, work with your health plan. Remember to have documentation (e.g., a log) to support your case.

Patient Rights

To be an informed medical consumer, it's important that you understand your rights and responsibilities and respect the fact that medical personnel must conform to their own professional code of ethics and practices. The American Hospital Association (AHA) has developed *Your Rights as a Hospital Patient,* a document that helps patients become aware of their rights and the hospital's responsibilities in treatment. Although written for hospital patients, most of these principles are important for all patients—hospitalized or not.

According to the American Hospital Association:

- You have the right to considerate and respectful care.

- You have the right to be well informed about your illness, possible treatments, and likely outcome, and to discuss this information with your doctor. You have the right to know the names and roles of the people who are treating you.

- You have the right to consent to or refuse treatment, as permitted by law, throughout your hospital stay. If you refuse a recommended treatment, you will receive other needed and available care.

- You have the right to have an advance directive, such as a living will or health care proxy. These documents express your choices about future care or name someone to make decisions if you cannot speak for yourself.

- You have the right to privacy. The hospital, your doctor, and others caring for you will protect your privacy as much as possible.

- You have the right to expect that treatment records are confidential unless you have given permission to release information or reporting is required by law.

- You have the right to review your medical records and to have the information explained, except when restricted by law.

- You have the right to expect that the hospital will give you necessary health services to the best of its ability. Treatment, referral, or transfer may be recommended. If transfer is recommended or requested, you will be informed of risks, benefits, and alternatives. You will not be transferred until the other institution agrees to accept you.

- You have the right to know if this hospital has relationships with outside parties that may influence your treatment and care. These relationships may be with educational institutions, other health care providers, or insurers.

- You have the right to consent or decline to take part in research affecting your care. If you choose not to take part, you will receive the most effective care the hospital otherwise provides.

- You have the right to be told of realistic care alternatives when hospital care is no longer appropriate.

- You have the right to know about hospital rules that affect you and your treatment and about charges and payment methods. You have the right to know about hospital resources, such as patient representatives or ethics committees, that can help you resolve problems and questions about your hospital stay and care.

Adapted from the American Hospital Association.

Advance Directives

Although medical technology sometimes can keep patients alive indefinitely, many people do not want heroic measures taken if there is little chance of recovery. Yet many people are unable to communicate their wishes at the time when a decision must be made. Health care professionals, bound by a duty to protect life, often are caught in a dilemma.

You can specify your wishes in advance through legal documents called "advance directives." These documents are prepared before you are faced with a life-threatening condition or major medical procedure.

Ideas that Work

- **Living will:** A living will states the kind of life support and measures you wish to receive if you're not able to make those decisions and your condition has been listed as terminal. Living wills also can specify what other medical procedures can be performed. It is a formal document that is signed, dated, and witnessed by two people who are not involved in your health care and are not heirs to your estate. It's recommended that a lawyer review your document, though it's not required.

- **Durable power of attorney for health care:** This is a formal document (also called a "health care proxy") in which you name another person who will make medical decisions for you in the event you are unable to make decisions on your own. A lawyer is not required to write a durable power of attorney for health care.

Things to Keep in Mind

- **Legality.** Most states recognize advance directive documents, but each state has its own requirements.

- **Which document?** Depending on requirements of the state where you live, one document or both may be recommended. Advance directives usually can be combined, specifying not only life support limitations, but also the type of care you wish to receive if you're unable to make decisions on your own.

- **Let your doctor know.** Your doctor must be made aware of advance directives. Generally you can assume that in extreme situations, if no advance directives are known, all measures will be taken to save your life.

- **Second thoughts?** You can cancel or change your directives at any time. Declining heroic measures will not affect the overall quality of your care, or change your doctor's decisions except in extreme situations.

- **No directives, what then?** If you have provided no advance directives and your illness prevents you from making care decisions, then your family, doctor, and hospital are responsible for your treatment plan. Sometimes a judge may be needed if there is disagreement about treatment options.

Resources

Choice in Dying
800.989.WILL

Eldercare Locator, for information on senior services
800.677.1116
www.eldercare.gov

Responding to Emergencies

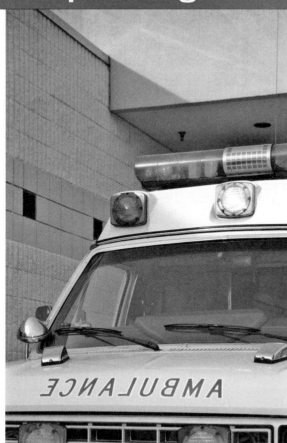

In this section:

- Identifying medical conditions that need emergency care

- Handling medical emergencies when you're away from home

- Responding to severe bleeding and shock

- Responding to a choking emergency

- Performing cardiopulmonary resuscitation (CPR)

- Responding to a drowning emergency

- Handling head injuries

- Responding to poisoning

Identifying Medical Emergencies

Most medical problems don't require urgent care. Avoiding the emergency room, whenever possible, saves time, stress, and money. However, it's crucial to be able to recognize true emergencies.

Conditions Requiring Emergency Care

Call 911 (if available) or the operator (dial 0) for an ambulance or emergency response team.

■ **Signs of a possible heart attack.** Severe pain in the middle of the chest, pain in the jaw or upper back, numbness (not alone), or pain that spreads to arms (especially left arm), shortness of breath, and cold sweats. *Do not delay calling for help in order to take an aspirin.* Wait for emergency personnel to advise you to take aspirin.

■ **Signs of a possible stroke.** Sudden fainting, dizziness, slurred speech, changes in vision, stupor, disorientation and/or marked weakness on one side of the face or in one or more extremities on the same side of the body.

■ **Signs of shock.** Pale, clammy skin; weak, rapid heartbeat with shallow, hurried breathing; lackluster eyes; cool extremities, confusion, and possible agitation. Until help arrives, have the person lie down, face up, with feet elevated (unless this causes pain or there is a suspected neck or back injury). Keep the person calm and still. See page 90.

■ **Loss of consciousness.** You are unable to awaken or arouse the person.

■ **Extreme difficulty breathing.** This may indicate a severe allergic reaction, an asthma attack, or something caught in the throat.

■ **The person is not breathing and has no pulse.** If you are alone and a phone is nearby, call for help first, then apply CPR. If you're not alone, send one person to call for help immediately and apply CPR. See page 93. If the person is choking, try the appropriate technique described on page 92. It is recommended that you learn CPR through your local chapter of the American Red Cross or American Heart Association.

■ **Possible spinal cord injury.** The person should not move or be moved if there is a possibility of an injury to the neck or back.

■ **Severe bleeding.** Call for help if bleeding is very severe or does not stop after you have applied direct pressure for 10 minutes. See page 90.

Other Situations Requiring Urgent Care
CALL THE EMERGENCY ROOM OR YOUR PRIMARY CARE PHYSICIAN IMMEDIATELY

- An infant less than 3 months of age has a fever of 103 F or higher (rectal temperature). This condition could indicate a serious infection and needs immediate attention.
- Severe vomiting or diarrhea, especially in infants.
- For poisoning, try to locate the toxic agent. Read the label and call the U.S. Poison Control Center at 800.222.1222—they will connect you to your local Poison Control Center. Follow instructions carefully. See page 96.
- A serious injury, such as possible broken bones, head injury (without loss of consciousness), or serious burns.
- Severe pain. Unexplained sudden pain that doesn't go away or gets worse.

Medical Emergencies on the Road

Whether you're traveling in the United States or abroad, it's important to get medical attention right away when you need it.

Your hotel may have a doctor on call. If you're in a foreign country, the nearest U.S. embassy will have a list of doctors in the area and will assist you in a medical emergency. If your medical problem is very serious, call a taxi or an ambulance immediately to take you to a hospital emergency room.

Ideas that Work

If you have a medical condition that may require attention while you're traveling away from home:

- **Consider a medical exam before leaving.** Be sure to have an examination if you plan to be out of the country for an extended period of time.

- **Health hazards abroad.** If you're planning a trip out of the country, check with authorities (see Resources, right) for areas with posted health alerts or quarantines for infectious disease (e.g., SARS, cholera).

- **Insurance.** Check with your employer or insurance carrier to make sure your health insurance will cover you at your destination.

- **Bring your medicine.** Carry enough medication to last the entire trip plus extra for unexpected delays returning home. Don't forget medication for colds, headaches, and allergies if you think you may need them. Carry all medications in their original containers and keep them in your carry-on luggage, pocket, or purse.

- **Take a copy of your medical records.** Include a list of all medications and dosages. Keep the list in a safe place other than where your medications are stored. Your doctor may be willing to provide you with a recent medical summary to alert others to your medical needs. If your condition puts you at risk for a medical emergency, make a plan ahead of time for how you would handle it away from home.

- **Identification.** Wear a medical information bracelet if you have a medical condition that warrants it.

- **Vision.** Take extra glasses, contact lenses, and lens cleaning solutions.

- **Make arrangements for your children.** If you are leaving children at home, make sure you sign an authorization for medical treatment and leave it with your children's caretakers.

- **Fees.** Many health providers require payment at the time of treatment for out-of-town patients. Be prepared to pay with cash, traveler's checks, or a major credit card.

Resources

Centers for Disease Control and Prevention Travelers' Health Hotline
877.FYI.TRIP
www.cdc.gov/travel

International Association for
Medical Assistance to Travelers
716.754.4883
www.iamat.org

Medic Alert
888.633.4298
www.medicalert.org

Uncontrolled bleeding, internal bleeding, or shock are serious emergencies that require prompt action. Blood loss can put a person into a life-threatening condition called shock.

Bleeding

Avoid infections by washing your hands (when possible) before and after administering first aid to someone who is bleeding. It's recommended that you wear gloves (latex or non-latex), if they are available.

> For serious bleeding and possible signs of shock (see right), call 911 or your local emergency response team. However, don't delay treatment.

- **Have the person lie down.** This will reduce the risk of fainting.
- **Apply direct pressure.** Applying direct pressure will stop most external bleeding. Do not remove any embedded object such as a knife or stick—this could increase bleeding. Using a sterile dressing or a clean cloth, apply direct pressure on the wound for at least 10 minutes. If the dressing becomes soaked with blood, do not pull the dressing from the wound— instead, place another clean dressing on top of the first cloth.

- **Elevate the injured area if you don't suspect a broken bone.** This helps slow down the bleeding.

- **If the bleeding doesn't stop, use pressure points.** Maintain direct pressure on the wound and also apply pressure to a "pressure point" above the wound (see right). Do not attempt to use a tourniquet except in a life-threatening situation or if you are trained to do so.
- **If you have assistance,** drive the person to the closest emergency room while your companion applies direct pressure to the wound.

Shock

Shock is life-threatening. It is caused by lack of blood flow to vital organs. Signs of shock: rapid, weak pulse; confusion, weakness, or unconsciousness; pale and/or clammy skin; shallow, rapid breathing.

> If the victim is showing signs of shock, call 911 or your local emergency response team immediately.

While you're waiting for help to arrive, do the following right away:

- **Check breathing, circulation (pulse), and airway.** Start CPR if necessary. See page 93.
- **Lay the victim flat and prop up the feet** 12 inches higher than the head. DO NOT move the person if there is a head, leg, neck, or spine injury.
- **Adjust for temperature.** Keep the person warm and comfortable. Loosen clothing.
- **DO NOT** give the person anything to eat or drink.

RESCUE BREATHING

Use rescue breathing if the person has a pulse *but is not breathing.* Call for help immediately.

Rescue breathing delivers air to the lungs if the victim is not breathing.

Assessing an Emergency

Assess the following to decide how to help:

Consciousness: Gently shake the victim and shout, "Are you OK?"

Circulation (pulse): Infants: Place your first two fingers on the inside of the infant's upper arm. Children and adults: Press your first two fingers on the victim's carotid artery (on either side of the Adam's apple).

Breathing: Listen for breathing by placing your ear next to the victim's mouth. Watch the chest to see if it rises and falls.

Rescue Breathing: Infants

Step 1: Lay the child on a flat surface. Tilt the head back *slightly* to open the airway.

Step 2: Place your mouth tightly over the infant's nose and mouth.

Step 3: Give 2 slow, gentle puffs, with a pause in between. The infant's chest should rise and fall as you breathe into the nose and mouth. If the chest does not rise, try 2 more breaths. *If chest still does not rise, the airway is probably blocked. See "Choking: Infants" on page 92.*

Step 4: Check for pulse. *Begin infant CPR if you do not feel a pulse. See "CPR: Infants" on page 93.* If the infant's chest rises with your breaths go to Step 5.

Step 5: Continue giving 1 breath every 3 seconds (or about 20 breaths per minute). Watch the chest as you give each breath to be sure air is getting into the lungs.

Step 6: Check pulse again and check for breathing. *Begin infant CPR if you do not feel a pulse.* Continue rescue breathing until the infant starts to breathe without your help, or until emergency help arrives.

Rescue Breathing: Children and Adults

Step 1: Tilt the victim's head back to open the airway.

Step 2: Check for breathing.

Step 3: Pinch the victim's nostrils closed and seal your mouth tightly over the victim's mouth.

Step 4: Give 2 slow breaths. The victim's chest should rise and fall as you breathe into the mouth. If it does not, reposition the victim's head and try 2 more slow breaths. *If the chest still does not rise, follow the procedure for "Choking: Children and Adults" on page 92, then try breaths again.*

Step 5: Check for pulse. If you feel a pulse but the victim is not breathing, go to Step 6. *If there is no pulse, begin CPR.*

Step 6: Give 1 slow breath every 4 seconds for a child/every 5 seconds for an adult, for 1 minute (about 12–15 breaths). Take your mouth away between breaths. Watch the chest as you give each breath to be sure air is getting into the lungs.

Step 7: Check pulse again, and check for breathing. *Begin CPR if you can't find a pulse.*

Step 8: Continue rescue breathing until the victim breathes on his or her own or until help arrives; check for pulse every minute.

CHOKING

For infants under 1 year of age who are choking and cannot cry, cough, or breathe.

Step 1: Lay the infant on his or her back on a firm surface. Remove any visible foreign object from the mouth. Check for signs of breathing. If the airway is clear but the baby is not breathing, begin rescue breathing. See page 91.

Step 2: If the infant's chest does not rise with rescue breathing, place the infant face down on your forearm, cupping his or her jaw with your hand. With your other hand, deliver 5 quick back blows between the shoulder blades.

Step 3: Turn the infant over, face up, with your arm supporting the back and your hand supporting the neck. Use your index finger and middle finger together to deliver 5 chest thrusts to the mid-chest, about 1/2-inch below the nipple line. Thrusts should compress the chest downward about 1/2 inch to 1 inch. Repeat steps 2 and 3 until the infant coughs up the object, begins to breathe, or becomes unconscious.

For children (over age 1) and adults who are conscious and choking or unable to breathe, talk, or cough.

Victim Standing or Sitting

Step 1: Wrap your arms around the victim from behind.

Step 2: Make a fist with one hand; grasp the fist with your other hand. Position your fist between the victim's navel and rib cage.

Step 3: Thrust your fist upward quickly and forcefully in an inward and upward motion.

Step 4: Repeat thrusts until the object pops out.

Victim Lying on the Floor

Step 1: Position the victim on his or her back.

Step 2: Kneel beside or straddle the victim.

Step 3: Keeping your elbows straight, put one hand on top of the other. With the heel of the bottom hand just above the waistline, deliver 5 quick upward thrusts.

Step 4: Repeat until the obstruction pops out.

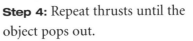

CPR

CPR combines rescue breathing with chest compressions to keep blood circulating. If the victim is unresponsive, call for help immediately.

CPR: Infants

Step 1: Give the child one breath.

Step 2: Place fingers on center of infant's breastbone, 1/2 to 1 inch below the nipple line. Compress chest rapidly 5 times, at least 1 to 1 1/2 times per second. Compressions should be about 1/2 to 1 inch deep.

Step 3: Feel for a pulse.

Step 4: Repeat a cycle of 5 compressions and 1 breath for about 1 minute (steps 1 and 2).

Step 5: Check for pulse and breathing.

Step 6: Continue a cycle of 5 chest compressions and 1 slow breath, checking for pulse and breathing every 3 minutes until the infant breathes without help, has a pulse, or until help arrives.

CPR: Children and Adults

Step 1: Check for consciousness.

Step 2: Kneel beside the victim.

Step 3: For an adult, place one hand on top of the other. Place the heel of the bottom hand 2 finger-widths above the notch of the victim's breastbone (where the bottom ribs meet in the center of the chest). For a child, place the heel of one hand 1 to 2 finger-widths above the notch of the breastbone.

Note: Use just one hand for a child; two for an adult.

Step 4: For a child, compress the chest 5 times to a depth of 1 inch; for an adult, compress the chest 15 times to a depth of 2 inches. Count your compressions aloud. Don't lift your hand(s) off the chest between compressions. Lock your elbow(s) straight during compressions and keep your shoulders directly over your hand(s).

Step 5: Tilt the victim's head back, lift the jaw forward, pinch the nose, and breathe into the mouth. Give a child 1 breath; give an adult 2 breaths, and watch for the chest to rise.

Step 6: Repeat the cycle of compressions and breaths (15:2 for an adult; 5:1 for a child) for 1 minute. Recheck for pulse and breathing.

Step 7: Continue giving CPR until the victim has a pulse or until help arrives.

For Your Information

Rescuer Safety

As a rescuer, there is a slight risk of being exposed to infectious diseases (e.g., hepatitis, HIV, AIDS, staph) by coming into contact with blood, saliva, and other body fluids. However, the American Red Cross recommends that you not delay giving emergency care such as CPR because of fear of getting a disease. Protect yourself by exercising these precautions, when possible:

- Wash your hands, if possible, before giving first aid. Always wash exposed skin afterwards.
- Keep a barrier mask with a one-way valve and gloves in your home and car first-aid kits.

DROWNING

ny near-drowning requires immediate action and prompt medical attention:

1. **Get the person out of the water.** This may be difficult in a large body of water. Call for help if needed. Depending on your own skills and the conditions, you may be able to swim to and retrieve the drowning person yourself. You could throw a rope or a buoyant object for the person to hold on to. Or, you could use a rowboat or canoe to get to the person. Once you reach the person, he or she can cling to the side while you row ashore; if you try to get the person in the boat, it may capsize.

2. **Begin resuscitation (see pages 91–93) as soon as possible if the person is not breathing.** If possible, start the process while you are removing the person from water, for example, in the shallow area of a lake. Don't waste time trying to drain water from the lungs.

3. **Call for emergency medical assistance.** Any near-drowning can lead to complications, so prompt medical attention is necessary.

4. **If the person is breathing, lay him or her down in the recovery position** (stomach down, head turned to side) and keep him or her warm with blankets until medical help arrives.

Resources

It is strongly recommended that you learn CPR from your local chapter of the American Red Cross or the American Heart Association.

For Your Information

Be Water-Wary for Your Child's Sake

- Adults should always supervise children near any body of water. Even a small amount of water in a bucket is a drowning hazard.
- If you have a pool, install a child-proof fence around it.
- Teach your child to swim, if he or she is at least 4 years old.* Reinforce the importance of never going in the water without an adult.
- Put a life preserver on your child whenever he or she goes boating.
- Secure toilet seats with childproof locks.
- Take a CPR course.

* American Academy of Pediatrics, 2004

HEAD INJURIES

The skull provides a lot of protection against most bumps and falls, so the majority of head injuries are minor and do not require hospitalization. Minor head injuries typically require rest for a few days. Refer to "Abrasions" (page 152), "Bruises" (page 159), or "Cuts" (page 162), as appropriate.

It is important to observe the injured person closely in the hours and days following a head injury. This may mean waking him or her periodically during the first night following the injury to be sure he or she can be awakened easily.

Call Your Doctor Right Away

■ If there is any change in the level of consciousness (from slight confusion to loss of consciousness), the person's pulse becomes slow (below 70 beats per minute) or irregular, his or her pupils are of unequal size, or if any other troublesome symptoms arise.

■ In the case of major head trauma, as may occur following a traffic accident or fall from a bike, seek emergency treatment. Keep the person lying down with the shoulders and head slightly elevated until help arrives. Do not move his or her neck.

Get Emergency Care Right Away

If the person:

• Is unconscious.

• Is not breathing. See "Rescue Breathing," page 91.

• Has severe head or facial bleeding. See "Bleeding," page 90.

• Has a deformed skull, bruising behind an ear or around eyes, pupils of unequal size, or bloody or clear discharge from ears or nose.

• Is confused, lethargic, vomits more than once, has a headache, speech difficulty, partial paralysis, partial memory loss, or convulsion either immediately following the injury, or in the hours or days following the trauma.

POISONING

Nearly 2.5 million poisonings occur each year, resulting in nearly 1,000 deaths. Most poisonings occur when someone swallows a poisonous substance, but also may result from exposure to a gas or absorption of a substance through the skin. Take the time to poison-proof your home—especially if you have young children.

Signs of Poisoning

Depending on the source of the poisoning, many body systems can be affected. If someone suddenly gets sick for no apparent reason, always suspect poisoning. Symptoms may include:

- Breath that smells like chemicals

- Nausea and vomiting

- Difficult breathing, cough

- Bluish lips

- Skin rash or burns

- Stupor or loss of consciousness

- Weakness, muscle twitching

- Heart palpitations, chest pain

Call Poison Control Right Away if:

You suspect poisoning; do not wait for symptoms to develop. Call the U.S. Poison Control Center at 800.222.1222—you will be connected immediately to your local Poison Control Center. You may also contact 911 or the emergency room (keep the phone number by all phones).

Responding to Poisoning

- **Check for pulse and breathing.** Call for emergency medical assistance.

- **Apply rescue breathing and CPR if needed.**

- **Provide information to the Poison Control Center** (e.g., victim's age, the name of the poison, when it was taken, whether the person has vomited).

- **Follow the instructions given to you.**

Do not induce vomiting unless instructed to do so by the Poison Control Center. Depending on what was swallowed, vomiting could cause more harm than good. Do not follow instructions on the label of the poison unless you're unable to contact the Poison Control Center.

For Your Information

Poison-Proof Your Home

- Keep medicines, household cleaners, cosmetics, and anything that contains alcohol out of sight, up high, and locked up.
- Be aware that child-resistant caps are not childproof—they just slow kids down.
- Never place poisonous liquids in other than original containers; they can be mistaken later for something else. Discard containers with damaged packaging or those with missing or illegible labels.
- Keep gasoline, pesticides, paint products, and antifreeze out of the reach of young children.
- Familiarize yourself with the plants in your home and yard. Remove toxic plants or any that have berries or leaves that might tempt a child.

Using Medications Wisely

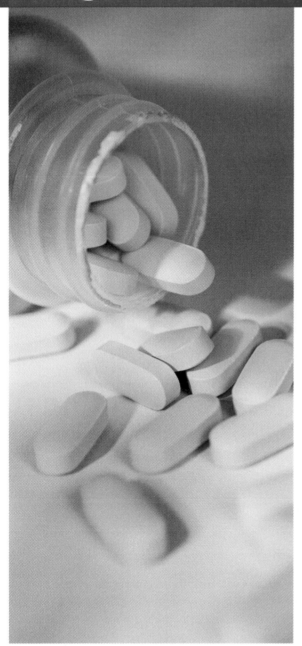

In this section:

- Using medications safely
- Medication use for older adults
- Stocking your home medicine cabinet
- Popular over-the-counter medications
- Understanding pain relievers
- Using antibiotics appropriately

Using Medications Safely

Medications, both over-the-counter (OTC) and prescription, need to be used wisely. Treat these drugs with respect by following the recommendations listed below.

Ideas that Work

- **When a medication is prescribed,** ask your doctor and/or pharmacist the following questions. It's a good idea to take notes.
  - ❑ Why has this drug been prescribed?
  - ❑ What side effects are possible?
  - ❑ Will it react with other drugs that I am taking?
  - ❑ How long will I need to take this drug?
  - ❑ What time of the day should I schedule my dose?
  - ❑ If side effects occur, what should I do?
  - ❑ Will this drug increase my sensitivity to sunlight?
  - ❑ What is the proper dosage?
  - ❑ Should I take it on an empty stomach?
  - ❑ Should I avoid alcohol or other foods or drinks?
  - ❑ How will I know if the drug is working?
  - ❑ How should this drug be stored?
  - ❑ Are refills allowed?
  - ❑ Can a generic brand be substituted for this drug?
- **Beware of overmedicating, or interactions with other drugs you may be taking.** Keep your doctor and pharmacist informed of all drugs you take, including herbal remedies and supplements.
- **Order by mail.** You could save up to 50 percent on a drug(s) for a chronic condition. Contact your health plan to locate mail-order suppliers. The supplier should maintain your medication files and have a toll-free number or Web site for questions and refill orders.

For Your Information

Taking Medication Safely

- Be sure you know the name and dosage of the drug(s) you are taking, including over-the-counter (OTC) medicines and herbal remedies.
- Be sure you are taking a drug properly (e.g., with water, on an empty stomach, the proper dosage, and how often you should take it).
- Learn whether any drugs (prescription and OTC medications) you're taking should not be taken with a new medication. Check with your pharmacist.
- Understand the common side effects of any and all drugs you take.
- Don't share your prescription drugs with another person or borrow someone else's.
- Don't change the way you take your medication without first talking with your doctor.
- Complete the full course of your prescription unless your doctor tells you otherwise.
- If possible, get all your prescribed medications from one pharmacy or chain so that one source will have a complete record of all your medications. This will help minimize the potential for adverse drug interactions.
- Understand that antibiotics don't help ailments that are caused by viruses. See page 104.
- When changing doctors or consulting a new specialist, either take a list of all your medications (including OTC, prescription, and herbal) or take them with you to your appointment so your doctor can review them.

Medication Use for Older Adults

ore drugs are prescribed for people over age 65 than for any other group in the United States. Older adults also are more likely to have problems with them. In fact, one in five older adults has experienced undesirable reactions to prescription medications.

There are a variety of age-related reasons that explain why seniors have twice as many adverse reactions to medications than do younger individuals. As we age, changes in the digestive and circulatory systems, kidneys, and body composition affect how the body is able to absorb, use, and eliminate medications. Decreases in the efficiency of the digestive tract can slow a drug's passage through the stomach and intestines.

For some drugs, such as Digoxin® and Warfarin®, this change in the amount of drug absorbed can be critical to its effectiveness. As we age, the liver is less able to filter toxic substances from the body. A drug that is filtered through the liver may have longer lasting and more severe effects in an older adult than in a younger person.

Remember, the best sources of information about your prescription medications are your doctor and your pharmacist. Take the time to understand the medication you will be taking. See page 98.

Among older adults, there are a few specific categories of prescription drugs that cause the most serious problems. They are summarized in the following table.

PROBLEM DRUGS FOR OLDER ADULTS*

Medication/Benefits	Common Brands	Adverse Reactions
DIURETICS –lower blood pressure –eliminate excess fluid and salt in tissues	Lasix®, Bumex®, Edecrin®, Diuril®, Hydrodiuril®, Aldactone®, Aldactazide®	–dehydration –low potassium –can worsen gout and diabetes
ANTIHYPERTENSIVES –lower blood pressure	Inderal®, Norvasc®, Aldomet®, Cozaar®, Vasotec®, Lopressor®, Minipress®, Plendil®	–headache –nausea –weakness/fainting –impotence –insomnia
CORTICOSTEROIDS –decrease inflammation	Decadron®, Cortef®, Cyclocort®, Hydrocortone®, Medrol®	–fluid retention –with long-term use, osteoporosis and impaired healing of wounds
SEDATIVES –aid sleep –reduce anxiety –promote relaxation	Valium®, Librium®, Xanax®, Dalmane®, Restoril®, Seconal®, Nembutal®, Ambien®, Equanil®, Halcion®, Prosom®	–memory loss –addiction –unsteadiness/falls –grogginess –agitation
OPIOID PAINKILLERS –treat pain –relieve diarrhea –cough	OxyContin®, Darvon®, Percocet®, Demerol®, Lomotil®, codeine	–addiction –tolerance to the drug –slowed breathing

*Do not stop taking any medication or change the dosage without talking with your doctor first.

Stocking Your Medicine Cabinet

This list will help you and your family stock your medicine cabinet. It includes basic items for the treatment and relief of common medical problems. But first, note these recommendations:

- Discard any over-the-counter or prescription medications that have passed their expiration date.
- Discard medications or supplies where packaging has been damaged (e.g., by water) or shows signs of tampering (e.g., safety lid is missing or loose).
- Never use another family member's prescription medication.
- Any drug can be harmful; read product information carefully and follow recommended dosages and schedules.
- Make sure all bottles are closed properly. Lock the cabinet and teach young children to stay out of the medicine cabinet. Never leave any drug within the reach of small children.

Supply Checklist

- ❑ Adhesive bandages, assorted sizes
- ❑ Gauze pads
- ❑ Disposable latex gloves (or synthetic, if you are allergic to latex)
- ❑ Cotton balls and swabs
- ❑ Chemical ice pack
- ❑ Elastic bandage
- ❑ Scissors
- ❑ Tweezers
- ❑ Safety pins
- ❑ Toenail clippers
- ❑ Thermometer. Include a rectal thermometer if there are young children in your household.

- ❑ Blood pressure cuff (sphygmomanometer) and stethoscope, especially if someone in your household has blood pressure problems
- ❑ Medications for fever, minor aches and pains, and headache. Aspirin, naproxen, or ibuprofen for reducing inflammation; ibuprofen or naproxen for menstrual cramps.

Note: Because of the risk of Reye's syndrome, aspirin should not be given to or used by children or teenagers who have or are suspected of having flu or chicken pox. Use acetaminophen.

- ❑ Antacid or sodium bicarbonate for treating an upset stomach or heartburn
- ❑ Antibiotic cream (e.g., Neosporin®) for minor cuts
- ❑ Antihistamines (e.g., Benadryl®, Claritin®) for treating minor cold symptoms and minor allergies such as hay fever; topical antihistamines (e.g., Caladryl®) to relieve insect bites
- ❑ Artificial tear drops to relieve dry or itchy eyes
- ❑ Saline solution to wash foreign matter from the eyes
- ❑ Hydrocortisone cream for the treatment of skin rashes and itching
- ❑ Colloidal oatmeal soap (e.g., Aveeno®) for rashes and itching
- ❑ Pectin substance (e.g., Kaopectate®) for controlling diarrhea
- ❑ Antifungal powder or spray to treat fungal infections such as athlete's foot and jock itch
- ❑ Sunblock or sunscreen (minimum 15 SPF) to prevent sunburn
- ❑ Zinc oxide preparation to prevent sunburn

Popular Over-the-Counter Medications

DRUGS/BENEFITS	COMMON BRANDS	POSSIBLE RISKS/DRAWBACKS

ALLERGY MEDICATIONS
• Oral antihistamine/decongestant preparations
  –Relieve and treat allergy symptoms
  –Relieve cold symptoms (e.g., congested nasal passages and runny nose)
  –Antihistamines can help relieve itching from rashes and swelling from insect bites
	Chlor-Trimeton®, Benadryl®, Claritin®, Allerest®, Sinutab®, Dristan®, Sine-off®, Sudafed®, Drixoral®, Tavist-D®, PediaCare®
	
	Some of these also contain acetaminophen.
		• Drowsiness and impaired function while operating machinery and driving
		• Decreased alertness and affected problem solving
		• Complicate existing prostate problems
		• Contact lenses difficult to wear
		• Agitation

Nose Drops/Sprays • Relieve and treat cold and allergy symptoms • Relieve nasal congestion	Afrin®, Dristan®, Neo-Synephrine®, Vicks Sinex®	• After several days, symptoms can become worse because nasal lining becomes dry and irritated, causing even more swelling • Agitation and/or rapid heart rate • Addiction
COLD/FLU MEDICATIONS • Relieve cold symptoms: fever, muscle aches, nasal congestion, runny nose	Contac®, Coricidin®, Dristan®, Dimetapp®, TheraFlu®, Triaminic®, Vicks Nyquil® *Some of these also contain acetaminophen.*	• Drowsiness/decreased alertness • Agitation • Possible upset stomach
COUGH PREPARATIONS • Expectorant preparations loosen mucus • Suppressant preparations reduce the cough reflex	Benylin®, Delsym®, Robitussin®, Romilar®, Cheracol-D®, Dimetapp®, NaldeconDX®, PediaCare®, Robitussin-DM®, TheraFlu®, Triaminic®, Vicks Formula 44® *Some of these also contain acetaminophen.*	• Drowsiness/decreased alertness • Constipation
LAXATIVE PREPARATIONS • Relieve constipation • Increase bulk to stool by drawing in water	Dulcolax®, Effer-Syllium®, Ex-Lax®, Metamucil®, Milk of Magnesia®, Phillips Liqui-Gel®, Senokot®, bulk laxatives that contain psyllium (e.g., Metamucil®)	• Diarrhea; dehydration with extreme cases of diarrhea • Tolerance to medications and constipation with prolonged use
DIARRHEA PREPARATIONS • Thicken the stool or slow bowel • Relieve severe cramping	Kaopectate®, Imodium A-D®, Pepto-Bismol®	• Nausea and sedation • Constipation in children
HEARTBURN/ANTACID PREPARATIONS • Neutralizes stomach acid • Blocks the production of stomach acid	Alka Seltzer®, Bromo Seltzer®, Gaviscon®, Gelusil®, Maalox®, Mylanta®, Pepcid AC®, Riopan®, Tagamet HC®, Tums®, Zantac®	• If you have high blood pressure or heart problems, watch the sodium content of absorbable antacids

Popular Over-the-Counter Medications

DRUGS/BENEFITS	COMMON BRANDS	POSSIBLE RISKS/DRAWBACKS
HYDROCORTISONE CREAM • Relieves itching and rashes from poison ivy, poison oak, and insect bites	Caldecort®, Cortaid®, Cortizone 10®, Dermarest®, Lanacort®	• Long-term use (more than 2 weeks) can lead to skin damage • Short-term use on face and genitals is not recommended
PAIN/FEVER RELIEVERS		
ASPIRIN • Relieves mild to moderate muscle pain • Reduces inflammation • Relieves tension headaches • Relieves arthritis pain • Reduces fever	Bayer®, Anacin®, Maximum Strength Anacin®, Maximum Strength Bayer®, Bufferin®, Alka-Seltzer®, Regular Strength Ecotrin®, Empirin OB®, Excedrin Migraine®, Aspergum®, BC Powder®, Goody's Powder®, Ascriptin®, Vanquish® *Some of these also contain acetaminophen.*	• Bleeding and bruising • Stomach upset, stomach and duodenal ulcers, or gastrointestinal bleeding • Reye's syndrome in children and teens • Increased risk to woman or fetus in last trimester of pregnancy • Aspirin poisoning
ACETAMINOPHEN • Relieves mild to moderate muscle pain • Relieves headaches • Does not irritate stomach • Recommended for children and teens with fever because there is no risk of Reye's syndrome • Relieves pain of osteoarthritis	Regular and Extra Strength Tylenol®, Anacin 3®, Excedrin P.M.®, Liquiprin®, Datril®, Midol®, Vanquish®, Fever All®, Percogesic®	• Liver damage in excessive amounts (greater than 5,000 mg) • Alcoholics are at greater risk for liver damage • Does not reduce inflammation • No effect on some types of arthritis
IBUPROFEN • Relieves muscle pain and soreness • Reduces inflammation • Relieves headaches • Useful for treating strains and sprains • Reduces fever • Relieves arthritis • Reduces menstrual pain	Advil®, CoAdvil®, Medipren®, Motrin®, Motrin-IB®, Midol Cramp®, Nuprin®, Pamprin-IB®	• Stomach upset, stomach and duodenal ulcers, or gastrointestinal bleeding • Potential kidney damage in people with kidney disease • Not recommended for pregnant women
NAPROXEN • Relieves fever, muscle pain • Reduces inflammation • Relieves headaches • Useful for treating strains and sprains • Night-time relief (lasts 8 hours) • Relieves arthritis • Reduces menstrual pain	Aleve®, Anaprox®	• Should not be used by children, heavy drinkers, pregnant women, or people who have aspirin sensitivity, ulcers, or asthma

Understanding Pain Relievers

For occasional, ordinary pain, the big four pain relievers (see page 102)—aspirin, acetaminophen, ibuprofen, and naproxen—work equally well in brand-name or generic forms. Keep in mind, however, that no over-the-counter (OTC) preparation will be very helpful for severe pain. Once you take a certain dose of any of these drugs you experience a ceiling effect: More pills won't kill more pain. If you have the kind of persistent pain that can't be reduced significantly or eliminated by an over-the-counter pain medicine, it's time to see your doctor.

Whatever pain reliever you choose, be sure to follow label instructions carefully (high dosages can be toxic). If one medicine gets to your pain faster and better than another, stick with it. Your body chemistry plays a big part in how a particular drug works for you.

Note: Because of the risk of Reye's syndrome, aspirin should not be given to or used by children or teenagers who have or are suspected of having flu or chicken pox. Use acetaminophen.

Hidden Pain Relievers

Acetaminophen is very effective for relieving pain and reducing fever, without the stomach problems that are common with aspirin and other nonsteroidal anti-inflammatory drugs. Yet, the FDA warns that too much acetaminophen causes serious and potentially fatal liver damage. This problem may occur if you take more acetaminophen than you realize when it is an ingredient in other OTC medicines you are taking, such as Nyquil® and Excedrin PM®. Taking medications that contain acetaminophen when you already are taking acetaminophen can cause an overdose that may damage your liver*.

To avoid an overdose of acetaminophen:

- Read all medication labels carefully.
- Always follow dosage instructions carefully. The common belief that "if one pill is good, then two must be better" could lead to an overdose. If you're not getting the relief you need with the standard dosage, don't take more—call your doctor.
- Do not take medication containing acetaminophen while you also are taking Tylenol®.
- Some prescription pain medications also contain acetaminophen. Tell your doctor if you already are taking acetaminophen or Tylenol®.
- Children's liquid acetaminophen and infant drops are not the same strength. To avoid giving an incorrect amount, read labels carefully.
- Alcohol also is toxic to the liver. Ask your doctor about the safety of using acetaminophen if you drink alcohol on a daily basis.

* Signs of liver disease include yellow skin and eyes, dark urine, light-colored stools, and loss of appetite. Other symptoms, such as feeling sweaty, achy, tired, and nauseous, can be mistaken for flu symptoms and may go unnoticed.

Using Antibiotics Appropriately

Antibiotics can be lifesavers. But overprescribing and overusing antibiotics has resulted in new and more powerful strains of antibiotic-resistant bacteria that are difficult to treat.

When you have a cold, the flu, or a sore throat, you may hope that after going to the doctor, you not only will feel better, but may be cured altogether. Some people may believe they'll get better if they ask their doctors to prescribe antibiotics to kill the germs that have made them sick. The problem is that antibiotics are effective only against bacteria. Colds and flu are caused by viruses, and antibiotics don't kill viruses. Antibiotics are not an appropriate treatment for a common cold or the flu. However, if your sore throat is caused by a streptococcal bacteria (strep throat), an antibiotic is the proper treatment.

Keeping Antibiotics Effective

- **Request a test** to determine whether your problem is caused by a virus, bacteria, or something else such as an allergy. Remember, antibiotics are not effective for viral illnesses such as colds, flu, and acute bronchitis, or for allergies such as hayfever.
- **If your problem is viral,** the infection must run its course. Try an over-the-counter medicine to relieve symptoms (e.g., runny nose, sore throat, nasal congestion) while your body heals. Talk to your doctor about specific antiviral medications for viral illnesses such as shingles and influenza.
- **If an antibiotic is prescribed,** use the entire prescription as directed. Do not stop early and save the medicine for later, because there's a good chance that some of the bacteria may not have been killed. This remaining bacteria may develop a resistance to the antibiotic, which will make it harder to treat in the future.

For Your Information

Generic Drugs

The notion persists that generic drugs don't work as well or that they somehow are not as good as familiar brand-name medications. However, since the 1980s, FDA regulations have required that generic drugs be as safe and effective as their brand-name counterparts.

A generic drug must contain the exact same active ingredients, in the same amounts, as the brand-name drug. In addition, the amount of the generic drug that gets into the user's bloodstream in a certain amount of time (bioavailability) must be the same as for the brand-name drug. Although the generic drug may be manufactured with different shapes, colors, flavorings, or fillers than the brand-name drug you are used to, these factors rarely affect the way the generic drug is going to work. Generic drugs are always less expensive as well.

In other words, the only real difference between generic and brand-name medicines is the price, and possibly, the taste and appearance. Before the prescription is written, ask your doctor if a generic-equivalent drug would be appropriate for you.

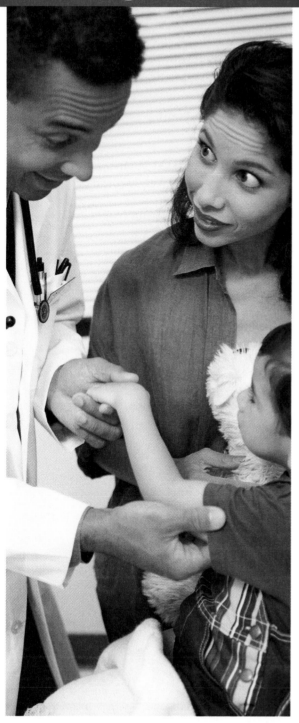

In this section:

- 145 common medical problems
- Determining if your problem needs medical attention
- HomeCare™ for medical problems that don't need a doctor's treatment

Introduction to Medical Self-Care

An estimated 80 percent of all common health problems—such as colds/flu, scrapes, and stomach upset—can be treated at home and do not require professional medical treatment. Medical self-care is an important skill that will help you make informed decisions about whether your problem needs emergency care, a call or visit to your doctor, or home treatment. Appropriate resources such as this book or a telephone nurse line will give you information for developing those important skills.

Among the many benefits of developing medical self-care skills are:

- **The power of knowledge.** The more you know about your own health, the more likely you are to take care of yourself.

- **Saving money.** When home treatment is appropriate, you can avoid unneeded doctor visits, which will save you out-of-pocket expenses (i.e., deductibles, copayments) and other costs, such as time away from work.

- **Greater confidence.** Making health-related decisions can seem very intimidating. However, by developing self-care and decision-making skills for common health complaints, you'll feel more confident as you work in partnership with your doctor to make all your health care decisions.

- **Becoming a partner with your doctor.** Your goal of medical self-care will encourage you to build an ongoing relationship with your doctor. By learning to recognize your symptoms, you can help your doctor get to the root of your problem quickly and develop a treatment plan that meets your needs.

Ideas that Work

- **Look in the Table of Contents** (pages iii–v) when you or a family member has a symptom (e.g., fever, sore throat) or health complaint (e.g., cut finger). You'll find your health complaint listed under "General Symptoms" or under a category such as "Conditions of the Head and Chest." Then turn to the page number listed. Topics also are listed in alphabetical order in the general index starting on page 294.

- **Do not delay in an emergency.** If you are told your problem requires immediate medical attention, DO NOT DELAY! Get emergency care right away.

- **When calling your doctor is recommended** or if your symptom or problem is not identified, call your doctor's office for instructions (e.g., come to the office immediately, make an appointment, watch symptom(s), continue HomeCare).

- **When medical treatment is not recommended** try the HomeCare listed for your condition.

This section is not a substitute for appropriate medical care. When in doubt, do not delay seeking medical attention.

Using the HomeCare Section

This section will help you decide if you need to see your doctor about your problem. After you review your signs/symptoms, decide whether you should:

Get Emergency Care Right Away If:

or

Call Your Doctor Right Away If:

or

Talk to Your Doctor If:

You're sure that your problem does not require medical attention. Then try:

HOMECARE

The HomeCare column has picture boxes (icons) that represent medication, fluids, rest, and other measures that may be used for treating your problem. Try the treatments in the order they are presented.

What Do the Self-Care Icons Mean?

Fluids

Recommendations for drinking adequate amounts of appropriate fluids, or avoiding certain fluids such as alcohol.

Medication

Recommendations for over-the-counter medications. It is important to keep the following points in mind:

- Use medication only as directed by the manufacturer or your doctor. Read the instructions on the side panel and insert.

- Be careful to take only the recommended dosage.

- If you have a health problem, such as high blood pressure, refer to the warning message on the label. If your problem is listed, call your doctor before taking the medicine.

Note: Because of the risk of Reye's syndrome, aspirin should not be given to or used by children or teenagers who have or are suspected of having flu or chicken pox. Use acetaminophen.

Rest

Recommendations to change or limit your overall level of activity.

Nutrition

Recommendations for special foods or a balanced diet.

Using the HomeCare Section

Heat/Cold

Recommendations for applying either heat or cold to the injured area.

• **Heat** is used in therapy to bring blood and nutrients to an injured area and help relax muscles.

• **Cold** is used to reduce pain, swelling, and discomfort. Ice therapy should be applied in intervals of 20 minutes on and 20 minutes off.

Note: Be careful of frostbite: white skin and numbness.

Clean

Recommendations for cleaning an injury or an area of the body exposed to chemicals or other external irritants such as poison ivy.

Cover

Recommendations for bandaging or covering a wound or injury.

Activity

Recommendations for either limiting physical activity to allow proper healing or for special exercises to speed recovery.

Note Well

This icon represents *"note bene,"* the Latin term meaning "note well." It will be followed by additional information about treating your problem at home.

Prevention

Recommendations and techniques for preventing the problem from recurring.

Cough

*C*oughing is an automatic reaction to an irritation in the throat, breathing tubes, or lungs. The irritation can be caused by dry air, tobacco smoke, allergies, a piece of food stuck in the airway, postnasal drip, gastroesophageal reflux disease (GERD), or chemical fumes; or can be a reaction to a viral (e.g., colds and flu) or bacterial infection. A productive cough (coughing up mucus) is your body's way of getting rid of infection. Viral infections need to run their course and usually don't need a doctor's attention. Bacterial infections, on the other hand, should be checked by your doctor.

Symptoms/Signs

- You may cough up yellow or white mucus if you have a viral infection.
- Green or rust-colored mucus often indicates a bacterial infection.

Get Emergency Care Right Away If:
The person coughs, then is unable to breathe. A foreign object may be lodged in the throat. See "Choking" on page 92.

Call Your Doctor Right Away If:

- Mucus is rust-colored, or is pink and frothy, and you have a fever of 102 F or higher.
- Your child has difficulty breathing, is wheezing, or is breathing rapidly.

Talk to Your Doctor If:

- Your infant (under 3 months) has a cough.
- You have a dry, nonproductive cough with no other symptoms, and it doesn't go away after 1 week.
- You cough up thick green mucus.
- Your cough hasn't gone away after you've recovered from a cold or flu.

HOMECARE™

If physician referral is not recommended at this time, try the following:

Fluids

- Drink plenty of fluids to help keep mucus thinner and easier to cough up.
- Avoid caffeinated drinks, such as coffee, soda, and tea, and alcohol, which increase urination.

Medication

- Experts recommend *not* using expectorants if your cough is productive. Try to loosen mucus by increasing your fluid intake.
- If your cough is nonproductive, try a cough suppressant that contains dextromethorphan. Take as directed.
- Try hard candy or throat lozenges to relieve an irritated throat.
- Try antihistamines or decongestants to control postnasal drip. Use as directed.

Note: Because of the risk of Reye's syndrome, aspirin should not be given to or used by children or teenagers who have or are suspected of having flu or chicken pox. Use acetaminophen.

Heat/Cold

- Try a vaporizer to increase the humidity in your home, especially your bedroom.
- A hot shower can help loosen mucus.
- Fill your bathroom sink with hot water. Lean over the sink and place a towel over your head to form a tent. Breathe in the steam for 10 minutes. Repeat as needed.

Prevention

- If you smoke, try to quit.
- Wash your hands frequently with antibacterial soap.

Diarrhea

Diarrhea is a common sign of a gastrointestinal infection. It's usually caused by a virus but also may be caused by bacteria (e.g., food poisoning, poor-quality drinking water). Diarrhea usually is preceded by abdominal gas and cramping and is the body's way of clearing the infection from the intestines.

Diarrhea can be a side effect of medications, especially antibiotics. Often, nervous tension stimulates the digestive system and brings on diarrhea. Chronic conditions such as irritable bowel syndrome (IBS) and certain food sensitivities (e.g., gluten, dairy) can cause cramping and diarrhea as well.

Symptoms/Signs

■ Loose or runny stools, usually preceded by abdominal gas and cramping.

Call Your Doctor Right Away If:

■ Your diarrhea is black* or bloody.

■ You experience the signs of dehydration: increased thirst, dark yellow urine, limited urination, and skin that may be wrinkled and have no tone.

Talk to Your Doctor If:

■ You experience severe abdominal pain with diarrhea.

■ Diarrhea continues for more than 48 hours after following HomeCare procedures.

■ You experience diarrhea that comes and goes for more than 1 week.

■ You have begun to take a new medication.

■ Your infant has any diarrhea episodes, is feeding poorly, appears listless, and is less responsive to you.

* *In the absence of other symptoms, black stools may result from taking iron supplements or medications containing bismuth, such as Pepto-Bismol®.*

Fluids

• To prevent dehydration, drink plenty of fluids, such as water and electrolyte solutions found in popular sports drinks. For breastfed infants, continue feeding as usual and offer extra water. For formula-fed infants, eliminate all but clear liquids (e.g., water or oral rehydration solutions: Pedialyte® and Infalyte®) for 24 hours.

Nutrition

• As tolerated, maintain a well-balanced diet from the major food groups including cereal, meats, cooked vegetables, and fruits.

• Greasy foods and milk products may make you uncomfortable.

Medication

• Over-the-counter preparations with pectin (e.g., Kaopectate®) solidify runny stools. Drink plenty of water with these preparations.

• Over-the-counter antimotility compounds, (e.g., Imodium A-D®) inhibit cramps and diarrhea. (Do not use if your temperature is above 101.5 F.)

• For children, the above over-the-counter preparations are not considered safe or effective.

Prevention

• To prevent food-borne infections, be sure that food is properly prepared and stored.

• Wash hands with hot water and soap before and after handling food.

• Decontaminate all areas where food is prepared (e.g., countertops, cutting boards, sinks) with antibacterial cleaning agents.

• Never drink untreated stream or lake water.

Dizziness

Your sense of balance is controlled by messages your brain receives from your body, including your eyes, your inner ears, and other nerves. When these signals are disturbed, you may feel:

- **Vertigo.** Ear inflammation, Meniere's disease, certain tumors, and even quick changes in motion (e.g., riding a roller coaster) can make you feel as though the room is spinning. Inner ear problems, balance disorders, and some medications can make you feel unsteady and off balance as you walk.
- **Lightheaded.** Anxiety, hyperventilation, or inner ear problems may produce feelings of spinning inside your head or that you are "spaced out."
- **Faint:** A drop in blood pressure, strokes, transient ischemic attacks (TIAs), and abnormal blood pressure can cause you to feel faint and lightheaded.

Symptoms/Signs

- Lightheadedness, possible sensation of blacking out.
- Dizziness that comes on suddenly and recurs (spells).
- Difficulty maintaining balance and/or the room seems to spin. Vertigo, possibly accompanied by vomiting, is sometimes caused by an inner ear infection, but often it's difficult to determine the cause.

Get Emergency Care Right Away If:

There is loss of consciousness or coordination, a rapid or irregular heartbeat, chest pain, trouble speaking, confusion, or shortness of breath.

Talk to Your Doctor If:

- You experience vertigo: balance problems and/or the room seems to spin.
- You suspect an inner ear infection. See page 133.
- Your lightheadedness keeps you from participating in your normal activities.
- You experience dizziness after using a new medication.

If physician referral is not recommended at this time, try the following:

Rest

- Learn to manage your stress and tension.
- Learn a relaxation technique. See pages 32-34.

Activity

- After vigorous activity such as running, cool down slowly by walking around for 2 to 3 minutes.
- Don't hold your breath when lifting heavy loads. Breathe out when moving an object.

Medication

- Follow directions for medication use (over-the-counter and prescription). Be sure to talk with your doctor before mixing a new medication with other drugs or alcohol.

Note: Because of the risk of Reye's syndrome, aspirin should not be given to or used by children or teenagers who have or are suspected of having flu or chicken pox. Use acetaminophen.

Prevention

- If you experience persistent spells, make note of symptoms, time of day, and possible causes—such as medication use, eating habits, changes in activity, periods of stress—and share your log with your doctor.
- Avoid jumping out of a chair or bed if you have episodes of lightheadedness upon rising.

Fatigue

Fatigue is a lack of energy and a general feeling of being tired. It can be linked to such physical causes as a viral infection, insomnia, autoimmune disorders, vitamin B deficiency, lack of physical conditioning, sleep apnea, and "over-training syndrome" found among many endurance athletes. Fatigue also can be a result of problems such as depression, anxiety, dehydration, or stress. Low blood sugar (hypoglycemia) is rarely a cause for ongoing or chronic fatigue. Most of us have our bouts of tiredness and low energy, lasting a few days. This usually is in reaction to a minor infection, overwork, or playing too hard. It is especially important for people with changing work schedules or who moonlight to get adequate rest and practice appropriate self-care skills.

Chronic fatigue syndrome (CFS) is an ailment that causes flu-like symptoms and extreme fatigue that is not relieved by rest. The cause of CFS is unknown, and there's no standard treatment. However, many doctors now prescribe carefully balanced periods of exercise and rest, directing patients to start out slowly and build gradually to find appropriate levels.

Symptoms/Signs

- Feeling tired all the time or having no energy.
- With chronic fatigue syndrome: overwhelming, ongoing fatigue, flu-like symptoms, aching muscles that don't feel better with exercise, and sometimes a low-grade fever.

Talk to Your Doctor If:

- Your fatigue is associated with a cold or flu and HomeCare doesn't reduce symptoms.
- Your fatigue doesn't go away after 3 weeks.
- You experience ongoing daytime fatigue, and you are a heavy snorer. See page 214.

If physician referral is not recommended at this time, try the following:

Rest

- Get 6 to 8 hours of sleep per night.
- See "Insomnia" on page 208 or "Snoring" on page 214, as appropriate.

Activity

- Slow down. Try to modify your schedule if you are burning the candle at both ends.
- Reduce your workouts for 2 weeks if you exercise heavily.

Fluids

- Avoid drinking too much alcohol.
- Limit drinks with caffeine.

Medication

- Do not rely on stimulants such as diet pills and amphetamines or illegal drugs such as cocaine to give you energy.

Nutrition

- Eat balanced meals.
- Drink plenty of fluids, especially during hot, humid days, and during strenuous exercise or other work.

Prevention

- Learn and practice relaxation and stress skills.
- Try to balance your work and play.
- Get enough sleep.

Fever

If physician referral is not recommended at this time, try the following:

Fever in itself is not a disease; it's part of the body's natural response to infection. Many bacterial and viral infections are destroyed by fever. It also may be a sign of a more serious medical problem. In infants and older adults, especially the frail elderly, fever could be a sign of a problem that rapidly could become more serious.

Symptoms/Signs

- A body temperature higher than 99.5 F measured with an oral (mouth) thermometer, or 100.4 F or higher measured with a rectal thermometer (used for babies and small children).
- Sweating, shivering, general weakness.

Call Your Doctor Right Away If:

- You have a high fever after traveling outside the U.S.; this could indicate SARS.
- Fever is combined with a stiff neck (difficulty touching chin to chest), confusion, and lack of energy.

Talk to Your Doctor If:

- **Infant under 1 month old:** Fever over 100.5 F rectally even if the baby doesn't seem sick.
- **Infant under 3 months old:** Fever of 100.5 F or a temperature of 99.5 F lasting more than 24 hours.
- **Child over 3 months old:** Fever over 101.5 F that lasts more than 3 days.
- **Children 3 months to 2 years:** Fever over 102 F even if the child seems fine.
- **Child:** Fever with signs of seizures or has a history of febrile seizures. See page 241.
- **Anyone age 4 or older:** Fever of 104 F or higher that does not come down after 2 hours of HomeCare.
- **Adult:** Fever of 100.1 F or higher that lasts more than 3 weeks.

Medication

- Aspirin, ibuprofen, or acetaminophen for reducing fever higher than 101 F. Use as directed.

Note: Because of the risk of Reye's syndrome, aspirin should not be given to or used by children or teenagers who have or are suspected of having flu or chicken pox. Use acetaminophen.

Fluids

- Drink plenty of water.
- Drink caffeine-free drinks such as fruit juices or ginger ale.

Heat/Cold

- Sponge the skin with lukewarm water (not cold water). Evaporation will have a cooling effect on skin. Stop if shivering occurs.

Rest

- Limit activity. Bed rest may be advisable in cases of high fever and other symptoms such as diarrhea.
- Allow your child to rest as he or she desires.

Note Well

- Remove extra layers of clothing.

Numbness

Most of the time, numbness is a harmless and temporary symptom associated with a minor injury, a pinched nerve, or arthritis. However, sometimes numbness is a sign of something more serious such as a stroke or diabetes. People with diabetes may experience numbness when their disease affects the health of nerve fibers, making them more prone to injury and infection. Numbness also can be a sign of toxicity of certain substances (e.g., mercury, lead, alcohol), medications, or deficiency of folic acid or vitamin B.

Whatever the origin of the symptom, it's important for you to know when to seek medical help.

Symptoms/Signs

■ Loss of feeling or sensation in any part of the body, sometimes accompanied by intermittent tingling or "pins and needles" sensation.

■ Numbness that is not associated with injury or another apparent cause.

Get Emergency Care Right Away If:

• Numbness comes on suddenly. It can indicate a stroke in progress—a life-or-death situation.
• You experience sudden numbness in your face or in the arm or leg (or both) on one side of your body.
• Sudden numbness is accompanied by vision problems, speech problems, dizziness, lack of coordination, difficulty swallowing, or a sudden and severe headache.

Call Your Doctor Right Away If:

■ Numbness comes on suddenly or is not clearly due to some minor cause.

■ Numbness is associated with injury to the neck or back, or weakness in any leg.

If physician referral is not recommended at this time, try the following:

Note Well

• For numbness in the hands and feet due to exposure to cold, see "Cold Hands and Feet" on page 161.
• Protect numb skin or other areas to reduce the possibility of injury.
• If you have diabetes, inspect your feet for cuts, scratches, blisters, or unhealed wounds.

Heat/Cold

• Keep areas of the body prone to poor circulation covered with warm, dry clothing.

Palpitations

It's not unusual to feel an occasional flutter in the chest or racing heart. Caffeine, alcohol, certain medications, tobacco, emotional excitement, anxiety, and stress all can cause palpitations.

You should be concerned when heart palpitations have no apparent cause or are accompanied by other symptoms. A congenital defect, heart disease, respiratory problems, and other disorders can stress the heart muscle. A visit to your doctor is the surest way to find out whether irregular heart rhythms are harmless "blips" on your cardiac screen or a wake-up call that may save your life.

Symptoms/Signs

■ Sensation that your heart is racing without cause, fluttering, missing a beat, or beating irregularly.

Get Emergency Care Right Away If:

- Palpitations or chest pain are accompanied by nausea, vomiting, cold sweats, shortness of breath, lightheadedness, or faintness.
- You experience chest pain that spreads to the neck, back, shoulder, or arms.
- Palpitations last more than 1 hour.

Call Your Doctor Right Away If:

■ You experience palpitations after you start or stop taking any medication.

■ You experience chest pressure or pain in the center of your chest (without nausea and vomiting and cold sweats) that lasts for more than a few minutes or that comes and goes.

■ You have a burning sensation that feels like severe heartburn or indigestion.

■ You have unexplained pain in your lower jaw.

Medication

- Avoid diet pills or other stimulants.
- Avoid certain over-the-counter cold or allergy medicines (check with your doctor or pharmacist).

Activity

- Exercise moderately and regularly. Check with your doctor before beginning a new exercise program, especially if you've been sedentary for a while. Then start slowly and increase intensity gradually.

Rest

- Get plenty of sleep; fatigue can increase anxiety and the effects of stress, which can increase the frequency of palpitations.

Fluids

- Drink six to eight glasses of fluids (preferably water) a day to stay well hydrated. Drink more if you're physically active.

Prevention

- Don't smoke. Avoid all tobacco products.
- Avoid alcohol and caffeine.
- Keep your weight in a healthy range; eat a balanced diet and exercise regularly.
- Practice stress-reduction techniques.
- Take medicines only as directed.
- Make sure that your doctor and pharmacist know about all the medications you're taking and whether you have any drug allergies.
- Do not use illicit drugs of any kind.

Runny Nose

A common source of a runny nose is a cold. It's your body's way of ridding itself of the virus that has invaded your respiratory system. If you don't have a cold, you may have allergic rhinitis—allergies to certain plants, pollen, or dust. In either case, the mucus usually is clear and watery. Gentle and frequent blowing will help keep nasal passages relatively clear.

Be careful using over-the-counter nasal sprays. Using them for more than 3 days can lead to a rebound effect, where the medication increases your symptoms or causes more congestion and can require a greater dose to be effective. A mild saline spray will wash away irritants and moisturize dry nasal passages. You can buy saline spray or make your own: Boil a mild saltwater solution of one-quarter teaspoon per 8 ounces of water; let it cool; and then inhale a small amount of the solution into your nose from your palm or through an inhaler.

Symptoms/Signs

■ Intermittent or continuous drainage of mucus from the nose.

Talk to Your Doctor If:

■ Your symptoms are accompanied by a fever of 103 F.

■ Nasal mucus is discolored (e.g., yellow or green) or has a foul odor. This may indicate a bacterial infection.

■ You suspect your runny nose is caused by seasonal allergies.

■ You have a runny nose without any other symptoms that lasts 3 weeks or longer.

■ You experience wheezing, shortness of breath, or difficulty swallowing.

■ Mucus is accompanied by severe facial pressure or pain that is not relieved with over-the-counter preparations.

If physician referral is not recommended at this time, try the following:

Medication

- Try an over-the-counter antihistamine or cold remedy.
- Use over-the-counter nasal spray medications for no more than 3 days, saline nasal spray as needed.

Note: Because of the risk of Reye's syndrome, aspirin should not be given to or used by children or teenagers who have or are suspected of having flu or chicken pox. Use acetaminophen.

Heat/Cold

- Breathe steam to loosen mucus and clear out nasal passages. Take hot showers. Or fill a basin with boiling water, drape a towel over your head, bend over the basin, and breathe. Drinking hot beverages helps, too.

Nutrition

- Eat a well-balanced diet with plenty of fruits and vegetables rich in vitamins C, A, and E.
- Avoid dairy products if they seem to make mucus thicker and more profuse.

Rest

- Get adequate rest to help re-energize your immune system.
- Limit activity in cold, dry weather.

Prevention

- If you have allergies, avoid offensive allergens. Use your home and car air conditioner during allergy season. Keep windows closed. Consider using a portable air filter.
- Keep your home well humidified.
- Don't smoke.

Sore Throat

A sore throat can result from factors such as dry air, smoking (including secondhand smoke), allergies, air pollution, or a viral or bacterial infection. Mild throat irritation is common in people who sleep with their mouths open or who have post-nasal drip.

Viral infections such as influenza and colds are common causes of sore throat. A viral sore throat usually includes other symptoms as well, such as a runny, congested nose, headache, and cough. These symptoms indicate a typical cold or influenza and rarely require a visit to your doctor. A more severe sore throat occurs with mononucleosis—a viral infection common among adolescents and young adults. A viral sore throat cannot be treated with antibiotics.

Sore throats also can be caused by bacteria, often from the streptococcal strain. Strep throat symptoms include fever, sore throat, and swollen neck glands. Untreated, strep can lead to rheumatic fever (mostly in children) or inflammation of the kidneys. Antibiotics are used to treat strep infections.

Symptoms/Signs

- Symptoms of mononucleosis include sore throat, extreme fatigue and swollen glands.
- Strep throat symptoms can be limited to pain, aching, and tenderness in the throat.

Talk to Your Doctor If:

- The throat is bright red, or pus or white spots are present on back of throat, and symptoms are limited to the throat only.
- You have a sore throat that is accompanied by fever of 101.5 F or higher.
- A mild sore throat lasts more than 7 days.
- You have difficulty breathing or swallowing anything, including saliva.

Rest

- With strep, get plenty of rest.
- Keep children home from school until the fever is gone.

Fluids

- Fluids will help relieve soreness.
- Try weak tea with honey and lemon to soothe the throat.

Medication

- Aspirin, ibuprofen, or acetaminophen for fever.
- Decongestants with or without antihistamines for runny nose.
- Cough drops to soothe a dry throat.
- Gargling with Cepacol® may relieve soreness.

Note: Because of the risk of Reye's syndrome, aspirin should not be given to or used by children or teenagers who have or are suspected of having flu or chicken pox. Use acetaminophen.

Note Well

- Saltwater gargles may ease soreness.
- Try a humidifier in your home, especially in bedrooms.
- A cool-mist vaporizer may help also.

Prevention

- If you smoke, quit. Smokers are more prone to upper respiratory infections.
- Avoid secondhand smoke.

Swollen Glands

Most cases of swollen glands involve the lymph nodes, or with mumps, the salivary glands of the neck.

Lymph nodes are small glands that help your body fight infections such as colds, ear infections, and those in small cuts. They become swollen, tender, and hard when an infection occurs and may remain hard after the infection has passed. You can feel lymph nodes in your neck, armpits, and groin area. Persistent swollen glands may indicate a serious health problem that may require medical consultation.

Viruses, such as the virus that causes mumps, can also cause swollen glands. Once a common childhood disease, mumps can now be prevented by immunization. See pages 44 and 240.

Symptoms/Signs

- Glands that are swollen or hard, and may be red and tender to the touch.
- **Mononucleosis:** swollen glands (especially in the back of the neck) with fever, sore throat, muscle aches, and fatigue.
- **Mumps:** one or both of the salivary glands (located below and forward of the ears) are swollen. Other symptoms include low fever, earache, headache, and/or fatigue.

Talk to Your Doctor If:

- The glands do not get smaller after 3 weeks.
- A single gland is getting progressively larger over 7 days.
- The skin covering the gland is red and inflamed.
- Swollen glands are accompanied by other symptoms such as fever and weight loss.
- You suspect mumps or mononucleosis.

HOMECARE™

If physician referral is not recommended at this time, try the following:

Note Well

- If lymph nodes are swollen, no treatment is required. Watch glands and other symptoms for 3 weeks.
- Evaluate and treat other symptoms as they occur, (e.g., fever, sore throat, cough). Refer to other conditions in this book.
- If you have, or suspect you have, mononucleosis, avoid contact sports because the spleen may be enlarged and could rupture.

Heat/Cold

- Apply a warm washcloth or a cold compress, according to which seems to provide the best relief.

Vomiting

Vomiting usually is your body's reaction to something that doesn't belong in your system: a virus, bacteria, food allergen, certain drugs, foreign objects, or poisons. Motion sickness, ear infections, emotional distress, pregnancy, or simply too much food or drink also can upset your stomach. Most mild vomiting can be prevented or alleviated with self-care remedies. But when vomiting is ongoing or severe, it could indicate a serious underlying medical problem such as gastritis, kidney or liver disorders, ulcer, some types of cancer, or an infection. Whatever the cause, vomiting is a clear signal that something is wrong internally. Knowing when to treat it at home and when to seek medical care is crucial.

Symptoms/Signs

- With viral gastroenteritis, viral stomach flu, or food poisoning: vomiting accompanied by fever, diarrhea, chills, headache, and extreme fatigue.
- When a foreign body is lodged in the throat or intestine: vomiting accompanied by no other symptoms.

Call Your Doctor Right Away If:

- Vomiting is prolonged, lasting more than 12 hours in adults or 4 hours in small children without improvement.
- Vomiting is accompanied by severe abdominal pain, earache, chest pains, or other unusual symptoms.
- Vomit appears bloody or looks like coffee grounds.
- Dehydration threatens. Symptoms may include dark yellow urine or lack of urination, sunken eyes, cold and clammy skin with poor elasticity, and, in infants, less than three wet diapers in 24 hours.
- You can't hold down fluids.

Fluids

- To help prevent dehydration, drink plenty of clear fluids: Water, hot broth, sports drinks; or chew on crushed ice. For breastfed infants, continue feeding as always, but offer extra water. For formula-fed infants, eliminate all but clear liquids (e.g, water or oral rehydration solutions: Pedialyte® and Infa-Lyte®) for 24 hours.

Nutrition

- With acute gastroenteritis or stomach flu, it's wise to avoid food for 24 hours. After 24 hours, eat small quantities of bland foods such as clear soups, bananas, rice, applesauce, dry toast, mashed potatoes, or plain pasta.

Medication

- Take acetaminophen for fever and body aches. Avoid taking aspirin or ibuprofen. They can irritate the stomach.
- Try Emetrol®, an over-the-counter stomach-settling syrup (not recommended for diabetics).
- Use over-the-counter preparations to prevent vomiting associated with motion sickness.

Note Well

- Reduce nausea by applying pressure with two fingers on the medial nerve, located on the inside of your wrist, below the little finger.

Prevention

- Make sure meat, seafood, poultry, prepared salads, dressings, and other foods are properly stored and prepared.
- Wash hands and work surfaces frequently during food preparation.

Wheezing

Asthma, bronchitis, pneumonia, emphysema, certain heart conditions, drugs, chronic lung disease, allergies, smoking, or airborne irritants—all can cause irritation and swelling in the lining of the airways, restricting the air passing through. When that happens, you hear wheezing: the coarse, whistling sound coming from the chest when you breathe out (exhale).

Symptoms/Signs

- Low-pitched or musical-sounding noise from the chest (not the throat) with every breath (exhaling).
- **Asthma:** shortness of breath; coughing that worsens at night or with exertion or cold air; tightness in the chest.
- **Bronchitis:** cold symptoms; coughing that produces green, yellow, or gray mucus; mild chest pain or fever.
- **Smoking-related respiratory problems:** shortness of breath; chronic coughing that produces thick mucus; limited lung capacity.
- **Children:** suspect a foreign object has been inhaled if there is sudden wheezing and shortness of breath without a previous history of asthma.
- **Generalized allergic reaction:** shortness of breath, tightness in the chest, or wheezing.

Get Emergency Care Right Away If:
- You become lightheaded or have difficulty breathing.
- You suspect a foreign body in the airway.
- You have symptoms of a generalized allergic reaction, including restricted breathing.

Talk to Your Doctor If:

- Mucus coughed up is streaked with blood.
- A cough persists for more than 2 weeks.
- Wheezing persists for more than 2 weeks or is accompanied by a persistent fever.
- You are experiencing wheezing for the first time.

If physician referral is not recommended at this time, try the following:

Medication

- With bronchitis, allergies, or colds, try a decongestant containing pseudoephedrine to relieve congestion. (Nonviral bronchitis sometimes requires prescription antibiotics.)
- Avoid aspirin or ibuprofen; take acetaminophen instead.

Note: Because of the risk of Reye's syndrome, aspirin should not be given to or used by children or teenagers who have or are suspected of having flu or chicken pox. Use acetaminophen.

Fluids

- Drink lots of fluids to keep mucus thin.

Activity

- With asthma, consult your doctor about how to remain active without triggering an attack. Otherwise, exercise normally unless exertion makes wheezing worse.
- With bronchitis, limit your activity.

Nutrition

- Avoid food triggers that may cause an allergic reaction.

Prevention

- Don't smoke, avoid respiratory irritants and allergens.
- Avoid foods or drugs to which you have an allergy.
- Treat colds and the flu quickly and effectively.
- Reduce and manage stress.
- Humidify and/or use a portable air filter in your bedroom for bronchitis.

Asthma

Asthma is a chronic upper respiratory disease that can be life-threatening. It is caused by inflammation and narrowing of the small breathing tubes of the lungs, which makes breathing difficult or impossible.

The airways of people with asthma are sensitive, swollen, or inflamed. During an asthma attack, exposure to specific triggers causes the linings of the breathing tubes to swell and become inflamed; mucus is produced, clogging the airways; and the muscles that surround the breathing tubes tighten, further restricting breathing.

Asthma triggers include allergens, irritants, respiratory infections, physical activity, strong emotions, and certain weather conditions.

If you have asthma, it's important to be aware of your exposure to triggers; be sensitive to the warning signs of an attack; and know what to do in acute asthma situations. See page 248.

Symptoms/Signs

- Labored breathing, wheezing, shortness of breath, tightness in the chest, and coughing.

Get Emergency Care Right Away If:

- You have an acute asthma attack and HomeCare does not reduce symptoms.

Talk to Your Doctor If:

- You have asthma symptoms for the first time.
- Your child has episodes of wheezing.
- You cough up green, yellow, or bloody mucus.

If physician referral is not recommended at this time, try the following:

Rest

- Reduce your activity when an asthma attack occurs.
- Try to remain calm. Stress can increase symptoms.

Medication

- Use prescribed medication only as directed by your doctor.
- Consult your doctor before using antihistamines if you have asthma.
- See your doctor if you are using your quick-relief inhaler more than twice a week. Your asthma may not be under control.

Fluids

- Drink plenty of clear fluids to help thin and loosen mucus.
- Coffee has been shown to help relieve attacks in some people.

Activity

- Stay physically active. If you have experienced exercise-induced asthma attacks, monitor the intensity of your exercise.

Prevention

- Know what factors (e.g., pollens, smoke, dust, fumes, cold air, dry wind, certain foods such as milk and eggs) cause your attacks.
- Avoid these agents or minimize your exposure by keeping your home dust free. Wash bedding weekly and remove carpeting, if possible.
- If you smoke, quit. Avoid smoke-filled areas.
- Try to reduce the stress in your life. Learn a relaxation technique. See pages 32-34.
- Install an air conditioner in your home and possibly an air-filtration system.

Bad Breath

Occasional bad breath (halitosis) is as natural as breathing itself. Indeed, you'd be hard pressed to find someone who has pleasant breath all the time. However, there may be cause for concern when breath is chronically offensive. The most obvious causes of bad breath—bad dental hygiene, smoking, poor diet—are easily treatable and should be treated because they eventually may lead to more serious medical problems. Problems such as liver disease, lung disease, respiratory infections, digestive disorders, and kidney failure can cause bad breath as well.

If your halitosis is particularly strong and won't go away no matter what self-care remedies you try, it's important to see your doctor to determine whether some underlying medical condition is to blame.

Symptoms/Signs

■ Foul mouth odor.

Talk to Your Doctor If:

■ Your breath ever smells like urine or feces.
■ Your breath has an unusually fishy or fruity odor.
■ Your bad breath does not go away regardless of the HomeCare procedures you try.

If physician referral is not recommended at this time, try the following:

Clean

- Brush and floss teeth two or three times daily, especially after meals. Don't forget to brush your tongue.
- If you can't brush or floss after a meal, rinse with water or mouthwash, or chew sugar-free gum.
- Have your teeth professionally cleaned and examined.

Medication

- Rinse mouth often with a medicated or antiseptic mouthwash.
- For temporary relief, try over-the-counter breath sprays or breath-freshening drops (remember, that such products only cover up bad breath for about 15 or 20 minutes).

Nutrition

- Chew on parsley, cloves, or fennel seeds after meals to freshen breath.
- Eat a balanced diet.
- Don't compound bad breath by eating foods that linger on your breath: garlic, onions, hot peppers, certain deli meats, and cheeses will leave an offending air for 24 hours after you eat them.

Fluids

- Drink plenty of water to keep your mouth moist (dry mouth is a leading cause of bad breath).
- Avoid coffee or other drinks that leave breath smelling foul.

Prevention

- Follow all of the above recommendations for treating bad breath. Most important: Practice excellent oral hygiene and visit your dentist twice a year.
- Don't smoke or use tobacco products.

Bleeding Gums

Left untreated, bleeding gums can slowly deteriorate and become a periodontal disease called gingivitis. The gums pull away from teeth, and eventually stop doing their part to keep your teeth where they belong. Signs include reddened, swollen gums, and loose teeth.

Dental disease is 100 percent preventable if you follow your dentist's advice about brushing, flossing, rinsing, and keeping appointments for regular check-ups. Your average time investment for lifelong dental health is about 10 minutes a day. That may not seem like a lot of time, but it's about 9 minutes more than most people spend on daily dental hygiene. See pages 46–47.

Symptoms/Signs

- Toothbrush bristles appear pink after brushing.
- Bloodstains on dental floss or toothpick.
- Bleeding during or after dental cleaning.

Talk to Your Dentist If:

- You notice pus near the gum line.
- Gums are swollen or bleed at times other than during brushing or flossing.
- Your gum recedes or pulls away from your tooth.
- Your teeth become loose or fall out.
- Bridgework or partials begin to fit differently, or your bite feels out of alignment.

HOMECARE™

If physician referral is not recommended at this time, try the following:

Medication

- Rinse with mouthwash after brushing and flossing. A mouthwash such as Listerine® or those containing cetylpridinium chloride or domiphen bromide have been proven effective.
- Always brush with a fluoride toothpaste.

Clean

- Brush and floss teeth two or three times daily, especially after you eat.
- If you can't brush or floss after a meal, rinse mouth with water or mouthwash, or chew sugarless gum to remove food particles and acids from teeth and gum surfaces.
- Along with regular brushing and flossing, try making a paste of baking soda and water to rub or gently brush on teeth and gums. Baking soda helps neutralize mouth acids.
- Have your teeth cleaned professionally every 6 months.

Nutrition

- Eat a well-balanced diet high in vitamins A and C (found in yellow fruits and vegetables, as well as green, leafy vegetables).
- Avoid sugary foods.
- Avoid sugary beverages, alcohol, and excessive amounts of fruit juices.

Prevention

- Don't smoke or use tobacco.
- Follow all of the above recommendations regularly to prevent gum disease.

Bronchitis

*I*t usually happens after the onset of the initial symptoms of a cold—your cough gets worse, you cough up yellow, green, or gray mucus, and you might have a slight fever. Bronchitis sets up shop in your lungs, clogging airways with mucus, and creating a rattling cough. Acute bronchitis will go away within a week or so. But when symptoms linger for weeks or months, the diagnosis is usually chronic bronchitis.

Smoking, allergies, exposure to chemical irritants in the air, or breathing too much dust can cause both chronic and acute bronchitis. In either case, don't ignore your symptoms because repeated or prolonged bouts of bronchitis can cause irreversible lung damage or pneumonia, or contribute to heart problems.

Symptoms/Signs

- **Acute bronchitis:** tightness in the chest; deep, heavy cough that brings up yellow or grayish mucus; slight fever; is associated with a severe cold; clears up within 5 to 7 days without treatment.
- **Chronic bronchitis:** persistent mucus-producing cough; no other condition to explain the cough; symptoms worse in the morning and in cold weather.

Get Emergency Care Right Away If:

You have a fever higher than 101 F, chest pain, shaking chills, shortness of breath, or night sweats with your bronchitis symptoms.

Talk to Your Doctor If:

- You have repeated bouts of acute bronchitis or your cough does not improve after a week.
- You cough up blood or mucus tinged with blood.

If physician referral is not recommended at this time, try the following:

Medication

- As long as your cough produces mucus, don't use cough suppressants; coughing removes secretions that harbor infection.
- Ask your doctor whether an over-the-counter or prescription bronchodilator (inhaler or tablet) would help relieve your symptoms.
- Take a cough expectorant if your cough does not bring up mucus.

Heat/Cold

- Breathe in warm, moist air (from a hot shower, a sink filled with boiling water, or a vaporizer) to loosen mucus and open airways.

Fluids

- Drink extra fluids to keep mucus thin and moving freely.
- Avoid alcohol and caffeine, which promote dehydration.

Note Well

- Quit smoking.
- Whenever possible, lie with your head lower than your chest to help clear your lungs of mucus. Ask your doctor what position would work best for you.
- Get adequate rest.

Prevention

- Avoid contact with people who have colds, flu, or respiratory infections.
- Avoid secondhand smoke, dust, and other air pollutants.
- Exercise regularly, but avoid exhaustion.

Canker Sores

Canker sores are painful ulcers that crop up on your gums, tongue, soft palate, or the inside of your cheek or lip. Most canker sores disappear within 5 to 10 days, but while they're active, you may have trouble eating, especially if you enjoy salty, spicy, or acidic foods. Sometimes the sores interfere with talking or sleeping.

Canker sores are not caused by viruses or bacteria so canker sores don't spread through person-to-person contact. Most doctors agree that mouth trauma, food allergies, hormone imbalances, or emotional stress may be factors that make some people more prone to have canker sores.

Symptoms/Signs

- **Early stage:** tingling or burning sensation on the tongue, soft palate, gums, or on the inside of the cheek or lip.
- **Middle stage:** small, round, reddish, swollen area(s) where tingling or burning occurs.
- **Eruptive stage:** painful rupture(s) on swollen area(s) covered by a white or yellow membrane with a red rim or halo.

Talk to Your Doctor If:

- Any mouth sore does not heal within 2 weeks.
- You have accompanying inflammation of the eyes or experience similar sores on your genitals.
- You have white spots in your mouth that are not canker sores.
- Sores interfere significantly with your ability to eat, speak, or sleep.
- High fever accompanies canker sores.

Medication

- Try sucking medicated lozenges or antacid tablets occasionally to decrease the acidity of your mouth.
- Use an over-the-counter medication containing carbamide peroxide (Gly-Oxide®, Amosan® or Cankaid®, for example) to speed healing.
- Gargle with an antiseptic mouthwash to relieve pain temporarily.
- For chronic problems, ask your doctor about using a prescription dental paste (such as triamcinolone) or antibiotic mouthwashes to help reduce inflammation and pain.

Nutrition

- Avoid chocolate, nuts, and foods that are spicy, salty, or acidic (tomatoes, citrus fruits, etc.).

Note Well

- Avoid scraping or biting mouth sores.
- Have your dentist repair rough or ragged tooth surfaces.

Prevention

- Avoid abrasive or irritating substances (tobacco, jalapeño peppers, very hot foods, hard pretzels, etc.).
- Use only a soft toothbrush.
- Practice stress-reduction techniques.

Chemicals in the Eye

For employees who work with solvents and other substances, exposing the eyes to chemicals is a serious risk. Home products such as cleaning products, paints, and fertilizers pose their own risks to both adults and children.

The best way to prevent exposure is to wear proper eye protection (shatterproof glasses or goggles) and to follow recommended procedures when handling caustic agents. It's important also to know the location of eye-wash stations in your workplace.

Symptoms/Signs

■ Pain, burning sensation, irritation, redness, excessive tearing of the eyes due to exposure to chemicals.

Get Emergency Care Right Away If:

You have been exposed to a strong chemical agent such as an acid (e.g., sulfuric acid) or a corroding agent (e.g., lye). *Flush the eye with water immediately and continue for at least 15 minutes. Go to the nearest treatment center.*

Call Your Doctor Right Away If:

■ You experience symptoms such as continued burning or irritation in the eye, blurred or poor vision, extreme redness or whiteness, watering or discharge.

■ HomeCare procedures fail to give relief and the eye continues to hurt after 30 minutes of treatment.

If physician referral is not recommended at this time, try the following:

Clean

• Flush the eye immediately with water. Hold the eye open as wide as possible and run water into the eye—under the faucet or from a clean container—for at least 15 minutes. If pain persists or vision is impaired, seek emergency care and do not bandage the eye.

Prevention

• Wear glasses or goggles.
• For chemicals, follow safety guidelines as specified by the manufacturer. Read labels.

Chest Pain

*C*hest pain is a symptom that should never be ignored, especially if you have a family history of heart disease or other risk factors such as high blood pressure, diabetes, high cholesterol, tobacco use, low physical activity, and excess body weight.

Chest pain also can be traced to heartburn, an ulcer, a hiatal hernia, lung infection, blood clots in the lung's blood vessels, acute bronchitis, gallbladder problems, a pulled muscle, or a broken rib.

Symptoms/Signs

The following are classic signs of a heart attack:

■ Uncomfortable pressure, fullness, squeezing, or pain in the middle of your chest that lasts more than a few minutes, or goes away and comes back.

■ Pain that spreads to the shoulders, neck, arms, or jaw.

■ Chest discomfort with lightheadedness, fainting, sweating, nausea, or shortness of breath.

Less common warning signs of heart attack, often noticed by women:

■ Chest, stomach, or abdominal pain.

■ Nausea or dizziness.

■ Shortness of breath or trouble breathing.

■ Unexplained anxiety, weakness, or fatigue.

■ Palpitations, cold sweat, or paleness.

Get Emergency Care Right Away If:

• You have one or more of the symptoms listed above.

• Your chest pain occurs after you have been bedridden due to surgery, illness, or injury.

Call Your Doctor Right Away If:

■ Your chest pain is due to a blow to the chest from a fall or other accident, and you have difficulty breathing or your ribs are sore to the touch.

HOMECARE™

If you have a muscle pull or strain, and your doctor has ruled out a heart attack or other serious condition, the following tips may be tried:

Note Well

• See page 137 for "Heartburn," as appropriate.

Activity

• Avoid activities that require bending, twisting, and lifting until pain is reduced.
• Try to breathe with diaphragm (e.g., belly breathing) only.

Medication

• For chest wall pain due to a pulled muscle: aspirin, ibuprofen, or acetaminophen may be tried. Rub-on salves such as Ben-Gay® also may help.

Heat/Cold

• A heating pad over the injured area may help.

Note Well

• Avoid wrapping the chest with elastic bandages; it may lead to pneumonia.
• Take deep breaths with your diaphragm and abdominal muscles to inflate your lungs fully, which will help prevent pneumonia. This is especially important if you're a smoker.

Colds and Flu

Colds and influenza (respiratory "flu") probably are the number one reason people see their doctors. Although severe symptoms are more likely with flu, there's little difference between the symptoms of a cold and flu. Because both are viral infections, they cannot be treated by antibiotics and usually need to run their course. See page 104, "Using Antibiotics Appropriately."

The best course of action, except for complications such as pneumonia or ear infection, is to treat the symptoms and reduce the discomfort. However, there may be certain situations where antiviral medications are indicated. Talk to your doctor.

Symptoms/Signs

Colds	Flu
■ Runny nose	■ Runny nose
■ Sneezing	■ Sneezing
■ Sore throat, coughing	■ Coughing
■ Headache	■ Headache
■ Low-grade fever	■ Fever
■ Red, itchy eyes	■ Fatigue
■ Congested ears	■ Muscle aches

Talk to Your Doctor If:

■ You have severe ear pain or trouble breathing or swallowing.

■ Cough is severe or lasts more than 10 days.

■ Mucus or sputum is thick, smelly, or green or rust-colored.

■ Fever stays at or above 102 F for 3 days.

■ You have a history of severe heart or lung disease.

If physician referral is not recommended at this time, try the following:

Fluids

• Drink plenty of fluids such as water, fruit juices, and caffeine-free drinks and teas.

Medication

• Aspirin, ibuprofen, or acetaminophen for fever higher than 101 F.
• Antihistamines or decongestants to help clear nasal congestion.

Note: Because of the risk of Reye's syndrome, aspirin should not be given to or used by children or teenagers who have or are suspected of having flu or chicken pox. Use acetaminophen.

Rest

• Reduce your activity.
• Bed rest may be needed depending on your symptoms.

Heat/Cold

• Stay warm.
• A vaporizer or humidifier can help keep mucous membranes moist.

Nutrition

• Hot broths such as chicken soup can help clear nasal congestion and soothe the throat.
• Try to eat balanced meals.

Prevention

• Influenza immunizations prior to flu season are recommended for those over age 6 months; those who wish immunity; and those under age 50 who suffer from chronic health conditions.
• Wash your hands often, especially if a family member has a cold or flu.

Cold Sores

Cold sores (also called fever blisters) are caused by the herpes simplex virus (HSV1), which, once you have it, stays with you for life. Experts estimate that from 50 to 80 percent of all people are infected with HSV1, but only about 10 percent of those who carry the virus ever experience a cold sore. It usually is spread through direct contact with the cold sores or saliva of an infected person.

If you are infected with HSV1, once you suffer through the first cold sore episode, future blister eruptions may be triggered by sunlight, hormones, stress, fever, or injury. However, with a little self-care and possibly prescription medications, the frequency and severity of cold sore outbreaks can be reduced significantly. Talk to your doctor.

Note: HSV1 is not the same virus that causes genital herpes (HSV2), although HSV1 can be spread to the genital area.

Symptoms/Signs

■ Tingling, itching, burning, sensitivity, swelling, or redness at blister site (before blister begins to form).

■ Painful, fluid-filled blisters appearing on the lips or around the mouth accompanied by a fever (usually only with first occurrence).

Talk to Your Doctor If:

■ You experience eye pain, sensitivity to light, or discharge from your eyes.

■ Any mouth lesion or blister does not heal after 2 weeks of home treatment.

■ Your cold sore attacks are especially frequent or severe.

If physician referral is not recommended at this time, try the following:

Medication

- Over-the-counter cold sore medications (usually topical lip balms) may reduce cracking, and alleviate pain.
- Orabase® ointment, Abreva® cream, or Acyclovir (prescription-only cream or pills) may speed healing; ask your doctor.

Heat/Cold

- Apply ice to affected area when you first notice tingling under the skin to help reduce inflammation and the severity of an outbreak.

Clean

- After a blister has broken, dab regularly with witch hazel or Domeboro® astringent (use a clean cotton ball or cotton swab each time).
- Wash your hands with soap before and after any contact with a blister.

Nutrition

- Eat more potatoes, dairy products, and brewer's yeast; the lysine in these foods has been shown to reduce the frequency of cold sores. Before taking any lysine supplements, however, check with your doctor. Pregnant or nursing women should avoid excess lysine, as it can interfere with fetal and infant growth.

Note Well

- Avoid sharing eating utensils with or kissing anyone with a cold sore.
- Manage stress in your life.
- If you have active blisters, avoid handling newborn or infant children.
- Wear a sunblock (SPF 15 or greater) on your lips when you go outdoors.
- Don't squeeze, pinch, or pick at any blister.

Conjunctivitis

Also known as "pinkeye," conjunctivitis occurs when the mucous membrane of the eyelid and white part of the eye becomes inflamed. If the conjunctivitis is caused by bacteria, your doctor can prescribe antibiotic eye drops or ointment to help clear up the condition. If a virus is the cause, antibiotics won't help, but eye drops to help manage symptoms of redness and congestion may be recommended. Allergic conjunctivitis causes severe itching around the eyes, which usually is relieved with antihistamines. However, most of the time, conjunctivitis will clear up on its own within a few days without the use of prescription medications or a trip to the doctor.

Symptoms/Signs
(in one or both eyes)

- Red, bloodshot appearance.
- Feeling of sand or dirt in the eye.
- Burning sensation.
- Excessive tearing.
- If viral, may have tender lymph glands in front of the ears.
- Crust around edges or in the corners of eyelids, especially upon waking.

Talk to Your Doctor If:

- You experience eye pain.
- Vision is impaired.
- Sensitivity to light is extreme.
- Your condition fails to improve after 3 days of HomeCare.

If physician referral is not recommended at this time, try the following:

Heat/Cold

- Apply warm compresses for 5 to 10 minutes, once or twice an hour. Use a clean compress for each treatment.

Note Well

- Children should stay home from school and away from other children until symptoms are gone.
- Adults need to stay home from work only if eye pain is severe or if there is excessive pus.

Clean

- For adults: To loosen and remove crust, wipe around the eyelids with a cloth moistened in a solution of 1 part baby shampoo to 10 parts warm water.
- During outbreaks, remove contact lenses and wear glasses until symptoms go away. Disinfect lenses or discard them. Ask your doctor.

Medication

- Apply prescription antibiotic eye drops or ointment as directed by your doctor.
- Use over-the-counter artificial tears eye drops or ointment to relieve sandy feeling and itching.

Prevention

- Keep your hands clean and away from your eyes.
- In order to avoid spreading the infection, do not reuse any cloths used to clean the eye.
- If you're prone to conjunctivitis, always wear goggles when you swim.
- Sterilize contact lens case regularly.

Contact Lens Irritation

Contact lenses can be a comfortable and attractive alternative to prescription eyeglasses. But wearing contact lenses comes with the extra responsibility of taking special care to clean, store, and wear your lenses properly. Otherwise, you place your eyes at risk for corneal abrasion, keratitis (inflammation of the cornea), corneal ulcers, and eye infections that can make your life miserable, or even threaten your vision permanently.

Depending on the visual correction you need, you can choose from a variety of lenses designed to suit your work and your lifestyle. Your eye doctor can help you choose the type that is best for you, but it's up to you to make a commitment to wear them in good health—and to take care of minor irritations before they become major problems.

Symptoms/Signs

- Red, irritated, burning, or dry eyes.
- Feeling that a foreign object is in your eye (excessive tearing and blinking).
- Blurred vision or sudden changes in vision.
- Secretions from either eye.

Get Emergency Care Right Away If:
You experience an eye injury while you are wearing contacts.

Talk to Your Doctor If:

- You develop irritation, redness, or burning that is not relieved quickly with HomeCare treatment.
- You develop any unusual or severe symptoms, such as pain, excessive eye secretions, or sudden changes in vision.

HOMECARE™

If physician referral is not recommended at this time, try the following:

Medication

- If your eyes are mildly dry or red, try an over-the-counter lubricating eye drop as recommended by your doctor.
- If your eyes are irritated due to abrasion (scratch) or infection, your doctor may prescribe antibiotic drops.

Clean

- If eyes become irritated, try cleaning your lenses. If cleaning does not solve the problem, proceed with enzymatic disinfection.
- Always wash your hands before handling your contacts. However, be sure to avoid soaps containing moisturizers, which can leave a residue on fingers that can be transferred to your lenses.
- Disinfect contact lenses each time you leave them out for any length of time. Never skip cleaning steps.
- Use fresh cleaning and disinfecting solutions; never store contacts in water or use saliva to wet your lenses. Throw out any solutions that have passed their expiration date.

Prevention

- Never wear dirty or damaged contact lenses.
- Sterilize your contact lens case once a week by boiling it in water for 10 or 15 minutes, as directed.
- Do not wear lenses beyond the time period for which they are designed: Replace them with fresh lenses as recommended by the manufacturer.
- Don't wear your contacts while you are sleeping, unless they are specifically approved to be used that way.
- Replace eye makeup every 6 months.

Dental Problems

Dental problems such as tooth decay and gum disease are caused by a buildup of plaque and bacteria around the teeth and gums. The main causes are infrequent brushing, failure to floss regularly, not using toothpaste that contains fluoride, and not seeing your dentist every 6 to 12 months for regular cleaning and inspection.

■ **Bacterial buildup** creates a film on your teeth called plaque. Plaque attracts sugars that in turn produce acids that can slowly decay the enamel tooth covering. Plaque also produces acid that inflames the gums or degrades the supporting bone.

■ **Toothache** usually is caused by a cavity in the tooth enamel that has irritated the nerve. An abscess is a serious infection that may cause fever, soreness, swelling in the jaw, and redness around the infected tooth.

■ **Bleeding gums** are an indication of periodontal disease, which affects the stability of the teeth and jaw. Though poor oral hygiene is the main cause, pregnancy, medications, and other health problems such as diabetes also may increase the risk. See page 123.

Call Your Dentist Right Away If:
Your tooth has been broken, damaged or knocked out.

Talk to Your Dentist If:

■ You have signs of an abscess: soreness, swelling in jaw, reddened gums, and fever.

■ You have a toothache or you can see or feel a cavity.

■ Your gums are bleeding or inflamed, or a tooth is loose.

HOMECARE™

If physician referral is not recommended at this time, try the following:

Medication

• Use ibuprofen, acetaminophen or aspirin to reduce toothache pain. Use as directed.

Fluids

• Avoid cold, or hot, beverages when you have a cavity.

Nutrition

• Avoid sugary foods and hard candies.
• Moderate your consumption of foods and beverages that contain sugar.
• Eat green and yellow fruits and vegetables.

Note Well

• Your dentist may recommend fluoride treatment or sealants.

Prevention

• Brush between meals with fluoride toothpaste.
• Floss every day.
• Limit your consumption of sugary foods.
• Visit your dentist every 6 to 12 months for preventive checkups.

Earache

Peaple who have allergies or are suffering from a cold often have earaches. When the eustachian tube, which connects the middle ear to the nasal passages, swells shut, fluid builds up behind the eardrum and causes pressure and pain. The fluid then can become infected. Fever and ear pain may indicate an ear infection. Usually, your doctor will prescribe antibiotics if a bacterial infection is discovered.

Children are especially prone to earaches because their eustachian tubes are smaller and swell shut more easily from upper respiratory problems. Also, bottle-feeding in bed increases the chances of ear infection.

Some earaches occur in the outer ear, as in the case of swimmer's ear (see page 143), excessive ear wax (see page 134), or if a foreign object is stuck in the ear canal. Sometimes, conditions that seem unrelated to the ear can cause earaches, as with arthritis of the jaw or some sore throats.

Symptoms/Signs

- Local pain and pressure in the ear with accompanying fever.
- In children, fever and pain and complaints of "fullness in the head" and partial hearing loss in the affected ear.
- In infants, irritability, crying, and rubbing and pulling the ears.
- Pain in the outer ear, especially when the earlobe is pulled.

Talk to Your Doctor If:

- Your infant shows signs of an ear infection: rubbing or pulling the ears, fever, crying, irritability, and trouble sleeping.
- You or an older child experience severe ear pain that is unrelieved by HomeCare.

If physician referral is not recommended at this time, try the following:

Heat/Cold

- To help loosen nasal mucus, take a hot shower or use a vaporizer.
- To relieve pain, place a cold washcloth over the ear for 20 minutes.

Note: Do not use any ear drops unless you are certain that your eardrum is not perforated. Ask your doctor.

Medication

- Adults: aspirin, ibuprofen, or acetaminophen to reduce pain and fever above 101 F.
- Antihistamines or decongestants may help relieve stuffiness and drain nasal secretions.

Note: Because of the risk of Reye's syndrome, aspirin should not be given to or used by children or teenagers who have or are suspected of having flu or chicken pox. Use acetaminophen.

Fluids

- Drink plenty of water or juices.

Activity

- Reduce your activity.

Prevention

- Don't give a baby a bottle while he or she is lying down.
- If you're prone to ear infections, use ear plugs when you swim, bathe, shower, or shampoo.
- Avoid cigarette smoking around children; it increases the risk of ear infection.

Ear Wax

The wax in your ears is a remarkable cleaning and protection system. Thick skin all along the external ear canal—containing oil glands and modified sweat glands—grows outward, excreting ear wax. Dust, dirt, dead skin, and anything else that gets into your ear is trapped in the wax and transported to the outer ear, where it eventually falls out on its own.

Unfortunately, thinking that ear wax is dirty and socially unacceptable, many people go to great lengths to remove the wax from sight. Using everything from cotton swabs to paper clips, they end up pushing dirt back into the ear canal, compacting the wax against the eardrum and risking injury to the skin that the wax is meant to protect. If you must remove wax from your outer ear canal, use only a damp washcloth wrapped around your index finger and use a gentle, circular motion to clear out only the wax that has made its way to the outermost regions of your ear. If you think your ear's natural cleaning system isn't working properly, see your doctor.

Symptoms/Signs

■ Wax that varies in color over time and appears at the mouth of the ear canal, or hard, brownish or amber wax that partially or fully blocks the ear canal.

Talk to Your Doctor If:

■ There is persistent itching or pain in your ear canal.

■ Any fluids or pus drain from your ear.

■ A painful, swollen, red bump appears in your ear canal.

■ You experience any hearing loss or ringing in your ears.

■ You know or suspect that an insect or foreign body is lodged in your ear.

If physician referral is not recommended at this time, try the following:

Do not use any ear drops unless you are certain that your eardrum is not perforated. Ask your doctor.

Medication

• If an insect becomes trapped in your ear canal, put a few drops of mineral oil in your ear canal to immobilize the creature until your doctor can remove it.

Clean

• Use only your middle finger wrapped in a damp washcloth to clean your outer ear canal. Never use cotton swabs or any other device to remove ear wax.

Note Well

• Never try to remove a foreign body lodged in your ear. Doing so may push the object farther into the ear canal and risk injury to the eardrum. Call your doctor.

Prevention

• Never insert any object other than your washcloth-wrapped finger into your ear canal.

Eye Injury

*I*njuries to the eyes can happen without warning and should be taken very seriously. Of course, prevention is the best medicine, so when you know your eyes are at risk for injury—at work, playing sports, or at home—use shatterproof safety glasses or goggles as your first line of defense.

- **For a blow to the eye,** place a cold, clean washcloth gently over the eye for 15 minutes. Always get emergency care in the case of a black eye because the inside of the eye could have been damaged as well.

- **If you get a speck or small foreign object in your eye,** carefully lift the upper eyelid up and then down over the lower lid. Blink a few times to stimulate tears and help wash the object away. See your doctor if your symptoms persist.

- **A cut or puncture injury** to the eye or lids is always an emergency. Do not wash out the eye or try to remove an object sticking out of the eye. Lightly cover the eye, apply no pressure, and get emergency care right away. As well, a chemical splash in the eye needs immediate care. See page 126.

Symptoms/Signs

- An object that penetrates the eye such as a sharp object.
- A "floating" object such as dirt, an insect, or sawdust that irritates the eye.
- Pain, irritation, and redness.

Get Emergency Care Right Away If:

- You see an object that has penetrated the eye.
- The eye appears bloody or torn.
- Flushing the eye does not relieve chemical splash injury.

Talk to Your Doctor If:

- HomeCare procedures have failed to remove the object.
- You have vision problems, pain, or discomfort 24 hours after removing a foreign body from the eye.

HOMECARE™

If physician referral is not recommended at this time, try the following:

Note Well

- Never rub the eye, which may cause the cornea to be scratched, increase the risk of infection, or push an object farther into the eye.
- Keep eye wash in your medicine cabinet.

Clean

- Wash the eye gently with water or a commercial eye wash solution.
- Lift the eyelid away from the eye to promote tearing.

Cover

- Don't bandage or patch your eye unless instructed to do so by your doctor.

Prevention

- Wear shatterproof safety glasses or goggles, especially in jobs or tasks that expose you to dirt, wood splinters/sawdust, glass, metal particles, or sparks.
- Wear sports goggles for high-risk activities such as racquet sports.

Hearing Loss

Nearly 30 million Americans have hearing loss that interferes with their ability to understand normal speech. The main cause of such hearing loss is, simply, exposure to too much loud noise. As well, hearing loss may be caused by injury, heredity, drugs, toxins, tumors, and inflammation.

Activities such as mowing the yard every week or going to an occasional rock concert can permanently damage your hearing. Shortly after being exposed to loud noises, you may notice a muffled sensation that goes away quickly. But, years down the road you may start to notice that it's harder and harder to understand what people are saying at parties or in a crowded restaurant. The real tragedy is that such hearing problems are almost always preventable.

Symptoms/Signs

- Ringing, humming, buzzing, roaring, or squealing noises that either come and go or are continuous, in one or both ears.
- Difficulty hearing high-pitched voices or understanding certain spoken words, especially those that contain S, F, SH, CH, H, or soft C sounds, or understanding words in a conversation when there's a lot of background noise.

Talk to Your Doctor If:

- You experience any sudden hearing loss.
- You notice signs of hearing loss in an infant or young child.
- You hear ringing or other sounds that either come and go or are continuous, in one or both ears.
- Ear noises are accompanied by ear pain, dizziness, vertigo, nausea, or vomiting.

HOMECARE™

If physician referral is not recommended at this time, try the following:

Clean

- Avoid cleaning your outer ear canal with anything other than your middle finger wrapped in a damp washcloth. Never stick any object—even a cotton swab—into your ear.
- If you need to have impacted ear wax removed from your ear canal, call your doctor.

Nutrition

- Reducing salt intake and avoiding caffeine and alcohol may reduce ringing in your ears.

Prevention

- Avoid loud noises, or wear adequate ear protection when you're exposed to them.
- For ear protection, never rely on cotton stuffed into the ear canal. Use high-quality ear plugs, regulation ear muffs, or a combination of both for maximum protection.
- Control your cholesterol and blood pressure levels.
- Exercise regularly to improve blood flow and normalize blood pressure, which can affect your hearing.

Heartburn

As part of the digestive process, the stomach produces hydrochloric acid. When that acid backs up into the esophagus (gastric reflux), the burning, painful sensation you feel is called heartburn. Factors that contribute to heartburn include being overweight, alcohol use, pregnancy, smoking, and eating certain offending foods (e.g., chocolate, peppermint, drinks containing caffeine, and spicy, acidic, and fatty foods).

Usually, heartburn doesn't require medical attention unless it occurs more than twice a week. Prolonged discomfort may suggest a medical condition such as gastroesophageal reflux disease (GERD), hernia, or ulcer, which should be evaluated by your doctor.

Symptoms/Signs

■ Burning sensation and discomfort just below the breastbone.

Get Emergency Care Right Away If:

You think you may be having a heart attack. See "Chest Pain" on page 127. *People having a heart attack may think they have heartburn.*

Talk to Your Doctor If:

■ Heartburn occurs more than twice a week or lasts more than 3 days with HomeCare.
■ You vomit black or bloody material.
■ Your stools are black and tar-like.

If physician referral is not recommended at this time, try the following:

Nutrition

- Avoid vinegar, chocolate, oranges, lemons, grapefruits, pickles, and tomatoes.
- Avoid fatty foods and peppermint.
- Avoid alcohol and caffeine.

Activity

- Stay mildly active for 2 hours after eating. An after-meal walk may aid digestion.

Rest

- Wait 1 to 2 hours after eating before lying down.
- If you need to rest, keep your shoulders 1 to 2 feet above hips.

Medication

- For chronic heartburn, try over-the-counter medications (e.g., Pepcid®, Tagamet®, and Zantac®) to reduce the production of stomach acid.
- Antacids in liquid or tablet form can relieve gastric discomfort.
- Avoid using aspirin, ibuprofen, or naproxen, which can further irritate the stomach.

Prevention

- Eat smaller, more frequent meals.
- Achieve and maintain your ideal weight.
- Try to manage stress.
- Stop smoking.
- Avoid tight-fitting clothing and belts that squeeze the abdomen or stomach.

Hoarseness

When your vocal cords become overstressed or obstructed in some way, the sound you create may be altered or even silenced altogether. Shouting at a sporting event or giving a long lecture can dry out mucous membranes and cause vocal cords to become irritated. Other problems—infection associated with a cold or the flu, smoking, digestive problems (see "Heartburn", page 137), polyps, allergies, chemical fumes, and tumors, to name a few—also can affect the vocal cords or throat muscles so that the sounds they produce are distorted.

In any case, most hoarseness is temporary and easily remedied with a few days of resting your voice and self-care. Be sure to see your doctor if any voice change is prolonged or recurring, or if you have other symptoms that could point to something more serious than simple "voice overload."

Symptoms/Signs

- A breathy, raspy, or whisper-like voice.
- Changes in voice volume (loudness) or pitch (how high or low the voice is).
- Throat may feel tight, dry, scratchy, or obstructed.

Talk to Your Doctor If:

- Hoarseness lasts longer than 2 weeks or has no obvious cause.
- You have throat pain not associated with a cold or the flu.
- You cough up blood.
- You have difficulty swallowing.
- You notice a lump in your neck.
- You lose your voice completely or have a pronounced change in your voice that lasts longer than a few days.

HOMECARE™

If physician referral is not recommended at this time, try the following:

Medication
- Use medicated throat lozenges or an over-the-counter throat spray.

Fluids
- Gargle with warm salt water or drink hot liquids.
- Drink plenty of water.

Nutrition
- Avoid spicy foods, caffeine, and alcohol.

Note Well
- Use a humidifier in your home, especially in your bedroom.
- Avoid speaking whenever possible until hoarseness disappears. Some cases require complete voice rest.

Prevention
- Avoid shouting, speaking in smoke-filled rooms, or talking a lot when you have a cold or the flu.
- Don't smoke. Avoid secondhand smoke.
- Limit alcohol consumption.

Migraine Headache

An estimated 18 million people suffer from migraine headaches, and women are three times more likely to have migraines than men. Migraine is a brain disorder caused by an interaction between the nerves in the brain and the blood vessels in the head.

Migraine headaches may be triggered by a variety of factors such as stress, certain foods, alcohol, hormone fluctuations, irregular or excessive sleeping patterns, excessive use of painkillers, tobacco, prescription medications, and withdrawal from caffeine and other drugs.

Your doctor may prescribe medications to prevent migraines; decrease the frequency of attacks; help stop an attack once it begins; or treat the symptoms of the migraine, such as pain or nausea.

Symptoms/Signs

- **Classic migraines:** severe throbbing pain, usually on one side of the head or behind one eye; nausea, vomiting, dizziness, sensitivity to light and sound, numbness in an arm or leg. At the onset of a headache, some people see an aura: stars, flashes of light, or blind spots.
- **Common or simple migraines:** pain throughout the head that is not accompanied by an aura.
- **Cluster headaches:** severe pain around or behind one eye that recurs off and on over days, weeks, or months. Other symptoms include nasal congestion, watery eyes, and pain, often developing during sleep.

Get Emergency Care Right Away If:
Your headache is associated with slurred speech, dizziness, or weakness in your arms and legs.

Talk to Your Doctor If:

- You suffer from migraine or cluster headaches.
- A headache continues after you've tried HomeCare.

If physician referral is not recommended at this time, try the following:

Medication

- An over-the-counter analgesic medication (e.g., Excedrin Migraine®) may provide relief for mild to moderate attacks.
- Talk to your doctor about discontinuing medications affecting female hormones (e.g., oral contraceptives).

Rest

- Get adequate sleep and rest, but avoid oversleeping.
- When headache occurs, go to a quiet, darkened room; lie down, and relax your body. See page 33.

Nutrition

- Avoid chocolate, aged cheese, red wine, and food additives such as nitrates and monosodium glutamate, which may increase symptoms.
- Track foods or situations that may trigger attacks in a migraine diary.

Fluids

- Drink plenty of water.
- Avoid drinks containing alcohol or caffeine.

Note Well

- Try to stay physically active.
- Learn relaxation techniques that may help reduce the number of headache episodes.

Prevention

- Get plenty of sleep and relaxation.
- Eat wisely.
- Be sensitive to and avoid your headache triggers such as alcohol, special foods, additives, or perfumes that cause symptoms.
- Learn to manage stress. See page 28.

Nosebleeds

Nosebleeds can be pretty scary. And while the amount of blood you may lose from one nosebleed can be quite alarming, it is not ordinarily dangerous. Because the septum (the cartilage wall that divides your two nostrils) contains many fragile blood vessels that are close to the surface, any physical blow to the nose can cause blood to flow. Some medical conditions such as hardening of the arteries, high blood pressure, sinus infection, or the common cold can cause minor nosebleeds, all of which usually can be stopped within 10 minutes or so. Long-term use of antihistamines also can cause minor bleeding because the nasal passages get too dried out.

If your nose bleeds only in the winter, make sure your home is well humidified and not too warm. Also, keeping nasal linings moist with petroleum jelly or saline nasal spray will help keep your nose from bleeding in cold, dry weather. Otherwise, take care not to blow your nose too hard.

Symptoms/Signs

■ Bleeding from one or both nostrils.

Talk to Your Doctor If:

■ You cannot stop the flow of blood from your nose after 20 minutes of HomeCare.

■ You have nosebleeds often but don't know why.

■ Your nosebleed is a result of being hit in the nose and is accompanied by a deformity in the shape or outline of your nose.

If physician referral is not recommended at this time, try the following:

Note Well

• To stop a nosebleed, remain in a sitting or standing position and do not tilt your head back. Blow your nose once gently to remove any blood clots that may be keeping tiny blood vessels open. Pack the bleeding nostril with gauze or cotton coated with petroleum jelly, then pinch your nose closed. Continue pinching for at least 10 minutes. If your nose is still bleeding after 10 minutes, apply pressure for another 10 minutes. Call your doctor if the bleeding doesn't stop within 20 minutes.

• Avoid blowing your nose at all for several hours after a nosebleed.

Heat/Cold

• Although many people apply ice packs to a bleeding nose, ice usually does nothing to slow blood flow.

Rest

• Avoid lying down when you have a nosebleed: Sitting or standing will help slow the flow of blood.

Prevention

• Discourage children from picking their noses.

• In dry weather, use a humidifier to add moisture to the air.

• If you are prone to nosebleeds, avoid taking aspirin because it thins the blood and makes bleeding harder to stop.

• Avoid blowing your nose too hard.

• Control your blood pressure. People with hypertension are more likely to have nosebleeds.

• Don't smoke, because smoking dries out nasal cavities.

• Avoid the chronic use of antihistamines.

Ringing in the Ears

For seven million people nationwide, loud and constant "ringing" in the ears (tinnitus) is a constant, bothersome companion that interferes with normal living.

Nearly all tinnitus sufferers have some degree of either temporary or permanent hearing loss. Often, if hearing can be restored or improved, tinnitus will either go away or decrease in intensity.

If you have sudden, occasional, or temporary tinnitus, check with your doctor to see if the cause (exposure to loud noises, impacted ear wax, allergies, infection or medications, for example) can be eliminated. If your tinnitus is constant or permanent, your doctor may be able to pinpoint the cause and recommend treatments that can at least help make the ear noises more tolerable.

Symptoms/Signs

■ Ringing, humming, buzzing, roaring, or squealing noises that either come and go or are continuous, in one or both ears.

■ Hearing impairment or loss.

Talk to Your Doctor If:

■ You have symptoms of tinnitus.

■ You experience any sudden hearing loss.

■ Ear noises are accompanied by ear pain or pressure, vertigo (loss of balance), or nausea and vomiting.

■ You suspect a particular medication is causing your tinnitus.

HOMECARE™

If physician referral is not recommended at this time, try the following:

Medication

• Avoid aspirin if possible. Taking too much or taking related compounds can cause tinnitus. Use acetaminophen instead.

Clean

• Avoid cleaning your outer ear canal with anything other than your middle finger wrapped in a damp washcloth. Never stick an object—even a cotton swab—into your ear.
• If you need to have impacted ear wax removed from your ear canal, talk to your doctor.

Nutrition

• Reduce salt intake.
• Limit alcohol and caffeine.

Note Well

• Surround yourself with noises that mask tinnitus sounds (e.g., a ticking clock, low-volume music or radio static, "white noise" machine, and ceiling fan).
• Talk with your doctor about using a special tinnitus masker and hearing aid. If you have hearing loss, this combination may be helpful.
• Practice relaxation techniques.

Prevention

• Avoid loud noises, or wear adequate ear protection when you're exposed to them. The noise from a lawn mower or personal stereo can be loud enough to damage hearing permanently.
• For ear protection, use high-quality ear plugs, regulation ear muffs, or a combination of both for maximum protection.
• Control your cholesterol and blood pressure.

Sinusitis

Usually, sinusitis develops when a cold, allergy, or other respiratory irritation causes nasal membranes to become so swollen that mucus no longer can flow freely out of the sinuses. Pressure increases, mucus builds up, and blocked sinus cavities become a breeding ground for bacteria. Once an infection sets in, antibiotics usually are the only way to rid sinuses of infection completely. Sometimes, however, chronic or severe sinusitis requires surgery to drain sinus cavities, or to repair bone or tissue abnormalities that keep infections coming back.

Symptoms/Signs

- Prolonged pressure or pain around the nose, forehead or cheeks, between and behind the eyes, or near the upper teeth.
- Yellow or green nasal mucus that may develop a bad odor or taste.
- Puffy eyelids.
- Coughing or difficulty breathing.
- Fever.

Talk to Your Doctor If:

- You develop thick, yellow, or greenish nasal discharge or if cold symptoms do not improve after more than 1 week.
- You have pain over the eyebrow, or below the eye, or in the upper teeth—usually on one side of your face.
- You have a severe headache that is not relieved by aspirin or acetaminophen.
- Swelling of the face increases.
- A fever over 101 F is accompanied by other symptoms.
- Vision changes or becomes blurred.
- There is no improvement after 3 days of HomeCare.

If physician referral is not recommended at this time, try the following:

Medication

- Use over-the-counter nasal decongestant sprays for no more than 3 days.
- Try an oral decongestant with pseudoephedrine to help clear nasal passages.
- Take acetaminophen or ibuprofen as needed for pain. Aspirin may promote more congestion in aspirin-sensitive individuals.
- Avoid antihistamines unless you have allergies that contribute to sinus inflammation.
- Try saline nasal sprays to help remove mucus.

Heat/Cold

- Apply warm compresses over your eyes and cheeks periodically to relieve pain.
- Inhale steam in a hot shower twice a day, or inhale steam from a sink of steaming water(drape a towel over your head to trap the steam).

Note Well

- Avoid air travel, swimming, diving, and high-altitude sports when you have symptoms.

Fluids

- Drink plenty of liquids, especially hot ones.
- Avoid drinks containing alcohol or caffeine.

Prevention

- Avoid or control airborne irritants and allergens such as dust mites.
- Blow your nose gently to avoid forcing mucus into sinuses or inner ears.
- Keep your nose lubricated with saline sprays or petroleum jelly.
- Use an air filter in your bedroom.

Swimmer's Ear

You don't have to go swimming to end up with "swimmer's ear"—an itchy infection of the outer ear canal. Water splashed into the ear canal during a shower or a shampoo can get trapped in the dark, warm environment near the eardrum, creating a perfect breeding ground for bacteria. As the bacteria take hold, the skin inside the ear begins to itch. Scratching the ear canal with your finger or a cotton swab will only result in removing the protective layer of bacteria-fighting ear wax. Without this protective coating, the bacteria continue to multiply, creating a full-blown infection that may have to be treated with antibiotics. The best way to prevent an outer ear infection is to keep the ear canal dry.

Symptoms/Signs

- Persistent itching or tickling in the ear canal (early stages).
- Pain in the ear canal, or pain when you touch or wiggle the ear lobe.
- Watery fluid draining from the ear.
- Feeling of fullness inside the ear.
- Crusting in the ear canal.
- Hearing impairment.

Talk to Your Doctor If:

- You experience persistent pain inside the ear canal.
- You have fluid draining from the ear.
- You have crusting in the ear canal.
- You notice any hearing loss or impairment.
- You have pain when you put drops in your ear.
- You have swelling of the external ear.

If physician referral is not recommended at this time, try the following:

Do not use any ear drops unless you are certain your eardrum is not perforated. Ask your doctor.

Medication

- Use over-the-counter ear drops that combat bacterial growth if your only symptom is ear itchiness.
- Take acetaminophen for ear pain only until you can get an appointment to see your doctor.

Heat/Cold

- Apply heat (use a heating pad set on low or a covered hot water bottle) to reduce pain until you can get an appointment to see your doctor.

Clean

- Clean your outer ear area daily, using your middle finger wrapped in a soft cloth.
- Never use any instrument to remove wax from the ear canal: Ear wax protects the ear from infection.

Note Well

- Don't scratch an itchy ear. Scratching can remove protective wax, irritate skin, and worsen an infection.

Prevention

- If you are prone to ear infection, use ear plugs whenever you swim or shower.
- If you are prone to ear infections, swim only in clean pools. Avoid swimming in lakes and ponds.
- Following a shower or a swim, use a dropper to put a mixture of 50 percent rubbing alcohol and 50 percent white vinegar into the ear canal while tilting your head so that your ear is facing the ceiling. Wiggle the outer ear gently to work the solution into the ear canal, then turn your ear toward the floor, allowing the solution to run out. This will help keep ears dry and kill germs.

Tension Headaches

Most headaches are caused by tense muscles in the scalp, jaw, neck, shoulders, and back. Tension headaches may stem from a reaction to personal or work problems, physical stress from working in one position for an extended period (such as word processing), and being exposed to excessive noise. Headaches also are a common symptom of viral infections such as a cold or flu, or bacterial infections such as sinusitis. In addition, they can be triggered by outside agents such as perfumes, mold, and noise.

Except for headaches caused by infections, the best way to manage headaches is to reduce the stress in your life and avoid your headache triggers. However, tension-type headaches also can be caused by depression (see "Depression," page 264). Periodic tension headaches rarely are an indication of other health problems, such as a brain tumor or high blood pressure. Also see "Migraine Headache," page 139.

Symptoms/Signs

■ Muscle tension in the scalp, face, neck, and shoulders.
■ Dull, steady pain that does not throb.

Get Emergency Care Right Away If:
- You have a headache and fever and stiffness in your neck (symptoms of meningitis).
- You have a headache and slurred speech, dizziness, or weakness in your arms and legs.

Talk to Your Doctor If:

■ Your headache is accompanied by vision problems.
■ Your headaches become much worse and more frequent.

If physician referral is not recommended at this time, try the following:

Medication
- Take aspirin, ibuprofen, or acetaminophen (at the first sign of pain) to relieve headache pain. Use as directed.
- To avoid *rebound headaches,* don't use pain relievers more than 3 consecutive days in a week.
- To reduce stomach upset, take pain medication with food and a full glass of water. You may try an antacid also.

Rest
- Learn a deep muscle relaxation technique. See page 33.
- Get adequate sleep.

Fluids
- Drink alcohol in moderation or not at all.
- Limit caffeine.

Heat/Cold
- Apply a heating pad or warm washcloth to the back of the neck.
- A long, hot shower or bath, followed by massaging the back of your neck, temples, and forehead may help.

Activity
- Exercise regularly. Regular physical activity has been shown to reduce stress and muscle tension.

Prevention
- Massage your neck muscles.
- Check your posture at work.
- Identify and learn to avoid your headache triggers.
- Learn to manage stress. See page 28.

Toothache

If you bite down and it hurts, chances are you have a decayed or abscessed tooth. Both conditions arise as a result of bacteria that has invaded the pulp (soft inner tissue) of the tooth, either through an injury to the tooth or from poor dental hygiene. Usually, warning signs (e.g., an increasing sensitivity to temperature or certain types of food; bad breath; red, swollen gums) precede an actual toothache.

Sometimes, tooth pain is a symptom of non-dental disorders such as sinusitis or neuralgia. Sinusitis usually is short-lived and responds quite well to home treatment (see page 142), if a bacterial infection is not present. Neuralgia (nerve pain), on the other hand, is difficult to treat with self-care measures and often requires prescription medication. In some cases, surgery is necessary to relieve the pressure of blood vessels that may be pressing on a nerve.

Symptoms/Signs

- Tooth sensitivity to heat, cold, and certain foods.
- A dull to throbbing pain at the tooth site that is made worse by chewing, shaving, or brushing teeth.
- Tooth pain that occurs only when you bite down on dense, tough, or crunchy foods.

Talk to Your Dentist If:

- You experience tooth pain that is not relieved after 1 week of self-care measures.
- Tooth pain is accompanied by fever; swelling in the face or neck; bloody nasal discharge; or pain, redness or swelling of an eye.

Medication

- Over-the-counter pain relievers (e.g., acetaminophen, ibuprofen, aspirin) may reduce or eliminate tooth pain temporarily until you're examined by your dentist. For severe pain or infection, your dentist may prescribe stronger medications.

Note Well

- Keep the affected tooth clean but avoid brushing the gums too briskly. Rinse your mouth often with warm salt water.
- Avoid chewing on the affected tooth.
- If your tooth falls out, rinse and wrap it in clean paper and take it to your dentist right away.

Prevention

- Practice proper oral hygiene; brush after meals with a fluoride toothpaste, floss daily, and see your dentist twice a year for a checkup.
- Limit starchy or sugary foods.
- Don't smoke or use tobacco products.
- Have broken or chipped teeth fixed right away; have loose or missing fillings and crowns fixed promptly.
- Make sure that partial dentures fit properly.

Vision Problems

Many vision problems are either temporary or completely treatable. However some conditions are sight-threatening and require medical care.

Some serious eye disorders do not produce any noticeable symptoms and can be detected only during an eye examination. It's important to have your eyes examined regularly by an eye care professional, particularly if you have diabetes or have a family history of glaucoma, age-related macular degeneration, or other chronic eye diseases.

Symptoms/Signs

- **Cataracts:** hazy or blurred vision; frequent changes in eyeglass prescriptions; glare or sensitivity to light.
- **Age-related macular degeneration:** difficulty reading and doing close work (not improved with glasses); blurry areas in visual field; straight lines appear wavy.
- **Glaucoma** (chronic open angle): progressive narrowing of the visual field (advanced stage, irreversible).
- **Nearsightedness or farsightedness:** problems seeing close up or far away.

Get Emergency Care Right Away If:

- Narrow angle glaucoma (acute angle closure): severe eye pain, nausea, redness in the eye, blurred vision.
- Hemorrhage or retinal detachment: seeing brown or red spots, a shower of star-like spots or bright flashes of light; sensation of a curtain covering vision; sudden loss of vision.

Talk to Your Doctor If:

- You injure your eye. See page 135.
- You have persistent eye pain.
- You notice a sudden change in your vision.
- You have red, crusted, or swollen eyelids.

If physician referral is not recommended at this time, try the following:

Medication

- For glaucoma, your doctor will prescribe eye drops that you will have to use every day to reduce pressure in the eye.

Cover

- Don't cover your eye unless your doctor tells you to do so.

Activity

- When sudden or permanent vision loss occurs, proceed cautiously with physical activity. Impaired vision may cause you to lose your balance or misjudge distances.
- You are more prone to retinal detachment if you are extremely nearsighted. Ask your doctor if your should avoid certain activities or sports where you might fall or receive a blow to the head.

Note Well

- Do not assume your eyes are healthy because you don't notice any problems. See your eye care professional regularly—*at least once a year if you have diabetes.*
- If you wear contact lenses, clean them regularly and according to your doctor's instructions.
- Wear sunglasses in sunlight or high-glare situations.
- Experiencing difficulty reading fine print after about age 40 is normal and usually is managed by using reading glasses. See your eye care professional.

Constipation

A general misconception about regularity is that daily bowel movements are an indication of well-being. The fact of the matter is that being "regular" is different for each person. Some people have bowel movements once a day, others just three times a week.

Constipation is defined as difficulty in passing stools, rather than not being able to "go" to the bathroom. It can be caused by hormone changes, medications, certain chronic conditions, or pregnancy.

You can relieve most constipation problems by increasing your fluid intake, eating more fiber, and getting regular exercise. And, by changing your dietary habits, you also will reduce your risk of colon cancer, diverticulosis, and hemorrhoids.

Symptoms/Signs

- Difficulty in having a bowel movement or having fewer than 3 per week.
- Feeling bloated.
- Abdominal discomfort.

Call Your Doctor Right Away If:

- Constipation occurs with weight loss, abdominal pain or swelling, or the passage of stools that are pencil-thin or have dark blood, or are black and tar-like.

Talk to Your Doctor If:

- Your constipation continues after you have tried HomeCare procedures for more than 1 week.

If physician referral is not recommended at this time, try the following:

Fluids

- Increase your intake of fluids such as water and fruit juices.

Nutrition

- Increase your intake of fruits, whole-grain cereals and breads, and vegetables.
- Limit caffeine and alcohol, which tend to cause dehydration.

Activity

- Increase your physical activity. Brisk walking, aerobic dance, and jogging have been shown to stimulate bowel movements.

Medication

- Avoid the frequent use of laxatives. If a laxative is used, try a bulk product that contains fiber. Don't use a laxative that contains phenolphthalein. See page 101, "Popular Over-the-Counter Medications."

Prevention

- Consume adequate fiber, drink plenty of water, and be physically active.
- If constipation continues to be a problem despite increasing fluids and fiber in your diet, consider adding bulk agents containing psyllium (e.g., Metamucil®) or stool softeners (e.g., Colace®). Talk to your doctor or pharmacist.
- Don't ignore the urge to have a bowel movement.

Hemorrhoids

Hemorrhoids, or "piles," occur when the veins around the anus become enlarged because of increased pressure. Certain conditions increase the risk of hemorrhoids, including excessive body weight, constipation, straining when trying to have a bowel movement, coughing or sneezing, and pregnancy. People in occupations that require long periods of sitting, such as truck drivers, have a higher incidence of hemorrhoids.

Typical symptoms of hemorrhoids are rectal pain, itching, and bleeding. Rectal bleeding can be a cause for concern, as it may suggest a more serious condition such as an ulcer or cancer. The blood from hemorrhoids is bright red and may be present on the outside of the stool or on the toilet paper.

Symptoms/Signs

- Rectal pain, itching, and bleeding.

Call Your Doctor Right Away If:

- You have rectal bleeding that makes your stools look black and tar-like. This may be a sign of significant blood loss from higher up in the digestive tract.

Talk to Your Doctor If:

- Minor hemorrhoidal bleeding doesn't stop after 3 weeks of HomeCare.
- Your child complains of rectal pain or itching, especially at night. This may indicate pinworms.
- Onset of hemorrhoids is associated with a significant change in bowel habits.

HOMECARE™

If physician referral is not recommended at this time, try the following:

Fluids

- Drink plenty of fluids—six to eight glasses of water per day.

Nutrition

- Eat more fiber, found in fruits, vegetables, and whole-grain cereals.

Note Well

- To avoid further irritation, use toilet paper gently. Use only white, nonperfumed paper that is super soft. Wetting the paper with warm water may help as well.

Medication

- Of the scores of hemorrhoid medications, none has proved to be more effective than any other. Ask your pharmacist. Consider trying more than one product and see which one gives you the best relief.
- If constipation continues to be a problem after increasing fluids and fiber in your diet, consider adding bulk agents containing psyllium (e.g., Metamucil®) or stool softeners (e.g., Colace®). Talk to your doctor or pharmacist.

Stomach Cramps

It could be something you ate or a virus you picked up at work. It also could be a symptom of sensitivity or intolerance to certain foods such as dairy or wheat products. Stomach cramps, sometimes accompanied by other symptoms—diarrhea, nausea, fever, and abdominal bloating—usually are a sign that your body is trying to handle something it doesn't like.

For the most part, stomach cramps that result from food poisoning, a stomach virus, or diarrhea are treatable at home. When stomach cramps are accompanied by diarrhea, take care to drink plenty of fluids, especially if you're very young, very old, or have a chronic condition that has compromised your body's ability to fight infection. See "Diarrhea," page 110.

Symptoms/Signs

■ Mild to severe abdominal pain that is episodic, intermittent, or rhythmic (as opposed to continuous and acute).

Call Your Doctor Right Away If:

■ Stomach cramps are accompanied by sudden, severe diarrhea, bloody diarrhea, or fever over 101 F.

■ Stomach cramps are localized in the lower-right abdomen. This is a sign of appendicitis.

■ Intermittent stomach cramps are accompanied by two or more of the following symptoms: vomiting, progressively painful abdominal swelling, progressive constipation (or total inability to move bowels or pass gas), weakness, dizziness, bloody/black stools, foul breath, or low-grade fever.

■ Stomach cramps are not relieved by HomeCare measures within 3 days.

HOMECARE™

If physician referral is not recommended at this time, try the following:

Medication

• When accompanied by diarrhea, try not to take any medication for the first 2 or 3 hours, because the diarrhea may be flushing infection or irritating substances from your body. After that time, try a bismuth preparation (e.g., Pepto-Bismol®) or an over-the-counter antidiarrhea medication (e.g., Imodium A-D®).

Nutrition

• Avoid heavy or greasy foods, dairy products, or foods rich in fiber while you have cramps and during recovery.
• Avoid foods to which you're sensitive (e.g., dairy, wheat, gluten).

Fluids

• Stay well hydrated when stomach cramps are accompanied by diarrhea: Try to drink 1 pint of water or clear broth or a drink such as Gatorade® to replace fluids and minerals you've lost.

Note Well

• Monitor your body temperature.
• Get plenty of rest as you recover.

Prevention

• Never eat undercooked meat or fish, mushrooms that you've picked yourself, or prepared salads or meats that have been unrefrigerated for more than an hour.
• Always wash your hands well with antibacterial soap before and after handling food.
• Decontaminate cutting boards and other kitchen surfaces regularly.
• Throw out any leftovers or canned food that you suspect may be spoiled.
• Manage stress.

Stomach Flu

S tomach flu (a type of gastroenteritis) often is a viral infection that brings on sudden stomach cramps, vomiting, nausea, and diarrhea. It is not caused by the influenza virus.

Stomach flu can be especially dangerous to infants, small children and the frail elderly because vomiting and diarrhea can cause rapid dehydration.

Symptoms/Signs

■ Stomach cramps, nausea, vomiting, and diarrhea that usually last less than 2 days.

Call Your Doctor Right Away If:

■ Excessive vomiting or diarrhea occurs in infants, small children, the frail elderly, or people with other health problems.

■ There are signs of dehydration: increased thirst, dark yellow urine, limited urination, and skin that may be wrinkled and have no tone.

■ Nausea, loss of appetite, fever, and general abdominal pain are followed by pain in the lower right abdomen.

Talk to Your Doctor If:

■ You have a fever higher than 101F for more than 2 days.

■ After only liquids are used, diarrhea continues for more than 2 days.

■ Diarrhea is bloody or black.

■ Vomiting continues on and off for more than 12 hours in an adult or 8 to 12 hours in a small child without significant improvement.

If physician referral is not recommended at this time, try the following:

Fluids

- Try crushed ice and sips of water for the first few hours.
- Drink clear liquids for the next 24 hours.
- **Breastfed infants:** continue feeding as usual and offer water or oral rehydration fluids too.
- **Formula-fed infants:** eliminate all but clear liquids (e.g., water or oral rehydration solutions) for 24 hours.

Nutrition

- Don't eat anything for the first 24 hours.
- Slowly introduce bananas, rice, applesauce, and toast (BRAT diet) on day 2.

Medication

- Try Ibuprofen or acetaminophen for pain.
- Do not give your child antidiarrhea medicine unless recommended by his or her doctor.

Note: Because of the risk of Reye's syndrome, aspirin should not be given to or used by children or teenagers who have or are suspected of having flu or chicken pox. Use acetaminophen.

Rest

- Reduce your activity. Bed rest may be needed.

Prevention

- Make sure meats are properly stored and prepared and all cooking surfaces are decontaminated.
- Avoid dressings, prepared salads, shellfish, poultry, and other meats left unrefrigerated more than 2 hours.
- Wash your hands before and after handling food, after using the bathroom, and after contact with someone who has the stomach flu.
- Disinfect cutting boards and all food preparation and cooking surfaces.

Stomach Ulcers

For decades, peptic ulcers (irritations in the stomach and small intestine) were thought to be caused by diet and stress. Today, doctors know that the majority of all such ulcers are caused by the *Helicobactor pylori* bacteria. A combination of antibiotics and other medications quickly eradicates the bacteria and relieves discomfort.

If you have ulcers that are not linked to *H. pylori* bacteria, you can speed relief and healing by avoiding aspirin or non-steroidal anti-inflammatory drugs (NSAIDs), such as ibuprofen and naproxen.

Symptoms/Signs

■ Gnawing or burning in the upper abdomen, usually worse on an empty stomach.

■ Upper abdominal pain made worse by drinking alcohol or eating spicy, heavy, or fibrous foods.

■ Possible bloating, nausea, vomiting, belching, indigestion, heartburn, weight loss, black or tarry stools, or feeling of fullness after eating small amounts of foods.

Get Emergency Care Right Away If:

You have symptoms of heartburn accompanied by shortness of breath, pain in your chest or jaw, or pain that radiates down your arm or to your back.

Call Your Doctor Right Away If:

■ Your bowel movements are black and tar-like.

■ You vomit black or bloody material.

■ You have periods of weakness, dizziness, or fainting.

Talk to Your Doctor If:

■ You suspect you have an ulcer.

■ Heartburn lasts more than 3 days.

Medication

• Avoid aspirin and anti-inflammatory drugs (NSAIDs) such as ibuprofen and naproxen.
• Ask your doctor if antibiotics will relieve or cure your ulcer.
• If you're on antibiotics to treat your ulcer, check with your doctor about using a bismuth medication (e.g., Pepto-Bismol®).
• Use antacids (as directed) to neutralize stomach acids.

Nutrition

• Avoid high-fat, high-fiber, or very spicy foods until your ulcer is healed.
• Eat six small meals a day instead of three large ones.
• Avoid taking iron supplements unless advised to do so by your doctor.
• Eat a well-balanced diet.

Fluids

• Drink lots of water to dilute stomach acids.
• Avoid drinking too much milk: It may soothe stomach acids temporarily, but it'll also cause your stomach to secrete more acid later.

Note Well

• Don't smoke.
• Restrict use of alcohol.
• Reduce stress whenever possible.

Abrasions

Skin abrasions, or scrapes, are surface wounds where layers of the skin are scraped or torn. Though generally not serious, abrasions can be painful and they may bleed a little. The most common cause of abrasions is falls. The hands, elbows, knees, and hips are the most common sites of injury. Be sure to wear gloves and protective knee and elbow pads when you engage in activities where falls are common. Be especially careful if you work in slippery areas (e.g., wet floors, icy walkways) or walk or climb in uneven terrain.

Symptoms/Signs

■ Torn or scraped skin with bleeding.

Talk to Your Doctor If:

■ There are signs of infection: increasing pain or tenderness, swelling and redness, red streaks coming from the injury, presence of pus, a fever of 101 F or higher without other causes, such as a cold or flu.

■ The date of your last tetanus shot is unknown, or your last tetanus shot was more than 10 years ago and the wound is not small and clean.

If physician referral is not recommended at this time, try the following:

Clean

- Rinse the wound with cool water.
- Wash the wound with soap and water. Although this may increase pain briefly, it is an important step.
- Use tweezers cleaned in alcohol to remove embedded dirt, glass, or gravel.

Cover

- Leave a small abrasion uncovered so it can air dry.
- If the wound is large, oozes blood, or is exposed to clothing or dirt, cover with an *occlusive* or *semiocclusive* bandage (see your pharmacist). This dressing keeps the wound moist—reducing scarring and speeding healing.

Medication

- Try aspirin, ibuprofen, or acetaminophen for pain.
- Apply antibiotic ointment.

Heat/Cold

- An ice pack or cool compress can be tried to help reduce pain.

Prevention

- Wear gloves and protective pads on knees and elbows when appropriate.
- Beware of slippery or uneven surfaces.
- A tetanus booster shot every 10 years is recommended. See page 44.

Acne

Nearly 8 out of 10 teens will develop acne, but pimples can continue to crop up for decades after you enter adulthood. Most experts agree that acne is linked to heredity and hormone levels. When hormones stimulate oil production in the glands around hair follicles, the ducts surrounding these follicles become clogged, and a whitehead or blackhead results. You get a raised, red pimple when one of these skin clogs becomes inflamed.

Occasional bouts of whiteheads, blackheads, or pimples usually can be cleared up rather quickly and painlessly with simple home treatment. For an unfortunate minority, however, acne can cause extremely painful, cyst-like lesions that leave deep scars. Such severe cases usually require medical treatment by a dermatologist.

Contrary to popular belief, diet plays a relatively minor role in acne frequency or severity. But certain drugs, stress, industrial chemicals, and some bacteria can trigger acne episodes. Avoiding such triggers can be a first step toward minimizing or eliminating acne altogether.

Symptoms/Signs

- Blackheads, whiteheads or red, swollen bumps on the skin (often the face, neck, chest, shoulders, or back).
- Bumps that come to a head, erupt, drain clear, yellowish, or pus-like fluid, and then crust over.
- A large painful cyst or pustule with red/purple inflammation, which may or may not erupt.

Talk to Your Doctor If:

- You suspect a cyst or pimple has become infected or inflamed (red or purple, swollen, painful, or does not get better with home treatment).
- Persistent acne is severe and leaves scars.

If physician referral is not recommended at this time, try the following:

Clean

- Keep all acne-prone areas very clean. Wash gently using mild soap and lots of water to rinse. Lukewarm or tepid water is best for not aggravating skin conditions. Pat skin dry—don't rub or scrub.
- Try over-the-counter soaps or astringents designed to dry the skin.

Medication

- Try over-the-counter acne medications, especially those containing benzyl peroxide, that promote skin peeling.
- For severe or recurrent problems, ask your doctor about prescription acne medications such as Accutane® or Retin-A® *(never take Accutane if you are pregnant or could possibly become pregnant)*.
- If your doctor prescribes Retin-A® for your acne, stay out of the sun as much as possible.
- Don't mix over-the-counter and prescription acne medications.

Cover

- Don't cover acne outbreaks with bandages or tight-fitting clothing.

NB
Note Well

- Keep skin clean.
- Manage stress and anxiety.
- Avoid acne triggers, such as certain makeups, drugs, and moisturizers.
- Use noncomedogenic or acne-free facial preparations.
- Replace makeup every 6 months.

Animal/Human Bites

Household pets—not wild animals or stray pets—cause most cases of animal bites. Even if the surface tear doesn't look bad, there could be damage beneath to the tendons and joints. Although less common, human bites should be taken as seriously as animal bites. You can get diseases (i.e., tetanus) and bacterial infections from animal or human bites. In addition, the human mouth is home to many bacteria and viruses, including the hepatitis B virus.

Any bite that breaks the skin should be attended to immediately by a health care professional. If a bite does not break the skin, treat it at home as a minor wound, but watch for signs of infection. An animal care or control professional should capture and observe a wild or stray animal to determine if it is infected with rabies.

Get Emergency Care Right Away If:

- Your tetanus immunizations are not current and you have symptoms of tetanus—stiffness and/or spasms of the jaw, neck, and other muscles; irritability; painful convulsions.
- The wound bleeds excessively. Apply pressure (see "Bleeding," page 90) to the bite area until you can get emergency medical treatment.

Call Your Doctor Right Away If:

- You have swelling, red streaks coming from the wound, excessive soreness, fever, or pus draining from the wound.
- An animal or human bite breaks the skin.
- A bite is from a wild or stray animal.
- You are bitten and have not had a tetanus shot within the past 10 years.
- You develop tingling or increased sensitivity in the bite area 3 to 7 weeks after a bite.

If physician referral is not recommended at this time, try the following:

Clean

- Clean a minor bite immediately and thoroughly with soap and water for 5 minutes, then apply an antiseptic such as hydrogen peroxide or alcohol.
- For serious bites, control bleeding first by applying pressure; do not clean a wound that is actively bleeding.

Medication

- If you are not current with your tetanus immunizations, the doctor will give you a tetanus shot immediately.
- If the biting animal has rabies or is suspected of having rabies, your doctor will prescribe a series of shots to prevent the disease.
- After cleansing a minor bite thoroughly, apply an antibiotic ointment.
- Your doctor may prescribe oral antibiotics to prevent infection.

Cover

- Cover minor bites (after cleansing) with a non-stick bandage.

Prevention

- Avoid contact with wild animals.
- Be careful around pets you don't know. Even an animal that seems friendly can become aggressive quickly.
- Make sure your pets' immunizations are complete and up-to-date.
- Be sure that your tetanus shots are up to date. See page 44.

Athlete's Foot

You don't have to run marathons or play tennis all day to suffer painful bouts of athlete's foot. Feet that are damp regularly from perspiration provide the perfect environment for the fungus that causes skin between toes and on the sides and soles of feet to crack, peel, itch, blister, and flake.

Athlete's foot takes about 4 weeks of aggressive home treatment to disappear completely. After it's gone, an equally aggressive routine often is necessary to keep athlete's foot at bay. Sweaty footwear, damp socks, and less-than-clean showering areas are all dank enough to harbor athlete's foot fungus. Avoiding those infection sites and becoming an otherwise ferocious fungus fighter usually are the only ways you can avoid future flare-ups.

Symptoms/Signs

- Itchy, cracked, burning, peeling, red, flaky skin on or between your toes (or, sometimes, between your fingers and on the palms of your hands).
- Itchy, blister-like bumps on the sides or soles of your feet.

Talk to Your Doctor If:

- Your foot is swollen, sore, blistered, red, or has pus in sores or blisters.
- Symptoms do not improve, or get worse, after treatment with antifungal preparations.
- You have diabetes or poor circulation in your feet and develop symptoms of athlete's foot.
- Inflammation of the skin makes it difficult for you to walk.
- Your legs swell and you have a fever.

If physician referral is not recommended at this time, try the following:

Medication

- Apply over-the-counter, antifungal preparations designed to combat athlete's foot fungus (Tinactin®, Desenex®, Aftate®), two or three times a day, until you have no symptoms for at least 2 weeks.

Clean

- Wash your feet and dry them thoroughly, every day.
- Remove dead skin from feet by scrubbing affected areas with a nail brush; pay special attention to the skin between each toe. Rinse and dry well, then apply antifungal powder.
- Keep shoes clean. Wipe the insides of athletic shoes with a damp cloth dipped in an antibacterial solution such as Lysol®, or spray Lysol® disinfectant inside shoes. Allow shoes to dry completely.
- Keep your shower or bathtub clean; spray or wipe down bathing areas with antibacterial cleansers regularly.

Prevention

- Avoid wearing shoes that are too tight or aren't breathable, especially those made from waterproof materials.
- Alternate shoes from day to day to give each pair time to dry out completely.
- Wear all-cotton or wool socks and change them two or three times throughout the day, if possible. Avoid synthetic fabrics that trap perspiration.
- Wear thongs or other foot protection when you're in public showers, spas, or pool areas.

Bed Sores

Although about half of people suffering from bed sores are more than 70 years old, anyone can develop bed sores simply from being confined to a chair or bed as a result of illness or injury. And while bed sores sound like a minor irritation or side effect, the truth is that thousands of people die from complications of bed sores each year.

Left untreated, bed sores (also known as pressure ulcers) break down skin and muscle tissue, eventually exposing bones and joints. For patients who already have compromised physical health or weakened immune systems, infection from advanced-stage bed sores can be deadly. Fortunately, simple preventive techniques can keep the skin and underlying tissue healthy.

Symptoms/Signs

- Reddened patch of skin that becomes a crater-like sore or ulcer; usually found where a bone is close to the skin (hips, shoulder blades, heels, elbows, etc.) or where skin is pressed against a bed or chair for long periods.

Talk to Your Doctor If:

- You have any red skin resulting from pressure that does not disappear when you press on it.

Prevention

All suspected or existing bed sores should be treated by a medical professional. Some of the following suggestions for preventing bed sores are intended for people who take care of bedridden or immobilized patients:

- Inspect skin daily for signs that a bed sore may be developing.
- Keep skin and bedding clean. Use lotions, creams, or gels to keep skin from drying out. Use cornstarch on skin to reduce friction from sheets or clothing.
- Change position every 2 hours (for people confined to bed) or every hour (for people confined to a chair). People confined to a chair who can shift their own weight should change position at least every 15 minutes. Remember to lift rather than drag anyone you're repositioning.
- Invest in a special mattress or cushion designed to prevent bed sores (such products usually contain air, foam, water, gel, or a combination of materials).
- For people confined to bed: Place pillows under legs from mid-calf to ankle to keep heels off the mattress (however, never position pillows only behind the knees). Use pillows or cushions to keep knees or ankles from touching each other.
- Incontinent people should wear absorbent pads/briefs with a quick-drying surface. Use a protective ointment to keep urine and bowel movements from irritating skin.
- Avoid using doughnut-shaped (ring) cushions.
- Avoid raising the head of the bed beyond 30 degrees.

Blisters

"I walked so far, my blisters had blisters" isn't necessarily a testament to the speaker's stamina or courage. Indeed, blisters usually are a sign that you're doing something you're not used to doing, or you're doing something the wrong way. Shoveling snow, knitting, wearing new shoes around the office, or running a marathon can give you blisters. In fact, any time you apply unusual amounts of friction to skin, you're likely to get a blister.

Although they look innocent enough and may not cause too much discomfort (as long as you stop doing whatever it was that gave you the blister in the first place), blisters can escalate into nasty infections that may have to be treated by your doctor. So do what you can to prevent blisters, and, failing that, do what you can to keep existing blisters from becoming more than just temporary nuisances.

Symptoms/Signs

- Reddish, painful, swollen area of skin with a fluid-filled bubble of skin near the center (blister has opened and fluid has drained if skin bubble is torn away).

Talk to Your Doctor If:

- Redness, swelling, or pain increases.
- Fluid from a blister has an odor or is thick or colored (normal blister fluid looks like water).

Clean

- Clean open blisters gently with soap and water.

Medication

- Apply Neosporin® or Bacitracin® ointment to an open blister that you've cleaned, before you put a bandage on it.

Cover

- Cover an unopened blister to protect it from further irritation. A moleskin "doughnut" can be used around the blister.
- Cover an open blister (after you've cleaned it) with a non-stick bandage. Change bandage twice daily, if it gets wet, or as needed.

Activity

- Avoid any activity that further irritates a blister.

Note Well

- Generally, avoid opening a blister.
- If you cannot protect a large blister (larger than a quarter) from further irritation, draining it may help: Sterilize a needle (using a flame or alcohol) and stick it into the side of the blister. Gently squeeze out all fluid, leaving the skin to act as a natural bandage. Coat blister with antibiotic ointment and cover with a non-stick bandage.

Prevention

- Wear shoes that fit.
- Wear soft, breathable socks. Wear work gloves when needed.
- Apply cornstarch or talcum powder before putting on socks or work gloves.

Boils

Boils are relatively common localized skin infections that usually pose no serious health threat. They can erupt around an inflamed hair follicle (folliculitis), usually on the face, scalp, underarm, thigh, or buttocks. Often, small boils arise and subside within a week or two. Deeper boils or boil sites with multiple pus-filled, pimple-like heads (carbuncles) are caused by a staph infection and can recur in cycles or erratically for years after the first eruption.

Most boils respond well to a relatively simple routine of very warm compresses and careful cleansing. Sometimes, however, boils fail to drain properly, or they become very painful and inflamed. In such cases, a visit to the doctor to have the area drained usually is necessary, and oral antibiotics may be prescribed.

Symptoms/Signs

- Red, painful, pus-filled abscess beneath the skin.
- Minor swelling around boil area.
- Appearance of a pimple-like head or multiple heads in center of swollen area(s) that sometimes erupt and drain fluid, pus, or both.

Talk to Your Doctor If:

- You have a boil on or near your lip, nose, armpit, groin, breast, or between buttocks.
- A boil is very large or causes significant inflammation of surrounding areas.
- You have boils accompanied by a fever.

HOMECARE™

If physician referral is not recommended at this time, try the following:

Heat/Cold

- At the first sign of a boil, apply very warm, wet compresses to the area for 20 minutes, three to four times a day for a week or until the boil comes to a head and breaks.
- Sit in a hot bath for 20 minutes daily until boil erupts.

Clean

- After a boil erupts, clean the area and apply an antibacterial cream or ointment (e.g., Neosporin® or Bacitracin®).

Cover

- Cover erupted or draining boils with a bandage to keep fluid from spreading infection or staining clothes. Change bandage often— three or four times a day.

Note Well

- Do not pinch or squeeze boils that are not fully drained. You may cause a deeper infection.

Prevention

- Bathe daily.
- Keep boil area or boil-prone areas very clean; wipe skin with a clean cotton ball soaked in alcohol or Betadine® antiseptic solution to keep infection from spreading.
- For boils on the face: Before shaving, wash your face with an antibacterial soap. After shaving, apply alcohol to affected areas. Immerse razors in alcohol between shaves, and don't share your razor.
- When you have a boil, use clean towels, washcloths, bed linens, and clothing daily; use hot water to launder all items that come in contact with a boil.

Bruises

You can be technical and call them "contusions," but bruises are just discolorations you sometimes get from bumping into something (or having something bump into you). The actual injury is to the deeper tissues beneath your skin; a bruise appears when blood from injured tissue accumulates near the surface of your skin. The bruised area may be tender or painful for a day or two, but the pain usually goes away as a bruise's color fades.

Every once in a while, athletes or people who overwork their bodies during exercise will notice an unexplained bruise a day or two after a hard workout. Those bruises result from tiny tears in the blood vessels under the skin and are no more serious than bruises caused by a bump or injury.

Symptoms/Signs

■ Discoloration of unbroken skin at the site of an injury (fresh bruises may be reddish at first, turning dark purple or blue within a few hours, then turning yellow or green after a few days as bruise heals).

Talk to Your Doctor If:

■ You have a bruise that swells or is extremely painful, especially if you take blood-thinning medication.

■ A bruise to a toe or finger results in a hemorrhage (collection of blood) under a toenail or fingernail.

■ You notice that you're bruising easily or for no apparent reason.

■ A bruise does not fade significantly within 10 days or fails to fade completely after 3 weeks.

■ You suspect medication may be causing your bruising.

■ You get a bruise on your abdomen or your head.

If physician referral is not recommended at this time, try the following:

Heat/Cold

• Apply cold compresses to the bruised area as soon as possible to reduce swelling and speed healing. Reapply for 15 minutes, once an hour for the first day or two if bruising is widespread or severe.
• After 48 hours, apply heat to increase blood flow to the bruised area.

Note Well

• If you have a large bruise on your leg or foot, elevate your leg as much as possible for the first 24 hours after the injury.

Medication

• Avoid taking aspirin to relieve pain, because aspirin inhibits blood clotting. Take acetaminophen instead.

Activity

• With large bruises to the limbs, you may need to restrict activity for the first 24 to 48 hours.

Prevention

• Avoid placing furniture by doorways or common walkways.
• Be sure that carpeting is secure and slip resistant.
• Be sure there are no electrical cords in open areas where they may trip someone.
• Keep floors dry and clear of clutter.
• Wear appropriate protective equipment (e.g., helmets) for your job, sport, or other physical activity.

Burns

If physician referral is not recommended at this time, try the following:

Burns are classified in three categories according to their severity. Third-degree burns are the most serious:

- **First-degree:** Limited to the skin's surface, first-degree burns (such as a typical sunburn, see page 180) are red and painful. They usually do not require medical attention.
- **Second-degree:** Splitting or blistering of skin is evident, indicating that deeper skin layers have been damaged.
- **Third-degree:** Severe tissue damage is evident involving the skin, fatty tissue, nerves, and other tissues deep below the surface. *Indications of third-degree burns include swelling, skin that is charred or white, and limited pain because nerves have been damaged or destroyed.*

Get Emergency Care Right Away If:

- Third-degree burns are evident.
- There are extensive second-degree burns or any second-degree burns on the face, hands, or feet.

Talk to Your Doctor If:

- Pain continues for more than 2 days.
- There are signs of infection: increasing pain, redness or tenderness; fever of 101 F or greater; the area becomes increasingly swollen.

Heat/Cold

- Apply cold compresses or cool water to the burn area right away. Continue for 5-10 minutes or until the pain is reduced.
- *Beware:* Applying ice compress may further damage tissue.

Medication

- Acetaminophen, ibuprofen, or aspirin to reduce pain. Use as directed.
- Antibiotic creams have questionable value.
- Aloe may help soothe the pain and discomfort.

Cover

- Do not cover a burn with a gauze dressing or bandage unless the area is irritated by clothing or other objects.

Fluids

- Drink plenty of water.

Note Well

- Avoid breaking blisters. Do not remove skin.

Prevention

- Avoid excessive sun exposure.
- Use sunscreen with a sun protection factor (SPF) of at least 15.
- Practice fire prevention. If possible, try to use the rear burners of your stove.
- Supervise children in the kitchen.

Cold Hands and Feet

"Cold hands, warm heart" isn't just what people with cold hands say to apologize for their chilling touch: It's actually true. When your body needs to maintain an adequate core temperature in cool weather, it simply reduces blood flow to your hands and feet to keep heat loss to a minimum. If you smoke, take certain medications, or have an iron deficiency, diabetes, or heart disease, chilled extremities can even be a problem in relatively mild temperatures.

Simple self-care and prevention usually is enough to keep your hands and feet from turning icy. If you have Raynaud's syndrome or acrocyanosis, self-care and prevention measures usually work, but you may have to talk to your doctor.

Symptoms/Signs

■ Cool or cold skin on hands and feet, sometimes accompanied by clamminess, perspiration, or mild numbness.

■ **Raynaud's syndrome:** fingers and toes suddenly turn blue or white upon exposure to cold, often accompanied by stinging pain. Common with lupus, scleroderma, and rheumatoid arthritis.

■ **Acrocyanosis:** hands and feet are sweaty, cool, and bluish in color.

■ **Circulatory disease:** occasionally chilled hands and feet, even in mild temperatures, sometimes accompanied by numbness.

Get Emergency Care Right Away If:
You lose feeling in any part of your arm or leg.

Talk to Your Doctor If:

■ Your (cool) hands or feet ache with use or when elevated.

■ Your hands or feet have poorly- or nonhealing sores.

■ Self-care measures fail to keep the hands or feet warm.

HOMECARE™

If physician referral is not recommended at this time, try the following:

Medication

• Use absorbent foot powders to keep feet dry.
• Avoid over-the-counter cold remedies and diet pills.

Heat/Cold

• Avoid putting your hands or feet in cold water.
• Use warm—not hot—water to warm chilled extremities slowly.

Nutrition

• Eat a meal (preferably a hot one) before going outdoors in cool weather.
• Eat iron-rich foods or talk to your doctor about taking iron supplements if you're anemic.

Note Well

• Wear gloves and moisture-wicking socks.
• Swing your arms in large circles or your legs in half-circles to move blood to your extremities.

Fluids

• Drink plenty of fluids throughout the day.
• Limit caffeine and alcohol.
• Drink hot cider, broth, or decaffeinated tea to warm hands and feet quickly.

Cuts

I t's important to decide if you need medical attention for a cut (laceration) that has one of the following characteristics: uncontrolled bleeding (see page 90); a jagged wound; possible damage to muscles, nerves, and other soft tissues; or possible infection. You may want to call your doctor if the cut is too large or deep for you to keep the edges together. Stitches provide the best insurance for holding the edges together, but they can cause scarring. Your doctor may suggest using butterfly bandages to minimize scarring.

Symptoms/Signs

■ Minor to uncontrolled bleeding.

Get Emergency Care Right Away If:
The wound cannot be closed and bleeding cannot be stopped or the wound is very irregular and there are flaps of tissue.

Call Your Doctor Right Away If:

■ There is weakness or numbness below the injury.

■ There is a long or deep cut to the face, chest, fingers, back, stomach, or palm of the hand, or over a joint.

■ There are signs of infection: pain, tenderness, swelling, redness, red streaks coming away from the injury, pus, or a fever of 100 F or higher without another cause, such as cold or flu.

Talk to Your Doctor If:

■ The date of your last tetanus shot is unknown, or your last tetanus shot was more than 10 years ago, especially if the wound is not small and clean.

■ The wound is very dirty or contains embedded foreign material that you can't wash away easily.

If physician referral is not recommended at this time, try the following:

Clean

- Rinse the cut with cool water.
- Wash around the wound with soap and water. Avoid getting soap in the wound.
- Use tweezers cleaned in alcohol to remove dirt, glass, or gravel that remains in wound.
- Do not attempt to remove any penetrating object sticking out of the wound.

Cover

- Apply pressure directly to wound with clean gauze pad until bleeding has stopped (see page 90).
- Apply an antibiotic ointment and a bandage to help prevent scarring and promote healing.
- Apply a butterfly bandage to a deeper cut after bleeding has stopped or slowed.
- Spray-on or liquid bandages may be useful for minor cuts.

Medication

- Take aspirin, ibuprofen, or acetaminophen for pain. Use as directed.

Prevention

- Be sure your tetanus immunization is up to date. See page 44.

Dandruff

*I*f you avoid wearing dark colors because of your dandruff, you're not alone. Nearly everyone has dandruff—which is little more than flakes of skin from the scalp. However, men and people who have excessively oily skin and hair are more likely to have troublesome dandruff.

The first line of defense is shampooing daily and using an over-the-counter dandruff shampoo. If you don't notice improvement after 3 or 4 weeks of home treatment, you could be dealing with a condition such as seborrheic dermatitis, which flakes like dandruff but has accompanying scalp inflammation that can weep or crust over. Seborrheic dermatitis can sometimes be helped by dandruff shampoos, and when appropriate, a prescription of a hydrocortisone cream or lotion may make a real difference.

Symptoms/Signs

- Itchy scalp.
- White or gray flakes that are obvious on hair and clothing.

Talk to Your Doctor If:

- Heavy dandruff does not improve after a few weeks of home treatment.
- You have very stubborn dandruff accompanied by scaly patches of skin on the sides of your nose, in your eyebrows, or on your chest.

If physician referral is not recommended at this time, try the following:

Clean

- Shampoo every day if possible, or at least five times per week. Use a mild, non-medicated shampoo to control scalp oil without irritating your scalp. If you don't see results, switch to an antidandruff shampoo. Use a conditioner to keep hair from drying out. Always rinse hair well.
- Try different over-the-counter dandruff shampoos until you find one that works for you. Preparations containing selenium sulfide or zinc pyrithione work quickly and slow down the flaking process. Those with salicylic acid and sulfur loosen flakes so they can be washed away more easily.
- Consult your doctor before using dandruff treatment products containing coal tar.

Medication

- If you're using a prescription scalp lotion or shampoo, or if you are using an over-the-counter coal-tar preparation, wear a hat to protect your scalp from excessive sunlight.
- For heavy, stubborn dandruff, your doctor may recommend a prescription dandruff shampoo or lotion.

Prevention

- Reduce your use of hair styling products.
- Manage stress.
- Eat a balanced diet.

Eczema

Eczema is a general term for inflammation of the skin, or dermatitis. The itchy rash of eczema can flare up for any number of reasons: contact with harsh detergents, rough fabrics, or cosmetics, as well as poor sleep habits, emotional distress, food allergies (about 10 percent of the time), poor circulation in the legs (stasis dermatitis), or a compromised immune system. Most of the time, bouts of eczema come and go, but during dry winter months eczema can linger for weeks and can be difficult to soothe. As a result, eczema sufferers have to look beyond typical dry-skin treatments in order to start healing broken skin and restoring moisture to affected areas.

Symptoms/Signs

- Mild to severe itching.
- Red, raised skin lesions.
- Cracked, dry, or scaly skin.
- Peeling skin.
- Swollen legs in some cases.
- Oozing and crusting (in severe cases).

Talk to Your Doctor If:

- Oozing or bleeding rash does not respond to HomeCare.
- Over-the-counter hydrocortisone creams do not satisfactorily control itching.
- You suspect childhood eczema is caused by an allergy.
- A scaly rash appears on your face and is accompanied by unusual joint pain and coughing.

If physician referral is not recommended at this time, try the following:

Medication

- Over-the-counter hydrocortisone creams and antihistamines to relieve itching.
- Calamine lotion for "weeping" eczema to help stop the oozing.

Nutrition

- In children, eggs, milk, and orange juice may cause skin rash; check with your doctor before eliminating foods from your child's diet.

Heat/Cold

- Apply cold, wet dressings to itchy areas. Cold water will do, but ice-cold milk is most soothing (be sure to wash skin after using milk).
- Avoid hot water whenever possible, especially at bath time.

Clean

- Keep skin moist and well lubricated. Apply a therapeutic lotion (Eucerin®, Keri®, Lubriderm®) or baby oil immediately after contact with water, before skin has had a chance to dry.
- Use soap sparingly, and choose non-soap or superfatted bath bars rich in lanolin, cocoa butter, or cleansing cream.

Note Well

- Avoid scratching, which could cause a secondary bacterial infection.
- Invest in a humidifier that ties into your home heating system.
- Avoid false fingernails: Acrylic and fingernail glue can aggravate eczema.
- Wear cotton or fabrics that don't irritate skin.
- Wear rubber gloves (avoid latex products if you have a latex allergy) when cleaning or doing dishes.
- Manage stress.

Frostbite

You don't have to go mountaineering in the dead of winter to get frostbite. Just shoveling snow or changing a tire on a cold day can freeze your skin to the point where, even after careful rewarming, there could be permanent tissue damage.

Simple common sense prevents frostbite: Don't venture outside in subfreezing temperatures. If you have to go out, dress appropriately. That means wearing mittens, warm socks, and a hat that covers your ears. Also, learn the signs of frostbite and what to do if they appear. Sometimes, for example, the method you use in an attempt to rewarm frostbitten skin can do more damage to tissues than the frostbite itself would do. It's also important to know that frostbite often is accompanied by hypothermia—a dangerous drop in the body's core temperature—that must be treated first, before you try to rewarm frostbitten skin. See page 167.

Symptoms/Signs

- Skin that is somewhat numb and white; may blister or peel when rewarmed (mild frostbite).
- Skin that is cold, hard, white or grayish, and numb; may turn blue or purple, or swell and blister when rewarmed (severe frostbite).

Talk to Your Doctor If:

- Symptoms of severe frostbite develop.
- Skin remains numb during and after rewarming.

If physician referral is not recommended at this time, try the following:

Note Well

- Find a warm area quickly.
- Never rub frostbitten skin.

Heat/Cold

- Use very warm water (100 to 105 F) to rewarm frostbitten skin quickly: Immerse in a tub or basin or apply compresses. Rewarming can be painful.
- Remove clothing from frostbitten areas and cover with blankets.
- Frostbitten skin burns easily so do not rewarm with a heating pad or too close to dry heat such as a campfire.

Note Well

- If you can't get to a warm area immediately, use your body to rewarm: Put frostbitten hands under your armpits. Rewarm frostbitten toes with your warm hands. Cover your face with your hands to warm your nose and cheeks.

Fluids

- Drink warm liquids (coffee, tea, broth, cocoa).
- Do not drink alcoholic beverages, which promote heat loss.

Rest

- Do not walk if your feet have been frostbitten and recently rewarmed.
- Rest with frostbitten areas elevated to minimize swelling of rewarmed tissue.

Prevention

- Dress appropriately outdoors.
- Go in at the first sign of overchilling.
- Don't drink alcohol in cold weather.
- Have your home heating unit checked annually.

Hyperthermia

You get hot, you sweat, and the sweat evaporates, taking heat away from your skin and keeping your core temperature at a proper level. But when you overload your "air conditioner," hyperthermia sets in.

The air temperature doesn't have to be extremely high for you to notice the first signs of hyperthermia. Even moderate air temperature when combined with high humidity can decrease your skin's ability to cool itself. Also, a chronic medical condition, such as high blood pressure, or the effects of certain medications (e.g., diuretics and antihistamines) can contribute to hyperthermia, even without much exertion or time in the sun.

Symptoms/Signs

- **Heat exhaustion:** increased thirst, weakness, mental or physical disorientation, nausea, profuse sweating, cold or clammy skin, visual disturbances.
- **Heatstroke:** confusion, bizarre behavior, strong and rapid pulse, extreme fatigue, rapid heartbeat, loss of consciousness, body temperature over 104 F, lack of sweating with dry, red skin (the very young or very fit may continue sweating, however).

Get Emergency Care Right Away If:
You or someone you are with has trouble remaining conscious or has other signs of heatstroke.

Talk to Your Doctor If:

- You or someone you are with experiences symptoms of heat exhaustion and does not respond to self-care measures within 30 minutes.

If physician referral is not recommended at this time, try the following:

Rest

- As soon as you notice any symptoms of hyperthermia, rest in a cool, shaded area with feet elevated. Remove excess clothing.
- Stop all activity at the first signs of hyperthermia.

Heat/Cold

- Splash skin with cool or tepid water, or apply cool towels or sheets to skin.
- If possible, move to an air-conditioned setting.

Fluids

- Drink lots of cool water, fruit juices, or sports drinks.
- Avoid alcohol and caffeine.

Note Well

- In hot/dry or warm/humid weather, dress in light-colored, loose-fitting clothes, wear a hat, drink plenty of fluids, stay out of the sun, and avoid strenuous activity.
- Use your air conditioner whenever possible or visit air-conditioned places such as shopping malls, movie theaters, and libraries during the hottest part of the day.
- Don't go shirtless, and change perspiration-soaked clothes often.

Prevention

- Increased alcohol consumption and overeating in hot weather increase the risk of heat stroke.

Hypothermia

The thermometer outside your front door doesn't have to register below freezing for winter weather to threaten your health. Temperatures up to 50 F can be deadly, particularly when accompanied by rain, wind, or your own physical exhaustion. In particular, the elderly and the very young are vulnerable to cool temperatures, even indoors.

Hypothermia—a mild to severe drop in the body's core temperature—can be prevented easily by checking the weather forecast and making sure you dress accordingly. Doing so can mean the difference between life and death. Severe hypothermia is a medical emergency. However, any amount of body cooling is serious and should be treated with caution and care.

Symptoms/Signs

- Shivering.
- Numbness of the hands and feet.
- Confusion, sleepiness, physical exhaustion, slurred speech, memory lapses.
- Slow and shallow breathing; a weak, slow heartbeat.
- Cool, pale skin; fingers, toes, and lips may be slightly blue.
- Cessation of shivering with diminished alertness or loss of consciousness, slow pulse and breathing (severe hypothermia).

Get Emergency Care Right Away If:
Anyone with symptoms of hypothermia suffers from diminished alertness, mental confusion, or loses consciousness.

Call Your Doctor Right Away If:

- HomeCare doesn't relieve hypothermia symptoms within 30 minutes, or if symptoms get progressively worse despite self-care.

If physician referral is not recommended at this time, try the following:

Heat/Cold

- Move to a warm, sheltered area.
- Use blankets or skin-to-skin contact (i.e., torso to torso) to raise body temperature or to keep warm.
- In cases of very mild hypothermia, a warm bath can help restore body temperature.
- Remove any wet clothes and put on dry clothes or cover with blankets. Keep the head covered.

Fluids

- Drink hot tea, broth, or water.
- Avoid alcohol.

Note Well

- Before spending time outdoors, find out what the forecast and weather conditions will be.

Prevention

- Always dress appropriately in cold weather: Wear layers of breathable clothing next to your skin, with wind-blocking or woolen outer layers. Always wear a hat and gloves.
- Never sleep outdoors in clothing you've worn earlier in the day.
- Keep clothes dry in cool weather; change from wet to dry clothes as soon as possible.

Ingrown Toenail

When you have an ingrown toenail, every step you take feels like one step too many. The soft skin that the nail has penetrated throbs, swells, turns red, and, without treatment, becomes infected. People with unusually curved toenails or who constantly suffer toe trauma (construction workers or ballerinas, for example) are at increased risk. Prevention is the key to pain-free feet.

Trim your toenails properly and choose shoes that fit properly, and you'll have a pretty good chance of avoiding a visit to your doctor with an infected toe.

Symptoms/Signs

- Toenail (usually on the big toe) growing into soft tissue next to the nail, causing pain and discomfort.

Talk to Your Doctor If:

- You have severe pain, swelling, and pus at the site where the toenail is ingrown.
- Any toenail becomes discolored and has crumbling edges.
- You have diabetes or poor circulation and have any pain, swelling, or redness in your toes or feet.

Medication

- If you suspect that your ingrown toenail is getting infected (swelling, redness, pus, etc.), soak your foot in an iodine solution. Apply an antibiotic cream (Neosporin®, Bacitracin®, Polysporin®) and cover it with a nonstick bandage.
- Try an over-the-counter product made to soften the nail and the skin around it for easier trimming. *Note: Do not use these products if you have poor circulation or diabetes.*

Clean

- Soak your feet in very warm water for 15 or 20 minutes to soften the nail for easier trimming.
- Keep the area around an ingrown nail very clean: Use alcohol, hydrogen peroxide, or antibacterial soap.

Cover

- Cover an ingrown toenail with a nonstick bandage only if you suspect that it is infected, you have applied antibiotic ointment, and you are waiting to see your doctor.
- Do not cover ingrown toenails that are not infected; if you must wear socks, wear only clean, white cotton socks and wide-toed, breathable shoes.

Prevention

- Trim your toenails regularly (about once a month) all the way to its edge and if possible, round-off sharp corners.
- Keep your feet and the area under toenails clean.
- Wear shoes that are not too tight or pointed excessively at the toe. Also, avoid wearing high heels.
- Avoid tight socks and panty hose whenever possible.
- If you're diabetic, practice good foot care.

Jock Itch

Jock itch, similar to athlete's foot, is caused by a fungus that thrives in warm, dark, moist places. Anyone—athlete or couch potato, male or female—can get jock itch, which is characterized by severe itching in the groin, thigh or anal area, and a raised circular rash with blisters that may ooze liquid or pus.

For both prevention and treatment of jock itch, keep your skin, clothes, athletic supporters, underwear, sheets, towels, or anything else that comes into contact with your groin area, clean and dry. This may seem simple, but we all forget to bring fresh gear to the gym every once in a while. And wearing yesterday's clothes for today's workout can be enough to start an infection.

Symptoms/Signs

- Severe itching on upper thighs, buttocks, genitals, or groin (males and females).
- Raised, circular rash with red edges (may appear ring-like) that may be accompanied by blisters that weep or ooze.

Talk to Your Doctor If:

- Jock itch symptoms do not get better after 2 weeks of HomeCare.
- You see signs of infection: fever, redness, swelling.

HOMECARE™

If physician referral is not recommended at this time, try the following:

Medication

- Apply over-the-counter antifungal preparations designed to combat jock itch fungus (e.g., Tinactin®, Lotrimin®, Desenex®, Aftate®), two or three times a day, until you have no symptoms for at least 2 weeks.

Clean

- Bathe daily. Wash the affected area well, dry completely with a fresh, clean towel, then apply antifungal powder or cornstarch to reduce irritation and prevent reinfection.

Note Well

- Avoid wearing too-tight underwear, and choose undergarments made from 100 percent cotton.
- Don't wear panty hose, Spandex shorts, or tights.
- Resist scratching the rash, which could lead to infection.

Activity

- During severe flare-ups, avoid activities that make you sweat.

Prevention

- Never share a towel with anyone.
- Never wear underwear, workout clothes, or an athletic supporter that hasn't been laundered since it was last worn.
- Follow all of the above recommendations for keeping areas prone to jock itch clean, dry, and protected from infection.

Puncture Wounds

Unlike scrapes and cuts, which usually are on the skin's surface, puncture wounds can be deep and pose a greater risk of bleeding and infection. Unfortunately, they're easy to ignore because of their small surface size. Deep puncture wounds can damage underlying blood vessels, nerves, and organs.

Puncture wounds are common in occupations such as construction, carpentry, medicine (needle sticks), and textile manufacturing.

It is important to clean all puncture wounds thoroughly to avoid infection.

Symptoms/Signs

■ A superficial to deep hole in the skin that was made by a sharp object. Bleeding may be slight (e.g., a few drops) or profuse (e.g., gushing, spurting). See page 90.

Get Emergency Care Right Away If:

- Indications of additional injury, such as loss of movement, numbness, profuse bleeding (spurting indicates that an artery has been injured).
- There are signs of shock: pale, sweating skin; dizziness; rapid, weak pulse.
- You cannot stop the bleeding.

Call Your Doctor Right Away If:

■ There are signs of infection: increasing pain or tenderness, swelling and redness, red streaks coming away from the injury, presence of pus, or a fever of 101 F or higher without another reason.

■ The object or debris remains in the wound.

■ The wound is in the hand, head, chest, back, eye, or abdomen.

■ It has been more than 10 years since your last tetanus shot; the date of your last tetanus shot is not known.

If physician referral is not recommended at this time, try the following:

Clean

- Rinse the wound with cool water.
- Wash around the wound with soap and water. Avoid getting soap in the wound.
- If the wound isn't too serious, encourage it to bleed to help bring material to the surface.

Heat/Cold

- Soak the wound in warm water two to three times a day, 10 to 20 minutes at a time, for 2 to 4 days.

Cover

- Apply an antibiotic ointment and a bandage to help prevent scarring and promote healing.

Medication

- Use aspirin, acetaminophen, or ibuprofen as directed for pain.
- Antiseptics such as hydrogen peroxide are not recommended. They can irritate the wound and cause further discomfort.

Prevention

- A tetanus booster shot every 10 years is recommended. See page 44.
- Store sharp objects carefully.
- Follow safety precautions when handling syringes and needles.

Rashes

If physician referral is not recommended
at this time, try the following:

Most rashes aren't serious and last only a few days, or up to a week. Some rashes—those caused by an illness or reactions to something you eat, medicine you're taking, or an insect sting—are signals from your body that something may be seriously wrong.

When a rash is caused by an allergy, try to avoid contacting the offending substance again, because subsequent contact can result in more severe reactions. Fortunately, with a little time and HomeCare you can treat a mild, localized rash, such as from an irritating soap, or from brushing up against a poison ivy plant.

Symptoms/Signs

- Raised, red patches of skin that may itch, burn, tingle, or feel sore or numb.
- **Contact dermatitis:** itchy, red skin that can be flaky or blistered. See page 182.
- **Hives or heat rash:** very itchy large, red welts in exposed areas. See page 185.
- **Rash from a virus** (e.g., chicken pox or measles): itchy, red spots or blisters all over the body. See page 176.
- **Rash from bacteria** (e.g., impetigo): small red bumps on the arms, legs, chest, or buttocks; may appear yellow as crust forms.
- **Rash from tick bite:** raised, red, ring-shaped or "bull's eye" rash at the site of a tick bite. See page 172.

Get Emergency Care Right Away If:
You feel warm and flushed, or experience dizziness, disorientation, or difficulty breathing.

Talk to Your Doctor If:
- Your rash has a distinct "bull's eye" appearance.
- You have a fever with a rash.
- Large areas of skin are affected.
- Progressive swelling occurs with the rash.

Medication

- Apply calamine lotion or an over-the-counter hydrocortisone cream to soothe prolonged itching. (Don't use hydrocortisone if you think the rash is infected.)
- Try a diaper rash ointment if the skin feels sore rather than itchy.
- For hives, try an over-the-counter oral antihistamine to relieve itching and inflammation.

Heat/Cold

- Apply cold compresses (not heat) to soothe itching and reduce inflammation.

Clean

- Wash the affected area with soap and water or alcohol, then pat dry. Apply a cornstarch-based body powder before dressing.

Cover

- Don't cover a rash.
- Wear loose, natural-fiber clothing so that air can circulate freely around affected area.

Activity

- Avoid activities that cause you to sweat profusely or get overheated.
- Don't go swimming when you have a rash.

Rashes, Adults

Rash	Signs/Symptoms	Cause
Psoriasis	Dry, red patches of skin with a top layer of thick, silvery scales or small, scaly spots; cracked skin, itching, some bleeding or joint pain may accompany rash.	Hereditary; additional, unknown factors
Seborrhea	Scaly, itchy, oily patches of skin on the scalp, face, neck, or chest. May be red or yellow and crusty. Profuse, itchy dandruff. See page 163.	May be hereditary; additional, unknown factors
Shingles	Pain or tingling followed by a painful red rash usually on one side of the face or trunk. Small blisters filled with clear fluid cloud and crust over after a few days; crust disappears within 2 or 3 weeks of first symptoms, but pain or skin sensitivity can linger for months. See page 178.	Reactivation of the varicella-zoster (chicken pox) virus
Athlete's Foot	Itchy, cracked, peeling, red, flaky skin on or between toes; sometimes appears between fingers and on the palms of the hand, or as itchy, blister-like bumps on the sides or soles of feet. See page 155.	Fungus, usually picked up in less-than-clean showering areas, that grows on moist skin Poor circulation
Jock Itch	In males or females: raised red rash on the groin, thigh, buttocks, or genital or anal area, accompanied by severe itching and red blisters that may ooze liquid or pus. See page 169.	Fungus that grows on moist skin
Lyme Disease Rash	Red, "bull's eye" rash radiating from the site of a tick bite, accompanied by chills, fever, muscle aches, fatigue, swelling of the joints.	Bacterial infection transmitted by a bite from a tick commonly called a deer tick, but which can be found on birds and rats as well.

When to See Your Doctor	HomeCare
If large areas of your skin are affected.	Psoriasis cannot be cured. Exposure to sunlight (without burning) and use of over-the-counter shampoos and other preparations for psoriasis can minimize symptoms. Avoid picking or scratching scales. Reduce stress and anxiety, which may worsen the condition.
If severe dandruff does not respond to regular use of dandruff shampoo, or if affected areas become infected (swollen and red with pus or radiating red lines present).	Shampoo hair often with dandruff shampoo; rinse hair thoroughly. Apply over-the-counter hydrocortisone cream to relieve itching in areas other than the scalp. If the condition persists, talk with your doctor.
If pain from shingles is severe, you have shingles symptoms on the upper part of the face, have eye pain, or you experience chronic pain long after a shingles rash has disappeared.	Take an over-the-counter analgesic for pain. Apply an antibiotic ointment to blisters. Depending on the severity, a consultation with your doctor may be appropriate. Do not use the over-the-counter shingles remedy Zostrix® until blisters have disappeared. Apply cool, wet compresses to affected areas to relieve pain. Keep blisters clean (use alcohol) and keep them covered until they crust over.
If your foot is swollen, sore, blistered, red, or has pus in sores or blisters; if you have diabetes or poor circulation in your feet and develop symptoms of athlete's foot; or if your legs swell and you have a fever.	Apply over-the-counter, antifungal preparations designed to combat athlete's foot fungus (e.g., Tinactin®, Micatin®, Desenex®, Aftate®, etc.), two or three times a day, until you have no symptoms for at least 2 weeks. Apply cool, wet compresses to ease pain and inflammation. Keep feet clean and dry. Remove shoes and socks whenever you can.
If symptoms do not improve with home treatment or if you have a fever with the rash.	Apply over-the-counter antifungal preparations (e.g., Tinactin®, Desenex®, Aftate®, Lotrimin®, etc.) two or three times a day, until you have no symptoms for at least 2 weeks. Keep area as cool as possible. Bathe daily. Avoid wearing too-tight underwear, panty hose, spandex shorts or tights. Avoid sharing a towel with anyone else. Avoid wearing underwear, workout clothes, or an athletic supporter that hasn't been laundered since it was last worn.
If you suspect you have Lyme disease.	Call your doctor. When detected early, Lyme disease can be treated with antibiotic therapy.

Rashes, Allergy

Rash	Symptoms	Cause
Contact Dermatitis	Red, itchy patches that may blister, drain, then crust over; limited to the area of the body that touched the irritating substance. See page 182.	Contact with a substance that causes allergic reaction and inflammation (e.g., poisonous plants, harsh soaps, jewelry, lotions, cosmetics, etc.)
Eczema (Atopic Dermatitis)	Reddish rash, cracked, scaly, or peeling skin that may bleed or ooze, mild to severe itching, a "pulled-tight" feeling to skin. See page 164.	Wide-ranging: may be hereditary, or associated with respiratory allergies, food allergies, and asthma
Poison Ivy/ Poison Oak	Raised, red patches or streaks on the skin with blistering and minor swelling, moderate to severe itching, watery liquid seeping from blisters. See page 187.	Contact with any part of poison ivy or poison oak plants
Rash from Medication	Allover itching, hives, red, raised patches on skin not limited to one area, blisters, swelling.	Reaction to over-the-counter or prescription drug. Symptoms usually occur after the first dose and get worse with subsequent doses, although it may take repeated doses to appear.
Food Allergy	Itching, swelling, hives, blisters. See page 183.	Reaction from consuming food to which you are allergic

SKIN CONDITIONS

When to See Your Doctor	HomeCare
If the rash becomes infected, has radiating red streaks, is accompanied by fever, or does not improve with HomeCare after 2 weeks.	Avoid the irritating substance. Keep the rash clean, but avoid soap; use alcohol or hydrogen peroxide instead. Take oatmeal baths or apply hydrocortisone cream for itch relief. Use plain calamine lotion to dry up weeping blisters.
If severe eczema does not respond to home care, or if itching is not satisfactorily controlled by over-the-counter hydrocortisone creams.	Apply cold, wet compresses or over-the-counter hydrocortisone cream to relieve itch. Use plain calamine lotion to stop the oozing. Avoid hot water, especially at bath time. Use moisturizing cream or lotion on nonweeping eczema to keep the area from drying and cracking. Avoid harsh soaps.
If you have a reaction involving your eyes, face, or genitals; if very large areas of skin are affected; if the rash is accompanied by fever or swollen lymph nodes.	Apply plain calamine lotion to soothe itch and dry blisters. Apply cold, wet compresses or over-the-counter hydrocortisone cream to relieve moderate itching. Use alcohol or soap and water to clean the rash after blisters have broken. Don't cover affected areas (except with loose, breathable clothing). Try an oral antihistamine (e.g., Benadryl®) for itching.
Seek emergency care if you have difficulty breathing, become dizzy or confused, or experience swelling in the face, throat, or tongue.	Stop taking over-the-counter medication if you suspect it caused the reaction. Call your doctor before discontinuing prescription medication. To relieve itch, apply cool compresses or hydrocortisone cream to the affected areas. Try an oral antihistamine that contains diphenhydramine (e.g., Benadryl®) for excessive itching or inflammation.
Seek emergency care if the rash is accompanied by swelling of the face, neck, tongue, or throat; severe abdominal pain or vomiting; fainting, wheezing, or difficulty breathing.	Avoid the food you suspect caused the reaction.

Rashes, Children

Rash	Symptoms	Cause
Cradle Cap	Thick patches of dry skin on an infant's scalp, hairline, eyebrows, eyelids, nose; some patches may appear crusty or yellow.	Unknown
Diaper Rash	Irritated, red skin of buttocks and thighs. See page 238.	Irritation from urine, bowel movements, or laundry detergents. In some cases, a fungal or bacterial infection is to blame
Chicken Pox	Red rash that develops blisters that ooze and scab over, accompanied by mild to severe itching and fever.	Virus (varicella zoster)
Ringworm	Red rings that progress from a center point on the skin or scalp. On the scalp, ringworm may cause bald spots.	Fungus, usually contracted from sharing hats, brushes, and combs, or from handling pets with ringworm
Roseola	Sudden high fever, swollen lymph nodes; red rash appears on trunk and neck as fever decreases.	Human herpes virus 6
Rubella (German Measles)	Mild, allover rash that disappears within 3 to 4 days, low-grade fever, swollen lymph nodes, itching.	Rubella virus
Rubeola (Measles)	Allover rash, fever, dry cough, red or swollen eyes, sore throat, runny nose, sensitivity to light, white spots on inside of cheek.	Rubeola virus
Prickly Heat	Tiny, white, pinhead bumps surrounded by red skin. Intense itching accompanied by tingling or prickly sensation. Common in infants and adults.	Excessive or prolonged perspiration
Scarlet Fever	Sandpaper-like rash on neck, chest, armpits, and groin accompanied by fever, sore throat and vomiting. Sometimes, tongue is swollen.	A type of streptococcal bacteria

Note: Because of the risk of Reye's syndrome, aspirin should not be given to or used by children or teenagers who have or are suspected of having flu or chicken pox. Use acetaminophen.

When to See Your Child's Doctor	HomeCare
If the condition does not improve with HomeCare treatment.	Shampoo the scalp daily with a mild dandruff shampoo or use a soft brush to remove excess scales and crust. Apply baby oil after shampooing. (See page 163.)
If the rash does not respond to home treatment, becomes bright red, crusty, or blistered, or if you suspect a fungal or bacterial infection.	Change the child's diaper as soon as it is wet or soiled; wash diaper area at every change and dry skin thoroughly. Expose affected areas to air as much as possible. Apply petroleum jelly or diaper ointment (e.g., A&D®, Desitin®) to protect skin that will be exposed to a soiled diaper for prolonged periods.
If fever over 102 F lasts for more than 2 days, skin appears bruised with no apparent cause, sores develop in the eyes, symptoms are accompanied by vomiting, extreme fatigue, and severe headache, or signs of infection (red streaks from the blister, pus, increasing pain or tenderness) appear.	Use acetaminophen to relieve fever (never give aspirin to children with chicken pox). Give tepid oatmeal or baking soda baths or apply cool, wet compresses or calamine lotion to relieve itching.
If ringworm spreads despite home treatment, or if the scalp is affected.	Use over-the-counter, antifungal preparations such as Tinactin® or Desenex®, or try iodine-based soaps or solutions (e.g., Betadine®).
If fever above 102 F causes convulsions **get emergency medical care right away.**	Use acetaminophen and cool, wet compresses (or tepid baths) to reduce fever.
If symptoms worsen daily, fever exceeds 102 F, severe headache is present, extreme fatigue sets in, or convulsions are present.	Use acetaminophen to relieve fever (do not use aspirin). Apply cool, wet compresses to relieve itching. Avoid exposing pregnant women to a contagious child.
If fever rises to 101 F or higher for more than 3 days, or the child has a sore throat, earache, discolored fingernails, discolored nasal mucus, convulsions, or difficulty breathing.	Use acetaminophen (not aspirin) to reduce fever. Try a cough medicine and plenty of liquids to relieve cough.
If rash becomes infected or does not improve after 1 week of home treatment.	Keep affected areas cool and dry. Keep your child from activities that cause excessive perspiration. Seek out an air-conditioned environment for your child. Apply plain calamine lotion or cornstarch to affected areas.
If you even suspect scarlet fever.	Use acetaminophen (not aspirin) to reduce fever, offer plenty of liquids, be sure your child gets plenty of rest, and see your child's doctor for prescription antibiotics.

Shingles

If you have had chicken pox, you are a candidate for developing its sister disease, shingles. That's because you never actually "get rid" of the chicken pox virus once you've had it: Remnants of the virus remain in your body for the rest of your life, waiting for an opportunity (when you're stressed or your immune system is suppressed) to reappear as shingles.

Unlike chicken pox, the discomfort you experience with shingles may not go away when your blisters disappear. Indeed, almost half of people over age 60 who experience a bout of shingles develop chronic neuralgia, a lingering soft-tissue pain that results from inflamed nerve endings. Because the medications to treat shingles (acyclovir and valacyclovir) work best in the disease's early stages, it's a good idea to see your doctor as soon as you suspect you have shingles.

Symptoms/Signs

■ Pain or tingling that is usually limited to one side of your face or running like a belt around one side of your body, from spine to chest. This is followed by a red skin rash with small blisters filled with clear fluid that cloud and crust over after a few days. Early-stage symptoms may be preceded by flu-like symptoms.

Talk to Your Doctor If:

■ Pain from shingles is severe.

■ You suspect shingles within 48 hours of the onset of a rash.

■ You experience shingles symptoms accompanied by any eye pain, tearing, or involvement of the nose.

■ You experience chronic pain long after a shingles rash has disappeared.

Medication

• Take an over-the-counter analgesic (aspirin, acetaminophen, ibuprofen, or naproxen) for pain.
• Apply an antibiotic ointment to blisters to keep infection at bay.
• In the first 48 hours, ask your doctor if a prescription for valacyclovir or acyclovir will speed recovery time.
• Do not use the over-the-counter shingles remedy Zostrix® until blisters have disappeared. Zostrix® is intended only for late-stage shingles pain and can cause great discomfort if applied to blistered skin.

Heat/Cold

• Apply cool, wet compresses to affected areas to relieve pain.
• Avoid heat and direct sunlight.

Cover

• Keep blisters covered until they crust over to avoid spreading the shingles virus to someone else.

Prevention

• If you've never had chicken pox, ask your doctor about receiving a chicken pox immunization.

Spots and Moles

Skin spots are common—moles, freckles, birth-marks, age spots, etc. Such discolorations are almost always harmless; some even come and go over the course of a lifetime. Still, it's important to pay close attention to all of your spots or moles, because a sudden or marked change in them can mean trouble.

Home treatment is not recommended when you notice an abnormality because unusual spots and moles sometimes can pose a serious threat to your health. *Do not delay seeing your doctor.* Many forms of skin cancer spread rapidly to underlying tissue or to other parts of the body and can be deadly if not diagnosed and treated early (see "Self-Exams for Cancer," page 45).

Symptoms/Signs

■ Moles that are larger than a pencil eraser; asymmetrical; irregularly shaped; have a border that is not clearly defined; or contain shades of red, blue, white, or black.

■ Skin tags (small skin "stalks" or flap-like growths usually on the neck, armpits, upper trunk, and body folds) that become red and inflamed.

■ Yellow, brown, or black growths on face, chest, shoulders, and back that are slightly raised, waxy, or gritty, and may be more than an inch in diameter.

Call Your Doctor Right Away If:

■ Your spots or moles exhibit any of the above signs.

■ Any spot or mole suddenly changes in size, height, shape, or color.

■ Any spot or mole bleeds, itches, or becomes painful.

■ A skin tag becomes irritated or infected.

If physician referral is not recommended at this time, try the following:

Prevention

• Avoid getting sunburned: Wear sunscreen daily of at least SPF 15.

• If you are swimming or sweating profusely outdoors, choose water-proof sunscreen and reapply it every hour or so.

• If you're going to be out in the sun, wear loose-fitting clothes that offer the greatest coverage to exposed skin; also, wear a broad-brimmed hat.

• Eat a well-balanced diet rich in vitamins C and E, and beta carotene.

• Check your skin every month or so for unusual spots or moles, or changes in either. Use a hand mirror to check your scalp, the tops of your ears, the back of your neck, your back, and your thighs.

Sunburn

By now, most of us know that the sun's ultraviolet rays damage skin, causing it to age prematurely and increasing your risk of skin cancer. Still, millions of people every year suffer sunburns that kill off healthy skin cells and injure blood vessels close to the skin's surface. And anyone who experiences one or more blistering sunburns in a lifetime doubles his or her chances of melanoma, the deadliest form of skin cancer that kills more than 7,000 Americans every year.

The best way to avoid the damaging effects of the sun is to avoid sun exposure whenever possible—which, for most active people, isn't always practical. The good news is that adequate sunscreen and protective clothing can act as an effective shield to keep skin healthy. Remember, too, that a tan is no protection against the ill effects of the sun: It's simply another form of damage to delicate tissues that you're better off avoiding altogether.

Symptoms/Signs

- Skin is reddened and warm to the touch.
- Minor swelling and itching in affected areas.
- Blistering in more serious burns.

Talk to Your Doctor If:

- You have nausea, fever, chills, or lightheadedness.
- Blistering is extensive and severe.
- You develop a rash or notice patches of purple discoloration.
- Your sunburn seems to worsen or spread 24 hours after exposure.

If physician referral is not recommended at this time, try the following:

 Medication
- Take aspirin, acetaminophen, or ibuprofen to reduce swelling and relieve pain.

 Heat/Cold
- Apply cool compresses (use water) several times a day.

 Clean
- Avoid soap or use only a mild soap to wash burned areas; rinse well.

 Note Well
- Apply aloe vera gel or moisturizer to burned areas immediately after bathing.
- Never peel areas of skin where blisters have broken or dried.

 Prevention
- Apply sunscreen with an SPF of at least 15 whenever you're outdoors. Reapply often if you swim or sweat. Replace your sunscreen once a year.
- Use sunscreen on infants less than 6 months of age when adequate clothing and shade are not available.
- Wear loose, light, protective clothing—a hat, long sleeves, etc.
- Avoid exposure when the sun is most intense (between about 11 a.m. and 3 p.m. daylight saving time).
- A wet cotton T-shirt does not provide adequate protection.
- Be aware that certain medications and cosmetics can increase your risk of sunburn. Read labels carefully, and check with your doctor.

Warts

Warts are caused by a common virus—fortunately not by contact with toads—that anyone can contract through an open cut, usually on the hand or foot. Left untreated, almost any wart will go away on its own. However, it can take 2 years for that to happen.

Most people don't want to wait that long, so they try an over-the-counter wart preparation or a folk remedy. With a little HomeCare, common warts can disappear within a few weeks or a couple of months. More aggressive cures include freezing, laser treatments, special injections, burning, or cutting warts off, all of which have to be performed by your doctor. Whatever course you choose, it's important to be sure that what you're treating is really a wart and not some other, more serious skin condition that wart preparations could make worse.

Symptoms/Signs

■ Raised, flesh-colored growths, usually small and granular, that feel hard or rough on the surface, have dark dots or specks in the center, and are not covered by a smooth or continuous layer of skin.

■ Growths may appear in clusters.

■ Not painful, except in the case of plantar (foot) and genital warts.

Talk to Your Doctor If:

■ You have warts or granular growths in your genital or anal area.

■ A wart drains fluid or becomes irritated, painful, or inflamed.

■ A wart appears on your face or neck.

■ You have any doubt that the growth is a wart.

■ Any wart fails to respond to HomeCare within 2 weeks.

If physician referral is not recommended at this time, try the following:

Medication

• Apply an over-the-counter wart treatment (typically they contain salicylic acid as the active ingredient). Follow directions carefully to avoid irritating or ulcerating healthy skin surrounding wart; do not use if you have diabetes or impaired circulation.
• For plantar (foot) warts, apply Zeasorb® powder as needed to keep feet as dry as possible.

Cover

• For some home treatment preparations, use an adhesive bandage to keep medication from becoming washed or rubbed away.
• To relieve pressure and reduce the discomfort of plantar warts, use a pad made from foam rubber that is designed to pad calluses or corns.

Note Well

• Apply vitamin E oil, vitamin A oil (fish liver oil), castor oil, vitamin C paste (made from crushed vitamin C tablets and water), or Vergo® vitamin cream to the wart daily; cover with an adhesive bandage.
• If the wart bleeds, apply pressure to the area until the bleeding stops.

Prevention

• Wear shoes or rubber thongs around pool, spa, or locker-room areas.
• Treat any cut or skin abrasion right away, especially those near your fingernail or toenail cuticles: Wash the wound thoroughly with soap and water or alcohol, then apply antibacterial ointment and a bandage until the cut is healed.
• Try not to touch any warts (yours or other people's) directly.

Contact Dermatitis

Contact dermatitis is a rash caused by skin contact with an external chemical allergen. Common sources of dermatitis are poison ivy, poison oak, and poison sumac; insecticides; solvents; caustic industrial chemicals; cosmetics; jewelry; and synthetic fibers. With dermatitis, the rash often takes the outline of the offending agent, such as the elastic bands from undergarments, or is localized on one part of the body. See page 174. If a localized rash appears, it's important to identify the possible cause:

- Have you been close to poison ivy, poison sumac, or poison oak?
- Have you changed laundry detergents, soaps, deodorants, shampoos, or cosmetics?
- Have you been exposed to insecticides or other chemicals (e.g., dry-cleaning solvents)?
- Have you been wearing new clothing or jewelry?

Symptoms/Signs

- Localized rash that often takes the shape of the allergic agent or is limited to one part of the body.
- Skin rash from an allergic reaction to chemicals or plant oils, such as poison ivy, that can spread to other parts of the body. See "Poison Ivy," page 187.

Talk to Your Doctor If:

- The rash does not improve after 1 week.
- The rash becomes bright red, seeps pus, or has red streaks that come away from the affected area.
- You become feverish.
- Itching is severe and does not respond to HomeCare procedures.
- Rash is near your eyes, especially if the eyes are reddened or lids are severely swollen.

If physician referral is not recommended at this time, try the following:

Clean

- Wash with soap and water immediately after contact to remove chemicals or other agents. A cleaning solution such as Cetaphil® is better than soap. For oily substances, use rubbing alcohol, then use soap and water.
- Follow manufacturer's guidelines for exposure to chemicals or insecticides.

Medication

- Apply cool compresses of Burrow's solution (see your pharmacist) for cases of poison ivy, oak, or sumac. Use as directed.
- Antihistamines to reduce itching. Use as directed.

Cover

- If practical, do not cover. Expose the rash to air. Don't scratch it for relief. Scratching can spread the rash and cause infection.

Note Well

- Use hypoallergenic cosmetics.

Prevention

- Avoid areas that are infested with poison ivy, sumac, or oak.
- Handle chemicals with care.
- NEVER burn poison ivy, oak, or sumac.
- Avoid contact with things you know will cause an outbreak.

Food Allergy

Food allergies can affect people of all ages. In particular, foods such as peanuts, strawberries, citrus fruit, seafood, shellfish, wheat, eggs, nuts, beef, and cow's milk are linked to allergic reactions. There is some evidence that suggests that breastfeeding helps protect infants from future allergies. However, a family history of allergies is the best predictor of future allergy problems.

As with any allergy, avoiding contact with the allergen is the best self-care strategy. The best way to identify the food that causes the reaction is through a process of trial and error.

Symptoms/Signs

- Wheezing.
- Swelling of the lips, tongue, or throat.
- Skin rash or fainting.
- Itching of the palms, soles of the feet, or other parts of the body.
- Runny nose.
- Gastrointestinal distress such as cramping, vomiting, or diarrhea.

Get Emergency Care Right Away If:

You have an acute allergic reaction that produces severe breathing problems; wheezing; dizziness; shock; choking or difficulty swallowing; swelling of the lips, tongue, or throat; tightness in the chest; hives; or fainting.

Talk to Your Doctor If:

- You experience a rash without the symptoms described in the box above.

If physician referral is not recommended at this time, try the following:

Medication
- Antihistamines may be used for mild to moderate reactions.

Note Well
- Blow mucus gently from your nose. Do not blow hard: An ear infection or bloody nose could result.

Activity
- Reduce your activity when you have an allergic reaction.

Rest
- You may need to rest after an allergic reaction.

Nutrition
- You may want to try a soybean milk substitute if your infant shows intolerance to cow's milk. Talk to your doctor.
- Identify foods that may cause a reaction and avoid them.

Prevention
- Breastfeeding may build resistance to some allergies in infants.
- If known, avoid foods that cause allergic reactions.
- When starting infants on solids, avoid foods that are more likely to cause allergies.
- Read food labels carefully to identify and avoid substances (e.g., peanuts, shellfish) to which you are allergic.

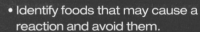

ALLERGIES

Hay Fever

Allergic rhinitis (hay fever) is the most common respiratory allergy and is a response to inhaled substances called allergens. For most people, allergy season is a period of moderate discomfort. But for others, pollen or dust can cause significant physical problems and be a year-round challenge.

Among adults, dust (especially dust mites), animal dander, molds, feathers, and pollen are the most common allergens. Among infants, animal dander and dust are the most common allergens.

In cases of severe allergy, professional medical consultation is recommended to determine the actual substances that cause the allergic reaction. Skin or blood tests may help determine the specific allergen. In some cases, hyposensitization injections help people with allergies become less sensitive to the allergen.

Most people who have mild to moderate hay fever can follow the HomeCare procedures listed. Whenever possible, avoiding the known allergens is the best course of action.

Symptoms/Signs

- Runny nose, sneezing.
- Watery, itchy eyes.
- Wheezing.
- Stuffy head, clogged sinuses, headache.
- Throat irritation, from postnasal drip.

Talk to Your Doctor If:

- You have difficulty breathing or severe wheezing.
- Nasal discharge is green or yellow.
- You would like more effective relief from your allergy symptoms than you are getting with HomeCare.
- Your symptoms are getting worse.

If physician referral is not recommended at this time, try the following:

Medication

- Antihistamines may help relieve your symptoms. *Use with caution; read the labels.*
- Nasal decongestants for stuffy head. (Don't use them for more than 3 days.)
- Cough drops will soothe your throat if it's irritated by postnasal drip.

Note Well

- Blow your nose gently to clear mucus. Do not blow hard, which may cause an ear infection or bloody nose.
- If cutting the lawn, gardening, dusting, or vacuuming aggravates your symptoms, wear an air-filtering mask while doing those chores.
- If you're allergic to molds, consider using an air conditioner with an electrostatic filter during the summer.

Rest

- You may need more rest when an allergic reaction strikes.

Prevention

- If possible, avoid contact with allergens that bother you.
- Keep house pets out of bedrooms.
- Try to keep your pet clean and groomed.
- Dust allergy can be reduced by wrapping your pillows and mattresses in special covers and washing sheets weekly in hot water (at least 130 F).
- Consider using a portable air filter in your bedroom.

Hives

Any time you have hives, your body is trying to send you a warning about something you've eaten or something that's bitten you. Insect venom, shellfish, nuts, certain berries, eggs, milk, antibiotics, and aspirin are common offenders. When an allergy-causing substance invades your system, your cells release chemicals called histamines, which in turn cause blood vessels to leak fluid into skin layers. The result is itchy, blotchy discomfort that can last for a few hours or a few days.

Hives by themselves generally are harmless and almost always respond to home treatment. The best treatment for all allergic reactions, of course, is to stay away from allergens.

Symptoms/Signs

- Raised, red, randomly distributed welts on the skin.
- Moderate to intense itching.

> ## Get Emergency Care Right Away If:
> - You have hives accompanied by tightness in the throat, wheezing, and shortness of breath.
> - You have hives in your mouth or throat.

Talk to Your Doctor If:

- You have chronic hives (a mild, lingering outbreak that lasts more than 6 weeks).
- You have a severe case of hives that does not respond to home treatment.

Medication

- Use an over-the-counter antihistamine such as Benadryl® to relieve itching.
- Apply calamine lotion to soothe itching.
- Hydrocortisone cream may relieve itching on a small area of the skin.
- If you're severely allergic to certain substances, ask your doctor if you should carry an allergy kit that contains injectable epinephrine to head off severe and potentially life-threatening reactions that usually begin with hives and shortness of breath.

Clean

- A lukewarm or tepid bath containing colloidal oatmeal (e.g., Aveeno®) can relieve itching temporarily.

Heat/Cold

- Cold compresses can help relieve itching.

Prevention

- If you are eating when an outbreak of hives occurs, stop. Chances are, something in the food is causing the reaction.
- Stay away from the substances to which you've had an allergic reaction in the past. Read food labels carefully.

Insect Bites and Stings

People react differently to insect bites or stings. In most cases an insect bite or sting is not serious, with discomfort limited to the area of the injury. However, some people may experience an extreme allergic reaction that requires immediate medical attention. This response can be caused by an individual's sensitivity to certain agents (e.g., bee venom) or by the toxicity of the agent, which causes a severe reaction in all victims.

Generally, there are two types of allergic reactions: a localized reaction and a generalized allergic reaction.

Symptoms/Signs: Localized

■ Swelling, itching, and redness that is limited to the site of the bite.

Get Emergency Care Right Away if:
You have a generalized (systemic) reaction, which may include hives covering the body, wheezing, tightness in the throat, shortness of breath, swollen eyes, and possible abdominal pain. **This is a life-threatening emergency.**

Talk to Your Doctor If:

■ You have a localized reaction that does not improve within 72 hours.

■ There are signs of infection after a localized reaction subsides (usually after 48 hours): fever, redness and swelling, and the presence of pus.

■ You think you may have been bitten by a mosquito and you have fever, headache, body aches, nausea, swollen lymph glands, weakness, tremors, and a skin rash on your torso. This may indicate West Nile virus.

If physician referral is not recommended at this time, try the following:

Note Well

- Bee sting: Remove the stinger as fast as possible to minimize the amount of venom it releases. Use tweezers, credit card, knife blade, fingernail, or fingers.
- Carry a kit containing epinephrine if you suffer generalized reactions and you regularly work or play outdoors. Instruct family and co-workers on its use, in case you're incapacitated. Talk to your doctor.
- Don't scratch an insect bite. This could cause infection.

Heat/Cold

- Apply ice or cold packs immediately following bite or sting.

Activity

- Reduce your activity immediately if you begin experiencing a generalized reaction.

Medication

- Try an oral or topical antihistamine to relieve itching.
- A paste made from baking soda or meat tenderizer also can be applied to the bite area.

Prevention

- Avoid places where insect bites and stings are more likely to happen.
- Use insect repellents that contain diethyltoluamide (DEET), especially at dusk and dawn.
- Avoid brightly colored clothes, as they may attract bees.
- Avoid using perfumes and scented soaps and shampoos when in grassy and wooded areas. These products attract insects.

Poison Ivy and Poison Oak

Skin rashes that develop as a result of contact with poisonous plants can range from mildly irritating to downright painful. Urushiol resin is present on the external parts of both poison ivy and poison oak. If your skin comes in contact with the resin, it becomes red and develops blisters that itch, usually within 24 to 48 hours after exposure. Neither fluid from broken blisters nor scratching will spread the rash. However, scratching can cause bacterial infection, which could lead to scarring. Severe cases may require medical treatment, but most of the time, rashes clear up on their own within 2 or 3 weeks. The best medicine: Learn to recognize and avoid poison ivy and poison oak (see the illustrations below). A general rule of thumb is: "Leaves of three, let it be."

Symptoms/Signs

- Raised, red patches or streaks on the skin.
- Blistering and minor swelling in affected areas.
- Moderate to severe itching at rash site.
- Watery liquid seeping from blisters.

Talk to Your Doctor If:

- You have a reaction involving your eyes, face, or genitals or that covers a large area.
- The rash is accompanied by fever or swollen lymph nodes, indicating an infection has set in.

Poison Ivy

Poison Oak

If physician referral is not recommended at this time, try the following:

Clean

- Wash thoroughly (within 5 to 10 minutes if possible) any skin that has come in contact with a poisonous plant. Use generous amounts of soap and water or isopropyl alcohol.
- Soap and water or alcohol can help keep the area free from infection after blisters have broken.
- *Never* clean skin with bleach or gasoline or other household chemicals.

Medication

- Plain calamine lotion (without antihistamines) may soothe the itch and act as a drying agent.

Heat/Cold

- Cold, wet compresses applied as needed will reduce itching and inflammation, especially after blisters have broken.

Cover

- Don't cover affected areas (except with loose, breathable clothing).

Prevention

- Remove poisonous plants from your property. Wear protective clothing, goggles, gloves, and a dust mask.
- Never burn poisonous plants. The smoke they produce carries urushiol resin dust.
- Avoid handling pets, clothing, or other objects that may have come in contact with poisonous plants.
- Try the over-the-counter barrier lotion Ivy Block® that can protect for up to 4 hours.

Achilles Injuries

Injuries to the Achilles tendon, which connects the calf muscle to the heel bone, are common among recreational and competitive athletes—especially those active in racket sports and long-distance running. Injuries to the Achilles tendon can cause a range of problems from tendinitis or bursitis, to complete rupture of the tendon.

Achilles tendon pain may come from overtraining and poor training techniques, insufficient blood flow to and within the tendon, mini-tears in the tendon, and over-pronation (rolling inward) of the foot.

Tenderness or pain in the Achilles tendon should be taken seriously because if you try to "play through the pain," it may rupture. Treatment for severe Achilles tendinitis involves reducing the inflammation first with medication and ice baths, and taking weight off the foot.

Symptoms/Signs

- Pain in the Achilles tendon (about 2 to 3 inches above heel), especially when running or jumping.

Talk to Your Doctor If:

- Discomfort and mobility do not improve with HomeCare.
- You experience a sudden, sharp pain in the Achilles tendon. You may hear a loud snapping or popping sound.
- Achilles tendon pain prevents you from putting some or all of your weight on the injured foot.

If physician referral is not recommended at this time, try the following:

Heat/Cold

- Apply ice packs for 20 minutes several times a day during the first 2 days, or for as long as the area is warm to the touch.
- Try applying heat packs to the injured area after inflammation has subsided.

Medication

- Try aspirin, naproxen, or ibuprofen for pain and inflammation.

Activity

- Decrease athletic activity by 50 percent.
- Once inflammation has subsided, exercise carefully with no force. Try stationary biking, rowing, stair climbing, and stretching.

NB Note Well

- Ask your doctor if you would benefit from adding a 3/8-inch heel lift to shoes during the recovery period.

Prevention

- Do regular conditioning exercises that include strengthening and stretching of all leg muscles.
- Warm up and cool down properly when exercising.
- Wear proper footwear that avoids overpronation of the foot. Consult a podiatrist if you have ongoing foot problems.
- Avoid overtraining and learn proper technique for your sport.

Ankle Injuries

The ankle is a hinge joint that connects the lower leg bones to the foot with many tough fibrous cords called ligaments. Because of these ligament "bridges," the ankle is quite strong and able to handle a lot of force and movement.

If you twist your ankle, these ligaments may be injured. An ankle **strain** occurs when the ligaments are stretched beyond their normal limit. An ankle **sprain** occurs when the ligaments are partially or completely torn.

You can twist your ankle by stopping suddenly or just putting your foot down the wrong way. People in occupations such as construction, ground maintenance, and surveying are prone to twisted ankles, as are those who engage in softball, basketball, and racquet sports.

Fortunately, most ankle injuries are not fractures or severe sprains, and can be treated using the self-care procedures listed under HomeCare.

Symptoms/Signs

- Swelling and pain in the ankle.
- General stiffness in the joint.
- Discoloration and/or a deformity in the joint.

Get Emergency Care Right Away If:
Your ankle appears bent or deformed in an odd way. This may indicate a fracture. Keep the ankle immobilized and apply ice.

Talk to Your Doctor If:

- You are unable to bear weight on the ankle or pain continues after 72 hours.
- Your ankle is swollen, black and blue.

HOMECARE™

If physician referral is not recommended at this time, try the following:

Heat/Cold
- Apply an ice pack to minimize swelling: Ice for 20 minutes; remove for 20 minutes. Continue for 2 to 3 hours or until the swelling is reduced.

Cover
- Wrap the ankle firmly in an elastic bandage for 24 to 48 hours, if the injury has significant swelling. Do not wrap it too tightly. It should provide comfort, not increase the pain.

Rest
- Rest the ankle for 12 to 24 hours; avoid putting weight on it.
- Keep the ankle elevated above heart level if swelling occurs.
- Expect limited range of motion for 2 weeks or longer.

Medication
- Aspirin, naproxen, or ibuprofen can be used to reduce pain and inflammation.

Activity
- Once pain and swelling have subsided, begin to rotate, flex, and extend the ankle gently three times a day to prevent adhesions.
- Use the ankle cautiously for 2 months after an injury.

Prevention
- Choose shoes with adequate ankle support.
- Beware of rough terrain that could cause a twisted ankle.

Arthritis

Arthritis is a painful condition of the joints (see pages 246–247). While there are more than 100 kinds of arthritis, most cases fall into one of these general categories:

- **Osteoarthritis.** The most common form of arthritis, it is characterized by a degeneration of the smooth cartilage that forms the surface of a joint (e.g., knee or hip). Developing symptoms of osteoarthritis usually is a by-product of aging. It also can result from an injury to the joint, or from repeated force that places an unnatural load on the joint.

- **Rheumatoid arthritis.** Rheumatoid arthritis is not a result of wear and tear on the joints. Although the direct cause is not known, researchers suspect that a virus may trigger a response by the immune system that causes inflammation in the joints. Besides inflammation and destruction of the joints, other body organs such as the heart, kidneys, lungs, skin, and eyes can be affected. It is more common in women between ages 20 and 50, but children also can get rheumatoid arthritis.

- **Gout.** Acute, severe pain and swelling in one joint (e.g., big toe) is caused by a buildup of uric acid crystals in the fluid that bathes the joint.

Symptoms/Signs

- Joint pain and stiffness, sometimes with heat and redness, and difficulty moving the joint(s).

Talk to Your Doctor If:

- You experience joint pain with flu-like symptoms (especially if you suspect a tick bite; see page 172).
- You can't move the joint through its range of motion because of pain, stiffness, or swelling.
- You have sudden onset of joint pain, swelling, and fever.

HOMECARE™

If physician referral is not recommended at this time, try the following:

Rest

- Rest the affected area when you experience flare-ups of inflammation.
- Balance rest with periods of activity.
- Those with rheumatoid arthritis may require up to 10 hours sleep per every 24 hours.

Heat/Cold

- Apply heating pads or hot towels to affected areas for 20 minutes.
- Ice packs can also be tried for up to 20 minutes at a time.

Medication

- Aspirin, naproxen, or ibuprofen can help arthritis pain. They also help with the swelling of rheumatoid arthritis. Acetaminophen can help arthritis pain, but not swelling.
- Over-the-counter lotions and creams containing capsaicin, camphor, or menthol may relieve minor joint pain of osteoarthritis.

Activity

- Gently move stiff joints through their ranges of motion, 3 times a day, 10 to 20 times per set.
- Activities such as water exercise and Tai Chi are excellent for many arthritic conditions. Consult your doctor if you've been inactive.

Note Well

- If you have difficulty with everyday activities (e.g., opening jars, holding utensils), consider buying user-friendly home aids.

Prevention

- Try to avoid heavy, repetitive strain on joints.
- Use proper equipment and techniques at work and play.
- Practice proper work posture.
- Try to keep your body weight within the recommended range. Excess body weight can place added stress on joints.

Back Pain

*I*t's estimated that more than two-thirds of all adults have had at least one episode of back pain. While most episodes of back pain will go away within a few days regardless of the treatment, for some people, pain management is an everyday concern.

Most lower back pain is caused by muscle spasm. Very few back problems are due to a slipped disk—when the disk bulges out and irritates the nerve roots.

Back problems can be traced to injury, poor posture, improper lifting techniques, repetitive twisting movements, sitting for long periods, vibration from vehicles and machinery, poor physical conditioning, and stress. See pages 251-255.

Symptoms/Signs

- Pain and stiffness in the back.
- Pain with other symptoms such as pain and numbness in a leg or foot or frequent urination.

Get Emergency Care Right Away If:

- Someone falls or is hit in the back and is unable to move his or her legs. Do not move the victim.
- You have low back pain with loss of bladder or bowel control.

Call Your Doctor Right Away If:

- You have low back pain with other physical symptoms such as painful or frequent urination, menstrual pain, flu, gastrointestinal distress, or abdominal pain.

Talk to Your Doctor If:

- Pain or numbness moves into the leg or foot.
- Pain is severe, even though you can still move.
- Low back pain is associated with weakness of any muscles in the leg or foot.
- HomeCare fails to provide relief after 72 hours.

HOMECARE™

If physician referral is not recommended at this time, try the following:

Rest

- Reduce your activity.
- For the first 24 to 48 hours with severe back pain, rest on a bed with your back flat and a pillow under your knees, or on your back on the floor with your lower legs bent 90 degrees and resting on a chair.
- Sleep on your side with your hips flexed 90 degrees and a pillow between your knees to prevent twisting of the spine.
- Recent studies have shown that prolonged bed rest aggravates back problems. Generally, getting up and about will speed recovery.
- Do flexibility stretches while resting.

Heat/Cold

- If you have an acute injury, apply ice packs (not a heating pad) for 20 minutes every hour, for the first 24 to 48 hours.
- Heat can be used for mild pain and discomfort.

Medication

- Aspirin, ibuprofen, or naproxen may help reduce pain and inflammation.

Prevention

- Practice proper lifting techniques. See pages 253-254.
- Keep back, leg, and abdominal muscles conditioned. See page 255.
- Use proper work posture.
- Do flexibility stretches. See pages 9-12.
- Practice aerobic conditioning and control your weight.
- Avoid sleeping on your stomach.

Broken Bones

Broken bones are classified in two categories: **closed fractures,** where the broken bone does not penetrate the skin; and **open fractures,** where the bone is forced through the skin, causing external injury and bleeding.

Consult your doctor if you suspect a bone fracture. However, every suspected fracture may not need immediate medical attention. Medical attention for simple fractures, such as those to the fingers, can be delayed for 24 hours if the affected area is immobilized with a splint. For example, you can tape the injured finger to the healthy finger next to it. Swelling can be treated with ice packs; pain can be reduced with aspirin or ibuprofen.

Symptoms/Signs

■ Limb or joint area may be deformed, sensitive to the touch or painful to move, have acute swelling, be discolored or cold, or have no feeling.

■ With an open fracture, the bone pierces the skin.

Get Emergency Care Right Away If:

• If there are signs of shock (see page 90).
• An open fracture is evident: The bone is sticking through the skin.
• The injury is to the neck or back and the victim is unable to move.

Call Your Doctor Right Away If:

■ The injury is deformed, sensitive to the touch, painful to move, shows acute swelling, is discolored or cold, or has no feeling.

If physician referral is not recommended at this time, try the following:

Rest

• If you're not sure you have a fracture and you don't have any serious medical conditions, rest and immobilize the area for 24 to 48 hours. See your doctor if your condition doesn't improve.

Heat/Cold

• Use ice packs in the first 24 to 48 hours if you're not sure there is a fracture.

Medication

• Aspirin, naproxen, or ibuprofen to reduce pain and inflammation.

Bursitis

You don't have to be an athlete or have a physically demanding job to suffer from bursitis. Bursitis can affect any one of the body's 150 bursae—tiny sacs of fluid found between moveable parts of the body (e.g., joints) that protect tissues (i.e., muscles and tendons) from friction. When you exercise too strenuously or too often, or when your work requires repetitive physical exertion, the friction from your movements can cause these sacs to become inflamed. The irritated bursae produce a chronic, dull ache that gets worse when you move. The resulting pain usually goes away within a week or so with proper treatment, but recurrent flare-ups are common and frustrating.

Symptoms/Signs

- Localized dull ache or stiffness, especially around joints.
- Pain is worse with movement.
- Affected area feels swollen or is warm or hot to the touch.

Talk to Your Doctor If:

- Bursitis pain is disabling or doesn't go away after 10 days of home treatment.
- You notice excessive swelling, bruising, or a rash in the affected area.
- Pain is sharp or shooting, especially when you exercise or exert yourself.
- Pain is worse in the morning, and you have a fever.

If physician referral is not recommended at this time, try the following:

Medication

- Take aspirin, naproxen, or ibuprofen for pain and inflammation.

Heat/Cold

- Apply ice packs for 20 minutes several times a day during the first 2 days, or for as long as the joint area is warm to the touch.
- After the joint is no longer warm, apply heat to stimulate blood flow.

Activity

- Stop any activity that you suspect has caused the pain or that makes the pain worse.
- Use stretching exercises to speed recovery and to restore full range of motion.

Note Well

If the joint is swollen:
- Wrap the injured area during waking hours with an elastic bandage.
- Elevate the injured joint above your heart to help reduce swelling.
- Do not massage the affected area.

Prevention

- Warm up and stretch before physical activity.
- If your work is physically strenuous, pace yourself and take breaks often.
- Avoid resting your elbow on hard surfaces (e.g., your desk).
- Use knee pads or a cushion when you kneel.
- Avoid shoes that don't fit or that have worn-down heels.
- Don't sit for long periods of time. Get up and move about.

Elbow Pain

lbow pain can be caused by bursitis (see page 193) at the tip of the elbow; an irritation of the tendon that slides over the elbow joint (tennis elbow); hyperextending (locking) the arm; or direct injury, such as chipping a bone or tearing the soft tissues around the joint.

In most cases, elbow pain results from repetitive movements that place strain on the soft tissues around the elbow. Tennis elbow is common in sports such as tennis or baseball, and in jobs that require rolling or twisting hand or arm movements, such as assembly, carpentry, or meat packing.

Symptoms/Signs

■ Severe pain at rest or during movement.

■ Swelling and redness in the joint.

■ Abrasion with bleeding and torn skin (see page 152).

Call Your Doctor Right Away If:

■ You have disfigurement and severe pain of the elbow joint due to a fall or collision.

■ You suspect a fracture or dislocation of elbow due to a fall or direct injury.

■ You cannot move your elbow (elbow seems locked).

Talk to Your Doctor If:

■ There are signs of infection: fever, redness, heat, and swelling in the elbow.

■ There is numbness or weakness in the hand.

■ Pain is not reduced after 2 weeks of HomeCare.

If physician referral is not recommended at this time, try the following:

Medication

- Aspirin, naproxen, or ibuprofen may help reduce inflammation and discomfort.

Heat/Cold

- For the first 48 hours, apply ice packs to the elbow for 20 minutes, several times a day.
- Heating pads are not recommended if swelling is present.

Rest

- Rest the elbow for 1 to 2 days; a sling may help.
- Avoid repetitive movements and stress on the elbow joint.

Activity

- After 48 hours, move the elbow through its full range of movement every hour.
- Strengthen and stretch the forearm and shoulder muscles once the pain has subsided, and before activity.

Prevention

- Use equipment that fits properly (e.g., a screwdriver handle that fits the hand or a tennis racquet with a grip and weight appropriate for you).
- Keep your forearm muscles strong.
- Take regular stretch breaks, especially if you do repetitive tasks.
- Maintain proper posture.
- Use proper technique when performing tasks that require repetitive movements.

Finger Pain

Almost all finger pain is related to arthritis. In fact, pain in the fingers can be one of the first signs of both osteoarthritis and rheumatoid arthritis. See pages 190 and 246–247.

Occasionally, sore fingers are not caused by arthritis. A mother will sometimes have sore fingers after the birth of her child; the pain can last up to a year, but usually diminishes over time. Gout, although most often associated with pain in the big toe, can affect a finger with sudden, intense pain, swelling, and redness.

Carpal tunnel syndrome, a nerve problem in the wrist, is a cause of numbness and tingling in the fingers and can seriously limit their use.

Symptoms/Signs

- Pain and swelling of finger joints.
- Overall aching or stiffness of finger joints.
- Pain or numbness in fingers after use or exertion.

Talk to Your Doctor If:

- HomeCare does not relieve discomfort after 6 weeks.
- You experience sudden or unexplained swelling and pain in finger joints.
- You have finger pain accompanied by fever.
- You cannot use your finger(s) as a result of pain or swelling.
- You have numbness in the fingers (except the little and ring fingers) and tingling in the fingers when the inside of the wrist is tapped. This may indicate carpal tunnel syndrome. See page 205.

HOMECARE™

If physician referral is not recommended at this time, try the following:

Medication

- Aspirin, acetaminophen, ibuprofen, naproxen may be used to relieve pain.
- Use acetaminophen for finger pain without inflammation.
- Over-the-counter lotions and creams containing capsaicin, camphor, or menthol may relieve minor joint pain of osteoarthritis.
- For severe and chronic pain, your doctor may prescribe corticosteroid injections or other drug therapies.

Heat/Cold

- Apply ice for 20 minutes several times a day if swelling is present.
- Apply warm compresses as needed to relieve stiffness.
- Keep hands warm and covered in cold weather.

Note Well

- Avoid overusing your hands and fingers whenever possible.

Rest

- Get plenty of rest. If you have rheumatoid arthritis, you may need about 10 hours of sleep in a 24-hour period.

Prevention

- Avoid repetitive activities that overuse the joints in the fingers.
- Use assistive devices such as faucet turners, openers for jars, and extended handles for grooming aids if you have trouble grasping objects.

Foot Pain

If physician referral is not recommended at this time, try the following:

There are many reasons for foot pain, however, the causes of foot pain in the elderly are the most serious. Gout, peripheral nerve degeneration caused by diabetes or rheumatoid arthritis, and blood vessel disease all can place a great deal of stress on the joints, muscles, and circulation of the feet. Unfortunately, in the advanced stages of some diseases, it is difficult to feel "warning" pain, so sores on the feet and circulatory problems are more likely. And, if left untreated, serious complications, such as tissue death, gangrene, and amputation, can follow.

If you have foot pain from any disease that could quickly compromise the health of your feet, take special care to avoid cuts, blisters, sprains, or fractures. Inspect your feet often for redness, swelling, or sores. Try to improve your general health so that your feet aren't as vulnerable to damage from infection or poor circulation.

Symptoms/Signs

- Pain, inflammation, swelling, or redness in one or more toe joints.
- Generalized muscle pain or sensitivity in the feet.
- Generalized foot pain that is preceded by tingling or numbness.

Talk to Your Doctor If:

- You have severe pain, swelling, stiffness, and redness in any toe joint.
- Foot pain from arthritis makes it difficult for you to perform daily tasks.
- You experience repeated pain in the arch of your foot.
- Moderate to severe foot pain is preceded by tingling and numbness in the foot, and is accompanied by loss of bladder or bowel control, weakness, or partial paralysis.

Medication

- Try nonsteroidal anti-inflammatory drugs (e.g., ibuprofen, naproxen) to treat the symptoms of gout and osteoarthritis, or relieve foot pain in general.
- Foot pain associated with peripheral vascular disease or rheumatoid arthritis may require prescription medication.

Heat/Cold

- Hot or cold compresses may relieve pain associated with rheumatoid arthritis.

Clean

- Keep your feet clean and treat any open sore or wound on the foot immediately, especially if you're diabetic.

Note Well

- Wear socks or support stockings and supportive shoes that fit properly.
- Rest inflamed joints, especially during severe episodes.

Prevention

- Don't smoke.
- Improve your general health: exercise regularly, eat a well-balanced diet, and manage stress.
- Climb stairs with your stronger leg (foot) first and with your weaker leg when descending.

Foot Pain
(Fasciitis)

Plantar fasciitis is a common foot injury among active people such as runners and dancers. The plantar fascia is a thick, fibrous band of tissue that runs along the bottom of the foot from the base of the toes to the heel. The fascia can become inflamed when excess stress is placed on this area, which causes the tissue to tear. Over time, scar tissue forms over the tears and makes the fascia stiff and less flexible. Bone spurs can form when the fascia begins to tear away from the heel bone.

Plantar fasciitis can be caused by high arches or flat feet that overpronate (the foot rolls inward too much when the foot is planted), rigid soles that cause the fascia to stretch, or worn-out footwear that doesn't provide enough support.

If you have heel pain related to fasciitis or a bruised heel, commercial heel pads can be just as effective as specially fitted orthotics. Persistent pain may require medical consultation. You may consider consulting with a podiatrist who is familiar with this kind of overuse injury. Treatment may include ultrasound, friction massage, and, perhaps, special shoe inserts (orthotics) that place the foot in a "neutral" position. In severe cases, surgery may be necessary.

Symptoms/Signs

■ Pain on the bottom of the foot in the mid-heel area that is more noticeable in the morning or at the beginning of an activity.

Talk to Your Doctor If:

■ HomeCare measures do not improve your condition after 4 weeks.

If physician referral is not recommended at this time, try the following:

Heat/Cold

- Apply ice packs for 20 minutes several times a day during the first 2 days, or for as long as the area is warm to the touch.
- Try warm whirlpool baths after pain and inflammation have subsided.

Medication

- Take aspirin, naproxen, or ibuprofen for pain and inflammation.

Activity

- Decrease athletic activity by 50 percent.
- Once inflammation has subsided: Sit on the edge of a chair with a towel spread out on the floor in front of you. In your bare feet, crimp your toes and grab the towel with them. Repeat this 5 to 10 times per session, 2 sessions per day.
- Stretch the front of your shin and calf muscles. Refer to page 12.

Note Well

- Take pressure off of a bone spur: Cut out a circle to fit your heel from foam that has adhesive backing on one side. Then, cut a hole out of the middle.

Prevention

- Wear footwear that provides adequate support.
- Avoid running on crowned roads (higher in the middle and lower at the shoulder).
- Strengthen the front of your shin and your calf muscles.
- Warm up and cool down properly when exercising.
- Avoid exercising on hard surfaces.

Knee Pain

Actions that twist or put excessive force on the inside or outside of the knee joint can easily stretch or tear the ligaments and damage the cartilage that support and protect the knee.

Knee pain also can be caused by a repeated force placed on the knee, such as during prolonged kneeling. Over time, the bursae (protective fluid sacs) of the knee can become inflamed and cause pain. See page 193.

Another cause of knee pain is runner's knee—a gradual wearing away of the cartilage behind the kneecap. Runner's knee usually is traced to weak thigh muscles, running on crowned roads (roads that slope from middle to edge), and pronation—the ankle tips inward.

Osteoarthritis is another cause of knee pain that usually is caused by general wear and tear of the cartilage over many years. Exercise will help stabilize the knee joint and reduce deterioration. When other conservative treatments fail, surgery or complete knee replacement is sometimes recommended. See pages 246–247.

Call Your Doctor Right Away If:

■ You have an injury that prevents you from walking or putting full weight on the injured leg, or your knee cannot be straightened or wobbles from side to side.

■ Your knee has rapid, extensive swelling.

Talk to Your Doctor If:

■ Knee pain is accompanied by fever.

■ You have dull pain or discomfort related to jogging, cycling, or prolonged kneeling, that's behind or around the kneecap and doesn't go away after 4 weeks of HomeCare.

■ You have pain or swelling in your calf muscle, below the back of your knee.

If physician referral is not recommended at this time, try the following:

Rest

• Avoid activities that may place stress on the knee.
• To prevent your knee from locking, sleep with a pillow under your knee, but change positions and straighten it periodically.
• A cane or crutches may help take weight off the injured knee.

Medication

• Aspirin, naproxen, or ibuprofen may help to reduce pain and inflammation.

Heat/Cold

• Apply an ice pack for the first 24 to 48 hours after injury: 20 minutes on, 20 minutes off.
• Hot bath or whirlpool may help thereafter.

Activity

• Avoid keeping the knee in a fixed position for extended periods of time. Every hour, gently straighten and flex the injured leg.
• Once the knee is healed, strengthen the front and back thigh muscles. See page 15.
• Consider consulting a sports trainer.
• Walking or doing pool exercises are excellent options.

Prevention

• Wear knee pads if your job requires prolonged kneeling.
• If you jog or run, wear the proper shoes; consider using orthotics; avoid uneven surfaces and crowned roads.

Leg Pain

Most leg pain or cramps result from sudden trauma, overuse, improper footwear, or poor technique during sports activities. And most occasional leg pain or cramps can be treated with self-care. However, leg pain can flare up suddenly for no apparent reason. Phlebitis, inflammation of a vein in the leg, can be life-threatening if blood clots form, break away, and lodge in the lungs.

Symptoms/Signs

- **Phlebitis:** the leg is painful, swollen, hot, and feels heavy.
- **Leg cramps:** muscle becomes tightly and painfully contracted (balled up), often during sleep.
- **Shin splints:** shooting or stabbing pain along the shins with each step. See page 202.
- **Mild strains:** extreme muscle tenderness. See page 200.
- **Sprains:** shooting pain, severe swelling, and bruising of the injured joint.
- **Tendinitis:** tenderness, warmth, swelling and/or pain in knees or ankles; pain is intense when you begin an activity, diminishes as you continue, and is sharp once you've stopped. See page 204.

Get Emergency Care Right Away If:
- You have signs of phlebitis (see above).
- You have shortness of breath or chest pain, with or without symptoms of phlebitis.

Talk to Your Doctor If:

- You have an injury to your leg with tingling, numbness, radiating pain, swelling or bruising that worsens after home treatment, or you are unable to put weight on the leg after 24 hours.
- You experience swelling or numbness in any part of the leg, or lingering leg muscle or joint pain that has no apparent cause.

If physician referral is not recommended at this time, try the following:

Rest

- Unless an injury is severe, rest for no more than 48 hours, since mild to moderate exercise will increase blood flow and encourage healing.

Heat/Cold

- Apply ice immediately to any injured area.
- Before exercising, apply warm compresses to affected areas.
- Apply ice to affected areas after exercise.

Cover

- Use a flexible brace or wrap only during and shortly after periods of activity.
- With an injury, compress affected area between icings to reduce swelling.

Medication

- Try aspirin, naproxen, or ibuprofen, which may help reduce pain and inflammation.

Prevention

- Warm up before and cool down after exercise. Stretch leg muscles. See page 12.
- Drink plenty of fluids.
- Vary your activities to avoid overuse.
- Moderate, daily exercise is safer than the strain of occasional strenuous activity.
- Use proper equipment and technique for every sport or activity.
- Jog on a running track instead of asphalt; play or work out on wood floors instead of concrete.

Muscle Strains

Your weekend softball game ends suddenly when, rounding first base, you feel sudden pain in the back of your thigh. Muscle strains such as this, often called muscle pulls, are tears or stretches in the muscle fibers or the tendons that connect muscles to bones. Strains can range from relatively mild injuries, with some muscle fibers being torn, to large muscle tears with swelling and bleeding present. Causes of muscle strain include:

■ **Muscle imbalance:** one side of the joint is stronger than the other, or while one muscle contracts, the opposite muscle doesn't relax, from either a lack of conditioning or overtraining one muscle group more than the opposing muscle group.

■ **Muscle fatigue** places additional stress on the muscle and tendons.

The more active you are, the greater your risk of injury. But, if you're not usually active, you are at greater risk when you suddenly engage in an activity.* It's important, therefore, for the *weekend warrior* as well as the serious runner to take the time to get into condition for their activities.

Symptoms/Signs

■ Pain, swelling, and tenderness in a muscle or joint that worsens with movement or pressure.

Talk to Your Doctor If:

■ Excessive swelling, bruising, and/or tenderness in the injured area lasts more than 48 hours.

■ Pain that prevents you from moving comfortably lasts more than 48 hours.

* *If you have been physically inactive or have a health problem, talk with your doctor before beginning any physical activity program.*

HOMECARE™

If physician referral is not recommended at this time, try the following:

Rest

• Reduce your activity. Avoid movements that place stress on the injured area.

Heat/Cold

• Apply cold pack or ice massage: 20 minutes on, 20 minutes off for 2 hours. Continue for 24 to 48 hours after the injury.
• Try heating pads, whirlpools, or analgesic balms on the third day if swelling is gone.

Cover

• Wrap the injured area with an elastic bandage—snugly, but not too tightly.

Note Well

• Elevate the injured area for 24 to 48 hours, depending on the severity of the injury.

Medication

• Aspirin, naproxen, or ibuprofen may help to reduce pain and inflammation.

Activity

• Try slow, gentle stretches if the strain is mild, but hold off for a few days if the injury is moderate or severe; try general movements (e.g., slow walking, gentle arm circles) to promote circulation.
• Condition properly for your activity.
• Use weight training to achieve adequate levels of strength in major muscle groups and their opposing muscles.

Neck Pain

Common causes of neck pain include poor posture, arthritis, injury, or stress. At work, sitting for prolonged periods of time in a fixed position can lead to occasional stiffness or cramping. This is common among people who do word processing or data entry. At home, a poor sleeping position may contribute to neck pain. Often, simply changing to a thinner pillow will correct the problem.

Many people respond to emotional stress by tensing the neck muscles. Over time this can lead to both neck pain and headaches.

Neck pain also can be caused by blows to the head and neck, as in the case of falls and motor vehicle accidents. Sudden twisting or snapping of the head (whiplash) can lead to muscle strain and ligament damage. A pinched nerve also can be a consequence of neck injury or arthritis.

Symptoms/Signs

- Stiffness and/or pain in the neck.
- Pain that radiates down the arm or tingling in the hands.

Get Emergency Care Right Away If:

- You have symptoms of meningitis: fever, headache, and a stiff neck that prevents you from touching the chin to the chest.
- Neck pain is related to an acute injury or blow to the head.

Talk to Your Doctor If:

- Pain radiates down the arm or you experience tingling in your hands.
- Pain does not lessen after 4 days.

If physician referral is not recommended at this time, try the following:

Medication

- Aspirin, naproxen, or ibuprofen to relieve pain and inflammation.

Heat/Cold

- Try hot showers, hot compresses, or a heating pad. Besides relaxing tense muscles, stretching is easier after muscles are warmed.

Note Well

- Fold a small towel lengthwise to form a 4-inch band. Wrap it around the neck before bedtime.

Activity

- Stay physically active.
- Practice neck stretches. See page 10.

Prevention

- If you have pain in the morning, try using a pillow with better support.
- Practice proper posture when doing repetitious tasks such as word processing and lifting. Take a break every hour.
- Do exercises that stretch the muscles of the neck and shoulders. See pages 10-11.
- Learn a general relaxation technique. See pages 33-34.
- Massage your neck muscles.

Shin Pain

Shin splints are the result of pounding too long on a surface that's too hard, especially when your legs aren't conditioned properly. Dancers, basketball players, runners, race walkers, or average people, who change their routine or get back into exercising after a long break are most susceptible.

When you perform a weight-bearing exercise, your leg muscles swell slightly and press against the bones in your lower leg. Too much exercise causes these muscles (as well as the surrounding ligaments, tendons, and bones) to become irritated and inflamed. When that happens, you have shin splints; when you really overdo it, you risk going beyond shin splints to a stress fracture.

Fortunately, shin splints aren't serious and almost never require medical attention. The best course of action is to take it easy and use HomeCare measures for 2 or 3 weeks to allow your muscles to heal.

Symptoms/Signs

■ Dull ache (at rest) or shooting pain (when bearing weight) on the shin, the long bone that runs along the front of the leg from knee to ankle.

Talk to Your Doctor If:

■ Home treatment does not relieve shin splints within 3 weeks.
■ You have a small area (about the size of a nickel) of stabbing pain on a bony area of your lower leg.

Rest

- Rest your legs from moderate- or high-impact activity for 2 to 3 weeks after the onset of pain.
- After the pain of shin splints has subsided, resume regular exercise and activity gradually and at a lower intensity. Never exercise "through the pain." Try non-impact activities such as bicycling or swimming until pain is completely gone.

Heat/Cold

- Apply ice to affected areas for first 24 to 48 hours to reduce swelling and inflammation.
- Apply warm compresses or low heat to affected areas to reduce discomfort and speed healing.

Medication

- Aspirin, naproxen, or ibuprofen may help to reduce pain and inflammation.

Cover

- For comfort and support, use a flexible brace or wrap (e.g., an Ace® bandage) only during and shortly after periods of activity.

Prevention

- Wear cushioned footwear with good arch support that fits properly. Replace worn shoes.
- Get into shape gradually.
- Jog or walk on a running track, grass, or dirt trail instead of asphalt or concrete; look for wood floors instead of concrete for basketball or aerobics workouts.
- Warm up before and cool down after each workout.
- Stretch shin and calf muscles daily. See pages 10–12.

Shoulder Pain

According to the old saying, "putting your shoulder to the wheel" might help you get the job done. However, every year, more than 4 million Americans see their doctors for painful shoulder conditions that interfere with their ability to do their jobs and enjoy recreational activities.

The shoulder joint has the widest range of motion of any joint in the body. Because of this, the shoulder joint is also unstable and can give rise to a variety of painful problems. While you may be able to trace your shoulder pain to a particular injury, most shoulder pain comes from strain, overuse, general wear and tear over time, or arthritis.

Symptoms/Signs:

- **Bursitis:** mild to severe pain with limited movement. See page 193.
- **Rotator cuff tear:** constant pain (especially with overhead activities), limited motion, pain at night, usually happens in your dominant arm.
- **Frozen shoulder:** feels stiff and tight; hard to lift arm overhead, reach behind back or across chest; limited motion.
- **Arthritis:** pain and swelling, limited motion. Joint may feel warm. See pages 190, 246–247.

Call Your Doctor Right Away If:

- Your arm is numb and weak and looks out of position, or you have pain and tenderness and a bump on the middle top of your shoulder. These may be signs of shoulder dislocation or separation.
- You have severe pain, bruising, and redness after an injury. This may indicate a fracture.

Talk to Your Doctor If:

- HomeCare measures don't bring relief after 1 week.

If physician referral is not recommended at this time, try the following:

Rest

- Rest an injured shoulder for 48 hours.
- If a certain activity aggravates your shoulder pain, let the joint rest for a few days before trying it again.

Heat/Cold

- Apply an ice pack to the injury for 20 minutes, four to eight times a day.
- For an old shoulder injury, warm the joint before activity and apply an ice pack afterwards.

Medication

- Try aspirin, naproxen, or ibuprofen for pain and stiffness.
- Your doctor may prescribe other anti-inflammatory medication, muscle relaxers, or injections to reduce symptoms.

Activity

- Try to keep joints flexible with regular activity and stretching. Limiting movement may cause your shoulder to become stiff and immobile.
- Before using a shoulder that has been injured, warm it up by moving at 70 percent of maximum effort, and then stretch it.
- Your doctor may prescribe physical therapy.

Cover

- If your shoulder is injured, keep it elevated (above the level of your heart) and wrap with an elastic bandage to reduce swelling and add stability.

Prevention

- Follow all safety (and ergonomic) practices associated with your job.
- Allow some time to get into shape for your activity. Being a *weekend warrior* stresses unconditioned joints.
- Learn proper form and technique for recreational sports.

Tendinitis

Anytime you overuse or misuse a muscle, you risk injuring the fibrous bands of tissue—called tendons—which connect that muscle to a bone. The resulting tendinitis (microscopic tears and an inflammation of the tendon), although quite painful and physically limiting, usually clears up if you give the damaged tissue time to heal. By playing, or working, through the pain without adequate rest, you risk damage that can require a long rehabilitation or even surgery to correct. If you have chronic tendinitis, it's possible that you may never regain full use of the affected joint area, even after therapy.

As soon as you notice pain or inflammation, ice down the sore area, give it a few days of rest, then gradually start exercising again to get the blood moving and speed healing to the tendon. Prevention that includes using proper conditioning, technique, and equipment is the best defense against tendinitis.

Symptoms/Signs

- Tenderness, warmth, swelling, and/or pain in joint areas (especially knees, wrists, shoulders, and ankles).
- Joint-area pain that is intense when you begin an activity, diminishes as you continue, and is sharp once you've stopped.

Talk to Your Doctor If:

- You have severe, radiating, or persistent muscle pain.
- You experience numbness or tingling.
- Pain worsens over time or persists for more than 10 days despite self-care measures.
- You experience sudden pain with a snapping sound such as in your Achilles tendon below the calf.

Rest

- Rest the injured area for no more than 48 hours or until swelling and pain has subsided (exercise will increase blood flow.) Try not to stress the injured area with too much repetition of movement.

Heat/Cold

- Apply ice to the injured area for 20 minutes on, 20 minutes off for the first 48 hours after injury.
- Try warm compresses or minimal heat to the injured area after swelling and pain have subsided.

Cover

- If the injury is severe, wrap the area with an elastic bandage or wear a brace.

Medication

- To reduce pain and inflammation, take aspirin, naproxen, or ibuprofen.

Activity

- Return to your activity gradually. Do not play or work through the pain.
- Stretch all muscle groups daily.
- Vary your activities to increase flexibility and avoid overuse.
- Get into condition for your activity, using proper technique and equipment.

Wrist Pain

The wrist consists of eight bones forming a stable platform that allows the hand to move freely. When the hand is bent back or dropped down, it places stress on the tendons and nerves that pass through the wrist. If the wrist is locked in either position for extended periods, damage and pain can occur. Therefore, for activities such as word processing or data entry keep your hands and wrists in a flat, neutral position.

Nerve entrapment, such as carpal tunnel syndrome (CTS), commonly occurs among people whose work requires them to do repetitive movements with their hands. Pregnancy also increases the risk of CTS. Other causes of wrist pain include rheumatoid arthritis, osteoarthritis, and injuries due to falls or trauma.

Symptoms/Signs

- Symptoms of nerve entrapment include pain in the wrist and forearm; weakness and loss of mobility in the hand; numbness in the fingers, except the little and ring fingers; and tingling in the fingers when the inside of the wrist is tapped.
- Severe pain, swelling, and discoloring after trauma to the wrist (e.g., falling on your wrist, hitting your hand).

Talk to Your Doctor If:

- You have fever, swelling, or severe pain even at rest.
- You have weakness, numbness, or tingling in your fingers that doesn't go away after 48 hours of following HomeCare.
- Your wrist is deformed, discolored, swollen, or sore to the touch after an accident.

If physician referral is not recommended at this time, try the following:

Rest

- Chronic wrist pain requires rest from the activity that caused the problem; 1 to 2 weeks is usually adequate.

Medication

- Aspirin, naproxen, or ibuprofen may help reduce inflammation.

Note Well

- Try a splint from a drugstore or medical supply house for a few days and then at night for 3 weeks.

Prevention

- Strengthen your forearm muscles. Squeeze a tennis ball 20 times, 3 times per day.
- Stretch your fingers and wrists every hour—but not if you experience pain in your wrists or hands.
- Use proper posture and technique for doing repetitive tasks.
- Consider using a wrist pad when you are typing.

Computer Posture

- Sit up straight with your lower back supported properly.
- Keep your wrists in a flat, neutral position.
- Rest your feet comfortably on the floor or on a footrest with your knees and ankles bent at 90-degree angles.

Anxiety

Fear and anxiety can be normal reactions to frightening or stressful situations. And, in small doses, anxiety can be helpful. It may motivate you to rehearse a speech, lock the front door, and file your taxes on time. But sometimes anxiety can become overwhelming, causing a sense of fear and dread for no apparent reason. Types of anxiety disorders include: generalized anxiety disorder (GAD), social anxiety (or phobia), panic disorder, obsessive-compulsive disorder (OCD), and post-traumatic stress disorder (PTSD).

Treatment for anxiety should involve psychological counseling (talk therapy) with or without medication. It's important to talk with your doctor about your concerns and fears.

Symptoms/Signs

- Feelings of excessive worry, helplessness, or unreality.
- Physical signs such as pounding heartbeat, headaches, dizziness, diarrhea, nausea, trembling, twitching, sweating.
- Sleep problems or ongoing fatigue.
- Restlessness, or feeling *keyed up*.
- Avoidance of situations that arouse fear.

Get Emergency Care Right Away If:

You experience chest pain, dizziness, shortness of breath, or an ongoing stomach problem.

Talk to Your Doctor If:

- Anxiety interferes with your ability to function normally (e.g., you stay home more, avoid certain everyday situations, etc.).
- Anxiety is associated with depression. See page 207.

If physician referral is not recommended at this time, try the following:

Activity

- Exercise every day to relieve tension and activate body chemicals that relieve anxiety, make you feel more calm, and improve sleep.

Rest

- Learn and practice relaxation techniques such as progressive muscle relaxation and breathing exercises to control anxiety symptoms. See page 33.

Note Well

- Confide in a friend or family member. It helps to share your feelings with someone you trust.
- If your home, work, or personal life is limited by your fears or anxiety, or if you feel depressed by these worries, consult with your company's employee assistance program (EAP) if available, a qualified counselor, or your doctor.

Prevention

- Avoid alcohol, caffeine, decongestants, antihistamines, diet pills, or other drugs that can worsen the symptoms of anxiety.

Depression

*I*f you find that you feel down frequently and have lost interest in activities that you usually enjoy, you may be depressed. If you have a chronic illness such as asthma, arthritis, diabetes, heart disease, or migraine, your risk of depression is higher. Depression can be mild, severe, or ongoing for 2 years or more.

Depression may be produced by a combination of genetic, psychological, and medical factors. Life events such as the death of a family member may lead to a depressive episode, but sadness and grief should not be assumed to be clinical depression. Medications (e.g., beta blockers, steroids, and cancer drugs) or withdrawal from stimulants (e.g., cocaine and amphetamines) also can trigger depression.

Most people with depression can be treated successfully with medication alone or combined with psychotherapy. See pages 264-265.

Symptoms/Signs

At least one of these first two:
- Feeling sad, blue, or down in the dumps.
- Loss of interest in things that were once enjoyable.

With at least four of the following, nearly every day:
- Losing or gaining weight.
- Feeling tired or having low energy all the time.
- Difficulty concentrating or making decisions.
- Racing thoughts or slowed thinking.
- Feeling worthless or guilty.
- Trouble sleeping, or sleeping too much.
- Thoughts of death or suicide.

Call Your Doctor Right Away If:

- You have any thoughts of suicide; or call a suicide prevention hotline, found in the local white pages.
- You see signs of depression in yourself or a loved one.

If physician referral is not recommended at this time, try the following:

Note Well

- Confide in a friend or family member. It helps to share your feelings with someone you trust.
- If your home, work, or personal life is limited by your depression, consult with your EAP (if available), a qualified counselor, or your doctor.
- Avoid using alcohol to cope with your problems.

Medication

- Avoid mood-altering drugs, especially illicit drugs such as marijuana, cocaine, amphetamines, or barbiturates.
- Use prescription drugs only as directed.

Rest

- Use a relaxation technique to help reduce tension. See pages 33-34.

Activity

- Exercise can boost your energy level and your sense of well-being. In particular, moderate exercise, such as walking, may help prevent depression or lessen its severity.

Nutrition

- Eat well-balanced meals to keep your energy level up.
- Be aware that overeating is common with depression.

Insomnia

People rarely take their sleep problems seriously, let alone talk about their sleep difficulties with their doctors. However, the consequences of sleeplessness—fatigue, low energy, and poor concentration—are significant causes of irritability, unhappiness, reduced work performance, and increased accidents.

Habits such as using caffeine, exercising close to bedtime, napping during the day, or feeling stressed or excited can disrupt sleep patterns. Drinking alcohol may make getting to sleep difficult or cause awakening shortly after getting to sleep.

The chronic use of sleep aids such as antihistamines or sedatives (sleeping pills) can create dependency and increased tolerance, producing a cycle of unnatural sleep patterns and more fatigue. If a sleep aid is prescribed by your doctor, it should be used short-term along with sensible stress management and HomeCare.

Restless legs syndrome can disrupt sleep as well. The legs (or feet or arms) feel uncomfortable at rest, but symptoms—an unpleasant creepy-crawly sensation— begin shortly after going to bed.

Sleeplessness may be a sign of chronic obstructive pulmonary disorder, congestive heart failure, or sleep apnea, and therefore may require an evaluation by a sleep specialist.

Symptoms/Signs

■ Inability to fall asleep or stay asleep, or waking too early.
■ Daytime fatigue, poor concentration, or irritability.
■ Abnormal snoring.

Talk to Your Doctor If:

■ The HomeCare recommendations do not improve your sleep pattern after 4 weeks.

HOMECARE™

If physician referral is not recommended at this time, try the following:

Fluids

• Avoid drinks containing caffeine such as coffee, tea, and colas in the evening.
• Don't use alcohol as a sleep aid.

Rest

• Practice a relaxation exercise. See pages 33-34.
• Have a fixed bedtime and wake-up time.
• Have a set bedtime routine that begins one-half hour before you go to bed.
• Do not watch TV in bed.

Heat/Cold

• A hot bath or warm shower promotes muscle relaxation.

Nutrition

• Eating a small amount of carbohydrates such as pasta can help promote relaxation and drowsiness.
• Warm milk also can help you become drowsy.

Activity

• Avoid heavy exercise in the late evening. Exercise earlier in the day.
• For symptoms of restless legs syndrome, walk around for 10 minutes and flex or massage muscles before going to bed.

Note Well

• If you can't sleep, get up and read in a chair until you feel drowsy.
• Avoid using sleep aids such as sedatives and antihistamines. Talk to your doctor about medication options if insomnia persists.

Jet Lag

Jet lag is that feeling of disorientation, fatigue, and sleeplessness that causes you to be staring at the walls of your hotel room at 3 a.m. when you should be getting a good night's rest. Jet lag occurs when your body's biological clock has trouble adjusting as you travel rapidly across time zones.

The natural hormone melatonin has been promoted as a natural sleep aid. While there is some evidence that melatonin promotes sleep, talk to your doctor first if you plan to use it. It is marketed as an over-the-counter supplement and has not been scientifically proven safe and effective for the relief of jet lag.

Symptoms/Signs

- Inability to fall asleep or stay asleep, or waking up too early.
- Daytime fatigue, poor concentration, disorientation, or irritability.

Talk to Your Doctor If:

- You travel extensively (especially internationally), ask about the short-term use of sleep aids while you adjust to a new time zone.
- HomeCare doesn't work.

If physician referral is not recommended at this time, try the following:

Rest

- Make your new sleeping environment as sleep-friendly as possible:
- Use ear plugs or blindfolds to block out strange sounds or lights.
- Close drapes and adjust the thermostat for your comfort.

Nutrition

- Eat sensibly. Try eating high-protein meals when you want to be alert and high-carbohydrate meals when you want to sleep.

Fluids

- Avoid alcohol in flight. The effect of alcohol can be twice as great at a high altitude. Drink plenty of water to prevent dehydration and headaches.

Prevention

- Get plenty of rest before your trip.
- Days before your trip, alter your sleeping hours to be closer to your destination time zone. Even 1 or 2 hours can make a difference.
- Set your watch to your destination time. While in flight, try to match your sleeping and eating schedule with that of your destination.
- Move around. Don't remain seated for the entire flight, as long as conditions are safe.
- Try not to schedule meetings immediately upon arrival; take time to relax, and, if possible, go to bed at your usual hour.
- Get a little sun, especially if you're traveling east, to help reset your internal clock. Try to spend some time outside during the first few days at your destination.

Memory Problems

Whether your age is 18 or 80, you can suffer from a poor memory. Alcohol, marijuana, some prescription drugs, depression, and thyroid problems all can make you more forgetful. You may have more memory troubles as you grow older. After age 20, the ability to recognize faces or find your car in a parking lot starts to decline; after age 35, it's more difficult to retrieve names.

Real memory problems, however, usually are associated with conditions far more serious than poor memory techniques or natural aging. One of the hallmarks of Alzheimer's disease, for example, is increasing forgetfulness and inability to name familiar objects or people. See pages 244–245. Memory loss resulting from a stroke, on the other hand, occurs suddenly and is accompanied by other serious physical symptoms. See pages 281–282.

Symptoms/Signs

- Inability to remember things or categories of things you've had no trouble remembering in the past.
- Increasing forgetfulness or short-term memory losses.
- Sudden memory impairment.

Talk to Your Doctor If:

- You notice a sudden and extreme change in memory.
- You have trouble remembering very recent events.
- You have trouble completing the steps it takes to perform familiar tasks (e.g., cooking a meal).
- You suspect a drug or drug dosage your doctor has prescribed is causing memory loss.
- You have symptoms of depression. See page 207 and pages 264-265.

If physician referral is not recommended at this time, try the following:

Medication

- If you suspect that your memory problems are caused by a prescription you are taking, check with your doctor before discontinuing it or changing the dosage.

Note Well

- Use memory cues and techniques to improve your memory. Use calendars or notebooks to write down important information, make lists, create routines (e.g., always put your car keys in the same place when you come home). Make a conscious effort to notice more details or be a more active listener, as in when you are introduced to someone.

Prevention

- Currently there is no way to prevent memory-robbing conditions such as Alzheimer's disease, but there are things you can do to keep your memory skills sharp. Keep up with mentally challenging activities (e.g., crossword puzzles, chess), play memory games, use memory aids, and make remembering a priority.
- If you drink alcohol, do so only in moderation. See pages 39-42.

Mental Confusion

Mental confusion is a symptom most often associated with illnesses or conditions of older people. However, people with diabetes, Alzheimer's disease, cirrhosis, and hypertension are at risk for mental confusion if their diseases are not well managed. Confusion is a sign of stroke, septic shock, transient ischemic attack (a temporary blockage in the artery supplying the brain), certain infections, and medication interactions.

If you think you're feeling confused, try to identify the cause quickly. Pay close attention to any physical changes. If you live alone, ask someone to check on you often, and note any unusual symptoms or changes.

Symptoms/Signs

- Physical disorientation.
- Impaired judgment.
- Inability to concentrate despite efforts to do so.
- Diminished ability to communicate with or understand others.

Get Emergency Care Right Away If:

- You are diabetic and mental confusion is accompanied by weakness, extreme thirst, abdominal pain, dry mouth, or labored breathing.
- Mental confusion is accompanied by a severe headache, high fever, or impaired speech or vision.
- Sudden confusion with trouble speaking or understanding. See Stroke on pages 281–282.

Talk to Your Doctor If:

- Mental confusion is accompanied by excessive thirst, frequent urination, unexplained weight loss, numbness/tingling of the hands and feet; or by increasing lapses in memory and distinct personality changes.
- You suspect mental confusion is a side effect of medication.

If physician referral is not recommended at this time, try the following:

Medication

- Be sure you are taking medications as prescribed. Call your doctor or pharmacist if you are unsure about dosage or have questions about drug interactions or allergies.
- If you are on insulin for diabetes, be sure to follow your doctor's instructions concerning dosage, monitoring blood glucose levels, etc.

Activity

- Do not drive a car or operate machinery during episodes of mental confusion.

Rest

- Get plenty of rest; fatigue can worsen symptoms of mental confusion.

Fluids

- Drink plenty of fluids; dehydration can contribute to increased confusion, disorientation, and agitation.
- Don't drink alcohol, or do so only in moderation.

Prevention

- Take all medications only as prescribed.

Shift Work

*O*ur habit of sleeping at night and being active during the day is primarily influenced by the effect of sunlight on our brains. When the body's natural clock and sleep patterns (called circadian rhythms) are changed, sleep problems can occur. It's hardest on night-shift workers, whose sleep time averages 2 to 4 hours less than day workers. Also, night shift workers report waking up feeling tired more often than day workers.

If you have trouble sleeping while on shift work, the guidelines in the HomeCare column to the right may help.

Symptoms/Signs

- Inability to fall asleep or stay asleep, or waking up too early.
- Fatigue, poor concentration, disorientation, or irritability during waking hours.

Talk to Your Doctor If:

- If HomeCare doesn't work or the above symptoms affect your productivity and safety.

Prevention

- If you have a choice, try to stay on one shift. If you need to rotate, 1 week is the minimum time recommended by experts to allow your body to adjust. Try to rotate clockwise, for example, nights to days, and days to evenings—this forward rotation is easier to adapt to than a counter-clockwise rotation.
- Bright lighting helps adjust your internal body clock by tricking the brain into believing it's daytime.
- In the morning light, wear sunglasses on your drive home. By decreasing the amount of sunlight to your eyes, your internal clock is fooled into believing that it's getting close to bedtime. However, if you feel sleepy while driving, keep your sunglasses off.
- Set a definite sleep time. Avoid lingering around the house or doing chores that eat into your sleep time. Establish a regular "lights out" and try to stick to it.
- Keep out the light and noise. If you sleep during the day, hang some room-darkening shades or a quilt over the window, or try wearing eye shades. The hum of a fan can help cover up outside noises.
- Make sure to get a commitment from family members to respect your sleep time.

Sleep Problems
(Children)

Sleep problems in children are a challenge for most parents. By 3 to 4 months of age, most babies will sleep for a 6- to 8-hour stretch at night. By 7 to 12 months of age, most infants sleep through the night consistently.

If your child is not a baby and is not ill, but still has trouble sleeping, you may need to help your child adjust his or her sleep habits. A regular bedtime schedule with a ritual of comforting activities will give your child cues that it's time to settle down. Once your child has gone to bed, resist responding to calls for water or a snack. Consistency is key.

Night terrors may occur at 3 to 4 years of age and can persist for several years. The child appears to be awake (or may be sleepwalking) and very afraid, often with crying or talking. It may be difficult to soothe the child during an episode, which may last several minutes to a half hour. The child will not remember the event the next day. Typically, night terrors occur in the first 2 hours of sleep, whereas nightmares occur later in the night.

Symptoms/Signs

- Inability to fall asleep or stay asleep.
- Frequent, frightening dreams, or terrors.

Talk to Your Doctor If Your Child:

- Has night terrors that are frequent, severe, or associated with an emotional or physical trauma the child is experiencing during the day.
- Has sleep problems that are disrupting family life and are not improved by HomeCare.

If physician referral is not recommended at this time, try the following:

Note Well

- Keep bedtimes regular and bedtime rituals quiet and brief.
- Add a warm bath to the bedtime ritual to promote muscle relaxation.
- Be gentle but firm about bedtimes and staying in bed. A security object, such as a blanket or stuffed animal, may ease the separation from you.
- If your child awakens, offer brief comfort in his or her own bed.
- If your child suffers a night terror, calm him or her in a dimly lit room until he or she responds to you.

Rest

- Don't let your child nap too long or too late in the day.

Activity

- Avoid stimulating activity in the late evening. Choose a more soothing activity such as reading a book to your child before bedtime.

Medication

- Antihistamines or decongestants your child takes may interfere with sleep. Talk to your doctor about an alternative.

Prevention

- If night terrors occur at the same time every night, waking your child 15 to 30 minutes prior to that time may prevent an episode.

Snoring

Snoring can disturb sleeping patterns and family members, and leave you less alert or productive during the day. Snoring often is caused by loose throat muscles, large tonsils, nasal obstructions, excessive body weight, allergies, pregnancy, smoking, or alcohol use. Fortunately, most snoring is remedied easily with some simple self-care methods.

On the other hand, obstructive sleep apnea is considered the most serious sleep disorder since it may produce fatal heart or lung events. With this condition, breathing stops because the airway closes after inhaling. As oxygen levels are reduced, the person rouses and catches his breath. These disruptions repeat through the night, leaving the victim feeling tired throughout the day. Sleep apnea is more common in men than women.

Obstructive sleep apnea needs to be assessed by a physician who is trained in the field of sleep disorders. Depending on the severity of the condition, treatment may involve the use of a continuous positive airway pressure (CPAP) device or the surgical removal of tissues in the nose and throat that are creating the obstruction.

Symptoms/Signs

■ Gurgling, snorting, or loud throat noises during sleep.
■ With apnea: loud snoring and breathing irregularities.

Talk to Your Doctor If:

■ You or your bed partner notice cycles of snoring, breathing cessation, and violent jerking or snorting.
■ You experience extreme fatigue, daytime sleepiness, or poor concentration despite having had what you think is a good night's sleep.
■ You experience no relief from snoring-induced sleep problems, no matter what self-care measures you try.

HOMECARE™

If physician referral is not recommended at this time, try the following:

Medication

• Avoid sedatives and antihistamines before bedtime.

Nutrition

• Avoid heavy meals within 3 hours of going to bed.
• Eat a well-balanced diet designed to keep your weight within a healthy range for your height, age, and body type.

Activity

• Exercise to help you tone muscles and maintain your ideal body weight.

Fluids

• Avoid alcoholic drinks 3 hours before bedtime.

Note Well

• If you suffer from allergies, reduce bedroom allergens (dust, pet dander, mold, etc.) to alleviate nasal stuffiness.
• Don't sleep with windows open: Use the air conditioner instead.

Prevention

• Establish regular sleeping patterns and avoid getting overtired.
• Keep your allergies in check.
• Sleep on your side.
• Use a humidifier in your bedroom if your bedroom is too dry.
• For severe apnea, ask your doctor if the continuous positive airway pressure (CPAP) mask is appropriate for you.

Incontinence

For about 12 million people, bladder control is a daily problem. The causes of urinary incontinence vary: hormonal imbalances, chronic cough, excess weight, childbirth, frequent constipation, neurologic disorders, the effects of certain medications, hyperactive bladder muscles, or an enlarged prostate can be at the root of the problem.

Fecal incontinence, the inability to control bowel movements, can be especially disheartening. For some, a mere sneeze or cough can cause leakage of soft stool.

The good news is that most cases of incontinence can be treated with behavior modification, medication, medical devices, and, in some cases, surgery.

Symptoms/Signs

- **Urinary incontinence:** Urine leaks as soon as you feel a strong need to urinate, or when you sneeze, cough, laugh, walk, exercise, get up from a chair, or get out of bed.
- **Fecal incontinence:** Stool leaks out when you are not trying to have a bowel movement.

Talk to Your Doctor If:

- You have symptoms of incontinence for more than a week.
- You have burning, pain, or bladder spasm upon urination.
- You have pain in the lower back or left abdomen, fever, nausea, or vomiting with symptoms of incontinence.
- Your urine contains blood.
- Your bladder is full but you can't release any urine.
- You have chronically impacted bowels and cannot correct the problem through self-care.
- Your stools are black and tarry or contain blood.
- You notice any sudden, major changes in normal bowel habits.

Nutrition

- Avoid spicy or greasy foods and products that contain artificial sweeteners, all of which can irritate the bladder.
- Increase whole grains and fresh fruits and vegetables in your diet to improve regularity.

Fluids

- Drink plenty of liquids, especially water—about 1 to 2 quarts throughout the day, tapering off intake close to bedtime.
- Avoid caffeinated and carbonated drinks, alcohol, and citrus juices, all of which can irritate the bladder.

Cover

- For chronic incontinence, use adult absorbent undergarments (e.g., Depends®).

NB
Note Well

- Do Kegel exercises that strengthen the muscles surrounding the opening of the bladder: These are the muscles that would stop the flow of urine midstream when you urinate. Try 20 to 30 repetitions, several times a day—but not while urinating.
- Sit on the toilet at the same time every day to encourage regularity.
- Try to increase the time between visits until urination can be controlled for longer periods.
- If you smoke, quit. Smoker's cough can damage pelvic muscles, and nicotine can interfere with bladder function.
- Lose excess weight.

Urinary Problems
(Men)

More than a third of men over age 50 have prostate conditions that cause urinary problems. Benign prostatic hyperplasia (BPH) is a noncancerous enlargement of the prostate that blocks the flow of urine. It is very common in older men. With prostatitis, or inflammation of the prostate gland, the prostate swells and presses on the urethra causing difficult, frequent, or painful urination. It may be caused by bacteria, a faulty immune response, or physical injury. Less commonly, prostate cancer can cause urinary problems. Fortunately, early detection makes prostate cancer highly treatable. See pages 279-280.

Urinary problems also may result from an infection or a sexually transmitted disease (see page 50). Genital herpes and gonorrhea, for example, can cause pain on urination. Bacteria introduced into the penis during intercourse also can cause inflammation of the urethra and of the prostate.

Symptoms/Signs

- Difficulty in starting urine flow.
- Increased urinary frequency.
- The sensation of not emptying the bladder completely after urinating.
- Pain or burning during urination.
- Pus or blood in the urine.

Talk to Your Doctor If:

- You have difficulty emptying your bladder or are unable to urinate.
- You have painful or unusually frequent urination.
- You have blood in your urine or semen.
- Any of the above symptoms with pain in the pelvis, lower back, or during ejaculation.
- You suspect you have a sexually transmitted disease.

If physician referral is not recommended at this time, try the following:

Fluids

- Drink cranberry juice at the first sign of a urinary problem to increase the acidity of your urine and flush out bacteria.
- Drink plenty of water—about 12 ounces an hour.
- Avoid alcohol and caffeine.

Medication

- If you have difficulty urinating, avoid taking antihistamines.

Prevention

- If you're age 50 or older, your doctor may recommend an annual digital rectal exam. Ask your doctor if an annual PSA (prostate-specific antigen) test is appropriate for you.
- Practice safe sex: Use a condom if you are unsure whether your partner may infect you with a sexually transmitted disease.
- Drink at least eight glasses of water a day.

Urinary Problems
(Women)

Bladder infections are the most common urinary problem among women. The female anatomy allows bacteria from the anal area to reach the urinary tract easily. Sexual activity can introduce unwanted bacteria as well. If the bacteria gain a foothold in the urinary tract, a bladder infection or kidney infection can result.

Less common but potentially serious causes of urinary problems in women include benign uterine fibroids and sexually transmitted diseases. See pages 50-51. Whether you experience painful urination, increased frequency of urination, or difficult urination, take care not to let urinary problems go untreated. You may risk damage to your bladder, your kidneys, and your health in general.

Symptoms/Signs

- Painful, difficult, or unusually frequent urination.
- Urine that contains pus or blood, or is unusually dark or discolored.

Talk to Your Doctor If:

- If you have painful, burning, or frequent urination, low-grade fever, cloudy urine, blood in the urine, lower back pain (dull or acute), fatigue, or nausea.
- If you notice pus or blood in your urine.

HOMECARE™

If physician referral is not recommended at this time, try the following:

Fluids

- Drink cranberry juice at the first sign of a urinary problem to increase the acidity of your urine and flush out bacteria.
- Drink plenty of water—at least 12 ounces an hour.
- Avoid alcohol and caffeine.

Clean

- Keep vaginal and anal area clean. Wipe from front to back after using the toilet.
- Do not douche unless advised to do so by your doctor.

Activity

- Abstain from sexual intercourse if it is painful or increases urinary discomfort.

Prevention

- Practice safe sex: Use a condom if you are unsure whether your partner may infect you with a sexually transmitted disease.
- Practice good hygiene: Wipe from front to back after using the toilet.
- Drink at least eight glasses of water a day.
- If you're susceptible to urinary tract infections, limit caffeine and alcohol intake.
- Drink a glass of water before intercourse, and urinate within 15 minutes after intercourse.
- Take showers instead of baths.
- Don't hold your urine: Urinate as soon as you feel the urge.

Balding/Hair Loss

Most balding is hereditary. Two out of every three men will eventually experience some form of balding, while an even higher percentage of both men and women will face some type of hair loss in their lifetimes. However, hair loss also can result from hormonal imbalances, acute illness, certain drugs, severe emotional stress, poor diet, even certain hairstyles. While this type of hair loss can be alarming, it's usually not permanent.

Medications for saving your hair are only moderately effective. Minoxidil (Rogaine®) and finasteride (Propecia®) have been proven to grow hair in bald areas. However, they may cause unpleasant or dangerous side effects, take months to show results, and they don't work at all for some people who try them.

Options such as hair transplantation offer more permanent solutions to hereditary hair loss, but their cost and relative risks are high.

Symptoms/Signs

- General thinning of scalp hair.
- Isolated bald patches on scalp (smooth, or accompanied by irritation or scaling).
- Generalized loss of body hair.

Talk to Your Doctor If:

- You have unexplained bald patches.
- You notice unusual and excessive shedding after combing or brushing.
- You experience sudden hair loss on any part of your body.
- You have ring-like bald patches that are red, scaly, and itchy.
- You are taking minoxidil (Rogaine®) and have itching, headaches, dizzy spells, or heartbeat irregularities.

HOMECARE™

If physician referral is not recommended at this time, try the following:

Medication

- If you have a heart condition, don't use minoxidil (Rogaine®), which is available over the counter.
- Women should never use or even touch finasteride (Propecia®) tablets.

Heat/Cold

- Avoid high-heat hair dryers or other styling appliances that can dry and damage your hair.

Clean

- Keep your hair clean, but avoid excessive shampooing, which can cause your hair to break.

Nutrition

- Eat a well-balanced diet with adequate protein and iron.
- Avoid high doses of vitamin A.

Note Well

- Avoid wearing tight-fitting hats or wigs for extended periods.
- Avoid wearing pulled-tight hairstyles (ponytails, braids, etc.) for extended periods.
- Avoid brushing or combing your hair excessively.
- Blot wet hair with a towel; avoid vigorous towel drying.
- Manage stress and tension. See pages 28-34.
- Be aware that certain hair products (e.g., perms) and treatments (e.g., hair straightening) may damage your hair.

Hernia

Hernia is a general term for any protrusion of organ tissue outside the area it normally occupies. But two of the most common types of hernias occur almost exclusively in men and involve part of the intestine pushing through a weakened internal opening into the groin (direct inguinal hernia) or scrotum (indirect inguinal hernia). Inguinal hernias usually result from physical overexertion or straining during lifting. They can be very painful or may go completely unnoticed until a routine physical exam uncovers the characteristic hernia bulge.

Often, your doctor will be able to push a hernia bulge back into place with relative ease, but this is only a temporary solution. When the hernia does not respond to physical manipulation, it is probably trapped or strangulated and may require surgery. Strangulated hernias that are not treated can result in the death of the trapped tissue, which then can become infected and require emergency, life-saving surgery.

Symptoms/Signs

- Unusual sensation of pressure in the groin.
- Abdominal or groin discomfort when lifting or bending at the waist.
- A painful lump or bulge in the groin or scrotum.
- Moderate to severe pain in the scrotum. See page 221.
- Swelling of the scrotum.

Talk to Your Doctor If:

- You experience any symptoms of a hernia.
- You have unexplained pain in the lower abdominal/groin area for longer than a week.
- You experience swelling or pain in the scrotum due to trauma to the groin.

If physician referral is not recommended at this time, try the following:

Nutrition

- Eat plenty of fiber to promote regularity.

Activity

- Avoid heavy lifting or any physical exertion that strains your abdominal muscles.
- If your job or exercise routine places a strain on your lower back or abdomen, use a back support belt.

Prevention

- Keep physically fit and maintain a weight that is within a healthy range for your age and frame.
- Avoid heavy lifting without proper back support.
- Avoid straining during bowel movements.
- Learn proper lifting techniques. See page 254.

Impotence
(Erectile Dysfunction)

It's not unusual for men to experience occasional difficulty achieving and maintaining an erection. Too much alcohol, stress, fatigue, and certain medications can put a damper on an ordinarily strong sexual response. Fortunately, most episodes of impotence (erectile dysfunction, or ED) are short-lived and can be remedied easily with HomeCare.

Repeated or chronic impotence can become a major stumbling block to intimacy or may be a sign of a physical problem. High blood pressure, heart disease, hardening of the arteries, diabetes, hormone imbalances, medications, and substance abuse may contribute to impotence.

In any case, it's a good idea to try to deal with psychological or emotional causes for impotence before seeking medical help. Learning how to relax, going slowly during sex, and talking to your partner about all aspects of intimacy often may be the only remedy you need.

If your problem turns out to be physical, your doctor can offer a number of effective treatments. For example, your doctor may prescribe a pill (e.g., Viagra®, Levitra®, Cialis®) that you can take prior to sexual activity. Note that these medications improve the quality of the erection but do not stimulate sexual arousal.

Symptoms/Signs

■ Inability to achieve or maintain an erection.

Talk to Your Doctor If:

■ You suspect that medication or a physical ailment may be causing your impotence.

■ After a few months of home treatment, you are not able to achieve or maintain an erection.

If physician referral is not recommended at this time, try the following:

Medication

- Ask your doctor to recommend another medication (e.g., high blood pressure medication) if the one you are taking seems to be causing your impotence.

Note Well

- Do not use recreational drugs (marijuana, amphetamines, opiates) and avoid excessive use of alcohol. These drugs are associated with increased impotence.
- Don't smoke.
- Find ways to relax, manage stress, and reduce anxiety.
- Work with your partner to minimize or lessen any psychological or emotional stress that affects your intimacy.
- Erection and ejaculation are not the only ways to achieve sexual success. Explore other ways to give and receive pleasure—options that may not lead to intercourse. Adopt a leisurely lovemaking pace, and become reacquainted with your body (and your partner's).

Activity

- Exercise aerobically three or four times a week (but avoid excessive exercise, which can interfere with sexual performance).

Prevention

- Reduce your risk of atherosclerosis (hardening of the arteries) by controlling your intake of fat and cholesterol, managing your weight, not smoking, exercising regularly, and controlling your blood pressure.
- If you drink alcohol, do so only in moderation.

Testicular Pain

Testicular pain can be so intense that it may cause nausea and profuse sweating. Most often, pain in the testicles is a result of blunt trauma—a good reason for men to wear a protective cup every time they participate in contact sports. Fortunately, permanent damage to the testicles due to injury is quite rare.

Other reasons men experience testicular pain include testicular torsion (the spermatic cord attached to the testicle becomes twisted), epididymitis (inflammation of the epididymis, a tube that transports sperm), varicocele (a mass of varicose veins in the scrotum), hernia, kidney stones, cysts, and tumors.

Testicular cancer usually strikes men between the ages of 15 and 40. Fortunately, testicular cancer has one of the highest cure rates of all cancers. See page 45, "Self-Exams for Cancer."

Get Emergency Care Right Away If:
- You experience sudden and excruciating testicular pain that is not caused by injury.
- An injury to the testicles includes puncture by a sharp object.

Symptoms/Signs
- Pain or tenderness in one or both testicles.

Talk to Your Doctor If:

- You experience pain in the scrotum that develops gradually but does not subside.
- You have pain with the elevation of one testicle in the scrotum, nausea, fever, or testicular swelling.
- Blunt trauma to the testicles results in pain, bruising, or swelling that does not subside within an hour.
- You notice a lump or any swelling in the scrotum that may or may not be painful or tender.

HOMECARE™

If physician referral is not recommended at this time, try the following:

Medication

- If your doctor determines that you have epididymitis, he or she may prescribe an antibiotic to kill the infection. You can take an over-the-counter pain reliever to ease the pain and inflammation.

Heat/Cold

- If your doctor determines that you have epididymitis, you can relieve some of the pain and swelling by applying ice packs to the scrotum periodically.

Activity

- If physical activity increases testicular pain, cease the activity.

Prevention

- Do an occasional testicular self-exam to establish familiarity with your normal tissue.
- Wear an athletic cup or supporter when participating in contact sports or any activity that may risk injury to the testicles, such as baseball or softball.

Breast Lumps

Whether it's a cyst, a swollen gland, some fibrous tissue, or an unusual lump you've never noticed before, any abnormality you feel in your breast tissue can be scary. Fortunately, most breast lumps that women find are not cancerous, and more than 90 percent of breast cancers are curable if they're found early.

Every woman should be familiar with what her normal breast tissue feels like so that she can recognize any unusual lumps or dense areas and report them to her doctor (see page 45). The keys to detection and prevention are regular breast exams by a medical professional, and mammograms every 1 to 2 years from age 40. About 11 percent of all women will develop breast cancer in their lifetimes—and those who survive usually are the women who detected a lump early, through regular screenings and mammography. See pages 256–257.

Symptoms/Signs

- A lump or hardness in the breast or armpit, a discharge from the nipple, and/or unusual changes to breast tissue.

Talk to Your Doctor If:

- You find a new lump or dense or fibrous tissue in your breast.
- You notice wrinkling, puckering, or dimpling of the skin on your breast.
- Your nipple retracts (pulls inward).
- You have a red, scaly rash or sore on your nipple.
- You notice any discharge from your nipple.
- There is a sudden and unusual increase in the size of one breast, or one breast appears unusually lower than the other.
- You are breastfeeding and experience flu-like symptoms, fever, and painfully swollen breasts.

If physician referral is not recommended at this time, try the following:

Prevention

- Become familiar with your normal breast tissue. See page 45.
- Have your doctor check your breasts during your regular checkup.
- Have regular mammograms if you're over 40. If you have a family history of breast cancer, consult your doctor for a screening schedule. See page 43.
- Exercise regularly.

Fluids

- Drink plenty of fluids.
- If you have a history of fibrocystic breast changes, avoid caffeine.

Nutrition

- Eat a well-balanced diet, low in fat.

Heat/Cold

- For abscesses, swollen glands, or clogged milk ducts, warm compresses can help reduce swelling.

Menopause

Not that long ago, the change of life was a time many women dreaded. Hot flashes, mood swings, depression, and many other symptoms of menopause often were assumed to be an inevitable package of misery that women had to endure at mid-life. However, women are finding that the cessation of their menstrual cycle can offer a newfound freedom— no more worrying about birth control, monthly menstrual discomfort, or medical conditions such as endometriosis. About 75 percent of all women either have no symptoms (except for the gradual cessation of menstruation) or experience only mild symptoms during this phase in their lives.

Menopause is a natural stage of womanhood that can bring out positive aspects of your personality you may not have noticed before. If you have more discomfort or symptoms than you expected, you may be able to manage them with HomeCare.

Some experts suggest trying alternative remedies such as black cohosh or vitamin E to help with hot flashes. Finally, consult with your doctor to discuss hormone replacement therapy (HRT) for short-term symptom relief, or for the prevention of osteoporosis.

Symptoms/Signs

- Hot flashes (flushed face and a sudden, allover warmth).
- Vaginal dryness.
- Uncomfortable or painful intercourse.
- Irregular menstrual periods.
- Mood swings, mild depression, listlessness, or insomnia.

Talk to Your Doctor If:

- You experience unusual or prolonged vaginal bleeding.

If physician referral is not recommended at this time, try the following:

- Eat a well-balanced diet rich in calcium. Eating five or six small meals a day instead of three big ones will help keep your metabolism and body temperature on an even keel.

- Keep cool: Use the air conditioner at home and in your car; invest in a small fan for your desk at work— anything that keeps hot flashes at bay.
- Wear loose-fitting, layered clothing. Remove a layer when you are hot.
- Water-soluble lubricants such as K-Y Jelly®, which are available over the counter, will help replace vaginal moisture during intercourse. Avoid petroleum-based lubricants.

- Drink plenty of water.

- Choose an exercise routine you enjoy and stick with it. Four or five sessions of aerobic activity each week can keep bones strong, regulate hormones, and help reduce insomnia.

- Talk with your doctor about using estrogen cream or a estrogen vaginal ring to improve vaginal tone and reduce symptoms of dryness.
- Hormone replacement therapy is not recommended for long-term treatment of menopausal symptoms. Talk to your doctor.

Menstrual Cramps

ramping in the lower abdomen is a common problem during a woman's menstrual period. Cramps are a result of strong contractions of the uterus during the menstrual period. Endometriosis, fibroids, pelvic inflammatory disease, or an IUD (intrauterine device) may cause menstrual cramping that lasts longer and begins earlier than ordinary menstrual cramps. In many cases however, cramping can be relieved through HomeCare.

Symptoms/Signs

■ Cramping in the lower abdomen.

■ Headache, backache, thigh pain, diarrhea, constipation, dizziness, and nausea also are common.

Get Emergency Care Right Away If:
You have symptoms of toxic shock syndrome (TSS)—a potentially fatal bacterial infection that is linked with diaphragms and superabsorbent tampons. Symptoms include a sudden high fever, headache, vomiting, diarrhea, weakness, and redness of the skin, mouth, and vagina.

Talk to Your Doctor If:

■ Cramping that lasts longer than is normal for you.

■ You have a fever, diarrhea, or a rash during your period.

■ Menstrual bleeding has been unusually heavy for several months.

■ After experiencing normal periods, you suddenly have painful cramping.

■ Cramping occurs with signs of major intestinal problems such as black, tarry stools, or blood in the stools.

If physician referral is not recommended at this time, try the following:

Medication

• Ibuprofen or naproxen are effective for relieving menstrual cramps. Aspirin also can be used.

Heat/Cold

• Take a hot bath; try to relax.
• Apply heating pads or hot water bottles to relax muscles and reduce cramping.

Nutrition

• Reduce your intake of salt and sodium products, especially the week prior to the start of your period.
• Increase your intake of magnesium and calcium to help reduce cramping.

Activity

• Physical activity has been shown to help reduce cramping for some women.
• Lie on your back with legs up on the wall. Lie still for 15 minutes and relax.

Prevention

• To help prevent TSS: Use sanitary napkins, or the lowest absorbency tampons made from natural fibers rather than synthetic materials. Change them every 4 to 6 hours.
• Do not keep diaphragms in longer than 24 hours.

PMS

Premenstrual syndrome (PMS) is the result of hormonal changes in the body, usually during the 2 weeks prior to menstruation. The physical and emotional changes associated with PMS can be mild for some women, severe for others. HomeCare measures usually will manage PMS symptoms effectively. However, in up to 10 percent of women with PMS, symptoms may be so disabling that medical treatment may be helpful.

Symptoms/Signs

- Weight gain, headaches, acne, bloating, breast tenderness, diarrhea or constipation, food cravings, dizziness, and fatigue.
- Mood swings, increased tension and anger, irritability, sadness, and unexplained crying.

Talk to Your Doctor If:

- Your symptoms are severe for several months and do not improve with HomeCare measures.

If physician referral is not recommended at this time, try the following:

Nutrition

- Decrease sodium intake in the days before your period.
- Increasing magnesium, vitamin E, and calcium intake may help reduce cramping. See page 224.

Medication

- For severe PMS, your doctor may recommend antidepressants, diuretics, or oral contraceptives. Talk to your doctor.

Note Well

- Discuss your PMS problems with your partner. Try to work together to deal with emotional and physical changes.
- Elevating your legs may reduce ankle swelling.

Fluids

- Limit your intake of caffeine as it can increase irritability and breast tenderness.
- Avoid alcohol, especially if depression is one of your symptoms.

Prevention

- Try to get extra sleep a few days before you usually experience symptoms.
- Learn a relaxation technique to manage stress and tension. See pages 33-34.
- Soak in a warm bath to help relax aching muscles.
- Increase aerobic exercise.

Prenatal Risks

*I*f you're planning to have a baby, it's important to understand that certain factors, most related to your lifestyle choices, can affect your health and the health of your baby. Consequences of poor lifestyle choices can range from miscarriage to delivery problems and, for your baby, from a low birth weight to birth defects.

Discuss any risk factors, described below, with your doctor. See pages 288-293 for more information.

For Your Information

The more high-risk behaviors you continue during your pregnancy, the greater your chances of having a premature baby or developing other serious health problems.

Reducing Your Prenatal Risks

Smoking

- Stop smoking before you become pregnant.
- Enroll in a stop-smoking program.
- Avoid smoke-filled areas (second-hand smoke).

Alcohol

- Don't drink if you're trying to get pregnant.
- Don't drink alcohol during pregnancy or while nursing your baby.
- If you think you have a drinking problem, seek help. See page 39.

Drug Use

- Abstain from all illegal drugs. See page 35.
- If you have a drug problem, get help before you become pregnant.
- Make sure your doctor approves any prescription or over-the-counter drugs you take.

Obesity

- Achieve a healthy weight before you get pregnant.
- Follow your doctor's recommendations for proper nutrition, exercise, and weight gain.

Eating Disorders

- Expect to gain 25 to 35 pounds during your pregnancy.
- Eat balanced meals.
- Don't try to lose weight during your pregnancy.
- Don't use diet pills.
- If you have an eating disorder (e.g., bulimia or anorexia), tell your doctor.

Sexually Transmitted Diseases (STDs)

- If you think you already have, or have been exposed to, any STD, see your doctor—if possible before you get pregnant.
- Avoid sexual contact with high-risk individuals. See page 50.

- If you have HIV, notify your obstetrician. The risk of transferring HIV to newborn children can be greatly reduced with medications.
- Use condoms if you are pregnant.

Age

- Pregnancies carry greater risks if you are under age 18 or over 35.
- If you have high blood pressure, diabetes or heart disease, see your doctor before you get pregnant.
- Get early prenatal care and ongoing medical supervision throughout your pregnancy.

Other

- For 3 months before getting pregnant and continuing throughout pregnancy, women should take a daily supplement of folate: 0.4 mg to prevent neural tube defects (e.g., spina bifida).

Note: these ideas are not a substitute for appropriate medical supervision.

Preventing Premature Labor

When a woman goes into labor 3 or more weeks before her baby is due. This is described as a preterm labor. A preterm (premature) baby is more likely to have health problems because his or her body is not fully developed.

You are at a greater risk for preterm delivery if you:

■ Suffer trauma (e.g., an automobile accident).

■ Are pregnant with more than one child.

■ Become pregnant less than 2 years after your last pregnancy.

■ Had a preterm baby previously.

■ Smoke, drink alcohol, and/or misuse drugs.

■ Are the daughter of a woman who took the prescription medication DES during her pregnancy.

■ Are younger than 18 or older than 40.

■ Are under a lot of stress and personal pressure.

■ Have had two or more second-trimester abortions or miscarriages.

■ Have had three or more urinary tract infections during this pregnancy.

■ Have a vaginal or cervical infection.

■ Are being abused by your partner.

Note: Inform your doctor if you have any of these conditions.

To reduce the chance of a preterm delivery:

■ Review your risk factors before you try to get pregnant. See page 226.

■ See a doctor as soon as you find out you're pregnant, and on a regular basis thereafter.

■ Don't smoke, drink alcohol, or use drugs. Check with your doctor before taking any medication.

■ Eat a well-balanced diet, gain the weight your doctor recommends, and get enough rest.

■ Drink 3 quarts of water a day (a 24-hour period).

■ Find support from people who care to help you when you are stressed or feel discouraged.

■ Use prenatal educational services sponsored by your health plan, employer, or local health provider.

■ Learn to recognize the signs of labor and what to do if you experience preterm labor.

For Your Information

Signs of Premature Labor

• Five or more contractions in 1 hour.
• Cramps that come and go or don't go away.
• Pelvic pressure: a feeling that the baby's head is pushing down; it may come and go.
• A low, dull backache (more than usual) that comes and goes or doesn't go away.
• Abdominal cramps with or without diarrhea.
• Leakage or bleeding from the vagina.
• Pressure in lower back, abdomen, or thighs.
• Changes in vaginal discharge. It may be more watery, have more mucus, or be blood-tinged.
• The baby is not moving as much as usual.

If you show signs of preterm labor:

Call your doctor, who may recommend that you:

■ Lie down on your left side for an hour.

■ Drink two to three glasses of water.

Call Your Doctor Right Away If:

The signs do not go away in 1 hour, or you have fluid leaking from your vagina. Getting help early is critical for preventing preterm delivery.

Resources

Your health care provider or local chapter of the March of Dimes.

Swollen Ankles

Swollen ankles are common in pregnancy and also are associated with many health problems. This occurs in pregnancy because fluid increases and accumulates in the body's tissues, especially in the hands and lower legs. Once a baby is delivered, the fluid levels will return to normal. Swelling during pregnancy is not a danger to the fetus or the mother, unless it is accompanied by symptoms of toxemia: elevated blood pressure, elevated urine protein levels, severe headaches, and swelling in the face, especially around the eyes. *Toxemia requires immediate medical attention.*

In people who are not pregnant, swollen ankles can be caused by liver problems, kidney malfunction, acute premenstrual syndrome, and circulatory diseases, which can cause fluid to pool in the ankles. If you are injured and notice sudden, unusual, or rapid swelling in your ankles or any other part of your body, it's a good idea to call your doctor right away.

Symptoms/Signs

- Swelling in ankles, feet, or lower legs.
- "Pulled-tight" feeling on skin around ankles.

Get Emergency Care Right Away If:
- You are unable to lie flat because you are short of breath.
- You have signs of toxemia.

Talk to Your Doctor If:

- You are pregnant and ankle swelling is accompanied by swelling in the face, especially around the eyes.
- Your ankle swells, becomes tender, and the skin appears red or purple.
- You have a chronic disease and notice any sudden or unusual swelling.
- Swelling is associated with pain in the back of the leg.

HOMECARE™

If physician referral is not recommended at this time, try the following:

Rest

- Whenever possible, relax with your feet elevated to reduce swelling.
- If your swelling is pregnancy-related, rest often on your left side.

Heat/Cold

- Seek out air-conditioned environments; becoming overheated will make swelling worse.

Nutrition

- Reduce your sodium intake. Be aware that processed foods and juices are high in sodium.
- Use the salt shaker sparingly.

Activity

- Avoid any physical exertion in hot weather.

Fluids

- Drink plenty of water throughout the day.
- Avoid alcohol and caffeine.

Note Well

- If your swelling is pregnancy-related and your work requires standing, take frequent breaks and elevate your feet. If you work at a desk, use a footrest to raise your feet as high as possible. Avoid crossing your legs.

Vaginal Bleeding

It's not uncommon for a woman to have unusual vaginal bleeding during her childbearing years. Changing hormone levels, weight gain or loss, heavy exercise, infections, difficulties with birth control methods (especially IUDs), certain drugs—even stress—can cause spotting or bleeding or cause menstrual periods to be heavier or last longer.

Vaginal bleeding also can alert you to such conditions as endometriosis (an overgrowth of the tissue that lines the uterus), uterine fibroids and polyps, ectopic pregnancy, miscarriage, certain types of cancer, and thyroid disease.

Symptoms/Signs

- Vaginal bleeding not associated with your regular menstrual cycle or a medical procedure.

Talk to Your Doctor If:

- You have unusual or severe pelvic pain, especially during menstruation.
- Menstruation becomes increasingly painful month after month, your flow lasts for more than 8 days, or your flow is very heavy and/or contains large clots.
- Your menstrual cycles shorten to less than 21 days.
- You have sharp pain deep in your pelvis during intercourse.
- You get weak, pale, and lightheaded while standing.
- You have any vaginal bleeding when you are past menopause and are not taking hormones.
- You have difficulty urinating, or you urinate frequently.
- You have unusual spotting or bleeding between menstrual periods, especially if bleeding lasts for more than 3 days or occurs for more than 3 months in a row.
- You are pregnant and have any bleeding or spotting.

If physician referral is not recommended at this time, try the following:

Medication

- Avoid taking aspirin during any episode of vaginal bleeding. Take acetaminophen or ibuprofen instead.

Nutrition

- Eat a well-balanced diet that contains plenty of sources of iron.

Cover

- Check tampons and sanitary pads when you change them to gauge your bleeding. Report noticeable changes in blood flow to your doctor.

Activity

- Stop doing any activity that increases abnormal bleeding.

Vaginal Dryness

The female reproductive system and its functioning is maintained by the body's delicate balance of hormones. When hormone levels change—either because of pregnancy, breastfeeding, menopause, or taking hormone medications that your doctor has prescribed—you'll probably notice many changes in your body. One such change, which is associated with a decrease in the hormone estrogen, is vaginal dryness.

Apart from hampering lovemaking, vaginal dryness is not a serious problem unless it is accompanied by other symptoms (see below). There are many products on the market designed to replace vaginal moisture, but those that most closely mimic normal vaginal secretions are water based (Lubifax® or K-Y Jelly®). Avoid oil-based lotions or creams, particularly if you are using a diaphragm or condom: Oil-based lubricants can destroy any contraceptive device made from latex and create a breeding ground for bacteria in the vagina.

Most of the time, vaginal dryness disappears when breastfeeding women wean their infants. Menopausal women may opt for an estrogen cream or ring to restore vaginal tissues.

Symptoms/Signs

■ Sensation of dryness or mild burning in the vagina.

Talk to Your Doctor If:

■ Vaginal dryness is accompanied by vaginal itching or redness.

■ You experience any abnormal vaginal discharge or bleeding.

■ You notice any blisters, lesions, or changes in vaginal skin texture.

HOMECARE™

If physician referral is not recommended at this time, try the following:

Medication

• If you are going through or have gone through menopause, ask your doctor about using estrogen vaginal cream.

NB Note Well

• Avoid nonlubricated intercourse, which can cause vaginal irritation or abrasion.
• Use a nonirritating lubricant during intercourse.
• If you use condoms during intercourse, buy the lubricated variety.
• Avoid using any petroleum-based lubricant with any condom or diaphragm; use water-based lubricants instead.

Vaginitis

The most common cause of vaginitis (inflammation of the vagina) is infection. Friction during intercourse can make the condition worse. Therefore, intercourse is not recommended until the infection has been treated. Vaginal dryness also can cause inflammation, pain, and irritation during intercourse. See page 230.

Infections of the vagina can be caused by yeast (also called monilia or candida), trichomonas, chlamydia, gonorrhea, and herpes. Although yeast infections are rarely spread during sex, the other four infections are sexually transmitted.

Yeast infections usually cause itching and a cheesy discharge. You are at a greater risk for yeast infections if you have diabetes, use birth control pills, are on hormone replacement therapy, or are taking antibiotics. Medications, which have a very good cure rate, are now available over the counter for treating yeast infections.

Symptoms/Signs

- Abnormal vaginal discharge, itching, and pain.

Talk to Your Doctor If:

- The problem is vaginal dryness and vaginal symptoms and discomfort don't go away after 1 month of stopping tampon use and using lubrication.
- You or your sexual partner have symptoms that suggest a sexually transmitted disease (e.g., painful discharge, pain on urination).
- It's the first vaginal infection you have had.
- You have tried over-the-counter medication for one episode of a possible yeast infection, with no success.

If physician referral is not recommended at this time, try the following:

Nutrition

- Reduce your intake of sugar. If you have diabetes, be sure to watch your blood sugar levels.

Medication

- Consider using an over-the-counter vaginal medication (e.g., Monistat®) for one episode if you have typical symptoms of a yeast infection (monilia vaginitis): itching, a cheesy discharge that may smell like baking bread, no pain, and no fever. See your doctor if symptoms persist.

Prevention

- Use tampons only during times of heavy menstrual flow, if at all. See page 224.
- For vaginal dryness, use a water-based lubricant (i.e., K-Y Jelly®) during sexual intercourse. Do not use an oil-based lubricant.
- Use only water when washing around the vagina. Soaps, bubble baths, and shampoos can strip natural oils from the membranes that protect the vaginal walls.
- Use a condom when there is risk of a sexually transmitted disease.
- Wear underwear made of cotton rather than polyester. Cotton breathes more and allows the skin to stay dry and cool.
- Sleep without underwear to allow adequate ventilation.
- Try using less absorbent tampons or pads if vaginal dryness is a problem.

Infant Feeding: Breast or Bottle?

Before your baby's birth, you and your partner should decide whether breastfeeding or bottle-feeding will be best for you and your baby. Consider that breastfeeding is strongly endorsed by health professionals. Breast milk:

- Is rich in antibodies to protect the baby from disease in the first few months. The baby may have fewer and milder illnesses and illnesses of a shorter duration.

- Is more easily digested, resulting in less colic and intestinal problems such as diarrhea and constipation.

- Aids in physical development. The hormones in breast milk may promote healthy digestive function.

- Adjusts to meet the baby's needs. Levels of fat, protein, minerals, and lactose in breast milk change to meet the growing baby's nutritional needs.

- Is less expensive than formula.

Be sure to let the doctor and the hospital staff know whether you will be breastfeeding or bottle-feeding your infant.

Breastfeeding

The learning period for breastfeeding varies from woman to woman, but may last 3 to 6 weeks. If you are getting discouraged or your baby is having difficulty latching on, your pediatrician, nurse-midwife, or a lactation nurse can give you helpful guidance during this period of adjustment.

A common cause of painful nipples during the first few days of breastfeeding is positioning. You'll be more comfortable if the entire nipple and as much of the areola as possible are in the baby's mouth.

When you nurse your baby, choose a quiet place so you both can relax and enjoy this time together. Nurse your baby whenever he or she is hungry, which may be every 2 to 3 hours during the first several weeks. Breastfed babies usually eat more frequently than bottle-fed infants because breast milk is digested more quickly than formula. Drink plenty of liquids and eat a well-balanced diet to keep up your supply of milk and keep yourself healthy.

If a breast becomes painful and hot, and you have a fever, you may have a blocked milk duct or a breast infection. Your doctor can help you with this problem.

Bottle-Feeding

Be sure to prepare the formula exactly according to directions. Do not dilute ready-to-feed formula. If you fill several bottles at a time with formula, keep them refrigerated until you're ready to use them so the formula doesn't spoil. Throw away formula left in the bottle after your baby has finished a feeding. Don't warm the formula in the microwave; the bottle could explode or get too hot and burn your baby's mouth or throat. Always test the temperature of the warmed formula on the inside of your wrist (before you feed it to your baby) to make sure it isn't too hot.

Resources

National Institute of Child Health and Human Development
800 370.2943; www.nichd.nih.gov

National Center for Education in Maternal and Child Health
703.524.7802; www.brightfutures.org

LaLeche League (breastfeeding information and support):
800.LALECHE; www.laleche.org

Breastfeeding and Returning to Work

Now that so many working mothers are choosing to keep nursing their babies after they return to work, some employers offer a room reserved for pumping breast milk, provide breast pumps, and have refrigerators for storing milk. Even if your company is not able to offer these benefits, you may be able to pump breast milk successfully at work. The following ideas may help:

- Buy or rent a good breast pump. Make sure the pump works well for you. A nurse or a lactation consultant can make suggestions.

- Find a quiet, private place to pump at work. Express your milk during your morning and afternoon breaks.

- Bring a small cooler with reusable ice packs to store your milk, or store the milk in a refrigerator. Breast milk can be refrigerated for up to 5 days and frozen for up to 4 months.

- Shirts and blouses with front openings and a nursing bra are convenient when you pump your breasts at work. Keep a spare top at work in case your breasts leak.

- Maximize your feeding time with your baby. Breastfeed right before you leave your baby and immediately after getting home. This will be a comforting, reassuring time for you and your baby, before and after your separation.

Resource

Nursing Mother, Working Mother: The Essential Guide for Breastfeeding and Staying Close to Your Baby After You Return to Work, by Gale Pryor. Boston: Harvard Common Press, 1997.

Bed-Wetting

Most healthy children over age 5 have control over their bowels or bladders and are able to stay dry through the night. Bed-wetting, or enuresis, may be caused by delayed physical development or gastrointestinal problems. Bed-wetting in a child who has been dry for at least 1 year may be related to stress.

Unless your child has other physical symptoms or has had a major change in his or her life, the best thing you can do is be patient. He or she needs your calm support and reassurance; punishment certainly will not help.

If your child is a girl older than 5 or a boy older than 6, your doctor may recommend medication to treat this problem.

Symptoms/Signs

■ Involuntary urination at night at least twice a month.

Talk to Your Doctor If Your Child:

■ Was previously dry at night and has other symptoms, such as fever, abdominal pain, increased frequency of urination, painful urination, or blood in his or her urine.

■ Has symptoms of diabetes, such as excessive thirst and hunger along with frequent urination.

■ Was dry for a year before the bed-wetting episodes began and HomeCare procedures have not helped.

■ Is still wetting the bed and she is older than 5 or he is older than 6, or is also wetting during the day.

■ Also has constipation or soils his or her underpants.

■ Has a neurological disorder or delay in development (e.g., in walking, talking, or toilet training).

■ You think bed-wetting is due to stress.

If physician referral is not recommended at this time, try the following:

Fluids

• Before your child goes to bed, limit the amount of fluids he or she drinks. Encourage intake earlier in the day and evening.
• Don't give your child drinks that contain caffeine (e.g., cola), which can irritate the bladder.

NB
Note Well

• Remind your child to urinate before going to bed.
• Don't wake your child at night to go to the bathroom.
• You may try a reward system, for example, a gold star on a calendar for a dry night. However, never punish for an accident.
• If you suspect stress is the cause, encourage your child to talk about what's troubling him or her.
• If your child is more than 2 years old, allow him or her to wear training pants instead of diapers. This shows confidence.

Colic

Colic is a common problem among infants from about 2 weeks to 3 months of age. A colicky baby's crying spells may last for several hours and frequently occur in late afternoon or evening. While no one is certain of the cause, it may be due to the baby's immature system and unusual sensitivity to the outside world. Colic also seems to be associated with abdominal pain. Babies with colic often draw their legs up toward their tummies, and their stomachs may appear bloated with gas.

If you have a colicky baby, everyone in your household suffers as well. Lost sleep, frustration, and added stress can make matters much worse. The added tension in your family can even cause your infant to become more irritable. If you can, have someone else watch the baby while you take a break—go for a walk, lie down, or just get out of the house for a while. With your peace of mind restored, you'll be able to deal with a cranky infant without becoming impatient or disheartened. Remember, whatever you do, the problem probably will go away within a few months.

Symptoms/Signs

■ Extended, recurring episodes of inconsolable crying in an infant. The baby may draw legs up toward the abdomen.

Talk to Your Doctor If Your Child:

■ Has crying episodes that are accompanied by diarrhea (see page 110), fever, or vomiting (see page 119).
■ Creates stress in your household that becomes overwhelming.
■ Has a crying episode that lasts longer than 4 hours.
■ Is more than 4 months old and crying bouts aren't diminishing.

If physician referral is not recommended at this time, try the following:

Nutrition

• Check to see that your baby is being fed enough.
• If you are breastfeeding your baby, avoid alcohol and foods that may produce gas (e.g., cabbage, onions, caffeine).
• Adopt a leisurely pace during feeding times.
• Change the brand of formula or substitute soy milk for cow's milk formula.

Note Well

• Check to see that the nipple hole on your baby's bottle is the proper size. Milk should drip at a rate of 1 drop per second.
• Rocking, walking, or riding in the car may soothe your baby.
• No medications have been proven safe and effective for colic.
• Be aware of your own feelings and ask family members or friends to take over for you if you feel overwhelmed. Taking a break and resting will revive your energy and restore your patience.
• Lay your baby face down, across your lap with his or her tummy resting on your knees. Sometimes this pressure relieves belly pain.

Heat/Cold

• Heat formula only to body temperature.

Prevention

• Burp your baby frequently during feeding.

Croup

C roup is an infection of the voice box and windpipe that usually affects children between the ages of 1 and 3 years. Commonly, the child has a cold in the days before croup symptoms appear. With home treatment, usually the symptoms will go away in 5 or 6 days.

Symptoms/Signs

- Loud, seal-like, barking cough.
- Increased effort required to breathe.
- Crowing noise from the throat upon breathing in.
- Fever.
- Hoarseness.
- Symptoms that are worse at night.

Get Emergency Care If Your Child:

- Has increasingly labored breathing, a high-pitched whistling or wheezing noise upon inhalation, or breathing that causes the area between the ribs to heave excessively or draw inward during inhalation.
- Gasps for air or breathes with his or her mouth open and chin jutting out.
- Drools excessively or has difficulty swallowing.
- Cannot bend his or her neck forward.
- Has blue lips or skin.
- Has a fever of 102 F and rust-colored or pink and frothy mucus.

Talk to Your Doctor If Your Child:

- Is less than 3 months old and has croup symptoms.
- Has a fever of 102 F or higher.
- Is very restless or agitated and cannot be calmed.

If physician referral is not recommended at this time, try the following:

Heat/Cold

- Use a cold-steam vaporizer or let your child breathe cool night air.
- If this is not effective, turn on a hot shower, close the bathroom door for 10 minutes, then bring your child into the bathroom; remain in the steam for 10 to 20 minutes.

Medication

- Give acetaminophen to reduce fever and discomfort.
- For certain types of infection, your child's doctor may prescribe antibiotics.

Note: Because of the risk of Reye's syndrome, aspirin should not be given to or used by children or teenagers who have or are suspected of having flu or chicken pox. Use acetaminophen.

Fluids

- Have your child drink plenty of clear, warm liquids to loosen mucus.

Rest

- Help your child sleep sitting upright or semi-reclining if lying down appears to make breathing more difficult. For infants, use a safety seat or swing, or hold your child while he or she sleeps.

Note Well

- Do your best to remain calm; your child will be very frightened and agitated and needs your reassurance.
- Don't allow anyone to smoke in the same house as a child with croup.
- Sleep in the same room with your child until croup symptoms are gone; symptoms can quickly worsen and require immediate medical attention.

Crying

*C*rying is an expression of displeasure or discomfort. Crying can be a healthy way to resolve inner upsets, and infants have no other way to communicate when things aren't going well for them. Most often, the issue is something as obvious as hunger, dirty diapers, or being startled by a loud noise. Or it may something more subtle: Does the child feel lonely? Need reassurance? Responding with sensitivity to your child's needs usually stops the crying.

A special type of crying occurs during the "fussy period." This is most common during the first 3 or 4 months of life, often beginning by 2 weeks of age. Typically, an otherwise happy baby will have episodes of crying usually around the same time every day. These episodes can last several minutes to several hours. With colic, babies seem to get tense abdomens and appear to double up in pain. See page 235.

Temper tantrums bring on a great deal of crying in toddlers and preschoolers. The tantrum usually is an expression of anger or frustration over a general lack of control over things. Depending on the parent's reaction to this type of behavior, it may become an effective but unhealthy way for a child to get his or her way. Your best bet is to ignore the tantrum, unless you need to physically restrain your child from hurting himself or herself or others. Overreacting or indulging the child will only serve to encourage this behavior. Teach your child that it's better to express feelings with words, not violence. Be a good role model for your child.

Talk to Your Doctor If Your Child:

■ Has symptoms other than crying that require medical care.

■ Has an unusually persistent crying spell.

■ Has severe, persistent tantrums.

If physician referral is not recommended at this time, try the following:

Note Well

- Check for sources of physical discomfort: clothing that's too tight, areas of injury to the body, dirty diaper.
- Try feeding, burping, rocking, comforting. If cramping seems to be the problem, try laying the child on his or her stomach, across your lap.
- Remain calm. A baby or child in the midst of a tantrum may become even more upset if you are upset and anxious too.
- If all possible causes have been eliminated, and the above treatment is unsuccessful, place the child in his or her bed. Keep the room and house quiet. Allow the child to "wind down" alone.

Medication

- If the child has had very hard stools recently or has not had a stool for a day or two, ask your doctor about using a glycerin suppository made for infants to induce a bowel movement.

Nutrition

- If you are breastfeeding, stick to a bland diet; avoid eating foods that may cause the baby to have gas. Avoid all alcohol and caffeine.
- For your bottle-fed baby, try a soy-based formula for 4 to 5 days.

Prevention

- Be sure that your baby is getting enough food, rest, and quiet time. Hungry, tired, or overstimulated children are fussier and more apt to throw tantrums.

Diaper Rash

Nearly every baby will have diaper rash every now and then. An infant's sensitive skin and the irritating nature of urine and feces are a perfect combination for causing a sore, red bottom.

Yeast infections, using harsh detergents for washing diapers, and other irritants also can cause a rash. If you try basic care for diaper rash and don't notice improvement, consider another course of action. Change detergents, try a barrier cream (avoid powders, which can be a health hazard if your baby inhales them) with every diaper change for 2 weeks. Probably the best remedy is to leave your baby's bottom uncovered for a while each day, whenever it's convenient for you.

Symptoms/Signs

■ Red, blotchy (sometimes raised) patches on buttocks, thighs, and genitals.

Talk to Your Doctor If Your Child:

■ Has diaper rash that contains blisters or crusty areas.

■ Has a diaper rash with bright red spots that together form a solid red area with a scalloped border.

■ Has a diaper rash that shows no improvement after 2 days of home treatment.

Clean

- Change diapers frequently.
- During each diaper change, use plain water or mild soapy water and a soft cotton cloth or cotton balls to clean baby's bottom. Pat dry with a soft cloth. Avoid disposable baby wipes that contain alcohol.

Cover

- Avoid bulky diapers that can create a hothouse effect next to baby's skin.
- Fresh air works wonders on diaper rash. Try to give your baby a good deal of diaper-free time each day.

Medication

- Though it may slow healing, you can try an over-the-counter diaper rash cream or ointment with zinc oxide.

Prevention

- Change diapers as soon as you know they are wet or soiled.
- If you use cloth diapers, opt for more breathable diaper covers than plastic or rubber pants.
- Use a mild detergent to wash diapers and rinse them twice.
- Be sure that the diaper does not fit your baby too snugly; a baby's bottom needs room to breathe.
- If your baby is especially prone to diaper rash, use a barrier cream (e.g., A&D Ointment®, Balmex®, Desitin®) with each diaper change to keep moisture away from his or her skin.

Head Lice

No matter how clean your child and his or her surroundings are, you still may have to fight at least one battle with head lice. Children are most susceptible because they spend so much time with other children, and they're more likely than adults to share combs, brushes, hats, and clothing. Getting rid of lice on your child and in your home requires quick recognition of the problem and immediate, full-scale treatment of everything with which the lice could have come in contact.

Head lice are tiny (1/8 to 1/4 inch), yellow-gray bugs with six legs. They are easiest to spot at the nape of the neck or near the ears. Female lice lay tiny, round, white eggs (called nits) on individual hairs, which are very difficult to remove. Eggs hatch in about 10 days and the lice live by sucking blood from your child's scalp; it's the bugs' saliva that causes the intense itching. Sometimes, a scaly rash forms on the scalp. At the first sign of itching, inspect for lice and eggs.

If you find evidence of lice, immediately begin home treatment. Any type of lice infestation may require more than one round of home treatment; be persistent for 10 days after you think you've licked the problem.

Symptoms/Signs

- Intense itching of the scalp.
- Tiny, red bite marks.
- Lice on scalp, clothing, hats, or bedding.
- Nits on hair shafts.

Talk to Your Doctor If Your Child:

- Still has lice after HomeCare procedures are followed.

If physician referral is not recommended at this time, try the following:

Medication

- Use over-the-counter shampoos or lotions, such as NIX® or RID®, to kill lice and nits. Follow directions very carefully. Repeat as needed.
- Ask your doctor about a prescription shampoo if over-the-counter preparations are not working well.

Note Well

- Use tweezers or a fine-toothed comb (usually provided with over-the-counter lice-removal shampoos) to remove lice and nits from your child's hair shafts. If this doesn't work well, try soaking hair in a solution of equal amounts of water and vinegar. Follow this with a shower and shampoo.

Clean

- Wash all clothing, towels, hats, scarves, bedding, combs, and brushes that have been used since the infestation. Use hot water and a disinfecting detergent. Repeat as needed.

Activity

- Keep your child at home until at least one treatment with medicated shampoo has been completed.

Prevention

- Tell your child not to use other children's combs or brushes, or wear their hats or jackets.
- Check your child's hair and scalp regularly for signs of lice and their eggs, especially during peak season (August to November).

Mumps

Mumps was a common childhood disease before widespread immunization was introduced. It causes the salivary glands below the ear to swell. If your child seems ill and has swollen glands that make it difficult to feel his or her jawbone, he or she may have mumps. Occurring most often in children ages 2 to 12, the symptoms rarely last more than 2 weeks. If your child has mumps, concentrate on symptom relief; the virus has to run its course. Your child will be contagious for about 1 week before and 2 weeks after the appearance of symptoms. Adolescent and adult males who have not had mumps and have not been immunized against it should avoid contact with a child who has mumps because of the risk of serious complications such as sterility.

Symptoms/Signs

- One or both of the salivary glands (located below and in front of the ears) are swollen.
- Low-grade fever, loss of appetite, muscle aches, headache, pain behind ear upon chewing or swallowing, and/or fatigue.

Get Emergency Care Right Away If:
Your child has a high fever, headache, stiff neck, lethargy, convulsions, or aversion to light after developing mumps.

Call Your Doctor Right Away If:
- Your child has upper abdominal pain, nausea, or vomiting after developing mumps.

If physician referral is not recommended at this time, try the following:

Fluids

- Offer plenty of fluids to prevent dehydration and soothe sore glands.

Rest

- Your child should rest in bed while he or she has a fever.

Heat/Cold

- Provide ice packs or a heating pad for swollen glands.

Medication

- Give your child acetaminophen to relieve fever and discomfort.

Note: Because of the risk of Reye's syndrome, aspirin should not be given to or used by children or teenagers who have or are suspected of having flu or chicken pox. Use acetaminophen.

Activity

- Keep your child at home, away from others, while he or she is contagious (for 14 days after symptoms appear).

Prevention

- Have your child vaccinated against mumps. See page 44.
- If your child is exposed to someone with mumps and does not have immunity against it, see your doctor within 24 hours for a vaccine.

Seizure/Convulsion

A seizure (convulsion) in a child who has never had one before typically is the result of a spiking fever. Overheating causes misfiring of electrical impulses in the brain. These seizures that are associated with fevers (febrile seizures) usually occur in children 6 months to 5 years old, last less than 5 minutes, and leave no lasting effect. Susceptibility to seizures tends to run in families.

If a convulsion occurs, your primary goal is to prevent your child from injuring himself or herself or inhaling vomit.

As soon as your child has recovered fully from a convulsion and is alert, do what you can to keep any fever down (see page 113) and keep him or her comfortable. Write down the details of the convulsion—how long it lasted, physical movements, body temperature, etc.—and report them to your doctor immediately.

Symptoms/Signs

- Rigid body, clenched fists and jaw, twitching in limbs or face.
- Eyes rolling back in head.
- Excessive salivation.
- Possibly, unconsciousness.

Get Emergency Care Right Away If:

- You suspect poisoning (see page 96).
- Normal breathing and pulse do not resume after a seizure. Call 911 immediately, See page 93.

Call Your Doctor Right Away If:

Your child:
- Has never had a seizure before.
- Has a seizure that lasts for more than a few minutes.
- Is younger than 6 months or older than 5 years.
- Has a seizure that is not associated with a fever.
- Has a fever of 102 F or higher that you cannot reduce.
- Has a seizure after taking a prescribed medicine.

HOMECARE™

If physician referral is not recommended at this time, try the following:

Note Well

During a seizure:
- Lay the child on a soft/padded surface. Do not restrain, but try to protect the child from injury.
- If your child vomits, turn his or her head to the side to prevent choking.
- Keep your child's mouth clear of all objects. There's no danger of his or her tongue being swallowed.

Medication

- Use acetaminophen to reduce and control fever.

Heat/Cold

- Use cool (not cold) compresses or a tepid sponge bath to cool your child slowly. Never put your child in a bathtub during a convulsion.
- Do not use ice baths or packs; body temperature will fall too quickly.

Cover

- As you try to bring the fever down, remove your child's clothes. After the fever is under control, dress the child lightly.

Fluids

- After the convulsion is over and your child is alert, give clear, cool (not ice-cold) fluids.

Prevention

- Reduce fevers of 102 F and higher: Use acetaminophen or children's ibuprofen and tepid baths.

Tonsillitis

Tonsillitis is the inflammation of the tonsils due to infection. Just a generation ago, doctors removed tonsils from children who had occasional bouts of tonsillitis because they thought tonsils served no real function. More recently, research has shown that tonsils catch infections before they cause more serious respiratory infections. Without the tonsils, the infection would settle in elsewhere.

Most common in children aged 5 to 15, tonsillitis usually goes away within 5 to 7 days of the first symptoms. HomeCare can alleviate many of the symptoms, which are similar to those of flu or a cold. But when a bacterial infection such as strep is the culprit, your child will need antibiotic treatment. A doctor will consider removing the tonsils only when a child experiences multiple (three or more), severe infections within a 12-month period.

Symptoms/Signs

- Severe sore throat, often with difficulty swallowing.
- Fever, possibly accompanied by chills.
- Headache.
- Fatigue or lethargy.
- Swollen, tender glands of the jaw and throat.
- Dark red and swollen tonsils, possibly with white specks, streaks, or spots.

Talk to Your Doctor If Your Child:

- Has difficulty breathing.
- Has symptoms of tonsillitis that do not improve after 48 hours, especially if accompanied by a high fever. See fever guidelines on page 113.
- Has symptoms of tonsillitis and a history of recurrent tonsillitis.
- Has a sore throat that worsens, especially on one side, despite the use of antibiotics.

If physician referral is not recommended at this time, try the following:

Medication

- If your child has tonsillitis resulting from a streptococcal infection, the doctor probably will prescribe a 10-day course of antibiotics.
- Use acetaminophen to reduce fever and relieve discomfort.

Note: Because of the risk of Reye's syndrome, aspirin should not be given to or used by children or teenagers who have or are suspected of having flu or chicken pox. Use acetaminophen.

Fluids

- Offer plenty of clear, warm liquids to relieve throat pain.

Rest

- Your child should get plenty of bed rest to help his or her body fight infection. He or she should remain home from school until fever is gone and symptoms are improving.

Note Well

- If your child is old enough, have him or her gargle often with warm salt water.

Prevention

- Teach your child to wash his or her hands with soap and water after direct contact with others, especially during cold and flu season.
- When possible, avoid contact with others who have colds and sore throats.

Special Health Issues

In this section:

- Information about specific health conditions
- Managing health problems and appropriate treatment options
- Questions to ask your doctor

Alzheimer's Disease

Alzheimer's disease is a common brain disorder that damages the cells in the brain responsible for intellectual functions, including memory, intelligence, judgment, and speech. Therefore, it affects a person's ability to carry out activities of daily living. The disease is costly when you include the loss of personal functioning, the extraordinary emotional and physical stress placed on caregivers, and the need for expensive and prolonged medical services.

What are the symptoms?

Alzheimer's can cause individuals to have trouble concentrating and making decisions. They may feel disoriented and show intellectual decline and emotional and personality changes. In addition, depression is common, brought on by the social isolation, the awareness of the loss of physical or mental abilities, or changes in brain chemistry. Unfortunately, depression can increase the patient's sense of isolation. See "Depression," pages 264-265.

What causes Alzheimer's disease?

Alzheimer's is caused by changes in brain cells and brain chemistry that seem to disrupt messages responsible for normal thinking and memory. In addition, a tangle of fibers and/or plaques form around the nerves of the outer layer of the brain. Why these abnormalities develop has not been determined, but there seem to be genetic links to both early- and late-onset Alzheimer's disease. Researchers are also investigating the link between Alzheimer's and certain risk factors for cardiovascular disease.

How is Alzheimer's diagnosed?

There is no single test for this disease. And, before a diagnosis of Alzheimer's disease can be made, other illnesses and drug reactions that may cause symptoms similar to Alzheimer's must be ruled out. After other diseases are ruled out, a diagnosis of Alzheimer's usually can be made based on medical history, mental status, and comprehensive physical, neurological, and psychiatric evaluations.

What treatments are effective?

The U.S. Food and Drug Administration has approved five drugs to treat Alzheimer's: Cognex® (tacrine), Aricept® (donepezil), Exelon® (rivastigmine), Reminyl® (galantamine), and Namenda® (memantine). Although these drugs are not cures, they seem to delay

Warning Signs of Alzheimer's

1. Asking the same question over and over.
2. Repeating the same story, word for word, again and again.
3. Forgetting how to cook, or how to make repairs, or how to play cards—activities that were previously done with ease and regularity.
4. Losing the ability to pay bills or balance one's checkbook.
5. Getting lost in familiar surroundings, or misplacing household objects.
6. Neglecting to bathe, or wearing the same clothes over and over again, while insisting that they have taken a bath or that their clothes are still clean.
7. Relying on someone else, such as a spouse, to make decisions or answer questions they previously would have handled themselves.

Alzheimer's Disease Education and Referral Center, a service of the National Institute on Aging, 2003

Alzheimer's Disease

the worsening of symptoms for a limited time and may help control behavioral symptoms. Other medications may help reduce symptoms such as anxiety, depression, and disturbed sleep patterns. In the meantime, research continues to provide hope. For example, non-steroidal anti-inflammatory drugs (e.g., ibuprofen, naproxen) and vitamin E appear to help slow the progression of Alzheimer's disease.

What about caregiving?

Living with and caring for someone with Alzheimer's is a challenge. These ideas may help:

- Proper nutrition and fluid intake are important, but special diets and supplements usually are not needed. Some people need to be encouraged to eat, while others seem to want to eat constantly.

- Activities should be kept as close to normal as possible. Changing the home environment (e.g., rearranging furniture, remodeling) may contribute to the patient's confusion and agitation.

- Communicate in simple words and phrases, using a calm, pleasant tone. Try not to speak as though you were talking to a child.

- Take advantage of support groups for families and friends of people with Alzheimer's disease.

- For the safety of the patient, try to take measures such as locking doors, windows, and cabinets, (exception: *remove* the lock from the bathroom door); and securing items such as medications, firearms, matches, knives, and household chemicals.

- As the disease progresses and the individual needs more care, a long-term care setting may be more appropriate.

Important Questions

Note: The following questions may be appropriate for the caregiver to consider, as well as the patient.

- Are regular checkups needed, or should I see my doctor only when I am having a problem?
- What can I do to slow the progress of the disease? What should I eat? Should I exercise?
- What medications will I be taking? How long will I need to take this drug(s) before I feel its effects? Will this drug affect other drugs I take? How?
- Are there any new treatment options we could try? What are the benefits, risks, and costs of these options?
- How can I make my home/environment safer?
- What support groups or organizations are available to help me (or the family) cope with Alzheimer's disease? How can I contact them?
- What happens if I do nothing? What are the risks? Are there any benefits to this approach?

Arthritis

We tend to think of arthritis as a condition affecting only older people. While its true that most people over age 75 have arthritis in at least one joint, the fact is that arthritis in its various forms can affect people of any age.

What is arthritis?

Arthritis is an inflammatory disease of the joints. To diagnose arthritis, your doctor will do a complete physical examination, paying special attention to your joints and your history of arthritis-like symptoms. In addition, X-rays, examination of joint fluids, and blood tests (for some forms of arthritis) are useful in making a diagnosis. While there are more than 100 different kinds of arthritic conditions, these are the most common:

Osteoarthritis (OA) occurs when the cartilage surrounding a joint breaks down. People who have spent a career overusing one or more of their joints (e.g., construction workers, athletes, dancers, miners) have a greater chance of developing osteoarthritis than does the rest of the population. That's why osteoarthritis is sometimes called "wear-and-tear" arthritis.

- **Symptoms:** Joint pain that is worse when the joints are being used, but gets better with rest. A joint may move through its range of motion with difficulty and it may make a grinding sound. Most people feel osteoarthritis in the knees and hips, but it can affect fingers, shoulders, and feet as well.

- **Managing OA:** Aerobic, strength, and stretching exercises (e.g., walking, for those with knee arthritis), eating a balanced diet, weight loss (extra body weight stresses joints), and soothing joints with creams such as Ben-Gay® or Capsaicin®.

- **Drug therapy:** Acetaminophen (e.g, Tylenol®), nonsteroidal anti-inflammatory medications (NSAIDs) such as ibuprofen, and COX-2 inhibitors (Celebrex®) reduce pain and improve mobility. More aggressive treatments include joint injections or joint replacement surgery.

Rheumatoid arthritis (RA) is less common and more baffling than osteoarthritis. The disease can appear at any age (even in children), but most new patients are women between the ages of 20 and 50. RA is a disease of the immune system (autoimmune disorder) that affects the whole body, not just the joints. The body's defenses attack tissue surrounding joints and then replace it with new, inflammatory tissue. Involved joints are gradually destroyed, causing pain and loss of movement.

- **Symptoms:** Joint pain, stiffness, and swelling. Joints are affected on both sides of the body (e.g., both knees, both hips). It also causes fatigue, fever, loss of appetite, and can affect other parts of the body (e.g., eyes, heart).

- **Managing RA:** Achieving a healthy body weight, balancing rest with appropriate exercise. Tai Chi and swimming are ideal activities because they don't place any extreme stress on the joints.

Stat Facts: Arthritis

- More than 40 million people in the United States have some form of arthritis.
- About 20 percent of adults have arthritis symptoms.
- Osteoarthritis is a leading cause of disability in the United States.
- Rheumatoid arthritis affects two to three times more women than men.

Source: Centers for Disease Control and Prevention

Arthritis

■ **Drug therapy:** Usually begun as soon as the disease is diagnosed, NSAIDs to reduce pain and inflammation are combined with Disease Modifying Anti-Rheumatic Drugs (DMARDs), which slow the destruction of the joints. More aggressive therapy may involve adding injections of drugs that work directly on the cells causing the inflammation.

Gout is caused by a buildup of uric acid in the body and the formation of uric acid crystals in the fluid that bathes the joint, causing severe pain and swelling in that joint. Gout is associated with obesity, high blood pressure, diabetes, high cholesterol, and kidney disease.

■ **Symptoms:** Sudden severe pain, swelling, and redness, usually in one joint—often the big toe.

■ **Managing gout:** Losing weight, managing blood pressure, and lowering cholesterol will help reduce gout attacks.

■ **Drug therapy:** NSAIDs for pain, and drugs that help remove uric acid (Probenecid®), or steroid medications to reduce inflammation.

Ankylosing spondylitis (AS) is arthritis of the joints of the spine that may eventually cause fusion or destruction of the joints. A gene has been identified that is found in most people with AS, but otherwise, its cause is unknown.

■ **Symptoms:** Stiffness and pain in the lower back and hip.

■ **Managing AS:** Exercising, practicing good posture, doing abdominal and back exercises.

■ **Drug Therapy:** NSAIDs may reduce pain and allow movement, which helps keep the bones of the spine from fusing.

How will I know if I am at risk for arthritis?

Arthritis tends to run in families and the older you are, the more likely you are to have arthritis. Women are affected three times more often than men.

What if I suspect I have arthritis?

You should call your doctor if: you have arthritis pain with fever, there is sudden unexplained swelling, redness or pain in any joint, the pain is so great that you cannot use the joint or it limits your regular activities, or the problem does not get better after 5 to 6 weeks and HomeCare is not working. See page 190.

If you have arthritis in one or more of its various forms, you may feel down and out from time to time. However, it's not healthy when symptoms of depression are more severe, longer lasting, and more disabling. See pages 264-265.

Important Questions

- What side effects are possible from the medications prescribed for arthritis?
- Are creams effective for relieving the pain of arthritis? What are the advantages and disadvantages of creams over oral medications?
- When is physical therapy helpful?
- What is the best exercise to help my arthritis?
- If joint replacement surgery is recommended, what should I expect?
- What assistive devices are available (e.g., canes, faucet turners, etc.) to help me with daily activities and to take pressure off my affected joints?

Asthma

Asthma is a chronic, potentially life-threatening illness that cannot be cured. However, asthma can be controlled. If you have asthma, it's important to work with your doctor to develop a treatment plan that prevents or relieves symptoms. It's also a good idea to carry medical identification such as a MedicAlert® bracelet or wallet card at all times.

What is asthma?

Asthma is a chronic upper respiratory disease caused by inflammation of the small breathing tubes (bronchioles) of the lungs, which makes it difficult or impossible to breathe. In asthma, the airways are always sensitive, swollen, or inflamed to some degree. During an attack, exposure to specific triggers causes the immune system to kick into high gear. The linings of the breathing tubes swell and become irritated. Mucus clogs the airways even more. In addition, the muscles that surround the breathing tubes tighten (called bronchospasm), further restricting breathing.

What causes asthma?

Asthma usually is triggered by: infections such as the common cold and influenza, allergens (e.g., pollens, molds, dust, animal dander, certain foods), cold air, tobacco smoke, strenuous exercise, air pollution, pesticides, chemical fumes, drugs (e.g., aspirin, acetaminophen, heart medications), and stress or strong emotions.

Some people have asthma symptoms when they exercise. However, exercise-induced asthma (EIA) is not a reason to be inactive. In fact, physical activity helps build and maintain lung function. Professional and Olympic athletes with EIA have excelled in their chosen sports with proper medical supervision.

Who is at risk for asthma?

Asthma seems to run in families. It is more common in children than adults, and more boys than girls have asthma. But in adults, more women than men have asthma. About 25 percent of children will outgrow asthma by adulthood. The most important thing to remember is that asthma at any age is a serious health condition that requires a doctor's care.

What are the symptoms of an asthma attack?

Symptoms of an asthma attack may start suddenly or they may take a long time to develop. In turn, symptoms can be severe, moderate, or mild.

- **Mild to moderate attack:** coughing, wheezing, shortness of breath, tightness in the chest, and spitting up mucus. When this happens, take your asthma medication and call your doctor if symptoms do not clear up within the time your doctor has told you they should, or if symptoms get worse.

- **Exercise-induced asthma (EIA):** tightness in the chest, shortness of breath, wheezing, coughing, fatigue, and difficulty recovering after exercise.

Get Emergency Care Right Away If:

You experience symptoms of a severe attack, which may include the inability to catch your breath or feeling breathless. You may have a hard time talking. Your fingernails may be bluish or grayish, neck muscles may be tight, and chest muscles (between the ribs) may feel sucked in and tight. Organs in your body may not be receiving enough oxygen. Take your asthma medicine right away.

Asthma

What does "the second wave" mean?

The second wave is a condition in which the air tubes continue to swell, even without symptoms for some people, after an initial asthma attack has eased. This reaction can last for days or for weeks and make the lungs more sensitive to triggers. A second-wave attack can be more severe and life-threatening than the first attack.

How is asthma diagnosed?

Your doctor will take your medical history to see if you have another health problem that may mimic asthma, such as allergies or an upper respiratory infection. Other tests may include a physical exam with chest X-rays, blood work, urine test, sputum test, tests that measure your breathing efficiency, or other evaluations such as allergy tests.

How can I monitor my asthma?

Apart from symptoms, you can tell if your airways are narrowing before an attack by using a peak flow meter, which measures lung efficiency. By blowing into the hand-held device, you can tell if your lung power is decreasing, which may be your signal of a potential asthma attack.

How is asthma treated?

There is no cure for asthma, but you can reduce or even prevent most attacks by managing your asthma conscientiously, every day. It's important to be under your doctor's supervision, because asthma attacks can be life-threatening if left untreated. Depending on the severity of your symptoms, there are many things you and your doctor can do to manage your asthma:

- **Reduce your exposure** to the things that trigger your asthma attacks. Keeping a diary or journal of your symptoms can help you identify your triggers.

- **Wise lifestyle choices.** Very simply, don't smoke (and avoid exposure to secondhand smoke). Drink plenty of water or breathe in warm, moist air to ease your breathing. Regular aerobic exercise such as brisk walking and swimming can help build lung capacity. (You may need to take medications before exercising to help open up airways.)

- **Monitor your lung function** with a peak flow meter.

- **Medications** for asthma are either used as long-term controllers or for quick relief from an attack.
  - Long-term controller medications (maintenance medicines) work by controlling inflammation or keeping the airways open. They are taken commonly as inhaled medications; however, some oral medications are included in this category. The most important thing about these maintenance medications is that, once prescribed, they must be used every day as directed by your doctor—even if you are feeling well and don't have any asthma symptoms. If you stop taking them, your asthma symptoms will get worse again.

Asthma

–Short-acting medications (rescue or quick-relief medications) stop an asthma attack once it starts. They act quickly to relax the muscles around the airways. Everyone with asthma needs to carry these medications at all times. This is true even if you take controller medicines. If your controller medications are working, a quick-relief medicine won't be needed every day—only if you have an asthma attack. If you use your quick-relief medicine more than one or two times a week, tell your doctor.

–For severe attacks your doctor may give you an injection of epinephrine (adrenaline), which provides short-term relief. Your doctor also may teach you how to self-administer epinephrine at home in case of emergency.

■ **Allergy shots** (hyposensitization therapy) expose you to certain allergens in small amounts over a long period of time. Your system becomes less sensitive to these allergens, thus reducing the chances of an asthma attack.

■ **Counseling and stress management** can help if your asthma attacks are triggered or complicated by emotional factors. Medications can be prescribed to reduce agitation, anxiety, depression, and unpredictable behavior, and to improve sleep.

What's the best way to control my asthma?

The American Lung Association recommends three things:

1. **See your doctor on a regular basis.** Share with him or her any changes in your symptoms, reactions to your medications, and any new triggers that cause symptoms.

2. **Take your asthma medications** as directed by your doctor. *Don't stop taking your medication, even if you feel well.*

3. **Stay informed about asthma.** Learn about asthma triggers and how you may avoid them. Also, be sure that your family understands what asthma is, its symptoms, and how to provide emergency care if you cannot do it yourself.

Important Questions

- What agents or situations trigger my attacks?
- How can I avoid these triggers?
- What do I need to do when an asthma attack occurs?
- What medications will I be taking? How should they be taken? What side effects are possible? Will this drug affect the other drugs I take? How? What medications should I carry at all times?
- How long does each drug take to relieve my symptoms? What should I do if my symptoms don't go away in the expected time?
- If I'm allergic to certain things, should I consider allergy shots?
- How do I use a peak flow meter to monitor my condition? What readings may indicate a potential attack?
- I hear that exercise is good for me, yet I have trouble breathing when I work out. What do I need to do in order to make exercise safe?
- Where can I get information on how to make my home and environment safer for me?
- What support groups or organizations are available to help me cope with asthma?

Back Pain

I't's estimated that more than two-thirds of all adults have had at least one episode of back pain. In fact, backaches are one of the most common reasons for a visit to the doctor.

What could place me at risk for back pain?

A number of factors increase risk: a sedentary lifestyle, being overweight, heavy tobacco use, injury, diseases such as osteoporosis or ankylosing spondylitis, stress, poor work posture, frequent heavy lifting, poor lifting techniques, vibration from vehicles and machinery, and aging.

Why is the back such a common place to have pain?

Your spine is constructed somewhat like a stack of round bones (vertebrae), separated by rubbery shock absorbers (disks). The spinal cord runs through the center of these bones, carrying electrical signals from the brain. A number of smaller joints, muscles, and ligaments provide strength, support, and flexibility to the spine as well. This complex system has to be flexible so it can withstand the stress of moving your body to stand, lift, walk, twist, bend, and turn.

What common situations cause back pain?

■ Sudden forceful twisting or jerking movements can cause supporting muscles to tear or spasm.

■ With age, wear-and-tear changes (arthritis) in the lower back limit flexibility and cause pain and stiffness.

■ Osteoporosis can cause the bones in the back to become weak and brittle so that stress from everyday activities may cause fracture(s).

Stat Facts: Back Pain

• For 85 percent of back pain sufferers, the primary site of pain is the lower back.
• Back pain is the second leading cause of absenteeism from work, after the common cold.
• Back injuries cause 100 million lost days of work annually.

Source: American Academy of Orthopaedic Surgeons

Is all back pain the same?

Symptoms may range from aching and soreness to severe pain, which may limit your ability to move and perform your daily activities. Arthritis pain may be a steady ache. Pain from strains and sprains in your back is acute and sharp. Osteoporosis pain usually has a sudden onset. In many cases, the cause of the pain may be unclear.

What should I do if I experience back pain?

In most cases, excessive bed rest (i.e., more than 2 days) isn't required. Also, it's dangerous to overuse prescription medications (such as Percodan® or Percocet®) to manage your pain. Getting well may be as simple as doing back exercises and limiting your activity (e.g., avoid lifting and twisting).

However, you should consult your doctor if you:

■ Have pain or numbness that moves from your back into your leg or foot.

■ Have severe pain, even though you can still move.

■ Experience low-back pain that happens with other physical symptoms such as painful or frequent urination, flu, gastrointestinal distress, or abdominal pain.

Back Pain

■ Feel low-back pain associated with loss of control of bladder or bowels.

■ Have tried self-care procedures and they fail to provide relief after 72 hours.

■ Find that your low-back pain is associated with weakness of any muscles in the leg or foot.

Get Emergency Care Right Away If:
You sustain an injury from a fall or being hit in the back and are unable to move your legs. Stay still until help arrives.

How will the doctor diagnose my back pain?

The doctor will ask you questions about your symptoms—what they are like, how and when they started—as part of a comprehensive medical history. The doctor also may do a physical exam focusing on the back and spine. You may be asked to show how much range of motion you have as you bend and twist. If you have symptoms such as weakness, numbness, or tingling in your arms and legs, the doctor also may perform a neurological exam such as testing the reflexes in your legs and feet. Finally, the doctor may order imaging studies (e.g., X-ray or MRI) to help pinpoint the cause of your back pain.

What's the best way to treat back pain?

Practice prevention. Back problems can be avoided with good lifting techniques, maintaining good posture, controlling your weight, not smoking, participating in regular exercise, and doing regular stretching exercises. See pages 10–12 and 255.

Your doctor may prescribe muscle relaxants, anti-inflammatory drugs and pain relievers, or refer you to a physical therapist for treatment.

If back pain does not require a doctor's attention, self-care treatments may include limiting activity, resting on a firm surface with your back flat (for no more than a few days), applying ice packs, and taking aspirin or ibuprofen as directed to reduce pain and inflammation.

Few people with back pain require surgery, such as the removal of a herniated disk. If surgery is recommended, ask sensible questions about available options and the costs, benefits, and risks of each option. A second opinion from another specialist may be advisable before you consent to surgery. See "Making Informed Medical Decisions," pages 78-81.

Important Questions

- What are the options for treating my back pain? What are the risks, benefits, and costs of each?
- If surgery is appropriate for me, what are the benefits? Are there risks? What are the costs? Success rate? Must it be done immediately or can it be delayed? How long? What will happen if I choose not to have surgery?
- Will I need rehabilitation? How much and for how long?
- Will I need to change my level of activity? How much and for how long?
- How will I know if I am taking too much medication?
- Will exercise help my back pain?
- What can I do to prevent episodes of back pain from recurring?
- Where can I get help for making lifestyle changes such as managing my weight and stress, exercising, or stopping smoking?
- Is it likely that my back injury will heal itself or that my pain will go away? How long might this take?

Back Care

Fortunately, 70 percent of those with back pain will get better within a month, and most will recover within 10 days. The following ideas and exercises will help you keep your back healthy and, if you have a back problem, will help you manage it. *Note: If you have a back problem, talk to your doctor before you try any of the exercises on page 255.*

Ideas that Work

■ **Stay active.**
  –Try to exercise 3 to 5 days a week, with aerobic activities such as brisk walking, swimming, cycling, and jogging. See pages 6-7.
  –Keep your abdominal and lower-back muscles strong. See page 255.
  –Warm up with simple stretches before you do lifting or twisting movements. See pages 10-12.

■ **Reach a healthy weight.** One extra pound on the abdomen puts as much as five extra pounds of stress on your lower back. See pages 22-23.

■ **Relax.** Practice relaxation techniques to help prevent or reduce stress and tension. See pages 33-34.

■ **Take a break.** If you sit or stand for extended periods of time, take hourly stretch breaks.

■ **Practice good posture,** both sitting and standing.

■ **After menopause,** women should monitor bone density to identify osteoporosis.

■ **Lift properly.** The leading cause of back injuries is improper lifting techniques. These tips may help:

–Clear the carrying path; note where the object is to be placed; and if possible adjust the height of the object. If the object does not have handles, lifting it from the bottom can be difficult.

–If the object is not fragile, tip it up to roughly knee height. The body is strongest from knee to shoulder height, peaking around hip height.

–When you're carrying a load, turn your whole body in the direction you need to go. Avoid twisting or jerking movements.

–Stack material you're carrying so that your view is clear while you're carrying it.

–If the load to be lifted weighs more than 30 pounds, use two people to make the lift or use mechanical means (hoist, etc.).

–Use handholds if the two-person load weighs more than 70 pounds.

–Two people carrying a long object should hold it at the same level, on the same side of the body.

–Setting the load down is just as important as picking it up. Lower the load by bending your knees, keeping your back straight.

–Avoid strain when lifting by storing heavy objects at least 12 inches above the floor.

–Don't overreach or overstretch to reach objects stored overhead. This can result in strains or falls.

–Wear shoes with firm, slip-resistant soles.

–Never hurry or run when you're carrying a load.

–Use mechanical aids such as hand carts if you can.

–When wearing gloves, make sure you have a firm grip before trying to lift.

–Consider wearing a lifting belt that supports the lower back.

Lifting Properly

■ Squat as though you're sitting in a chair, with your feet flat on the floor and your knees bent (even with, or behind, your toes). Keep your head forward and your body weight shifted back over your heels to counter the weight of the object.

■ For leverage, hold the load between your legs, about 10 inches above your feet.

■ Keep your head and back aligned, tuck your chin and keep a slight inward curve in your low back.

■ Get a firm, secure grip. Be especially careful if you're wearing gloves.

■ Take a second to get set and then stand up smoothly using your legs rather than your back or arms to produce force. Avoid jerking the load, or twisting or bending to the side.

■ To put a load down, just follow these steps in reverse—keep the load close to your body, keep your head and back aligned, bend at the knees, and place the load down between your legs.

Note: If the load is too heavy or hard to handle, use a handcart or get help.

Lifting Awkward Loads

Odd-sized loads. Carry long objects supported on your shoulder, keeping the front end higher than the back end.

Overhead loads. If the object is above shoulder level, use a ladder to prevent overreaching. If it's under 25 pounds, slide it to you and hug it to your body as you descend.

Reaching into a bin. Stand with your feet shoulder-width apart, bend your knees, and squat, bending at your hips, not at your waist. Slide the object as close to your body as you can and raise yourself up using your leg and hip muscles. Tighten your stomach muscles as you lift and rest your knees against the side of the container. Be careful not to jerk the object out.

Back Conditioning

Abdominal Curls

- Lie on your back with your knees bent and your feet flat on the floor about 12 inches from your buttocks.
- Fold your arms across your chest.
- Keep your chin tucked in, tighten your stomach muscles and press your lower back against the floor as you lift your head and chest slightly off the floor. Keep the motion controlled and smooth. Breathe out as you lift.
- Lower yourself with control to the resting position.
- Do 15 to 20 repetitions. Repeat 2 to 3 times. Rest for 2 minutes in between.

Single Knee-to-Chest Stretch

- Lie on your back with your feet flat and your knees bent.
- Grasp one leg just below the knee.
- Let your back muscles relax.
- Pull your leg toward your chest until you feel a gentle stretch. Try to relax away the tightness.
- Hold for 15 seconds.
- Repeat 2 to 3 times. Alternate with each leg.

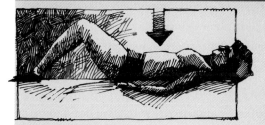

Back Press

- Lie on your back with your knees bent and your feet flat on the floor.
- Relax your arms at your sides.
- Tighten your stomach muscles and press the small of your back against the floor as you exhale.
- Hold for 6 seconds, then relax.
- Repeat 3 to 5 times.

Back Extension

- Stand with your feet shoulder-width apart.
- Place your hands on the small of your lower back.
- Extend your shoulders back gently to a point of tension.
- Hold for 6 seconds, relax.
- Repeat 3 to 5 times.

Breast Cancer

reast cancer remains the most common and second most deadly form of cancer (after lung cancer) in women. Fortunately, if you are diagnosed with breast cancer, the earlier it is caught the better your chances for survival.

What is breast cancer?

Lumps, thickening, or tumors in the breasts can be malignant (cancer) or benign (not cancer). Breast cancer cells can damage the tissues near the tumor. The cells also can break away from the tumor and spread throughout the breast tissue, into the lymph nodes, and to other parts of the body. Without treatment, cancer cells continue to grow, crowding out and replacing healthy cells.

Stat Facts: Breast Cancer

- More than 38,000 women in the United States will die from breast cancer this year.
- One of every eight women can expect to get breast cancer.
- About 180,000 women will be diagnosed with breast cancer next year.

Source: National Cancer Institute

What causes breast cancer?

While the exact cause is not known, bumping or bruising the breast tissue does not cause breast cancer. The process by which cancer develops in the body usually takes years (see "Cancer" page 258). However, there are risk factors that increase your chances of developing breast cancer.

What are the risk factors for breast cancer?

■ Risk factors you may be able to control include:

–**Obesity after menopause.** Postmenopausal women who have excessive body fat have more estrogen in their bodies. Elevated estrogen levels may lead to a higher risk of getting breast cancer.

–**Physical inactivity.** If you're physically inactive, you're more likely to gain weight, especially after menopause. One study found that the risk of breast cancer was lowest in lean women who exercised at least 4 hours per week.

–**Alcohol use.** The more alcohol you drink, the more your risk for breast cancer increases.

–**Hormone replacement therapy.** Taking estrogen alone or estrogen with progestin for more than 5 years may increase your risk of breast cancer.

■ Risk factors you may *not* be able to control include:

–**Age.** Breast cancer occurs more often in women over age 60, less often before menopause. Most diagnosed breast cancers are in women with no known risk factors, other than growing older.

–**Family history.** Your risk is higher if your mother, sister, daughter, or another close relative has had breast cancer. Families with a high incidence of breast cancer seem to have changes in certain genes that make breast cancer more likely.

–**Race.** The incidence of breast cancer is highest in Caucasian women.

–**Your history.** You are at increased risk if you: began having menstrual periods before age 12; went through menopause after 55; or never had children.

Breast Cancer

How can I take an active role in the health of my breasts?

1. **Evaluate your risk** with your doctor's help.

2. **Have a clinical breast exam** performed by your doctor or other health professional every year.

3. **Have a mammogram.** This is the surest way to detect cancer in its earliest stages. Low-dose X-rays can show breast lumps when they are too small to be felt. All women over age 40 should have one every 1 to 2 years, and every year after age 50. *Note: If you have significant risk factors, your doctor may recommend screenings at an earlier age, including mammogram, ultrasound, and MRI.*

4. **Breast self-exam.** You may choose to examine your breasts regularly (see page 45). This is the best way to become familiar with your normal breast tissue. Report any changes you find to your doctor.

What are the signs of breast cancer?

■ Size and shape of the breast changes.

■ Skin looks scaly, red, or looks pitted, like the skin of an orange.

■ Discharge (fluid) coming from the nipple.

■ Nipple appears inverted (pulled in) or feels tender.

■ A lump or thickening in the breast, near the breast, or in the underarm area.

How is breast cancer diagnosed?

If you find any changes in your breast, see your doctor right away. Your doctor will be able to find out if the changes you report are cancer or not. If your doctor suspects a problem, further testing will be done, which may include X-rays, MRI, ultrasound, or a biopsy, which removes fluid or tissue from the breast so it can be examined for cancerous cells.

How is breast cancer treated?

Depending on the type and severity of the breast cancer, treatment choices may include the following four standard therapies:

■ **Surgery** to either remove the cancer but save the breast (lumpectomy or partial mastectomy) or to remove the breast, the surrounding tissue, and the lymph nodes (total, radical, or modified radical mastectomy).

■ **Radiation therapy.** X-rays or other forms of radiation are used to kill cancer cells.

■ **Chemotherapy.** Strong drugs are given to kill the cancer cells or stop them from growing.

■ **Hormone therapy.** Drugs are given to remove or block hormones and stop the growth of the cancer.

Depression is common among women facing breast cancer. You'll manage your battle with cancer more effectively if you treat your depression as well. See pages 264-265.

Important Questions

- What is my level of risk for breast cancer?
- When should I begin having mammograms?
- If it's needed, what kind of diagnostic test is best for me? What are the risks?
- What type of cancer do I have? How advanced is it?
- Who will help me decide on a treatment plan?

Cancer

One out of every two men and one of every three women in the United States will get some form of cancer at some point in his or her life. Over 500,000 Americans die from cancer each year.

At least one-third of cancer deaths in the United States are linked to smoking, and another 35 percent are associated with diet. And there has been a great increase in cases of malignant melanoma, a form of skin cancer. The good news is you can reduce your risk of getting cancer or dying from it by modifying your lifestyle habits and taking advantage of early detection and screening programs.

What is cancer?

Cancer occurs when cells in the body grow abnormally and divide to create more abnormal cells, eventually forming a growth or tumor. Without treatment, these cells continue to grow and crowd out the healthy cells, invading and damaging the tissues. They also may spread to other parts of the body (metastasis). Although all cancers have similar characteristics, each is different in its own way. Some are easy to cure, others are not. Some are slow growing, while others take over the body rapidly.

Stat Facts: Cancer

- The four leading cancers are lung, breast, prostate, and colorectal.
- Cancer accounts for nearly 25 percent of the deaths in the United States.
- In 2000, there were 9.6 million cancer survivors in the United States, with an average age of 65.

Source: National Cancer Institute

What causes cancer?

Cancer is the result of changes in certain genes. Normal genes stimulate cells to start dividing, some halt this process, and others repair damaged genes. Usually, a delicate balance keeps cell growth in check. But in cancer, this process is upset when the genes mutate and abnormal cells grow out of control. Most of these mutations are caused by environmental or lifestyle factors, but some are inherited. Viruses may cause certain leukemias and lymphomas, cancer of the nose and pharynx, liver cancer, and cervical cancer.

What are the risk factors for cancer?

The following may increase your risk of developing cancer:

- **Tobacco use.** 85 percent of all lung cancer deaths are caused by smoking. Smokeless tobacco (chew, snuff) causes cancers of the mouth and esophagus. Secondhand smoke raises the chance of a non-smoker getting lung cancer.

- **Diet.** Research has shown a link between cancers of the colon, prostate, and uterus and a high-fat diet. A high-fiber diet may reduce your risk of colon cancer.

- **Ultraviolet radiation.** Excessive exposure to the sun or the use of sunlamps and tanning booths can lead to changes in the skin that cause skin cancer.

- **Alcohol.** Heavy drinking can cause cancer of the larynx, liver, mouth, throat, and esophagus. Women who drink moderately may increase their risk for breast cancer slightly.

- **Chemicals, metals, pesticides.** These may act alone or with other cancer-causing agents (smoking) to cause cancer.

Cancer

■ **Hormone replacement therapy.** Researchers have found that HRT can increase the risk of cancer in some situations. Talk to your doctor about the safety of short-term HRT to manage menopausal symptoms.

■ **Family history.** Your risk for developing cancer is higher if any close relatives have had colon, melanoma, breast, ovary, or prostate cancer.

What are some of the signs of cancer?

■ Change in bowel or bladder habits.

■ A sore that does not heal.

■ Unusual bleeding or discharge.

■ Thickening or lump in breast or elsewhere.

■ Indigestion or difficulty swallowing.

■ Obvious changes in a wart or mole.

■ Nagging cough or hoarseness.

■ Unexplained weight loss.

How is cancer detected and diagnosed?

You can screen yourself for the changes described on page 45. Follow your doctor's recommendations for cancer screening. See page 43. If you have any of the signs and symptoms above, contact your doctor. Depending on the examination, imaging tests (MRI, CAT scan, ultrasound) may be ordered. He or she may recommend a biopsy or tissue sample of the area examined to look for abnormal cells. If cancer is diagnosed, it is categorized (staged) by severity on a scale from 1 to 4—from localized to metastasized.

What about treatment options?

Treatments will vary by type of cancer; however, they may include:

■ **Surgery.** Removes the cancer, surrounding tissue, and lymph nodes.

■ **Chemotherapy.** Kills cancer cells with powerful drugs.

■ **Radiation.** Destroys cancer cells.

■ **Hormone therapy.** Prevents cancer cells from getting the hormones they need to grow, either with drugs, or by removing the organs that produce hormones.

■ **Immunotherapy.** Helps the body's immune system fight the disease with biological agents.

■ **Bone marrow transplantation.** A cancer patient receives new stem cells (immature blood cells) to replace those lost in chemo or radiation therapy.

Finally, cancer patients may become clinically depressed, which can make battling cancer far more difficult. See "Depression," pages 264-265.

Important Questions

• Considering my age and family history, what cancer-screening tests should I have? How often?

• If I have cancer, what are my treatment options? What are the benefits and risks of each option?

• If I have cancer, what stage is it? What does this mean in relation to my treatment options and the likelihood of survival?

• How can I learn more about a specific cancer and available treatment options?

• Where can I find support groups to help me?

Cataracts

As part of the aging process, most of us will experience changes in vision. A gradual decline in the ability to read small print or to focus on close objects is normal by about age 50. Although some changes in your vision are expected as you grow older, there are other eye conditions, such as cataracts, that should be evaluated and treated. In fact, cataracts are relatively common in older adults, and 90 percent of people over age 75 have some type of cataract.

What is a cataract?

A cataract is a change that happens to the lens of your eye. The lens is located in the front of the eye, just behind the iris (the colored part). Light travels into the eye through the lens, which normally is crystal clear. But with a cataract, the lens becomes thick, cloudy, and stiff. The cloudy lens blocks or distorts the light entering the eye just as a smudge on a camera lens would decrease the amount of light coming into the camera.

What causes cataracts?

Most cataracts are caused by normal changes in the aging eye. Cataracts also may be present at birth, or they can be caused by overexposure to sunlight, an injury to the eye, chemical burns, electrical shocks, certain drugs, or radiation. You also are more likely to develop cataracts if you smoke cigarettes, have taken corticosteroid medications, or have diabetes.

How will I know if I have a cataract?

Cataract symptoms develop gradually and painlessly in one or both eyes. They can include:

- Foggy, blurry, fuzzy vision.

- Difficulty driving at night because of glare from oncoming car headlights.

- Hazy vision in bright sunlight.

- Double vision.

- Frequent eyeglass prescription changes.

- The lens of the eye appears milky, with very dim vision (later stages).

How are cataracts diagnosed?

Cataracts can be diagnosed by an ophthalmologist (a medical doctor and surgeon who specializes in disorders of the eye) or an optometrist. He or she will do a comprehensive exam, after your eyes have been dilated, to look at the lenses and the insides of your eyes.

What treatments are available for cataracts?

Surgery is the only effective treatment for cataracts. In the past, surgery was delayed until the cataract was very cloudy, or "ripe." Now, surgery is usually recommended much earlier—as soon as you feel your decreased vision is interfering with your work or daily activities. There is a high success rate for cataract surgery (approximately 98 percent). The procedure

Stat Facts: Cataracts

- More than 20 million people in the United States over age 40 sought medical care for cataracts in 2000.
- Cataracts are slightly more common in women than men.
- The federal government spends more than $3 million on cataracts annually through Medicare.
- More than 1 million cataract surgeries are performed every year.

Source: National Eye Institute

takes less than an hour, usually is done under light anesthesia, and can be done on an outpatient basis.

Cataract surgery involves removing the cloudy lens through a tiny opening on the front of the eye. Once the cataract is removed, an artificial lens called an intraocular lens implant (IOL) is placed in the same position as the natural lens. This new lens restores clear distance vision and cannot be felt. In rare cases where an IOL may not be appropriate, your doctor may recommend using a contact lens or glasses to restore vision after cataract removal. You may need eyeglasses, especially for reading, after cataract surgery.

Will the cataract ever grow back?

Once the cataract is removed, all of the lens material is removed, so the cataract cannot return. However, about half of all people who have a cataract removed may experience the return of hazy vision again at some point after surgery. This often is caused by a clouding of the natural capsule surrounding the lens implant. If this happens, an opening can be made in the cloudy tissue to allow light to pass through unobstructed once again. This painless procedure is done with a special laser and does not require hospitalization.

Is there anything I can do if I know I have a cataract but don't feel that my vision is bad enough to need surgery?

To help compensate for changes in your vision, be sure to have plenty of light indoors, especially on steps and stairs where falls can occur. Use more than one light in a room; standard lights seem to work better than fluorescent. Cut down on glare by using blinds or shades on windows; when outdoors, wear yellow-tinted lenses and a large hat or sun visor. Position your TV screen so it doesn't reflect glare. Large-print books and newspapers and magnifying glasses or lenses can help you read more easily.

Is there any way to prevent cataracts?

The U.S. Public Health Service preventive care guidelines recommend eye exams every 2 to 4 years for adults between the ages of 50 and 60 and every 2 years for people over the age of 60. In addition, you can protect your eyes from damaging ultraviolet radiation, which can contribute to the formation of cataracts, by wearing sunglasses.

Important Questions

- What are the treatment options for cataracts? Must I have surgery? When is the best time to have the surgery? What happens if I decide not to have surgery?
- What's the best way to prepare for surgery?
- What are the risks and benefits of the surgery?
- What can I expect during the normal recovery process after surgery? How soon will my vision return to normal? Will I still need to wear glasses after surgery?
- Are there signs of complications I should watch for after this procedure? What are they? What should I do if they occur?

Chronic Obstructive Pulmonary Disease

*C*hronic obstructive pulmonary disease (COPD) is a term that describes airway and lung diseases including emphysema and chronic bronchitis. These two separate but closely related and often coexisting conditions damage the lungs and prevent them from bringing oxygen to the body and getting rid of carbon dioxide effectively. As a result of COPD, the airflow in and out of the lungs gradually becomes more and more limited.

What is emphysema?

Changes in lung tissue caused by emphysema limit the flow of air in and out of the lungs. Emphysema affects the smallest air passages: tiny air sacs in the lungs called alveoli. Eventually, many of these air sacs are destroyed, and the lungs are less able to function efficiently. In addition, the heart has to work harder to deliver the oxygen to the body. If you smoke, you are 10 to 15 times more likely to be disabled by emphysema than someone who does not smoke.

What is chronic bronchitis?

Chronic bronchitis occurs when the bronchial tubes in the lungs become inflamed. This inflammation thickens the walls of the bronchi and increases the production of mucus. This results in a narrowing of the air passages.

What causes COPD? What are the risk factors?

Cigarette smoking is the major cause of COPD. Seventy-five percent of those with chronic bronchitis have a history of heavy smoking. Exposure to air pollution can irritate the lungs, also. Although either of these may cause COPD, their combined effects are stronger than exposure to either one separately. Other risk factors include gender (men are more susceptible than women), family history of the disease, and age (COPD is more prevalent in those over age 50, especially if they are heavy smokers).

What are the symptoms of COPD?

Symptoms may appear gradually. Early signs include:
■ Mild shortness of breath.

■ A slight cough, especially in the morning.

■ Wheezing.

■ Greenish sputum when you have a cold.

Signs of more advanced stages of the disease include:
■ Severe breathlessness and fatigue.

■ Chest pains and palpitations.

■ Bluish skin and lips.

■ Insomnia.

■ Headache.

■ Impaired thinking and irritability.

Stat Facts: COPD

- Over 123,000 people died of COPD in 2001.
- COPD is the fourth leading cause of death in the United States.
- An estimated 16 million Americans have COPD.
- Men are seven times more likely than women to develop COPD.

Source: The Centers for Disease Control and Prevention

Chronic Obstructive Pulmonary Disease

How do I know when to get help?

Contact a health professional if you have a sudden increase in shortness of breath; sharp chest pain with coughing; a productive cough with green, yellow, or rust-colored sputum; wheezing; changes in the nature of your cough; a cough that is so severe it is exhausting; or a cough that lasts longer than 7 to 10 days without improvement.

How is COPD diagnosed?

Your doctor will gather a thorough history of your symptoms, including a history of any smoking habits. You may undergo various lung function tests that measure the volume, force, amount of air expelled, and the amount of air remaining after exhaling. Tests also may be ordered to monitor the levels of oxygen and carbon dioxide in your blood.

How is COPD treated?

Treatment focuses on two areas: slowing the progress of the disease and relieving the symptoms.

■ **Lifestyle practices** such as not smoking, avoiding polluted air or environments where the air is too hot, too cold, or too thin, and taking precautions to protect yourself against respiratory infections can help slow the advance of the disease. Increasing fluid intake will thin mucus secretions.

■ **Antibiotics** can control respiratory infections.

■ **Corticosteroids and bronchodilators** may be prescribed to prevent respiratory attacks and improve air flow.

■ **Respiratory therapy techniques** such as percussive massage (clapping the chest and back, while lying in certain positions) and controlled coughing techniques assist in bringing up secretions from the lungs.

■ **Physical conditioning** can tone respiratory muscles and slow the respiratory rate.

■ **Correct breathing techniques** help make the best use of limited lung capacity.

■ **Oxygen therapy** may be needed in advanced stages of the disease.

Be aware that COPD patients are susceptible to depression. See pages 264-265.

Important Questions

- What can I do to slow the progress of this disease? Which options are most effective? What are the disadvantages of each?
- What things can I do at home to make myself more comfortable? To breathe more easily?
- What tests are needed? What does each do? How often will I need to have these tests? How will they help my treatment?
- What can I do to help protect myself against respiratory infections?
- Should I wear a surgical mask to help reduce respiratory complications when I'm in public places or doing yard work?
- Will I be on medications for this condition? How will they help me? What side effects can I expect?
- What should I do on "bad air" days to help me breathe more easily?
- Do I need respiratory therapy? How will it help?

Depression

We all have emotional ups and downs. But if you find that you feel down frequently and have lost interest in activities that you usually enjoy, you may be depressed. It is estimated that up to 12 percent of men and 25 percent of women experience at least one episode of clinical depression during their lifetime. Fortunately, an estimated 80 percent of those with depression can be treated successfully and usually begin to feel better within weeks of beginning treatment. It's important to discuss your feelings with your doctor if you feel you may be depressed.

What is depression?

Depression is an illness that affects a person's moods, thoughts, body, and behavior. Depression is not a sign of personal weakness, and it's more than the blues. A person does not just "snap out of it."

Stat Facts: Depression

- Twice as many women experience depression as men.
- Depression affects about 6 million elderly people, but only 10 percent ever receive treatment.
- The incidence of depression in people with chronic illness is over 30 percent.

Source: National Mental Health Association

How is depression diagnosed?

Your doctor will do a complete physical examination and review your family history of health problems or mental illness, other factors such as recent stressful events, prescription medications, and alcohol or drug use. Depression is diagnosed if you are experiencing at least one of the following two symptoms, every day, for 2 weeks or more:

- Feeling sad, blue, or down in the dumps.
- Loss of interest in things that were once enjoyable,

With at least four of the following, nearly every day:
- Losing or gaining weight.
- Feeling tired or having low energy all the time.
- Difficulty concentrating or making decisions.
- Racing thoughts or slowed thinking.
- Feeling worthless or guilty.
- Trouble sleeping, or sleeping too much.
- Thoughts of death or suicide.

Are there different kinds of depression?

Depression is classified by the number of symptoms present, their severity, and their persistence.

- **Major depression** includes a combination of symptoms that interferes with a person's functioning. Episodes can occur once or several times within a lifetime. Sometimes in older adults, depression is overlooked because sadness is not reported. This is **atypical depression**, where the typical signs of sadness or depressed mood are not present.

- **Seasonal affective disorder (SAD)** is a type of major depression that arises from a person's sensitivity to the limited amount of daylight available as the days grow shorter. Symptoms typically begin in the fall, worsen in the winter, and improve in the spring.

- **Dysthymia** is defined as chronic depressive symptoms that are not disabling. Usually symptoms are milder, but last for at least 2 years. Approximately 10 percent of those with dysthymia have episodes of major depression as well.

264

Depression

■ **Bipolar disorder** (formerly known as manic-depressive illness) A person with a bipolar disorder will have cycles of depression (with irritability) and mania (periods of extreme mood swings). During a manic episode, the person will show at least three of the following signs:

–Being extremely talkative

–Increased energy and bursts of activity

–Decreased need for sleep

–Grandiose notions and an inflated sense of self-esteem

–Distractibility

–Racing thoughts

–Involvement in high-risk activities that can be dangerous

What causes depression?

In most cases, the cause of depression is unclear. Experts believe that depression may be produced by a combination of genetic, psychological, and medical factors. However, there does seem to be an imbalance of certain chemicals called neurotransmitters (e.g., norepinephrine, serotonin, and dopamine) in the brains of people with depression. Due to this biochemical connection, antidepressant medications are successful in treating this imbalance. Life events such as the death of a family member may lead to a depressive episode, but sadness and grief should not be immediately assumed to be clinical depression. Other factors such as the use of medications (e.g., beta blockers, steroids, and drugs used to treat cancer), withdrawal from stimulants (e.g., cocaine and amphetamines), or a health problem can trigger depression.

If you have a health problem such as diabetes, asthma, or cancer, it's important not to accept depression as a natural outcome of the illness. Bring any symptoms of depression to your doctor's attention.

How is depression treated?

■ **Medication.** Antidepressant medications treat depression by changing the chemical balance in the brain. More severe cases of depression are best treated with medication.

■ **Psychotherapy** (talk therapy) helps sort out psychological or social issues related to depression.

■ **Light therapy.** Some with seasonal affective disorder have success with phototherapy, using a special light box that has the harmful UV light screened out.

■ **Exercise.** Moderate physical activity for 30 minutes most days of the week helps prevent and manage episodes of mild to moderate depression.

■ **Electroconvulsive therapy (ECT)** is an accepted treatment for major depression, or it may be used when a patient is an immediate threat to himself or herself.

Important Questions

- Could my symptoms be the result of a physical illness or related to seasonal changes (SAD)?
- Can my family doctor treat my illness?
- Could I try psychotherapy alone (without medication) to treat my illness?
- If medication is prescribed, how long will I need to take it? What are the side effects?
- Will my treatment change as my condition improves?

Diabetes

Diabetes is a complex metabolic disorder that can cause a cascade of serious complications. Living with diabetes requires conscientious day-to-day management of diet and exercise, an ongoing partnership with your health care professionals, and using the medications prescribed to manage symptoms and complications.

What is diabetes?

When we eat, our food is converted into glucose, a kind of sugar that our bodies can use for energy. Normally, our bodies produce just the right amount of insulin to pull the glucose from the blood and turn it into energy. However, in diabetes the body doesn't make enough insulin or doesn't use the insulin properly. When the level of glucose in the blood stays at an abnormally high level—called high blood sugar—blood vessels thicken and leak, and fatty substances build up on artery walls. This sets the stage for many serious and potentially life-threatening complications. (Blood sugar levels can get high enough to cause coma or even death.) Left untreated, diabetes can damage blood vessels, kidneys, eyes, and the nervous system; and lead to a higher risk for stroke, atherosclerosis, hypertension, heart disease, kidney failure, loss of limb, and visual problems such as blindness.

Stat Facts: Diabetes

- In 2001, more than 71,000 Americans died of diabetes and its complications.
- Each day, about 2,700 people are diagnosed with diabetes.
- There are nearly 1 million new cases of diabetes each year.

Source: American Diabetes Association

How many kinds of diabetes are there?

There are four main diabetic conditions:

- **Type 1 diabetes** usually develops during childhood or young adulthood, but it can develop at any age. It is an autoimmune disease, but it also may be caused by heredity, viruses, or environmental factors. The body does not produce the insulin necessary to use glucose properly.

- **Type 2 diabetes** is the most common form of diabetes. It usually develops in people over age 40 and is associated with obesity. With the increase in childhood obesity, many younger people are developing type 2 diabetes as well. Early in this disease there is enough insulin, but the body is unable to use it efficiently. Eventually, the production of insulin may drop off and the result is the same as for people with type 1 diabetes.

- **Gestational diabetes** develops during pregnancy and usually goes away after the baby is born. Mothers who have had gestational diabetes have a higher risk of developing type 2 diabetes later in life.

- **Pre-diabetes** develops when blood glucose levels are high enough to begin causing changes to the heart and circulatory system. Exercise and strict dietary management can lower blood glucose levels and delay or eliminate the onset of type 2 diabetes.

What are the risk factors for diabetes?

- Family history of diabetes.

- Overweight by at least 20 percent.

- High blood pressure and/or elevated cholesterol.

Diabetes

- People of African-American, Hispanic, Native American, Asian-American, or Pacific Islander descent are at higher risk for diabetes.

- Personal history of diabetes in pregnancy, or of giving birth to a baby weighing more than 9 pounds.

What are the symptoms of diabetes, particularly of type 1 diabetes?

Consult your doctor if the following symptoms begin and seem to persist, or get worse over a few days:
- Frequent urination.

- Excessive thirst.

- Weight loss.

- Blurred vision.

- Fatigue.

Other symptoms may include increased appetite, skin infections, slow-healing wounds, recurrent vaginitis, difficulty with erections, and tingling or numbness in the hands or feet.

How is diabetes diagnosed?

Testing for diabetes can be done by measuring glucose levels in the blood or the urine.

How is diabetes treated?

It's critical to keep your blood glucose level tightly controlled. Be sure to monitor your blood glucose level through daily self-testing and have HbA1c blood tests every 3 to 6 months. The HbA1c tests measure your blood sugar more accurately over the long term so you can control your blood sugar more effectively. In addition, the following will help you manage your diabetes:
- Eat sensibly. Follow your doctor's recommendations.

- Exercise to manage weight and lower blood sugar.

- Stop smoking.

- Control cholesterol and blood pressure with medication if your doctor recommends it.

- Check your feet for cuts, blisters, or sores that won't heal.

- Have regular eye, kidney, and foot examinations, and tell your dentist you have diabetes.

- Take medications as prescribed—either oral medications to help lower your blood sugar, or insulin to replace insulin lost as a result of the disease.

Be alert for signs of depression, which occurs three times more often in people with diabetes than in the general public. See pages 264-265.

Important Questions

- What is a normal blood sugar level? What should I do if I think my blood sugar is too high or too low?
- What type of treatment is best for my condition? Are there other options? What are the risks, benefits, and costs of each option?
- Why is foot care important? What are the danger signs for foot problems?
- How should I treat cuts, blisters, and sores?
- How often should my doctor measure my HbA1c levels?
- Should I modify my diet? What will happen if I don't change my current diet?
- How does exercising affect my blood sugar?
- Where can I find resources, support groups, and more information about diabetes?

Heart Disease

*H*eart disease is a general term that refers to a problem with the heart's ability to pump blood. If the heart muscle doesn't get a constant supply of nutrients and oxygen from the blood, or if the heart itself does not function properly, it cannot deliver blood to the rest of the body effectively.

What causes heart disease?

The most common cause of heart disease is **coronary artery disease (CAD)**. Fortunately, this form of heart disease, and your risk of developing it, can be modified by your lifestyle—behaviors such as quitting smoking, eating a sensible diet, exercising regularly, managing stress, and limiting alcohol use.

In CAD the arteries that supply blood to the heart are diseased. Deposits of fat and cholesterol—called plaque—build up and thicken the walls of the arteries, causing artery walls to grow thick and irregular, narrowing the openings further. Eventually the flow of blood to and from the heart is restricted and blocked. Recent studies have shown that CAD also may arise from an inflammatory process that narrows the vessels. The severely reduced blood flow may result in physical signs and symptoms. These complications of coronary artery disease are called coronary heart disease, including:

Stat Facts: Heart Disease

- Heart disease is the number one cause of death in the United States.
- In 2000, more than 2 million adults in the United States, (nearly 11 percent) had heart disease.
- Heart disease caused more than 700,000 deaths in 2001.
- One person dies of heart disease every 33 seconds in the United States.

Source: Centers for Disease Control and Prevention

- **Angina:** Dull or crushing pain behind the breastbone that may radiate to the left arm, then go away with rest, often brought on during exercise.

- **Arrhythmia:** Noticeable irregularities (racing or pounding) in the heart rhythm.

- **Heart attack (myocardial infarction)*:**
  - Chest pain, usually in the center of the chest lasting more than a few minutes, or that goes away and comes back. It may feel like pressure, squeezing, fullness, or pain
  - Pain or discomfort in the jaw, neck, back, arm, or shoulder
  - Sweating, anxiety, nausea, vomiting
  - Shortness of breath, dizziness, fainting

* Note: Women may experience their symptoms as indigestion, anxiety, lightheadedness, feeling of impending doom, and discomfort that may not feel as though it is behind the breastbone.

However, sometimes, heart disease is caused by diseases or by defects in the structure or function of the heart itself. These may include:

- **Congestive heart failure.** The heart works harder than it should normally and becomes inefficient. The heart's chambers enlarge, its muscle mass increases, and it beats faster. Over time, the heart becomes weakened by this extra work. Fatigue, weakness, swelling, and lung congestion (fluid) result when the body no longer is getting the blood it needs.

- **Viruses** that damage heart structure or function.

- **Congenital malformations (birth defects).**

- **Defective heart valves.**

- **Heart damage from rheumatic fever.**

Heart Disease

What are the risk factors for CAD?

■ **Age.** Over age 45 for men, 55 for women.

■ **Family history** of early death from heart disease.

■ **Smoking.**

■ **High LDL (bad) cholesterol and low HDL (good) cholesterol.**

■ **Physical inactivity.**

■ **Overweight and obesity.**

■ **Diabetes.**

■ **Metabolic syndrome.** A combination of elevated cholesterol and triglycerides, high blood pressure, waist size larger than 40 inches (for men) or 35 inches (for women), and insulin resistance.

■ **Diet** high in saturated and trans fats, and low in fiber, fruit, and vegetables.

What should I do if I think I'm having angina or a heart attack?

Unless you are under a doctor's care and have specific instructions otherwise, call 911 immediately, or have someone else call for you. Do not drive yourself to the hospital unless you have no other option. Discuss with your doctor ahead of time what you should do if you have symptoms. Make sure family members know what symptoms to look for and how to call 911.

How is heart disease diagnosed?

Your doctor may take your pulse and blood pressure and use a stethoscope to listen to your heart and lung sounds. Your doctor also will consider your medical history and risk factors for CAD (see left). Other common diagnostic tests may be used:

■ **X-ray.** Detects heart enlargement.

■ **Blood enzyme test.** Evaluates damage to the heart muscle.

■ **Electrocardiogram (ECG/EKG).** Records the heart's electrical activity, shows irregular heart rhythms, and provides information for determining the extent of injury to heart tissue caused by a heart attack.

■ **Exercise stress test.** Blood pressure, breathing, EKG activity, and oxygen levels are measured during exercise. This test detects problems that occur when the heart is pumping blood harder than usual.

■ **Nuclear scan.** Nuclear material is injected into a vein and the heart is viewed with a special camera. This scan can detect a problem with the heart's pumping action as well as areas of the heart that are damaged or have poor blood flow. This procedure is sometimes done during a stress test.

■ **Coronary angiography:** A special dye is injected into a tiny tube inserted into the blood vessels of the heart. X-rays show blockage of the arteries.

■ **Intracoronary ultrasound.** Shows the quality and thickness of the walls of the coronary arteries to help evaluate blockages and blood flow.

How is coronary artery disease treated?

■ **Lifestyle changes.**
  –Quit smoking.
  –Control blood pressure and cholesterol.
  –Eat a balanced diet, low in saturated fat.
  –Achieve and maintain a healthy weight.
  –Engage in 30 minutes of moderate physical activity, most days of the week.

–Manage diabetes. Control blood sugar levels.

–Take any medications prescribed by your doctor.

■ **Medications.** Your doctor may prescribe medications to control your heart disease.

–Aspirin reduces clotting and inflammation. It may be recommended to prevent a heart attack if you are at risk or if you already have had one.

–Digitalis slows fast rhythms and improves heart contractions.

–ACE inhibitors treat high blood pressure and reduce strain on the heart.

–Beta blockers slow the heart and lower blood pressure so the heart doesn't have to work as hard.

–Nitroglycerine and calcium channel blockers relax vessels and stop angina pain.

–Clot-busting drugs dissolve blood clots to restore blood flow. They must be given within 1 hour after a heart attack to be effective.

–Statins reduce cholesterol and help prevent the recurrence of heart attacks.

■ **Procedures** clear out plaques that are narrowing the arteries.

–Coronary angioplasty (balloon angioplasty). A tiny balloon inflated inside the artery widens a narrowed area and improves the blood flow. Often a wire mesh tube, called a stent, is inserted into the enlarged place to help keep it open.

–Laser angioplasty. A laser inserted into the artery vaporizes the plaque. This is sometimes used in combination with balloon angioplasty.

–Atherectomy. Areas of plaque are shaved off and removed. A stent or balloon angioplasty may be done at the same time.

■ **Surgery** provides an immediate alternate route around blocked coronary arteries. In coronary artery bypass graft (CABG) or bypass surgery, a section of a healthy artery is taken from another part of your body and stitched to the diseased artery, increasing the quantity of blood to the heart.

Depression is common in people with heart disease. People with both heart disease and depression are more likely to have a heart attack than those without depression. If you have any signs of depression, talk to your doctor or mental health professional. See pages 264–265.

Important Questions

- Can I be treated with approaches such as physical activity, dietary management, relaxation exercises, and drug therapy?
- What diagnostic tests do I need? How accurate are they?
- What medication will I need to treat my condition? Will this drug(s) affect any other medication(s) I am taking?
- Do I need to be on a special diet? Do I need to take cholesterol-lowering drugs?
- What are the benefits and risks of angioplasty and CABG?
- Should I take aspirin every day?
- After a heart attack, when can I resume normal activities (e.g., yard work, leisure activities, sexual intimacy)?

High Blood Pressure

ore than 50 million Americans have high blood pressure severe enough to benefit from monitoring and treatment. High blood pressure, although a common medical condition, can have serious consequences if left untreated. These include coronary artery disease, stroke, and kidney failure. Even borderline hypertension can damage the heart and blood vessels and increase the risk of heart attack.

What is high blood pressure?

Blood pressure is the amount of force blood exerts against artery walls as it flows through them. If you have high blood pressure, or hypertension, your heart has to work too hard and blood vessels are damaged, which increases your risk of heart disease, stroke, kidney disease, and blindness.

What causes high blood pressure?

Ninety percent of the time, the cause of high blood pressure cannot be determined. This type of high blood pressure is referred to as "essential hypertension." The remaining 10 percent is caused by such conditions as kidney disease and tumors.

What are the risk factors for high blood pressure?

Risk factors for high blood pressure fall into two categories:

■ Risk factors you can't control:
  –Previous family history.
  –Gender (affects more males than females).
  –Race (affects African-Americans more than other ethnic groups).
  –Age (high blood pressure occurs most often in men over age 35 and women over age 45). Risk increases with age.

■ Risk factors you can control:
  –Smoking (narrows blood vessels and makes the heart beat faster, causing your blood pressure to rise).
  –Excessive weight.
  –Stress.
  –Lack of exercise (regular exercise tones your heart, blood vessels, and muscles and keeps your blood pressure lower).
  –Excessive alcohol consumption.
  –Excessive sodium (salt) consumption.

What are the symptoms of high blood pressure?

Most people with high blood pressure have no symptoms. Therefore, you should have your blood pressure checked at least every 1 to 2 years.

How is high blood pressure diagnosed?

Blood pressure is easily checked with a pressure cuff, gauge, and stethoscope. It is measured and recorded as two numbers: **systolic pressure**, the peak force when the heart beats (contracts) and **diastolic pressure**, the force against the artery walls when the heart is at rest or between beats. If you buy your own equipment, your doctor can teach you the proper way to measure

Stat Facts: High Blood Pressure

• One in five people in the United States has high blood pressure.
• In more than 90 percent of cases, the cause isn't known.
• One-third of those with high blood pressure don't know they have it.

Source: American Heart Association

your blood pressure at home. Even if you take your own blood pressure, have it checked as recommended by a health professional. See page 24 for guidelines.

How is high blood pressure treated?

You can manage or prevent high blood pressure with the following lifestyle changes:

■ Eat a diet rich in fruits, vegetables, and whole grains, which are naturally low in sodium. The DASH diet (Dietary Approaches to Stop Hypertension: National Heart, Lung, and Blood Institute) is designed to help lower blood pressure. This sensible plan is low in total fat, saturated fat, and cholesterol, and stresses fruits, vegetables, and low-fat dairy foods. It also emphasizes whole-grain products, fish, poultry, and nuts, and limits red meat, sweets, and sugary drinks. The DASH diet also has been shown to reduce levels of cholesterol —a risk factor for cardiovascular disease.

■ Maintain your ideal weight.

■ Increase aerobic physical activity. Aim for 30 minutes on most days.

■ Limit daily sodium intake to no more than about 1 teaspoon. Researchers found that reducing sodium (salt) along with the DASH diet reduces blood pressure even further.

■ Include foods that contain potassium (e.g., bananas, lentils, cantaloupe) each day.

■ Don't smoke.

■ Limit alcohol to no more than two drinks per day for men, one per day for women. Pregnant women should not drink alcohol.

■ Practice stress management techniques.

Based on your blood pressure readings and your risk factors, your doctor may recommend treating your condition with medication. Standard antihypertensive drugs include diuretics (which increase urination), beta blockers, calcium channel blockers, alpha blockers, and angiotensin-converting enzyme (ACE) inhibitors. Tell your doctor about any side effects you may experience such as headaches, fatigue, and extra or skipped heartbeats.

Important Questions

- Can diet and lifestyle changes help to control my high blood pressure? If so, what can I do?
- Do I need to limit my sodium intake? What foods should I eat? What should I avoid?
- Does increasing my calcium and potassium intake help to control blood pressure?
- How often should I get my blood pressure checked? Should I check it myself?
- Will medication help to control my hypertension? What type of drug will work best for me? How does it work? What side effects can I expect? Should I take it with food? Do I have to take it at the same time each day?

Osteoporosis

Osteoporosis, meaning "porous bone," is a bone condition that affects millions of Americans. Its impact on health, lifestyle, and emotional well-being can be far-reaching. Osteoporosis can result in bone fractures which, in turn, cause pain, disability, and loss of independence.

What is osteoporosis?

When levels of calcium and phosphorus—the minerals essential to bone formation—are not sufficiently incorporated into the bones, the bones become weak and brittle and are more likely to break. The bones of the hip, spine, and wrist seem especially vulnerable. Estrogen loss after menopause accelerates the loss of calcium. Taking steroid medications also can lead to osteoporosis. Certain female elite athletes, dancers, and others who restrict their diets and overtrain, run the risk of lowering their estrogen levels so much that they begin to develop osteoporosis—in some cases, at very young ages.

What are the risks?

■ **Gender.** Women are much more likely than men to develop osteoporosis. In fact, during the first 5 years after menopause, women lose as much as 25 percent of their bone mass.

Stat Facts: Osteoporosis

- Ten million people in the United States have osteoporosis.
- Eighty percent of all osteoporosis patients are women.
- Osteoporosis results in 1.5 million bone fractures each year.

Source: National Osteoporosis Foundation

■ **Age.** Bones weaken and get thinner as you get older.

■ **Smoking.** It interferes with calcium absorption.

■ **History.** If you or your mother have a history of fractures as adults, your risk of having reduced bone mass is more likely.

■ **Race.** Caucasian and Asian women are more susceptible to osteoporosis.

■ **Lifestyle.** Excessive alcohol use, not getting enough exercise, and not consuming enough calcium and vitamin D can increase your risk for osteoporosis.

■ **Being thin and/or having a small frame.** Women who are thin and/or have a small frame are more likely to develop osteoporosis.

What are the symptoms?

Usually there are no symptoms until a fracture occurs. The first sign may be sudden pain in the back or hip, or painful swelling of a joint after a minor fall. See your doctor if your sprain does not improve after 4 days of home treatment, or if you have a lot of swelling or bruising after even a minor fall.

What can I do to prevent osteoporosis?

The two major strategies for helping reduce the risk of osteoporosis are:

■ **Proper nutrition.** Adults should consume 1000 mg of calcium and 200 IU of vitamin D daily. If you are female and past menopause, 1500 mg of calcium and 400 IU of vitamin D is recommended. Excellent sources of calcium include skim milk, low-fat yogurt, chopped collards, broccoli, and canned sardines with bones. You may need to take supplements to reach sufficient levels. See page 17.

Osteoporosis

■ **Regular weight-bearing exercise.** Weight-bearing exercise places stress on the bones, which encourages bone growth. Excellent exercises include walking, jogging, aerobic dance, and tennis. Recent studies suggest that weight training also helps maintain bone density.

How is osteoporosis diagnosed?

If you get an X-ray for a suspected fracture, it may reveal changes in the bone caused by osteoporosis. The density of your bones, typically the spine, hip, wrist, or ankle, can be measured painlessly with a Bone Mineral Density test (BMD). Osteopenia is a condition where your bone mass is lower than normal for your age, but not low enough to be considered true osteoporosis. If osteopenia is identified with a BMD, you will have the opportunity to take a more active role in managing your risk factors (e.g., exercising more, consuming more calcium, quitting smoking) and your doctor may prescribe medication to slow or stop bone loss before your bones get dangerously thin.

How is it treated?

■ **Lifestyle.** Eating a balanced diet with adequate levels of calcium and vitamin D and engaging in regular weight-bearing exercises have been shown to increase or maintain bone density.

■ **Antiresorptive medications.** Biophosphonates (Fosamax®, Actonel®, Calcitonin®) reduce bone loss and increase bone density.

■ **Hormone replacement therapy (HRT).** HRT preserves bone density after menopause. However, HRT is associated with an increased risk of certain cancers, so talk to your doctor about the relative risks and benefits of using HRT.

■ **Selective Estrogen Receptor Modulators (SERMS)** such as Evista® increase bone formation without some of the side effects of estrogen replacement therapy (HRT).

■ **Parathyroid hormone.** This more recent therapy (Fortéo®) stimulates new bone formation and increases bone density.

■ **Joint replacement.** Surgery to replace joints destroyed by osteoporosis helps to decrease pain and restore independence.

Finally, because osteoporosis can be painful and threaten independence, feelings of isolation and depression are common. See pages 264-265.

Important Questions

- Can osteoporosis be prevented? How? Is it too late to start?
- Should I be screened for osteoporosis if I have a family history?
- How can I increase my consumption of calcium-rich foods? Will calcium supplements help? How much should I take? How often? Are there any precautions?
- Is a biophosphonate drug appropriate for me? How do I take it? How effective is it? What are the risks? Side effects? Are there alternatives?
- When is joint replacement surgery indicated? What are the risks? What benefits can I expect? Will I need rehabilitation? For how long? What if I don't have the surgery?
- How do I develop an exercise plan that will be effective against osteoporosis?

Parkinson's Disease

Parkinson's disease is an incurable condition that affects the nervous system, movement, and the ability to communicate. It is a progressive disorder characterized by the deterioration of specific cells in the brain. In these cells, the neurotransmitter dopamine is no longer produced. Dopamine normally transmits the signals from the brain that control body movements.

People with Parkinson's disease develop rigid muscles, jerky movements, rhythmic tremors, and loss of reflexes. They can have difficulty living independently as the disease progresses because of significant physical and intellectual changes.

What causes this condition?

The exact cause of this disease is not known. However, researchers believe that genetics, viruses, or environmental factors such as exposure to pesticides, herbicides, and heavy metals may cause Parkinson's.

What are the risks to my health if I develop Parkinson's disease?

Due to the progressive nature of the disease, eventually your ability to live and care for yourself independently may decrease to the point where you may not be able to live alone. In severe and late stages of the disease, you may become immobile and require constant nursing care.

What are the symptoms of this disorder?

The early symptoms such as mild tremors, stiffness, and fatigue may go unnoticed. As the disease progresses, tremors increase and posture becomes stooped and pitched forward—resulting in a shuffling and unsteady gait. Joint and muscle stiffness increase. Movements become slower. When walking, it becomes difficult to stop and change direction. It may be hard to start a muscle movement. The face may have a fixed, mask-like expression and the eyeblink reflex diminishes.

Stat Facts: Parkinson's Disease

- Parkinson's affects more than 1.5 million people in the United States.
- The average age of onset of Parkinson's is 55, but there is an alarming increase of younger patients.

Source: National Parkinson Foundation

What should I do if I think I may have Parkinson's disease?

You should make an appointment to see your doctor, even if symptoms are mild. Recognizing and treating Parkinson's disease in the early stages may help slow its progression.

How is Parkinson's disease diagnosed?

Your doctor will begin by doing a complete health history and physical exam. A thorough neurological exam also may be done, including a variety of tests that measure changes in movement, balance, and intellect. No specific lab work is useful in making a diagnosis. Your doctor will ask you and family members to describe your symptoms and the history of the problem.

How is Parkinson's treated?

Although there is no cure for Parkinson's, home treatment, medication, lifestyle modifications, and appropriate medical care can help slow the progress of the disease.

■ **Self-care.** Eat regular and well-balanced meals, control stress, and get regular exercise, based on your doctor's advice. When physical activity is maintained, Parkinson's seems to progress more slowly and side effects may decrease.

■ **Medication.** The standard drug for Parkinson's disease is levodopa, although it causes unwanted side effects. The dose of the drug must be adjusted frequently, and its effectiveness can dwindle over time. Other medications can be added to prolong the effect of levodopa, reduce its side effects, or slow the progression of symptoms early in the illness.

■ **Other approaches.** Deep-brain stimulation is a recently approved surgical treatment that involves implanting an electrical wire in the brain to stimulate selected areas. Other surgical techniques destroy or disconnect areas of the brain that are causing symptoms. These treatments may be appropriate for those who are no longer satisfied with the level of control they are getting from medication alone. Promising research involving fetal stem cell transplants is underway, but the safety and effectiveness of such treatment for humans isn't known yet.

■ **Special concerns.** Physical therapy and regular exercise can prolong mobility. Canes, walkers, and wheelchairs may be helpful as balance and movement decline. It helps to stay involved in social activities and hobbies for as long as possible. But feelings of hopelessness, fear, and depression are common in Parkinson's. Dealing with a progressive, degenerative disease is very stressful for both the individual with Parkinson's and for his or her family as well. Share

your concerns and questions with your doctor or a mental health provider. See pages 264-265.

Important Questions

- What can I do in my daily life and activities to slow the progression or lessen the symptoms of this disease? How should I exercise? What should I eat? Is there anything I can do to reduce symptoms? How can I modify my living environment to make it safer?
- What medications will I be taking? When? How? What are the side effects? How can the side effects be reduced? Will these drugs affect any other drugs I might be taking?
- Are there any new treatment options? How successful have they been in cases like mine? What are the benefits, risks, and costs?
- If my condition worsens and I can no longer live alone or without assistance, where can I get assistance? What are my homecare options?
- What happens if I do nothing and accept the progression of this disease? Are there any risks to my health and well-being? Are there any benefits to doing nothing? If I change my mind later, will it be too late?
- Are there any home treatments that can help me deal with the changes I will experience as the disease progresses?
- How will the progression of this disease affect my communication skills? How can I get help in coping with decreased verbal ability? What communication aids are available?

Periodontal Disease

Periodontal or gum disease is the main cause of tooth loss in older adults, and nearly half of all older adults show signs of gum disease.

What is periodontal disease?

Periodontal (meaning "around the tooth") disease is an infection that attacks the gums and structures that support the teeth and keep them in place. In the beginning stages, the gums become inflamed. As the disease progresses, infection takes hold and the underlying tissues and bone also deteriorate. With nothing to anchor them, the teeth grow loose and fall out.

Surprisingly, the consequences of gum disease can extend beyond your mouth. The bacteria associated with periodontal disease can travel through the bloodstream to other parts of the body. Gum disease may:

■ **Contribute to heart disease.** In one scenario, a person with gum disease injures the gum tissue while chewing or brushing. Bacteria enters the bloodstream and accumulates on the heart valves, which leads to a potentially fatal infection. In another scenario, bacteria in the oral cavity enters the bloodstream, attaches to fatty plaques, and contributes to the formation of dangerous blood clots.

■ **Increase the risk of preterm, low birth-weight babies.** The process of infection in gum disease produces chemicals that may trigger early labor. The mother's infection also may lead to lower birth weight in her baby.

■ **Pose a threat to people with diabetes.** People with diabetes are more likely to have gum disease and lose their teeth than those without diabetes. Periodontal disease also can raise blood sugar and make it more difficult to control.

■ **Pose a threat to people with respiratory diseases.** Bacterial secretions in the mouth and throat can be inhaled and drawn into the lower respiratory tract. This can cause infections, such as pneumonia, or worsen existing lung conditions, such as chronic obstructive pulmonary disease (COPD).

Stat Facts: Periodontal Disease

- Most adults have periodontal disease but don't know they have it.
- More men than women have periodontal disease.
- About 50 percent of Americans ages 34 to 44 have been diagnosed with periodontal disease.
- Most of the estimated 25 million Americans who have lost all of their teeth are the victims of periodontal disease.

Source: Healthy People 2010

What causes it?

Plaque is a sticky film that builds up on the teeth and gums. Unless the film is removed from the teeth, it can irritate the gums and create pockets between the teeth and gums. Bacteria invading these pockets leads to an infection—gingivitis or periodontitis.

What are risk factors for gum disease?

■ Tobacco use, including smokeless forms.

■ Certain health conditions, including diabetes and pregnancy.

■ Crooked teeth and broken fillings.

■ Some medications, including steroids, oral contraceptives, and cancer drugs.

Periodontal Disease

■ Poor oral hygiene and lack of professional care from a dentist.

What are the symptoms?

Signs include reddened, swollen gums, loose teeth, and bleeding upon brushing. In addition to getting regular dental checkups (every 6 months), you should consult your dentist if your gums are red and swollen, if your gums bleed when you brush your teeth, if your teeth are loose or seem to be moving apart, if you notice a change in the way your teeth fit together, or if there are changes in the way your dentures fit.

How is it diagnosed?

Your dentist will determine if you have periodontal disease based on his or her examination of your teeth and gums. This may include some probing to detect bleeding or pockets along the gum line. An X-ray may detect bone loss in advanced stages of the disease.

How is it treated?

Early stages of the disease can be treated with correct brushing and flossing of the teeth every day and can be monitored by dental checkups every 6 months. At these checkups, a professional cleaning of your teeth will remove plaque and calculus (hardened bacterial plaque). Your dentist also may prescribe a mouthwash containing chlorohexidine (e.g., Peridex®, Perioguard®) to treat symptoms.

More advanced periodontal disease may be treated by either eliminating the pockets of diseased tissue or by cleaning the affected roots using a process known as scaling and root planing. Surgery may be used in some instances. If your dentist suggests surgery first, ask about scaling or planing.

Can it be prevented?

Periodontal disease can be prevented with these simple measures:

■ Brushing regularly.

■ Flossing regularly.

■ Seeing a dentist for regular checkups and professional cleaning.

The dentist can detect disease before you notice any warning signs. Also, your dental professional will be able to clean your teeth more thoroughly than you can, no matter how conscientious you are in your home dental routine.

Important Questions

- Can periodontal disease be slowed or reversed? How? What can I do to prevent further disease?
- Will changing the types of foods I eat help prevent this condition?
- Is brushing with a fluoride toothpaste helpful in preventing periodontal disease?
- How should I be brushing and flossing my teeth? How often? Do I need a special type of brush or floss?
- How often should I have a dental checkup if I have this condition? What will happen if I don't see a dentist regularly? What will be done at these checkups?
- What will be my options if the disease worsens? Is scaling and planing an option for me? What are the benefits? Risks? What will happen if I do not have this procedure?
- When is dental surgery appropriate?

Prostate Problems

The prostate—a doughnut-shaped gland that surrounds the bladder opening and urethra in men—is located at the bottom of the bladder, about halfway between the rectum and the base of the penis. In most prostate problems, the gland enlarges and narrows the neck of the urethra (the tube through which urine flows out of the body), producing an array of troubling symptoms that are uncomfortable and inconvenient. And, in the case of prostate cancer, the symptoms signal something far more serious.

How are prostate problems diagnosed?

A doctor can evaluate the size, texture, and firmness of the prostate gland with a digital rectal examination (DRE). The PSA test measures the level of prostate-specific antigen (PSA) in the blood, which gives the doctor information about prostate health. PSA rises in prostate cancer, but also in prostatitis and benign prostatic hypertrophy (BPH). All men over 50 and those with a family history of prostate cancer should discuss with their doctors the need for regular PSA testing and DRE.

What are the most common prostate problems?

As men age, the prostate can develop three problems: **Prostatitis** is an inflammation that is usually caused by a bacterial infection, but sometimes the cause isn't known.

■ **Symptoms:** Difficult, painful, burning urination, low-back pain, and sometimes chills and fever.

■ **Treatment:** If bacteria are the cause, then antibiotics will clear up the infection.

Benign prostatic hypertrophy (BPH) is a non-cancerous enlargement of the prostate. The incidence increases in men after the age of 50. Normally about the size of a walnut, the prostate enlarges, narrowing the size of the urethra, making urination difficult. BPH usually is not serious unless urination becomes extremely difficult or the incomplete emptying of the bladder causes bladder infections or kidney problems. A blocked urethra, through which no urine can flow, is a medical emergency.

■ **Symptoms:** Despite a powerful urge to urinate, the stream is often hard to start and is reduced to a dribble. The bladder may never feel really empty.

■ **Self-care treatment:** For mild symptoms, the following may help:

–Limit fluids (e.g., alcohol, water) in the evening.

–Limit caffeine, which can irritate the bladder.

–Take time to empty the bladder as completely as possible.

–Ask your doctor whether any medications you are taking might contribute to BPH.

Stat Facts: Prostate Problems

• Up to 75 percent of men have cancerous changes in the prostate by age 75.
• The prostate cancer death rate among African-American men is twice that of Caucasians.
• By age 60, about half of all men will have signs of enlarged prostate.

Source: National Cancer Institute

Prostate Problems

Only about half of those men who have symptoms eventually need more treatment, which may include:

- **Drug therapy.** Medications to relax and smooth the muscles of the prostate and neck of the bladder (e.g., Cardura®), and allow the urine to flow more freely. Another medication acts on an enzyme affecting the male hormone testosterone (Proscar®), reducing symptoms and increasing urine flow. Some research indicates that using both drugs works better to improve symptoms than using either drug alone.

- **Surgery.** A slender instrument is inserted into the urethra to trim away prostate tissue using either a tiny blade or radio-frequency energy. These procedures, done on an outpatient basis, increase the flow of urine quickly, usually within weeks. Surgical removal of part of the prostate (prostatectomy) is another option, usually reserved for extremely enlarged prostates, about 5 percent of all cases.

Prostate cancer You are at higher risk for prostate cancer if you are 65 or older, African-American, or if your father had prostate cancer. Prostate cancer typically is relatively slow-growing compared with other cancers. It has been shown that measuring how fast the PSA levels increase over time (PSA velocity) can be a predictor of aggressive prostate cancer. In addition, obese men with prostate cancer are more likely to have more aggressive tumors and have more recurrence of their cancers than men of normal weight.

- **Symptoms:** Early prostate cancer grows so slowly that you may not notice any symptoms. When you begin to have symptoms, they are similar to those of BPH. Prostate cancer spreads to the bone, so bone pain, particularly in the back, may be a symptom of prostate cancer as well.

- **Treatment:** As with any cancer, the diagnosis is confirmed through biopsy of the tissue. Treatment may include surgery to remove the prostate gland, radiation, chemotherapy, cryotherapy, or hormone therapy. Watchful waiting and monitoring a small tumor carefully with regular exams and screenings is sometimes an option, especially for men over age 75.

Note: Incontinence, erectile and ejaculatory problems, and/or infertility are risks associated with prostate treatments.

Finally, an estimated 25 percent of cancer patients develop depression. Depression can make battling prostate cancer far more difficult. See pages 264-265.

Important Questions

- Given my risk factors, what screening tests are recommended?
- If I have prostatitis and it is not caused by a bacterial infection, what self-care can I do to feel better?
- If I have BPH, is no treatment the best option for me? What should I do if the symptoms get worse? Will medication help?
- When is surgery needed for BPH? What are the risks? Benefits? How long is the recovery period?
- If I have been diagnosed with prostate cancer, what treatment options are recommended? What are the risks, benefits, success rates, and major side effects of each?
- Is watchful waiting an option for me?
- What other factors do I need to think about when considering cancer treatment options (e.g., stage of disease, age, health problems)?

Stroke

Stroke is a serious medical emergency that affects more than 700,000 people each year. The good news is that the survival rate for stroke victims is improving.

What is a stroke?

A stroke is the death of an area of nerve cells in the brain, which occurs when the blood supply to the area is blocked. When the brain tissue is deprived of oxygen this way, the cells begin to die. Transient ischemic attacks (TIAs) or "mini-strokes" cause less damage but can serve as a warning sign that a more serious stroke could occur. One of three people who has a TIA will have a stroke within the following 5 years if he or she does not get treatment. Also, whether large enough to cause symptoms or not, strokes are a major cause of dementia.

What causes strokes?

- TIAs usually are caused by a **narrowing of blood vessels** in the neck (carotid arteries) because of a buildup of plaque. (See pages 268-270.)
- A **blood clot** can form around deposits that stick out from the arterial wall and block the flow of blood, causing a stroke.
- A **cerebral embolism (brain stroke)** occurs when a clot in the bloodstream gets stuck in one of the arteries in the brain, completely blocking it.
- If a weakened artery bursts inside the brain, the resulting **cerebral hemorrhage (brain bleed)** also can cause a stroke.
- A **brain aneurysm** occurs when a weakened blood vessel or artery in the brain bulges and bursts, causing severe damage or death.

What increases my risk of having a stroke?

Individuals experiencing TIAs are at increased risk for stroke. After TIAs, important risk factors are:
- High blood pressure.
- High cholesterol.
- Heart disease.
- Gender (men are more susceptible than women).
- Family history.
- Race (African Americans are more vulnerable).
- Diabetes.
- High level of red blood cells, sickle cell disease.
- Smoking.
- Chronic stress.
- Obesity.
- Migraine sufferers should undergo treatment to relieve their migraines and to reduce their risk factors for stroke.

Stat Facts: Stroke

- Every 45 seconds, on average, someone in the United States has a stroke.
- Heavy smokers are twice as likely to have a stroke than non-smokers.
- Stroke is the third leading cause of death in the United States, behind heart disease and cancer.

Source: American Heart Association

Stroke

What are the symptoms of a stroke?

■ Sudden blurred or decreased vision in one or both eyes.

■ Numbness, weakness, or paralysis of the face, an arm, or a leg, on one or both sides of the body.

■ Difficulty in speaking or understanding.

■ Dizziness, loss of balance, or an unexplained fall.

■ Difficulty swallowing.

■ Headache that is severe and comes on abruptly, or unexplained changes in a pattern of headaches.

Get Emergency Care Right Away If:
You have any of the symptoms above.

Do not ignore these signs, even if they seem temporary. You may be having a TIA—a warning of a stroke to come. A TIA lasts only a few minutes and symptoms usually disappear within 24 hours.

How is this condition diagnosed?

Your doctor may diagnose a stroke through physical examination, medical history, EEG, and CAT scan. Your doctor also can diagnose narrowing of the carotid arteries (on either side of the neck, leading to the brain), which can cause TIAs, by examining the arteries using a stethoscope, ultrasound, or arterial angiography.

What treatment options are available?

Eighty percent of strokes are caused by arterial blockages. The goal of stroke treatment is to clear or open the artery and restore blood flow. If given within 3 hours of a stroke or heart attack, "clot buster" medicines (e.g., t-PA) may increase the likelihood of recovery. However, they also increase the risk of bleeding. Aspirin or other blood-thinning medicines may be prescribed to help fend off future strokes. A surgical procedure called carotid endarterectomy may be effective by removing excess fatty plaques from the arteries of the neck. In addition, balloons, stents, and coils are used in newer techniques (cerebral angioplasty) to widen the artery and increase blood flow.

When brain tissue is affected by a stroke, varying amounts of disability may result, and the rehabilitation process may be difficult. Stroke survivors may feel discouraged and depressed. Up to 27 percent of post-stroke patients suffer from depression. If these feelings are overwhelming or interfering with daily activities and relationships, seek advice and support from your doctor and family members. See pages 264-265.

Important Questions

- How often should I have my blood pressure checked?
- If I have high blood pressure, what medications do I need to reduce my risk of stroke?
- If I am having TIAs, what should I do?
- What diagnostic tests are recommended?
- If I have had a stroke, what kind of rehabilitation do I need? How long will it take?
- What other treatment options are available?
- Will I need adaptive devices to help me maintain daily activities? What kind?
- What type of support and assistance is available for those who will be helping me care for myself? How can I find these services?

Family Medical Records and Resources

In this section:

- Maintaining family medical and immunization records
- Recording and tracking medication use
- Contacting organizations for more information on specific health topics

Personal Medical Record

Photocopy the following pages for each family member and file them in a safe place.
Keep these records up to date and take them with you if you change doctors.

Name: _____

Date of birth: _____

Problems at birth: _____

_____

Blood type: _____   **Rh factor:** _____

Childhood Diseases

Chicken pox   Date _____

Measles   Date _____

Mumps   Date _____

Whooping cough   Date _____

Rubella (German measles)   Date _____

Other Illnesses:

Illness: _____ Date: _____

Comments: _____

_____

Illness: _____ Date: _____

Comments: _____

_____

Illness: _____ Date: _____

Comments: _____

_____

Illness: _____ Date: _____

Comments: _____

_____

Personal Medical Record

Allergies:

Type: _____ Medication: _____

Allergic to what? _____

_____

_____

Type: _____ Medication: _____

Allergic to what? _____

_____

_____

Type: _____ Medication: _____

Allergic to what? _____

_____

_____

Hospitalizations:

Reason: _____ Date: _____ to _____

Doctor: _____

Hospital: _____

Comments: _____

_____

_____

_____

Reason: _____ Date: _____ to _____

Doctor: _____

Hospital: _____

Comments: _____

_____

_____

_____

Personal Immunization Record

Name: _____

Date of birth: _____

Immunization	Date	Doctor's Name	Comments
Diphtheria Pertussis Tetanus (DPT)	_____ _____ _____ _____ _____	_____ _____ _____ _____ _____	_____ _____ _____ _____ _____
Adult Diphtheria and Tetanus	_____ _____	_____ _____	_____ _____
Oral Polio (OPV)	_____ _____ _____ _____	_____ _____ _____ _____	_____ _____ _____ _____
Chicken pox	_____	_____	_____
Measles, Mumps and Rubella (MMR)	_____ _____ _____ _____	_____ _____ _____ _____	_____ _____ _____ _____
Hemophilus B	_____ _____ _____	_____ _____ _____	_____ _____ _____
Influenza	_____ _____	_____ _____	_____ _____
Pneumonia	_____	_____	_____
Hepatitis B	_____ _____ _____	_____ _____ _____	_____ _____ _____
TB Skin Test	_____	_____	_____
Other	_____	_____	_____

Note: Keep a separate record for each family member.

Medication Use Record

Make a photocopy of this form and take a copy with you whenever you visit your doctor. If a prescription or over-the-counter medication is recommended, have your doctor fill out the information below. Be sure you understand the instructions. Do not change your treatment schedule without first consulting your doctor.

Name: _____

Name of drug? _____

Date prescribed? _____

Doctor's name? _____

Used to treat what problem? _____

How much? _____

How many times a day? _____

For how long? _____

With food or on an empty stomach? _____

Fluids recommended? _____

Alcohol prohibited? _____

Do not take with other drugs? _____

What foods/drinks to avoid? _____

What should I do if I miss a dose? _____

Name of drug? _____

Date prescribed? _____

Doctor's name? _____

Used to treat what problem? _____

How much? _____

How many times a day? _____

For how long? _____

With food or on an empty stomach? _____

Fluids recommended? _____

Alcohol prohibited? _____

Do not take with other drugs? _____

What foods/drinks to avoid? _____

What should I do if I miss a dose? _____

Resources

Alcohol/Drug Abuse

AA—Alcoholics Anonymous
P. O. Box 459
Grand Central Station
New York, NY 10163
212.870.3400
www.aa.org

Al-Anon/Alateen Family Group
Headquarters
1600 Corporate Landing Parkway
Virginia Beach, VA 23454-5617
757.563.1600
www.al-anon.alateen.org

American Council for Drug
Education
174 W. 74th St.
New York, NY 10023
800.488.3784
www.acde.org

MADD
Mothers Against Drunk Driving
511 E. John Carpenter Frwy.
Suite 700
Irving, TX 75062
800.438.MADD (6233)
www.madd.org

Narcotics Anonymous
P.O. Box 9999
Van Nuys, CA 91409
818.773.9999
www.na.org

National Clearinghouse for Alcohol
and Drug Information
P.O. Box 2345
Rockville, MD 20847-2345
800.729.6686
www.health.org

National Institute on Alcohol Abuse
and Alcoholism
6000 Executive Blvd., Suite 409
Bethesda, MD 20892-7003
301.443.3860
www.niaaa.nih.gov

Partnership for a Drug Free
America®
405 Lexington Ave., Suite 1601
New York, NY 10174
212.922.1560
www.drugfreeamerica.org

Allergies

American Academy of Allergy,
Asthma, and Immunology
611 E. Wells St.
Milwaukee, WI 53202
800.822.2762
www.aaaai.org

National Institute of Allergy and
Infectious Diseases
6610 Rockledge Dr., MSC 6612
Bethesda, MD 20892-6612
www.niaid.nih.gov

Alternative Medicine

National Center for Complementary and Alternative Medicine
P.O. Box 7923
Gaithersburg, MD 20898
888.644.6226
www.nccam.nih.gov

Alzheimer's Disease

Alzheimer's Association
225 N. Michigan Ave., 17th floor
Chicago, IL 60601-7633
800.272.3900
www.alz.org

Alzheimer's Disease Education &
Referral Center
P.O. Box 8250
Silver Spring, MD 20907-8250
800.438.4380
www.alzheimers.org

Arthritis

Arthritis Foundation
P.O. Box 7669
Atlanta, GA 30357-0669
800.283.7800
www.arthritis.org

National Institute of Arthritis and
Musculoskeletal and Skin Diseases
1 AMS Circle
Bethesda, MD 20892-3675
877.22NIAMS
www.nih.gov/niams

Resources

Asthma

Asthma and Allergy Foundation
of America
1233 20th St. N.W., Suite 402
Washington, DC 20036
202.466.7643
www.aafa.org

National Heart, Lung, and
Blood Institute
P.O. Box 30105
Bethesda, MD 20824-0105
301.592.8573
www.nhlbi.nih.gov/health/public/
lung/index.htm#asthma

Breastfeeding

La Leche League International
1400 N. Meachum Rd.
Schaumburg, IL 60173-4808
800.LALECHE
www.lalecheleague.org

Cancer

American Cancer Society
1599 Clifton Road N.E.
Atlanta, GA 30329
800.ACS.2345
www.cancer.org

National Cancer Institute
6116 Executive Blvd.
MSC 8322
Bethesda, MD 20892-8322
800.4CANCER
www.cancer.gov

Skin Cancer Foundation
245 Fifth Ave., Suite 1403
New York, NY 10016
800.SKIN.490
www.skincancer.org

Child Care

Child Care Aware
1319 F Street N.W., Suite 500
Washington, DC 20004
800.424.2246
www.childcareaware.org

National Child Care
Information Center
243 Church St. N.W., 2nd floor
Vienna, VA 22180
800.616.2242
www.nccic.org

Children's Health

American Academy of Pediatrics
141 North West Point Blvd.
P. O. Box 927
Elk Grove Village, IL 60007-1078
800.433.9016
www.aap.org/family

Maternal and Child Health Center
Health Resources & Services
Adminstration
5608 Fishers Lane
Rockville, MD 20857
www.ask.hrsa.gov/MCH.cfm

National Institute of Child
Health & Human Development
P.O. Box 3006
Rockville, MD 20847
800.370.2943
www.nichd.nih.gov

Diabetes

American Diabetes Association
1660 Duke St.
Alexandria, VA 22314
800.232.3472
www.diabetes.org

National Institute of Diabetes and
Digestive and Kidney Diseases
NIH Building 31, Room 9A04
MSC 2560
Bethesda, MD 20892-2560
www.niddk.nih.gov

Dental Health

American Dental Association
211 E. Chicago Ave.
Chicago, IL 60611-2678
312.440.2500
www.ada.org

National Institute of Dental and
Craniofacial Research
31 Center Dr.
NIH Building 31, Room 2C35
MSC 2290
Bethesda, MD 20892
301.496.4261
www.nidr.nih.gov

Resources

Environmental Health

National Institute of Environmental
Health Sciences
P.O. Box 12233
Research Triangle Park, NC 27709
919.541.3345
www.niehs.nih.gov

U.S. Environmental
Protection Agency
1200 Pennsylvania Ave. N.W.
Washington, DC 20460
202.2272.0176
www.epa.gov

Exercise/Fitness

American Alliance for Health,
Physical Education, Recreation
and Dance
1900 Association Dr.
Reston, VA 20191-1598
703.476.3400
www.aahperd.org

American College of Sports
Medicine
P.O. Box 1440
Indianapolis, IN 46206-1440
317.637.9200
www.acsm.org

President's Council on Physical
Fitness and Sports
200 Independence Ave. S.W.
Washington, DC 20201
202.690.9000
www.fitness.gov

YMCA of the USA
Health and Physical Education
101 N. Wacker Dr.
Chicago, IL 60606
800.USA.YMCA
www.ymca.net

Family Health

U.S. Department of Justice
Office on Violence Against Women
810 7th St. N.W.
Washington, D.C. 20531
800.799.SAFE (hotline)
www.ojp.usdoj.gov/vawo

National Council on Family
Relations
3989 Central Ave. N.E., Suite 550
Minneapolis, MN 55421
888.781.9331
www.ncfr.com

General Health

American Academy of Family
Physicians
11400 Tomohawk Creek Parkway
Leawood, KS 66211-2672
www.familydoctor.org

American Heart Association
7272 Greenville Ave.
Dallas, TX 75231-4599
800.AHA.USA1
www.americanheart.org

American Lung Association
1740 Broadway
New York, NY 10019
212.315.8700
www.lungusa.org

American Medical Association
515 N. State St.
Chicago, IL 60610
312.464.5000
www.ama-assn.org

American Public Health Association
800 I St. N.W.
Washington, DC 20001-3710
202.777.APHA
www.apha.org

American Red Cross
225 E. St. N.W.
Washington, DC 20006
202.303.4498
www.redcross.org

U.S. Department of Health and
Human Services
Office of Disease Prevention and
Health Promotion
200 Independence Ave. S.W.
Room 738G
Washington, D.C. 20210
www.odphp.osophs.dhhs.gov

National Heart, Lung,
and Blood Institute
P.O. Box 30105
Bethesda, MD 20824-0105
301.592.8573
www.nhlbi.nih.gov

U.S. National Library of Medicine
8600 Rockville Pike
Bethesda, MD 20894
www.nlm.nih.gov

Hearing

National Institute on Deafness and
Other Communication Disorders
31 Center Dr., MSC 2320
Bethesda, MD 20892-2320
800.241.1044
800.241.1055 (TTY)
www.nidcd.nih.gov

HIV/AIDS

CDC Divisions of
HIV/AIDS Prevention
P.O. Box 6003
Rockville, MD 20849-6003
800.342.2437
www.cdc.gov/hiv/pubs/facts.htm

Johns Hopkins AIDS Service
Johns Hopkins University Division
of Infectious Diseases
www.hopkins-aids.edu

Immunizations

Centers for Disease Control
and Prevention
National Immunization Program
Mail Stop E05
1600 Clifton Road N.E.
Atlanta, GA 30333
800.232.2522
www.cdc.gov/nip/default.htm

Infertility

American Society for Reproductive
Medicine
1209 Montgomery Hwy.
Birmingham, AL 35216-2809
205.978.5000
www.asrm.com

RESOLVE: National Infertility
Association
1310 Broadway
Somerville, MA 02144-1731
888.632.0744
www.resolve.org

Medications

American Pharmaceutical
Association
2215 Constitution Ave., N.W.
Washington, DC 20037-2985
202.628.4410
www.pharmacyandyou.org

Center for Drug Evaluation
and Research
5600 Fishers Lane, HFD-240
Rockville, MD 20857
888.INFO.FDA
www.fda.gov/cder

Mental Health/Stress

Anxiety Disorders Association
of America
6000 Executive Blvd., Suite 513
Rockville, MD 20852
301.231.9350
www.adaa.org

National Institute of Mental Health
6100 Executive Blvd.
Room 8184, MSC 9663
Bethesda, MD 20892-9663
866.615.6464
www.nimh.nih.gov/

National Mental Health Association
2001 N. Beauregard St., 12th Floor
Alexandria, VA 22311
800.969.NMHA
www.nmha.org

Panic Disorder Information Line
800.64.PANIC

National Self-Help Clearinghouse
365 5th Avenue, Suite 3300
New York, NY 10016
212.817.1822
www.selfhelpweb.org

Neurological Disorders

National Institute of Neurological
Disorders and Stroke
P.O. Box 5081
Bethesda, MD 20824
800.352.9424
www.ninds.nih.gov

National Stroke Association
9707 Easter Lane
Englewood, CO 80112
800.STROKES
www.stroke.org

Nutrition

American Dietetic Association
National Center for Nutrition and
Dietetics
216 W. Jackson Blvd.
Chicago, IL 60606

Consumer Nutrition Hotline
800.366.1655
www.eatright.org

Center for Food Safety
and Applied Nutrition
5100 Paint Branch Parkway HFS-555
College Park, MD 20740-3835
www.cfsan.fda.gov/list.html

Pregnancy

National Healthy Mothers,
Healthy Babies Coalition
121 N. Washington St., Suite 300
Alexandria, VA 22314
703.836.6110
www.hbhm.org

March of Dimes
1275 Mamaroneck Ave.
White Plains, NY 10605
www.modimes.org

International Childbirth Education
Association
P.O. Box 20048
Minneapolis, MN 55420
952.854.8660
www.icea.org

Primary Care

National Clearinghouse for Primary
Care Information
2070 Chain Bridge Rd., Suite 450
Vienna, VA 22182
800.400.BPHC
www.bphc.hrsa.dhhs.gov

Safety

U.S. Consumer Product Safety
Commission
4330 East-West Hwy.
Bethesda, MD 20814-4408
800.638.2772
www.cpsc.gov

National Center for Injury
Prevention and Control
4770 Buford Hwy. N.E.
Atlanta, GA 30341-3724
770.488.1506
www.cdc.gov/ncipc

National Fire Protection Association
1 Batterymarch Park
Quincy, MA 02169-7471
617.770.3000
www.nfpa.org

National Highway Traffic Safety
Administration
400 Seventh St. S.W.
Washington, DC 20590
Auto Safety Hotline:
888.DASH.2DOT
www.nhtsa.dot.gov

National Institute of Occupational
Safety and Health
200 Independence Ave. S.W.
Washington, DC 20201
800.35.NIOSH
www.cdc.gov/niosh/
homepage.html

National Safe Kids Campaign
1301 Pennsylvania Ave. N.W.
Suite 1000
Washington, DC 20004
202.662.0600
www.safekids.org

National Safety Council
1121 Springlake Dr.
Itasca, IL 60143-3201
630.285.1121
www.nsc.org

Sexually Transmitted Diseases (STDs)

American Social Health Association
P.O. Box 13827
Research Triangle Park, NC 27709
919.361.8400
www.ashastd.org

National Center for HIV, STD, and TB Prevention
1108 Corporate Square
Atlanta, GA 30329
404.639.8040
www.cdc.gov/nchstp/od/nchstp.html

STD National Hotline
800.227.8922

Senior Support

Administration on Aging
Department of Health
and Human Services
One Massachusetts Ave.
Suites 4100 and 5100
Washington, DC 20001
202.619.0724
800.677.1116 (eldercare locator)
www.aoa.dhhs.gov

American Association
of Retired Persons
601 E St. N.W.
Washington, DC 20049
888.OUR.AARP
www.aarp.org

National Council on Aging
300 D St. S.W.
Washington, DC 20024
202.479.1200
www.ncoa.org

Sleep

American Academy of Sleep
Medicine
One Westbrook Corporate Center
Suite 920
Westchester, IL 60154
708.492.0930
www.aasmnet.org

The Better Sleep Council
501 Wyethe St.
Alexandria, VA 22314-1917
www.bettersleep.org

Vision

American Foundation for the Blind
11 Penn Plaza
Suite 300
New York, NY 10001
800.232.5463
www.afb.org

National Eye Institute
31 Center Drive, MSC 2510
Bethesda, MD 20892-2510
301.496.5248
www.nei.nih.gov

Work and Family

The Women's Bureau
U.S. Department of Labor
200 Constitution Ave., N.W.
Room S-3002
Washington, DC 20210
800.827.5335
www.dol.gov/dol/wb/welcome.html

Family and Work Institute
267 Fifth Ave., 2nd Fl.
New York, NY 10016
212.465.2044
www.familiesandwork.org

Index

■ **A bold entry indicates a medical emergency.** ■ **A blue entry indicates a primary discussion.**

Index

■ **A bold entry indicates a medical emergency.** ■ **A blue entry indicates a primary discussion.**

Index

■ A bold entry indicates a medical emergency. ■ A blue entry indicates a primary discussion.

Index

■ **A bold entry indicates a medical emergency.** ■ **A blue entry indicates a primary discussion.**

Index

■ **A bold entry indicates a medical emergency.** ■ **A blue entry indicates a primary discussion.**